SUBVERSIVES

Antislavery, Abolition, and the Atlantic World

R. J. M. Blackett
James Brewer Stewart

SERIES EDITORS

ANTISLAVERY COMMUNITY IN

SUBVERSIVES

WASHINGTON, D.C., 1828–1865

STANLEY HARROLD

Louisiana State University Press
Baton Rouge

12 11 10 09 08 07 06 05 04 03

5 4 3 2 1

Designer: Amanda McDonald Scallan
Typeface: ACaslon Regular
Typesetter: Coghill Composition Co., Inc.
Printer and Binder: Thomson-Shore, Inc.

ISBN 0-8071-2805-8 (cloth)
ISBN 0-8071-2834-4 (paper)

The paper in this book meets the guidelines for permanence and durability of the Committee on Production Guidelines for Book Longevity of the Council on Library Resources. ∞

For Judy

CONTENTS

CONTENTS

ILLUSTRATIONS

ILLUSTRATIONS

ACKNOWLEDGMENTS

In writing this book, I have enjoyed the help, advice, and encouragement of many extraordinary scholars, librarians and archivists. I have also had the assistance of two great institutions: the National Endowment for the Humanities, which awarded me a fellowship during the 1996–1997 academic year, and South Carolina State University, which provided me financial support during that same year and has otherwise encouraged my scholarly pursuits.

Librarians and archivists provided generous assistance in locating and accessing documents. Jo Cottingham, James Brooks, and the rest of the staff of the Interlibrary Loan Department at the University of South Carolina's Cooper Library were essential to the project. Andrew Penson of South Carolina State University's Whittaker Library was invariably helpful. Carolyn Mahin of the University of Central Oklahoma Library went out of her way to help me get some hard to acquire material. I also thank Charles Arp of the Ohio Historical Society; Mary Ellen Chijioke and Patricia C. O'Donnell of the Friends Historical Library of Swarthmore College; Mary Beth Corrigan, Bonnie Hedges, and Gail Redmann of the Historical Society of Washington, D.C.; Robert S. Cox of Clements Library, University of Michigan; Joelle El-Bashir of the Moorland-Spingarn Research Center, Howard University; Lynne Farrington of the Olin Library, Cornell University; Ken Grossi of Oberlin College Archives; Janie C. Morris of the Special Collections Library, Duke University; Karen Ross of Haverford College Library; Judith Ann Schiff and Virginia H. Smith of the Massachusetts Historical Society; and Christine Weideman of Yale University Library. The efficient and professional manuscript department staffs at the Library of Congress, the National Archives, Historical Society of Pennsylvania, and the Congregational Library, Boston, were also very helpful.

As for scholars, I thank Frederick J. Blue, Lawrence J. Friedman, and James Brewer Stewart for supporting my NEH grant application in 1995. I am equally grateful to those who read part or all of the manuscript and offered encouragement. Among them are Victoria E. Bynum, Merton L. Dillon, William C. Hine, James L. Huston, James Brewer Stewart, and Judith Wellman. Professor Huston has my everlasting thanks for pointing out that I could not stop the book at 1860 as I had planned. I also thank Norrece T. Jones Jr. and Shirley J. Yee, who commented on a version of Chapter Three during a session at the meeting of the Organization of American Historians in 1998.

Several scholars gave me helpful information, documents, or advice. They include Robert H. Abzug, Robert Ellis, Josephine Pacheco, Mary Kay Ricks, Hilary Russell, Loren Schweninger, Mark J. Stegmaier, Paul Verduin, and Donald Yacovone. Two nonhistorians, Emily Harrold and Judy Harrold, provided technical assistance.

An earlier version of Chapter Eight appeared as an article in the December 1996 issue of *Civil War History* and an earlier version of Chapter Three in the Summer 2000 issue of *The Journal of the Early Republic*. I thank these journals for permission to republish portions of those articles.

Finally I thank the team at Louisiana State University Press. Richard J. M. Blackett and James Brewer Stewart, who edit the *Antislavery and Abolition in the Atlantic World* series, provided insightful critiques of the manuscript. The anonymous outside reader read the manuscript very closely and provided excellent advice. Acquisitions Editor Sylvia Frank Rodrigue saw the manuscript through its early stages at the Press. Michael K. Smith's careful editing greatly improved my prose. Associate Director and Editor-in-Chief Maureen G. Hewitt coordinated the entire process with unfailing good cheer.

I alone am responsible for my interpretations and errors. But I have depended on a community.

Stanley Harrold
Orangeburg, South Carolina

ABBREVIATIONS USED IN NOTES

AMAA	American Missionary Association Archives, Amistad Research Center, Tulane University
AP	*Albany* (N.Y.) *Patriot*
AS	*Ashtabula Sentinel* (Jefferson, Ohio)
ASR	*Anti-Slavery Reporter* (British and Foreign Anti-Slavery Society)
BSV	*Baltimore Saturday Visiter*
CA	*Colored American* (New York–Philadelphia)
CG	*Congressional Globe*
DMC	*Daily Morning Chronicle* (Washington, D.C.)
DANB	*Dictionary of American Negro Biography*
DTD	*Daily True Democrat* (Cleveland)
E	*Emancipator* (New York and Boston)
EHP	Emily Howland Papers, Cornell University
FDP	*Frederick Douglass' Paper* (Rochester)
GSP	Gerrit Smith Papers, Syracuse University Library
GUE	*Genius of Universal Emancipation* (Baltimore-Washington)
JRGP	Joshua R. Giddings Papers, Ohio Historical Society
L	*Liberator* (Boston)
LTP	Lewis Tappan Papers, Library of Congress
MASS	Massachusetts Anti-Slavery Society
MMP	Myrtilla Miner Papers, Library of Congress
NA	National Archives
NASS	*National Anti-Slavery Standard* (New York)
NE	*National Era* (Washington, D.C.)
NR	*National Republican* (Washington, D.C.)
NS	*North Star* (Rochester)
NYDT	*New York Daily Tribune*

NYH	*New York Herald*
PF	*Pennsylvania Freeman* (Philadelphia)
RCHS	*Records of the Columbia Historical Society*
TL	*Tocsin of Liberty* (Albany, N.Y.)
WHSP	William H. Seward Papers, Rush Rhees Library, University of Rochester

If laws and Constitutions exist, that take away rights, it is the duty of every human being to use all his influence to change, or to subvert them. . . . And when the Government ceases to answer the great ends for which it was formed, it is the right, it is the *duty* of the people to subvert it, "peacefully if they can, forcibly if they must."
　　—First Annual Report of the Albany, New York, Vigilance
　　　Committee, December 12, 1842.

We, the people of Charles County, in the State of Maryland, hav[e] watched with deep concern the tendency of the . . . reckless efforts of fanaticism in the Northern portion of the United States, to subvert the institutions of the State, and ruthlessly to invade the peace of our people by the sacrifice of our property at the risk of our lives, and the destruction of our constitutional rights.
　　—Slaveholders' Meeting, Port Tobacco, Maryland,
　　　July 15, 1845.

INTRODUCTION

Slavery and Its Opponents at a Vulnerable Point

Slavery was the most powerful institution in early-nineteenth-century America. Although concentrated in the South, those who owned human property exercised enormous economic, social, and political influence over the entire country. Their staunch opponents—the minority of Americans who advocated the abolition of slavery—sought not only to undermine and destroy that power but to free millions of enslaved African Americans. Most abolitionists labored in the North, where there were almost no slaves. But a few of them went into the South to ally themselves with African Americans and small groups of white southerners in a desperate struggle to *subvert* slavery on its own ground.

Slavery's vital economic role established its great power. Slave labor produced tobacco, rice, sugar, hemp, wheat, lumber, and, most important, cotton—the country's leading export and most remunerative product. This productivity, plus the control slaveholders exercised over the people they held in bondage, made them America's wealthiest class. Northerners also profited from an economy based on slave labor and shared with white southerners a compelling interest in defending that labor system. Meanwhile slavery anchored white racial supremacy. Most white Americans—both northern and southern—regarded slavery as the best means of controlling a growing black population that they regarded as alien, inassimilable, and dangerous.[1]

---

1. For a concise history of American slavery from its origins through its abolition, see Peter Kolchin, *American Slavery, 1619–1877* (New York: Hill and Wang, 1993).

1

Slavery's economic and social power translated into political power. The prevailing interpretation of the United States Constitution promoted its interests. Slaveholders enjoyed advantages that allowed them to dominate the nation's government at Washington, D.C., a slaveholding city carved out of the slave states of Maryland and Virginia. Between 1789 and 1850 all but three United States presidents were slaveholders. The master class constituted a powerful bloc in Congress, controlled the Democratic party from its founding in 1828, and dominated the Supreme Court.[2] Yet slavery was for three reasons vulnerable in Washington and the surrounding Chesapeake region. First, it outraged the moral sense of visitors from the North and abroad. Second, it appeared to have brought economic and cultural decay to the region. Third, while it thrived elsewhere in the South, it was in decline in and about Washington.

From 1800, when the national government moved to Washington from Philadelphia, until 1846, when Virginia reclaimed the portion of the District of Columbia to the southwest of the Potomac River, the capital city shared the District of Columbia with two other municipalities. To the northwest, on the northeastern shore of the Potomac River, was the market center of Georgetown. On the Virginia side of the river was the port city of Alexandria. It was Washington, nevertheless, that became the focal point of the sectional struggle over slavery.

The moral and cultural shock outsiders experienced in traveling to this southern city is evident in the writings of British author and social critic Harriet Martineau, who embodied a major ethical perspective in the Atlantic world. When Martineau visited the United States during 1834 and 1835, she felt at home in the North but recoiled from what she observed in Washington. "In Philadelphia," she recalled, "I had found perpetual difficulty in remembering that I was in a foreign country." In Washington the food, the so-

---

2. Don E. Fehrenbacher, *The Slaveholding Republic: An Account of the United States Government's Relation to Slavery*, Ward M. McAffee ed. (New York: Oxford University Press, 2002); Paul Finkelman, *Slavery and the Founders: Race and Liberty in the Age of Jefferson* (Armonk, N.Y.: M. E. Sharpe, 1996); Finkelman, *An Imperfect Union: Slavery, Federalism, and Comity* (Chapel Hill: University of North Carolina Press, 1991); Leonard L. Richards, *The Slave Power: The Free North and Southern Domination, 1780–1860* (Baton Rouge: Louisiana State University Press, 2000).

2

ciety, the manners, and especially the pervasiveness of human bondage indicated that she was indeed in a strange land.

When during her visit to the city she first saw an enslaved person—a young girl—she felt "a horror" that "sickened [her] very soul." She believed that enslavement doomed the child "to ignorance, privation, and moral degradation." The physical desolation she observed in Washington also shocked her. "The approach to the city is striking to all strangers from its oddness," Martineau wrote. "I saw the dome of the Capitol from a considerable distance . . . but, though I was prepared by the description of preceding travellers, I was taken by surprise on finding myself beneath the splendid building, so sordid are the enclosures and houses on its very verge."[3]

Fifteen years later, Jane Grey Swisshelm, a journalist from Pittsburgh, recorded a similar impression of Washington and its environs. The condition of slaves appalled her and, while she declared the Capitol Building to be "sublime," it seemed to her to be located "in the midst of wilderness." Compared to the "garden-like plantations of eastern Pennsylvania," the area of Maryland that nearly surrounded Washington appeared to be a wasteland. "It is very wonderful to see the old State lie inactive . . . at the very foot of the Capitol, stretching out in primitive wilderness or exhausted barren wastes," she reported.[4]

The capital city's residents took pride in the impressive Capitol, the Library of Congress, and several theaters. The city's elite enjoyed a vigorous social life. By the 1850s there were gaslights and horse-drawn trolleys. The diplomatic corps and the presence of Americans from all sections of the country gave the city a cosmopolitan character. But the promise of urban grandeur encompassed in Pierre Charles L'Enfant's 1791 plan for Washington remained unfulfilled during the antebellum period. One resident recalled that the city was "a place of wide, unbuilt areas of land, oftentimes dreary commons, wide open spaces, creeks and rills, cutting across unexpected places, few buildings of any pretensions; not a sewer anywhere, surface drainage with a shallow, uncovered stream carrying off the refuse to the Potomac." Swisshelm in 1850 remarked the mud, pigs, and garbage in the city's streets. She

3. Harriet Martineau, *Retrospective of Western Travels*, 2 vols. (New York: Harper, 1838), 142–4.

4. Swisshelm to Horace Greeley, 10 April [1850] in *NYDT,* 12 April 1850.

noted the prevalence of tobacco-spitting and coarse language in the halls of Congress.[5]

Martineau and Swisshelm assumed that slavery caused the economic and social decay they observed in Washington and in the surrounding Chesapeake region.[6] They also realized that slavery generated gut-wrenching misery among local African Americans. This combination of local decline and black despair, they and other abolitionists believed, put slavery in Washington and its vicinity at risk. A successful challenge to human bondage at this symbolic and strategic point, they concluded, would have major repercussions.

Slavery was declining and free wage labor advancing in the Chesapeake during the four decades prior to the Civil War. Wheat had begun to replace tobacco as the region's principal crop, and local masters sold excess bondpeople into the Deep South, where a cotton boom created a market for them. These developments had a profound impact. In the District of Columbia in 1820 there were 6,277 slaves in a total population of 33,039. By 1860 there were only 3,185 slaves in a total population of 75,080. In the portion of Virginia to the west of Washington, northern settlers began during the early 1840s to purchase worn-out farms and ro work them with free labor. Meanwhile, free labor became dominant in Delaware and northern Maryland. To a greater degree than Washington, Baltimore, the region's major city, became a wedge for economic and social revolution. Rivaling Philadelphia as a major port, by the 1830s this slaveholding and slavetrading city employed mostly free laborers—many of them black.[7]

5. *Planters' Advocate* (Upper Marlboro, Md.), 26 January, 16 February, 21 December 1853; Constance M. Green, *Washington*, 2 vols. (Princeton: Princeton University Press, 1962), 198–9; P. P. [Torrey] to Editors, 4 December 1841, in *New York Evangelist*, 11 December 1841; Joseph T. Kelly, "Memories of a Lifetime in Washington," *RCHS* 31–2 (1930): 123 (quotation); Jane Grey Swisshelm, *Half a Century*, 2d ed. (Chicago: Jensen, McClerg, 1880), 128.

6. Barbara Jeanne Fields points out that large wilderness areas in the Chesapeake were not necessarily direct results of slavery's decline. See Fields, *Slavery and Freedom on the Middle Ground: Maryland during the Nineteenth Century* (New Haven: Yale University Press, 1985), 70–1.

7. Constance M. Green, *The Secret City: A History of Race Relations in the Nation's Capital* (Princeton: Princeton University Press, 1967), 33; Gary Lawson Browne, *Baltimore in the Nation, 1789–1861* (Chapel Hill: University of North Carolina Press, 1980); Fields, *Slavery and Freedom*, 1–8, 15–9, 60–2; Jane N. Garrett, "Philadelphia and Baltimore, 1700–1840: A Study of Intraregional Unity," *Maryland Historical Magazine* 55 (March 1960): 1–13; Patience Essah, *A House Divided: Slavery and Emancipation in Delaware, 1638–1865* (Charlottesville: Univer-

This weakening of unfree labor in the Chesapeake shaped proslavery policy locally and nationally. The Chesapeake area, including the states of Delaware, Maryland, and Virginia, as well as the District of Columbia, constituted a crucial portion of a larger region of the United States—variously known as the *border South,* the *borderlands,* and the *middle ground*—stretching from the Atlantic coast westward through Kentucky to Missouri. Slaveholders feared that if economic change and abolitionism forced slavery to retreat from the Chesapeake—if Delaware, Maryland, the District of Columbia, and Virginia embraced emancipation—maintaining human bondage in Kentucky and Missouri would become untenable as well. Worse yet, pressure on the next tier of slaveholding states would ensue. These were horrifying prospects because southern whites believed abolitionist activity would lead to slave revolt and race war.[8]

As northern abolitionist Charles T. Torrey noted in 1842, slaveholding politicians were also determined to defend slavery in Washington as "a point of honor." The existence of slavery in the national capital, he maintained, provided "a sort of symbol and proof of its control over the government of the country." Slavery in Washington made it a *southern* city and legitimated bondage as an American institution. Termination of slavery in this city would destroy this symbolism and could be the first step toward general emancipation. Paraphrasing slavery's most famous defender, Massachusetts abolitionists asserted in 1846 that "Mr. [John C.] Calhoun assures us that the District is THE KEY OF SLAVERY. And when we have gained this Gibraltar, we shall need no prophet to promise us the whole land." When in 1850 the state

---

sity Press of Virginia, 1996); William H. Williams, *Slavery and Freedom in Delaware, 1639–1865* (Wilmington: Scholarly Resources, 1996); *AP,* 21 February 1844; Samuel M. Janney, *The Yankees in Fairfax County, Virginia* (Baltimore: Snodgrass and Wehrly, 1845); Richard H. Abbott, "Yankee Farmers in Northern Virginia, 1840–1860," *Virginia Magazine of History and Biography* 76 (January 1968): 56–66.

8. Fields, *Slavery and Freedom,* 6–7, 19–20; Lawrence H. McDonald, "Prelude to Emancipation: The Failure of the Great Reaction in Maryland, 1831–1850," (Ph.D. dissertation, University of Maryland, 1974), 55–6; *Richmond South,* quoted in *PF,* 1 June 1848; Anita Louise Aidt-Guy, "Persistent Maryland: Antislavery Activity between 1850 and 1864" (Ph.D. dissertation, Georgetown University, 1994), 38, 68–9; *Richmond Enquirer,* 4 & 28 December 1849. Aidt-Guy confuses proslavery prevarication with gradual abolitionism, but her sources indicate slaveholders' fears.

of Georgia listed possible northern actions that would require it to secede from the Union, it put the abolition of slavery in the District first.[9]

One might imagine that the decline of slavery in and about Washington constituted an unalloyed benefit to the enslaved people of the city and its region. Contemporary observers reported that slavery in the area was more "mild" than it was farther south. Slaves appeared to be relatively well fed and well clothed. Unlike their counterparts in the Deep South, Chesapeake slaves during the 1830s, 1840s, and 1850s could still sue for their freedom and their masters could still manumit them. Many of them lived away from their masters' supervision and worked for wages. Some of them had, by arranging to purchase their freedom over time, transformed themselves into term slaves rather than slaves for life.[10]

But economic decline also put at risk what advantages local bondpeople enjoyed. After 1830, Chesapeake planters often avoided bankruptcy by disposing of their excess human property through the interstate slave trade. The *Richmond Enquirer* lamented in 1846 that selling "negroes" was "the only reliable means of liquidating debts." Some masters broke manumission agreements in order to sell their slaves and kidnappers preyed on the local black population to supply the Deep South market. As Washington became a major depot in the trade, residents grew accustomed to coffle gangs trudging along city streets on their way to southerly destinations. Thousands of people,

9. *TL,* 27 October (first & second quotations), 3 November 1842; Mary Tremain, *Slavery in the District of Columbia: The Policy of Congress and the Struggle for Abolition* (New York: G. P. Putnam's Sons, 1892), 80–3, 88; "Address of the Massachusetts Liberty State Committee," n.d., in *AP,* 9 September 1846 (third quotation); *Southern Banner,* 21 August 1851, quoted in James L. Huston, "Southerners against Secession: The Arguments of the Constitutional Unionists in 1850–51," *Civil War History* 46 (December 2000): 298. See also Fehrenbacher, *Slaveholding Republic,* 363 n.129.

10. W[illiam] S[lade] to Editor, 18 February 1839, in *PF,* 14 March 1839; *LP,* 25 May 1848 (quotation); Letitia Woods Brown, *Free Negroes in the District of Columbia, 1790–1846* (New York: Oxford University Press, 1972), 57–8, 61–3, 97–127; Tremain, *Slavery in the District of Columbia,* 32–9, 54; Worthington G. Snethen, *The Black Codes of the District of Columbia in Force September 1st 1848* (New York: William Harned, 1848), 24, 30; Ira Berlin, *Slaves without Masters: The Free Negro in the Antebellum South* (New York: New Press, 1974), 29–36, 101–2, 138–57, 185. T. Stephen Whitman, *The Price of Freedom: Slavery and Manumission in Baltimore and Early National Maryland* (Lexington: University of Kentucky Press, 1997), 11–5, 49–57, 105–6, 111–7; Fields, *Slavery and Freedom,* 27–8, 47–9.

Slave auctioning in Washington. From the 1830s through the 1850s abolitionists used woodcuts such as this to contrast Washington's symbols of liberty with its reality as a slave-holding and slavetrading city. *Mirror of Slavery* (New York: AASS, 1833).

Swisshelm charged, had "dragged their manacled limbs away, away to return no more."[11]

In December 1830 these appalling scenes prompted an outburst from the slaveholding editor of the *American Spectator,* a literary journal published in Washington. The editor mainly worried that "colored human beings, hand-cuffed in pairs, and driven along" by slavetraders on horseback undermined the city's pretensions as the capital of a liberty-loving nation. But he also included a verse depicting the wrenching emotional impact sale had on African Americans as they left the city on slave ships destined for the Deep South:

> The tender ties of father, husband, friend,
> All bonds of nature in that moment end,

11. *GUE,* 19 February 1830; *Enquirer* 13 November 1846, quoted in *NE,* 15 April 1847 (first quotation); Fields, *Slavery and Freedom,* 14–7, 24–7, 38–9; Tremain, *Slavery,* 48–54; Green, *Washington,* 1:186–7; George Howard Connaughton, "The Anti-Slavery Movement in the District of Columbia" (master's thesis, Ohio State University, 1934), [13–6]; Frederic Bancroft, *Slave Trading in the Old South* (Baltimore: J. H. Furst, 1931), 45–66; William Slade to

And each endures, while yet he draws his breath,
A stroke as fatal as the scythe of death;
They lose in tears, the far receding shore,
But not the thought that they must meet no more![12]

Such tragedies eroded whatever benefits enslaved African Americans enjoyed as a result of the *mildness* of slavery in the Chesapeake. There were also laws that oppressed both slaves and free blacks. It was illegal for African Americans to vote, hold office, testify against whites, serve on juries, or own firearms. An 1827 Washington ordinance subjected them to a 10:00 P.M. curfew. An 1836 ordinance attempted to restrict them to the most menial work. In Washington, Virginia, and Maryland—as in most southern jurisdictions—the law presumed that all black people were slaves unless they could prove otherwise. This presumption supported the arrest of African Americans who could not document their free status. It led in Washington to the sale into slavery of some free blacks in order to pay the cost of their imprisonment on false charges that they were slaves.[13]

African Americans responded to these conditions in a variety of ways. They attempted to protect or to gain their freedom by going to court. They sought to purchase the freedom of relatives. Their most desperate option was to escape to Baltimore or the North. These efforts further weakened slavery in the Chesapeake, not least because African Americans who sought freedom attracted the support of few whites. Among them were antislavery congressmen and abolitionist journalists, as well as some local attorneys, businessmen, Quakers, and evangelicals. They were all to varying degrees influenced by the northern antislavery movement, which held human bondage to be sinful as well as economically outmoded.

Editor of the *E*, 12 October 1838, in *PF*, 1 November 1838; Swisshelm to Horace Greeley, 10 April [1850], in *NYDT*, 12 April 1850.

12. *American Spectator*, 4 December 1830, quoted in *L*, 1 January 1831.

13. U.S. Congress, House, *Special Report of the Commissioner of Education on the Condition and Improvement of Public Schools in the District of Columbia*, 41 Cong., 2 sess., H. Exec. Doc. 315, Serial 1427 (1870), 308–17; Brown, *Free Negroes*, 140; Walter C. Clephane, "The Local Aspect of Slavery in the District of Columbia," *RCHS* 3 (1900): 231–2; Tremain, *Slavery*, 35–45; Snethen, *Black Codes of the District of Columbia*, 11; Connaughton, "Anti-Slavery Movement," [19, 31–4].

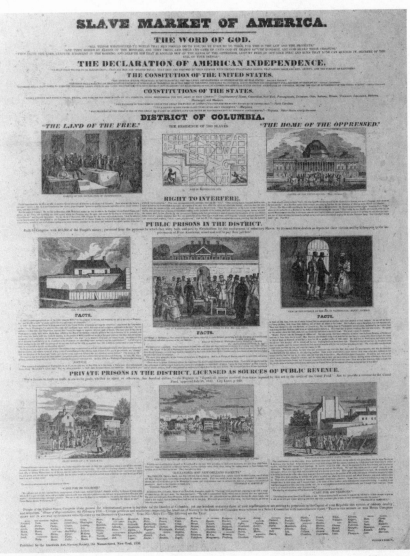

This broadside presents scenes associated with the slave trade in Washington. They include a slave coffle passing the U.S. Capitol, a slave jail in Alexandria, an auction outside Washington Jail, a slave mother and child in the jail, and two slave-traders' headquarters. *Slave Market of America* (New York: AASS, 1836). With permission from the Historical Society of Washington, D.C.

9

At first the abolitionists had called for gradual emancipation and supported the efforts of the American Colonization Society (ACS) to send former slaves to Liberia, in West Africa. But by the late 1820s they had begun to demand the *immediate* emancipation of the slaves and equal rights for African Americans in the United States.[14] The whites in Washington who represented these aims shared Martineau and Swisshelm's perception that slavery was weak in the region surrounding Chesapeake Bay. Together with local African Americans, and backed by northern antislavery activists, they aggressively sought to destroy the institution. This effort involved enormous risks to the blacks and whites who committed themselves to it. The law, local public opinion, and pervasive racism aided slavery's increasingly determined defenders. Those who challenged slavery and racism risked beatings, mob violence, imprisonment, and death.

Nevertheless, by the 1820s, northern antislavery literature circulated widely if not freely among African Americans in the area, and this continued to be the case through the 1850s. Several northern abolitionists conducted speaking tours. Among them was Lucretia Mott of Philadelphia, who in 1844 told a group assembled in a Washington church, "I am aware of the place in which I stand; I know there are many who will not allow any thing to be said in behalf of the slave. But I believe it to be my duty to plead the cause of the poor and of the oppressed." Others stayed longer and went beyond pleading. "I regard it as important," declared Torrey in 1842, "to make more vigorous assaults than ever, upon slavery in this District."[15]

In 1848 William L. Chaplin, a white northern abolitionist residing in Washington, proclaimed that "the existence of slavery has become precarious

14. Charles G. Sellers, *The Market Revolution: Jacksonian America, 1815–1846* (New York: Oxford University Press, 1991); James Brewer Stewart, *Holy Warriors: The Abolitionists and American Slavery,* 2d ed. (New York: Hill and Wang, 1997); Philip J. Staudenraus, *The African Colonization Movement* (New York: Columbia University Press, 1961).

15. Antislavery literature: Merton L. Dillon, *Slavery Attacked: Southern Slaves and Their Allies, 1619–1865* (Baton Rouge: Louisiana State University Press, 1990), 140, 145–6; *GUE,* 15 January 1830; *L,* 8 & 15 October 1831; Nancy Day to George T. Downing, 18 June 1855, MMP. Speakers: David L. Child to [editor], 3 January 1843, in *NASS,* 12 January 1843; *AP,* 9 February 1843; *PF,* 1 February 1844 (first quotation), 28 October 1847; Anna Davis Hallowell, *James and Lucretia Mott: Life and Letters* (Boston: Houghton Mifflin, 1885), 210–9, 235–41. Torrey: *TL,* 27 October 1842 (second quotation).

in this District at all events." By helping black families defend themselves against sale south, Chaplin maintained, abolitionists engaged in "an assault upon the slave system at a vulnerable point." He hoped that such activities would "drive it from the Capital." In 1850 white abolitionist educator Myrtilla Miner told United States Senator William H. Seward that an effort in behalf of the "colored people" would be "most felt in the City of Washington."[16]Visiting there in December 1845, abolitionist poet John Greenleaf Whittier expressed a similar hope concerning the strategic role of the city in furthering the southward progress of abolitionism. First Whittier wrote of the horrors of Washington's slave trade and the willingness of the city's inhabitants to sacrifice humanity and morality for "Wealth and Pride." Then he relented and turned more optimistic about the struggle against slavery there despite the great dangers faced by abolitionists:

> Nay, my words are all too sweeping:
> In this crowded human mart,
> Feeling is not dead but sleeping;
> Man's strong will and woman's heart
> In the coming strife for Freedom yet shall bear their
> generous part.
> And from yonder sunny vallies,
> Southward in the distance lost,
> Freedom yet shall summon allies
> Worthier than the North can boast,
> With the Evil by their hearth-stones grappling
> at severer cost.[17]

That slavery was both weak and vicious in Washington is at the heart of this book. The threat of sale south and the hope of freedom led local African Americans to seek out sympathetic whites. Empathy for black families facing dismemberment and an opportunity to strike a telling blow against slavery at

16. Chaplin to Pat, n.d., in *AP*, 22 March 1848 (first–third quotations); Miner to Seward, Dec. 25, 1850, WHSP (fourth & fifth quotations).

17. Whittier, "Lines Suggested by a Visit to the City of Washington in the 12th Month of 1845," in *PF*, 12 February 1846.

a strategic and symbolic location led antislavery whites to respond positively. Together they formed a subversive community that flourished in and about the city from the late 1820s through the mid-1860s. While some of the people involved in this biracial community wielded power as politicians and journalists, most were obscure even in their own time. Black and white women played an important role. Legally barred from political participation, they needed only bravery and determination to engage in subversive antislavery activities in the Chesapeake. Together with their male colleagues, they purchased the freedom of slaves, undertook court action, enlisted support from sympathetic northerners, and helped slaves to escape.

The subversives' activities influenced—and were influenced by—local and national government actions and political parties. But their heretofore untold story demonstrates that Washington's homes, places of business, and streets, not just its halls of government, constituted focal points of the antislavery struggle. As desperate African Americans drew a few whites into antislavery action in this very important southern city, they together had a profound impact. Simply by engaging in interracial cooperation, the subversives raised a radical challenge to the existing social order. The overt and covert means they employed to destroy slavery in and about Washington made them a threat to powerful slaveholders. The subversives' story clarifies the character of the antislavery movement, nineteenth-century race relations, and the antebellum struggle over the vital border region.

ONE

Chesapeake Origins

HE formation of a subversive antislavery community in Washington and its vicinity depended on two things: the desperate efforts of African Americans to preserve their families and the arrival of northern whites who were willing to assist them. Yet this reform community would have emerged under different circumstances, or not at all, if a tradition of interracial antislavery cooperation had not existed in the Chesapeake. From the 1780s through the 1820s, a few whites cooperated with blacks to counteract some of slavery's more oppressive features. The issues they dealt with and the conditions they faced foreshadowed those of the three decades before the Civil War. Not until the 1830s did Washington emerge as the center of these subversive antislavery activities.

In the Chesapeake—as elsewhere—antislavery efforts among blacks, both slave and free, antedated biracial abolitionism. In this region, where slavery originated in America, most whites had long assumed that their own freedom required that all blacks be slaves. Yet there had been since the colonial period some black people who were free. Until the last decades of the eighteenth century, most of them were mulattoes who had been manumitted by their slaveholding fathers, but others had purchased their freedom, won it in court, or had escaped. They received little help or sympathy from a white antislavery movement confined to Quaker abolitionists.[1]

1. Edmond S. Morgan, *American Slavery American Freedom: The Ordeal of Colonial Virginia* (New York: Norton, 1975), 363–87; Ira Berlin, *Slaves without Masters: The Free Negro in the*

The Revolutionary era stretching, from the 1760s through the 1780s, produced both greater white involvement and a growing class of free blacks. As American colonials came into conflict with British authority, asserted their independence, and fought a long war to achieve it, they embraced an ideology that conflicted with perpetual slavery for African Americans. The Revolutionary claim that all men had rights to life, liberty, and private property led many whites to reconsider the legitimacy of black slavery. African Americans, under the influence of the same idea, asserted their right to freedom and took action to make that right a reality.[2]

In the North, state governments either abolished slavery or provided for its gradual abolition. In the Chesapeake, where the country's largest concentration of free blacks already lived, revolutionary ideology—combined with regional economic conditions and rising numbers of slave escapes—led many masters to manumit their bondpeople. As tobacco yields declined in the region and wheat cultivation—which did not require a permanent labor force—expanded, planters turned increasingly to free labor. Simultaneously, industrial growth in Baltimore and other urban areas encouraged the growth of a free black class. During the early 1790s some observers predicted that Delaware, Maryland, and Virginia would follow the northern states in providing for general emancipation, leaving the Deep South alone clinging to perpetual black slavery.

But this was not to be. Revolutionary-era manumissions in the Chesapeake—based on ideology and economic self-interest rather than on blood lines—produced not only a larger free black class but one with a darker complexion. Soon whites perceived a threat in this growing and presumably alien population.[3] They believed that the enlarged free black class in their midst bore responsibility for a series of aborted revolt conspiracies that culminated in 1800 with the slave Gabriel's plan to attack Richmond. Most whites also

Antebellum South (New York: New Press, 1974), 3–12; Jean R. Soderlund, *Quakers and Slavery: A Divided Spirit* (Princeton: Princeton University Press, 1988), 3–31; Gary B. Nash and Soderlund, *Freedom by Degrees: Emancipation in Pennsylvania and Its Aftermath* (New York: Oxford University Press, 1991), 41–73.

2. Gary B. Nash, *Race and Revolution* (Madison, Wis.: Madison House, 1990); Berlin, *Slaves without Masters*, 15–50.

3. Letitia Woods Brown, *Free Negroes in the District of Columbia, 1790–1846* (New York: Oxford University Press, 1972), 49–51.

regarded free blacks as an immoral, criminal class that endangered property and chastity. Whites claimed as well that free black laborers debased the status of white laborers and impaired their work ethic.

Unlike their counterparts in the Deep South, the state and district governments of the Chesapeake never outlawed manumissions. They realized that changing economies required free black workers. But manumission became more difficult, especially in Virginia where traditional agricultural interests remained most powerful. Some masters who earlier might have freed their slaves began to sell them south. Other masters perpetuated bondage by requiring individual slaves to purchase their freedom over a term of years. As attractive as self-purchase over time was to black men and women seeking freedom, the practice kept them under their masters' control and left their children in slavery. Meanwhile, during the early 1800s, whites in Maryland and Virginia periodically initiated campaigns to force free African Americans to leave their states. While none of these campaigns realized their objectives, they represented formidable white resistance to manumission and black freedom.[4]

As enthusiasm for the Revolutionary era's natural rights doctrines waned during the early 1800s and masters became more vigilant, slave escapes declined. Only young men continued to attempt escape in substantial numbers. A few went to the North. The great majority settled in Baltimore, increasing that city's free black population. Others sought refuge in the District of Columbia.[5] As a result, Washington, Georgetown, and Alexandria became—along with Baltimore—centers of black antislavery efforts essential to the formation of a biracial subversive community in the Chesapeake. By the 1810s and 1820s African Americans in all four of these municipalities could protect

4. Berlin, *Slaves without Masters*, 84, 138–57; T. Stephen Whitman, *The Price of Freedom: Slavery and Manumission in Baltimore and Early National Maryland* (Lexington: University Press of Kentucky, 1997), 101; Whitman, "Slavery, Manumission, and Free Black Workers in Early National Baltimore (Maryland)" (Ph.D. dissertation, Johns Hopkins University, 1993), 176–9; Lawrence Herbert McDonald, "Prelude to Emancipation: The Failure of the Great Reaction in Maryland, 1831–1850" (Ph.D. dissertation, University of Maryland, 1974), 19, 24.

5. Whitman, *Price of Freedom*, 69–73; Brown, *Free Negroes*, 46–8, 60–1; Berlin, *Slaves without Masters*, 102–3. For a general survey of slave escapes see John Hope Franklin and Loren Schweninger, *Runaway Slaves: Rebels on the Plantation* (New York: Oxford University Press, 1999).

Elisha Tyson (c.1749–1824) was a northern-born Quaker who worked with African Americans in Baltimore from the 1790s to the 1820s. [John S. Tyson], *Elisha Tyson, the Philanthropist* (Baltimore: B. Lundy, 1825), frontispiece.

their own freedom and promote freedom for others. Informally and illegally, free black families harbored fugitive slaves. Formally, wealthier black residents organized churches, schools, and benevolent societies. They protested against schemes designed to force them out, correctly understanding that such schemes aimed to strengthen the slave system.

On occasion, African Americans went to court to contest government efforts to limit their freedom. In 1821 William Coston filed in the District of Columbia the best known of these suits. Coston, a member of Washington's black elite, challenged a city ordinance that required all free African Americans to post a twenty-dollar bond for their good behavior. He won a limited victory when United States Circuit Court Judge William Cranch ruled that while the ordinance was constitutional it could not be applied retroactively to include persons such as Coston who already lived in the District.[6]

Earlier a few local whites had begun to aid Chesapeake blacks in their an-

6. [John S. Tyson], *Elisha Tyson, the Philanthropist* (Baltimore: B. Lundy, 1825), 126–31; Constance M. Green, *The Secret City: A History of Race Relations in the Nation's Capital* (Princeton: Princeton University Press, 1967), 23–7.

tislavery and antidiscrimination efforts. Starting during the 1780s and influenced by Pennsylvania's antislavery Quakers, a series of weak state-level gradual-abolition societies came into existence in Delaware and Maryland. There were also ephemeral local Quaker-dominated gradual-abolition organizations in Baltimore, Alexandria, and Washington. Inconsistency on racial issues marked these organizations. Patterned on the Pennsylvania Society for Promoting the Abolition of Slavery, they aided individuals and families gain to freedom in court. They also encouraged manumission, sought to ameliorate conditions of enslavement, and resisted kidnapping of free blacks into slavery. They invoked the Bible and natural rights theory to criticize slavery. But members of these societies adopted a condescending tone when addressing black audiences. Often they presented themselves as acting in behalf of the political, economic, and moral interests of whites. Especially after the formation of the ACS in 1816, they endorsed plans to send free blacks to Liberia or to other locations beyond the borders of the United States. This linkage of emancipation and expatriation put the societies at odds with most black leaders during the 1820s.[7]

The two leading white gradual abolitionists active in the Chesapeake during these years, Elisha Tyson and Benjamin Lundy, nevertheless anticipated later biracial antislavery efforts by cooperating closely with black abolitionists. Both of these men were northern-born Quakers. Tyson, who was probably born in 1749, moved from Philadelphia to Maryland at "an early age." He established himself as a flour merchant in Baltimore and from the 1780s until

7. Alexandria Society for the Relief and Protection of Persons Illegally Held in Bondage, "To the Honorable General Assembly of Virginia," 1795 and George Drinker to Joseph Bringhurst, 10 December 1804 in Pennsylvania Abolition Society Papers, Historical Society of Pennsylvania, Philadelphia; *Alexandria Gazette,* quoted in *Freedom's Journal* (New York), 25 May 1827; Monte A. Calvert, "The Abolition Society of Delaware, 1801–07," *Delaware History* 10 (October 1863): 295–320; Alice Dana Adams, *The Neglected Period of Anti-Slavery in America (1808–1831)* (1908; reprint, Gloucester, Mass.: Peter Smith, 1964), 116–36; Gordon E. Finnie, "The Antislavery Movement in the Upper South before 1840," *JSH* 35 (August 1969): 320–7; Merton L. Dillon, *Benjamin Lundy and the Struggle for Negro Freedom* (Urbana: University of Illinois Press, 1966), 10–2, 108–9; Dillon, *Slavery Attacked: Southern Slaves and Their Allies, 1619–1865* (Baton Rouge: Louisiana State University Press, 1990), 92–106, 117–8; Berlin, *Slaves without Masters,* 22–9, 81–5; Brown, *Free Negroes,* 54–8, 60; Basil Hall, *Travels in North America in the Years 1827 and 1828,* 2 vols. (Philadelphia: Carey, Lea, and Curry, 1829), 2:142–43; *GUE,* 27 November 1829, 2 April 1831.

his death in 1824 engaged in a variety of benevolent enterprises, including biracial efforts to protect free blacks and weaken slavery. Among the black leaders with whom Tyson worked were future African Methodist Episcopal (AME) bishop Daniel Coker, who taught at the African School that Tyson helped establish, and George R. McGill, a local preacher, teacher, and entrepreneur.[8]

Lundy, born in New Jersey in 1789, was considerably younger than Tyson and more influential. A transitional figure between gradual and immediate abolitionism, Lundy published his weekly *Genius of Universal Emancipation* in Ohio and Tennessee prior to moving it to Baltimore during the year of Tyson's death. There, his newspaper became a focal point in strengthening ties between antislavery whites and blacks in the Chesapeake. Local black abolitionists Jacob Greener, William Watkins, and Hezekiah Grice—at least two of whom had earlier cooperated with Tyson—were among Lundy's closest associates.[9]

Greener, a housepainter and teacher, helped Lundy print the *Genius* and acted as the paper's local agent. Watkins was a teacher and preacher who published articles in the *Genius* and became, during the 1820s and 1830s, Baltimore's leading opponent of the ACS. Grice, a former butcher, like Lundy combined criticism of the ACS with advocacy of other colonization schemes. In 1830 Grice became the principal founder of the National Black Convention Movement, a northern black abolitionist organization.

8. Tyson, *Tyson*, 1–77 (quotation, p. 3), 99; Leroy Graham, *Baltimore: Nineteenth Century Black Capital* (Washington: University Press of America, 1982), 1–92; Christopher Phillips, *Freedom's Port: The African American Community of Baltimore, 1790–1860* (Urbana: Illinois University Press, 1998), 49. Many years later, McGill remembered Tyson with "admiration." See McGill to Moses Sheppard, 16 May 1854, Moses Sheppard Papers, Friends Historical Library, Swarthmore College. Both Coker and McGill supported colonization efforts.

9. The discussion in this and the following paragraphs is based on these sources: Dillon, *Lundy*, 1–84, 132–64; Graham, *Baltimore*, 93–125; Wendell Phillips Garrison and Francis Jackson Garrison, *William Lloyd Garrison, 1805–1889: The Story of His Life Told by His Children* 4 vols. (New York: Century, 1885–89), 1:145–50; *Anglo-African Magazine* 1 (October 1859), in Herbert Aptheker, ed., *A Documentary History of the Negro People in the United States*, 2d ed. (New York: Citadel, 1963), 98–101. Hepburn and Watkins's exchange: *GUE*, 13 & 27 November, 11 & 18 December 1829. Impact on Garrison: Robert H. Abzug, *Cosmos Crumbling: American Reform and the Religious Imagination* (New York: Oxford University Press, 1994), 146, 150–1.

It was as a facilitator of exchanges of views among black and white abolitionists that Lundy made his major contribution to antislavery community in the Chesapeake. In 1829 he published a running debate between Watkins and black nationalist John B. Hepburn of Alexandria on the issue of African colonization. That same year Lundy brought the young white reformer William Lloyd Garrison from Boston to Baltimore as associate editor of the *Genius.* Garrison had already begun questioning gradualism when he agreed to work with Lundy. But the months he spent in contact with Greener, Watkins, and other local black leaders helped shape his concept of immediatism. As early as 1827 Baltimore's black Friendship Club had demanded *"Emancipation* without *emigration,* but equal rights on the *spot."*[10] Garrison's time in Baltimore convinced him of the appropriateness of these principles and initiated decades of direct ties between northern abolitionists and the black people of the Chesapeake.

Tyson, Coker, McGill, Lundy, Greener, Watkins, Grice, and Garrison established an agenda for the future. Tyson, Lundy, and McGill were patient and legalistic. They were not immediate abolitionists and, during the 1820s, neither was Coker, Greener, Watkins, Grice, nor Garrison. But they pioneered antislavery tactics that later characterized Washington's subversive community. Prior to 1830 antislavery whites in Baltimore and Washington joined blacks in confronting slavetraders and kidnappers. They helped purchase freedom, supported blacks in numerous freedom suits, and promoted black schools. Tyson, Lundy, and Garrison empathized with suffering African Americans, took physical risks, and earned the esteem of their black contemporaries.[11]

This was most clear in their efforts against the slave trade, which galvanized antislavery action among local blacks and a small minority of local whites from the 1790s through the 1820s. The trade and its auxiliaries—kidnapping, slave pens, and sales into slavery of *alleged* escapees—encouraged interracial cooperation among slavery's opponents. Far more than was the case farther north, the barbarity of the trade led antislavery blacks and whites to confront the slave system. Interracial cooperation began in Baltimore be-

10. *Freedom's Journal,* 20 July 1827.

11. Earning respect of blacks: *Freedom's Journal,* 20 July 1827; Tyson, *Tyson,* 122–5; Graham, *Baltimore,* 82–4.

cause it, prior to the late 1820s, greatly surpassed Alexandria and Washington as a slave market.[12]

In his biography of his uncle, published in 1825, John S. Tyson remarks that this domestic slave trade "gave rise to most of the difficulties with which Mr. Tyson had to contend." As the Chesapeake economy changed during the late eighteenth century, the trade provided local masters with a profitable alternative to manumission. It was not, however, an awareness of a link between the slave trade and the continuation of slavery itself in the Chesapeake that motivated Elisha Tyson. Rather it was black resistance to the trade. Those threatened with sale south faced "a separation like that of death between the nearest and dearest relatives," banishment from "their native soil," and cruel treatment from the traders. Therefore, as John S. Tyson recalled, they used "all the means in their power to avoid so terrible a destiny."[13]

Although Washington and Alexandria developed more slowly than Baltimore as slave trade depots, the brutality associated with the trade in these cities also aroused the emotions of some whites. In 1804 George Drinker, an antislavery Quaker residing in Alexandria, reported to a northern colleague that "our feelings wher [sic] often shock'd with a view of 50 or 60 of these poor objects handcuff'd & chained to gether, taking leave of their friends & relatives never to meet again." During a visit to Washington in 1815, Philadelphia abolitionist Jesse Torrey stood at the door of the Capitol observing "a procession of men, women and children, resembling that of a funeral . . . bound together in pairs, with ropes, and *chains*." According to Torrey, "several hundred people, including not legal slaves only but many kidnapped freemen and youth bound to service for a term of years, and unlawfully sold as slaves for life . . . [were] annually collected at Washington (as if it were an emporium for slavery) for transportation to the [Deep South] slave regions."[14]

12. William Calderhead, "The Role of the Professional Slave Trader in a Slave Economy: Austin Woolfolk, a Case Study," *Civil War History* 23 (September 1977): 195–211.

13. Tyson, *Tyson,* 7–9. During the early 1820s the president of the Maryland auxiliary of the ACS sold fifty-four slaves south rather than colonize them. See Calderhead, "Woolfolk," 196.

14. Calderhead, "Woolfolk," 200; Frederic Bancroft, *Slave Trading in the Old South* (Baltimore: J. H. Furst, 1931), 47, 49, 58; Michael Tadman, *Speculators and Slaves: Masters, Traders, and Slaves in the Old South* (Madison: University of Wisconsin Press, 1996); Drinker to Joseph Bringhurst, 10 December 1804, Pennsylvania Abolition Society Papers, Historical Society of Pennsylvania, Philadelphia (first quotation); Jesse Torrey, *A Portraiture of Domestic Slavery in*

From the time of his arrival in Baltimore, Lundy denounced the slave trade, and in 1826, in anticipation of abolitionists in Washington, began forcing himself to attend slave sales. Seeking to inculcate sympathy among whites for suffering blacks, he described the public auction of a woman and her four children in the "christian city of Baltimore." He reported that "the spectacle was well calculated to awaken all the sympathies of our nature. The mother, a most respectable and interesting woman, was in tears [and the children] wept with a pathos that would have melted a heart of stone."[15]

Such emotional appeals to whites to recognize their common humanity with blacks were new during the 1820s when nearly all antislavery whites rejected "intimate social contact between the races." According to John S. Tyson, the difficulty to be overcome was that "the [white] man who would practice [benevolence toward African Americans], must struggle against the most violent prejudices in himself, and antipathies in others." Whites, Tyson contended, had been "taught to despise" the "quarter of the world" from which black people had originated. Whites also imagined that African Americans lacked not only "human beauty but even . . . human nature." Therefore whites were "irresistibly inclined to regard them as an inferior race of beings, born to toil for the benefit of others, and predestined to oppression."[16]

It is a tribute to their own humanity and that of the black people with whom they cooperated that white abolitionists made progress in overcoming such deep-set prejudices—and tremendous social pressures—in order to form a subversive community. In 1804 Drinker distributed antislavery literature "to the free people of color" in Alexandria. In 1812 Elisha Tyson attended a meeting at Daniel Coker's African Institute to hear black colonizationist Paul Cuffe speak. Then, when a local tavern refused to provide lodging to Cuffe, Tyson invited Cuffe to spend the night at his home. In 1829 Lundy and Garrison shared a boardinghouse with Watkins and Greener. By 1830 it seemed

---

the United States 2d ed. (Ballston, Pa.: [Torrey], 1817), 63–4 (second quotation), 73 (third quotation). John S. Tyson credits his uncle with the decline of the slave trade in Baltimore, Calderhead credits the establishment of Franklin and Armfield's business in Alexandria. See Tyson, *Tyson*, 11–2.

15. *GUE* 1 (13 May 1826): 292–3.
16. Tyson, *Tyson*, 4.

appalling to Garrison that the slaveholding chairman of the House of Representatives's committee on the District of Columbia showed no sympathy for black families separated by the slave trade.[17]

This dawning sense of interracial community led white abolitionists in a slaveholding and slavetrading city to make common cause with African Americans in direct physical action against slavery. Unlike some of Washington's more radical abolitionists of the 1840s and 1850s, Tyson, Lundy, Garrison, and others acted nonviolently within the existing legal system. Yet a confrontational style exposed them to the same dangers that accompanied later black-white cooperation.

Tyson, who was a large man, intervened physically only in behalf of individuals who had been illegally deprived of their freedom. But this limited commitment led him personally to rescue free blacks from kidnappers and slavetraders. According to his nephew, Tyson once went alone and unarmed at night to a tavern where five slavetraders were holding six free African Americans. When one of the traders threatened him with a pistol, Tyson reportedly faced him down by replying, "'Shoot if thee dare . . . but thee know, that the gallows would be thy portion.'"[18]

In another instance, having received written documentation of the free status of a black man who was about to be shipped by sea to New Orleans, Tyson went with two constables to Baltimore's harbor. There, while the constables remained on the wharf, he boarded a ship, argued with its knife-wielding captain, and rescued the man. But, true to his legalistic view of antislavery action, Tyson flatly refused to help a man who came to his home seeking to avoid being sold south. When the man could not prove that he had paid $250 toward purchasing his freedom, Tyson told him, "The law is against thee, and thou must submit. I can do nothing for thee." The man,

17. Drinker to Joseph Bringhurst, 10 December 1804, Pennsylvania Abolition Society Papers (quotation); Graham, *Baltimore*, 70; James Brewer Stewart, *William Lloyd Garrison and the Challenge of Emancipation* (Arlington Heights, Ill.: Harlan Davidson, 1992), 43; *GUE*, 8 January 1830.

18. Tyson, *Tyson*, 19–23, 78–83. Tyson's efforts in behalf of kidnap victims: Tyson to Isaac Hopper, 10 July 1811, Tyson to William Masters, 18 July & 12 December 1811; 9 April, 20 August, & 11 November 1812, Pennsylvania Abolition Society Papers.

who cried "I cannot live away from my wife and children," subsequently killed himself.[19]

Later antislavery activists better remembered Lundy and Garrison's physical confrontations with slavetraders and slaveholders than they did Tyson's. When Lundy arrived in Baltimore in 1824, he denounced Austin Woolfolk, the city's leading slavetrader. In January 1827, Woolfolk responded by waylaying Lundy and beating him severely. When Lundy pressed charges, Woolfolk pled guilty. But the judge ruled that the slave trade was a beneficial enterprise, that Lundy had insulted Woolfolk, and that therefore "Lundy had received no more than merited chastisement." Woolfolk had to pay a one dollar fine plus court costs.[20]

Two years later Garrison revived the controversy by challenging Woolfolk to assault him. When the slavetrader did not respond, Garrison declared that one of Woolfolk's slave ship captains was a robber and murderer. Convicted on charges of "malicious libel" and unable to pay a fine of fifty dollars, Garrison spent forty-nine days in Baltimore Jail. Finally, the New York abolitionist leader Arthur Tappan secured Garrison's release. This was only the first of several such efforts undertaken by northern abolitionists in behalf of their associates in the Chesapeake.[21]

Before he regained his liberty, Garrison demonstrated a willingness similar to Tyson's to confront slaveholders physically. Enjoying "considerable freedom within the walls" of the jail, Garrison observed an allegedly brutal master and several companions come to retrieve an escaped slave. When the slave refused to return voluntarily, Garrison stepped forward. With his "blood boiling" and his "limbs trembling with emotion," he declared that—despite a legal title—the master had no right to the slave. He contended that the master was a thief and a kidnapper and that blacks were morally and intellectually equal to whites.[22]

---

19. Tyson, *Tyson*, 83–4, 95–6. Leroy Graham maintains that Elisha Tyson harbored escaping slaves and engaged in an early underground railroad operation, but I am not convinced by the evidence he cites that this was the case. See Graham, *Baltimore*, 27–9, 48–9.

20. Dillon, *Lundy*, 118–20; Calderhead, "Woolfolk," 195–211. Long after his death, abolitionists recalled that Tyson too had a physical confrontation with Woolfolk. See Graham, *Baltimore*, 84–5.

21. Garrison and Garrison, *Garrison*, 1:168–71.

22. Ibid., 1:175–7.

This was an important turning point. Garrison's *words* anticipated the justification for later *illegal* action against slavery in Washington and its vicinity: that since slavery itself violated God's law, one might righteously break state and national laws designed to protect it. It took courage for Garrison to speak as he did. Yet this was also his last confrontation with a slaveholder on southern soil. He soon determined that the true theater for antislavery action was back in Boston. Rather than Garrison and his associates, it was a more aggressive group of abolitionists, hailing from upstate New York, that refined the doctrine of the illegality of slavery and acted on it in the Chesapeake.

Even without such a doctrine, however, court proceedings during the late eighteenth and early nineteenth centuries were more effective than physical confrontation in freeing people in the region. Courtroom ventures also involved more extensive interracial cooperation. Beginning during the Revolutionary era, African Americans took advantage of their access to the courts in Maryland and Virginia to bring freedom suits against their masters.[23] Such efforts became biracial during the 1790s as state and local gradual abolition societies provided financial and legal assistance. This support became the main work of the societies and created a bond between antislavery whites and blacks that lasted into the Civil War years.

From 1789 to 1796 the Maryland Society for Promoting the Abolition of Slavery and Relief of Free Negroes and Others Unlawfully Held in Bondage concentrated on freedom suits, earning in 1791 a vote of censure from the Maryland legislature. Elisha Tyson acted for the Society in these court cases and organized a protection society in 1816. In 1817 he succeeded in convincing Maryland's legislature to prohibit the selling of suspected escapees to cover the costs of jailing them. He worked closely with black petitioners in tracing genealogies back to free maternal ancestors. He went to court with them and had "extraordinary success." In 1787 a local antislavery society on

---

23. During the 1790s, Maryland and Virginia passed laws making such litigation more difficult. See: Maryland, *Laws of Maryland. Made and Passed at a Session of Assembly, Begun and Held at the City of Annapolis [Nov. 1–Dec. 22, 1790]* (Annapolis: Md., 1791), c. 75; Samuel Shepherd, comp., *The Statutes at Large of Virginia from October Session 1792, to December Session 1806*, 3 vols. (Richmond: Samuel Shepherd, 1835), 1:363–5, 2:77–9. See also, Brown, *Free Negroes*, 56–8.

Maryland's eastern shore claimed similar results, having helped liberate sixty people in seven years.[24]

White abolitionists also supported successful black freedom suits in the District of Columbia. In 1827 local Quakers Samuel M. Janney and George Drinker, both of whom remained active for many decades in antislavery efforts, joined fourteen other members of the Benevolent Society of Alexandria in successfully supporting twelve African-American petitioners in court against slavetraders. In 1831 Lundy helped a black family of five or six win freedom in a district court.[25]

But earlier there had been devastating losses in those courts. In 1797 Drinker reported from Alexandria to the American Convention of Abolitionist Societies that he doubted the local Society for the Relief and Protection of Persons Illegally Held in Bondage could win in fourteen out of twenty-six cases it undertook that year. In 1800 the Society failed badly in an effort to secure the freedom of a family of five that had been sold by its *former* master to a slavetrader. Not only was the family reenslaved, but court costs, including those incurred in defending against a counter suit, were so high as to impair the Society's ability to function. Such losses were especially heart-rending because African Americans who undertook freedom suits had to endure imprisonment until a court ruled in their case. During the winter of 1825, Representative Alexander Thomson of Pennsylvania noted that four children in a Washington jail awaiting a court decision "were almost naked; one of them sick, lying on the damp brick floor without bed, pillow, or covering."[26] For children to suffer and then lose was a difficult experience for parents and friends.

24. Graham, *Baltimore*, 58; Brown, *Free Negroes*, 55; Tyson, *Tyson*, 13–23 (quotation), 94–9; Calderhead, "Woolfolk," 204; Thomas E. Drake, *Quakers and Slavery in America* (New Haven: Yale University Press, 1950), 120; American Convention, *Minutes of the Proceedings of the Fourth Convention of Delegates from the Abolition Societies* (Philadelphia: [American Convention], 1797), 38.

25. American Convention, *Minutes of the Twentieth Session of the American Convention for Promoting the Abolition of Slavery. . . .* (Baltimore: American Convention, 1827), 53; *GUE*, vol. 2, ser. 3 (May 1831): 5–7.

26. American Convention, *Proceedings of the Fourth Convention* (1797), 4–5, 38–40; *Proceedings of the Seventh Convention*, 31–3; Tyson, *Tyson*, 94; *Register of Debates in Congress*, 19 Cong., 1 sess. (1 March 1826), 1480–1 (quotation).

Concern for black children also promoted biracial educational efforts aimed to remedy the negative impact of slavery and discrimination. Once again following the lead of Quaker abolitionists in Pennsylvania, white abolition societies in the Chesapeake initiated the region's first black schools. In Alexandria, Baltimore, Georgetown, and Washington there were, starting during the 1790s, a wide variety of such schools for black children and adults. They ranged from Sunday schools designed to teach Bible-reading to academies providing a classical education.

During the first decade of the nineteenth century, African Americans began to assume responsibility for these schools. In 1802 black leaders purchased Baltimore's African Institute, which had been established by the Maryland Abolition Society. Former slaves established Washington's first black school in 1807 and blacks took control of similar schools in the other Chesapeake cities. But schools for African Americans, taught and administered by whites, continued to exist, as did white support for schools taught by blacks. During the 1820s, associates of Elisha Tyson established a Sunday school for slaves. The encouragement of black education later became part of the program of the Washington Abolition Society as well as of Lundy and Garrison.[27]

Schools supported by the ACS insisted on educating only those who intended to migrate to Africa, and in some instances white-supported schools for blacks emphasized "suitable" education for black children as industrial workers. But generally, antislavery advocates and their proslavery opponents assumed that the education of African Americans encouraged abolitionism. After a visit to one of the schools in 1829, Garrison declared, "We should like to have those who persist in debasing the intellect and capacity of our colored population, to step into [t]his school, and try if they can argue against fact." The link between the schools and abolitionism became explicit in 1830 when

27. American Convention, *Proceedings of the Fourth Convention* (1797), 34–6; Graham, *Baltimore,* 22–3, 62–3, 93, 142; Nash and Soderlund, *Freedom by Degrees,* 128; U.S. Congress, House, *Special Report of the Commissioner of Education on the Condition and Improvement of Public Schools in the District of Columbia,* 41 Cong., 2 sess., H. Exec. Doc. 315, Serial 1427 (1870), 195–206; Robert C. Smedley, *History of the Underground Railroad in Chester and Neighboring Counties in Pennsylvania* (1883; reprint, New York: Arno, 1969), 260; *NI,* 25 March 1828; Garrison and Garrison, *Garrison,* 1:149.

a Washington court sentenced a British man who taught "a large colored school" to "a term in the penitentiary" for "assisting a slave to his freedom."[28]

The proliferation of black schools also provided formal roles for black and white women in an emerging biracial community. In Baltimore John Needles, a Quaker associate of Elisha Tyson, provided housing for a school taught by Prudence Gardner, a local black woman. In Georgetown and Washington during the first four decades of the nineteenth century there were several schools for black children taught by women. Prior to 1810 Anne Maria Hall, an African American from Maryland, opened a school on Capitol Hill. During the 1810s and early 1820s, Mary Billings, a white Englishwoman, conducted schools for black children in Georgetown and Washington. Young women from prominent free black families taught other schools. Among them were Louisa Parke Costin, daughter of William Costin, and Maria Becraft, a former student of Billings.[29]

By cooperating in black education, in promoting or protecting black freedom, and in confronting slavery's defenders, early black and white abolitionists established a framework for the future. They strengthened local black institutions. They encouraged interracial trust among the opponents of slavery. They publicized the oppressiveness of slavery in a region where it reputedly existed in a mild form. In all, they anticipated the more aggressive biracial antislavery community that flourished in Washington from the late 1830s into the Civil War years.

Sometimes there was personal continuity between the earlier and later periods. Mary Billings taught the black man who established the school that Washington black leader John F. Cook Sr. conducted from the 1830s to the 1850s. When northern abolitionist Joshua Leavitt first visited Washington in 1834, an aged George Drinker accompanied him on a tour of Franklin and Armfield's slave pen in Alexandria. Charles T. Torrey revered the example of Elisha Tyson and during the 1840s worked with Tyson's son Isaac. In 1850 John Needles endorsed a note for William L. Chaplin's bail following

28. Graham, *Baltimore,* 97; Green, *Secret City,* 33–4; *GUE,* 20 November 1829 (first quotation), 6 November 1829 (second quotation); House, *Special Report,* 199 (third–fifth quotations).

29. Graham, *Baltimore,* 96; U.S. House of Representatives, *Special Report,* 198–9, 203–5; Edward Needles Wright, ed., "John Needles (1786–1878): An Autobiography," *Quaker History* 58 (Spring 1969): 3–21.

Chaplin's arrest on charges of helping slaves escape. When Myrtilla Miner faced persecution in Washington during the early 1850s, she took refuge in the Georgetown home of Maria Becraft's family.[30]

Important discontinuities, however, separated the two eras. Among them were the rise of immediate abolitionism, Washington's replacement of Baltimore as the center of the regional slave trade, and the impact of a great proslavery reaction. The emergence of Washington as the center of interracial antislavery cooperation in the Chesapeake was of particular importance. Both persistence and change shaped the antislavery community's development.

Black leaders in Baltimore and Washington helped lead the opposition to the ACS that presaged *immediatism* in the United States. They characterized colonization as an effort to strengthen slavery by expatriating its free black opponents. During the 1820s many black and white abolitionists, including Elisha Tyson, Lundy, Garrison, and Grice were inconsistent concerning their goals. They often combined advocacy of elevating African-American status within the United States with grudging support of the ACS expatriation plan. Vocal black opposition to this plan and black insistence on rights as American citizens made such equivocation increasingly difficult. Watkins was especially outspoken during the late 1820s and in 1831 Washington's leading black educator, John W. Prout, led a "large and very respectable meeting" at the city's AME church in expressing deep distrust of efforts to encourage blacks to leave "their only *true and veritable home.*"[31]

Garrison's northern evangelical background, his embrace of moral absolutes, and his firsthand experience with slavery in Baltimore made him especially receptive to anticolonizationist arguments, and to immediate (as opposed to gradual) abolitionism. That anticolonization arguments came from Watkins, Jacob Greener, and Garrison's other black associates in the city

30. Cook, John Francis Sr., q.v. *DANB;* Drinker and Leavitt: *GUE* 14 (March 1834): 39–41. Tysons and Torrey: Torrey to Isaac Tyson, n.d. and Tyson to Torrey, 15 January 1842, Charles T. Torrey Papers, Congressional Library, Boston; Torrey to Gerrit Smith, 3 August 1844, GSP. Needles and Chaplin: Gamaliel Bailey to Lewis Tappan, 12 March 1851, GSP. Elijah Tyson's son Isaac also endorsed the note.

31. Phillips, *Freedom's Port*, 220–4; *NI*, 4 May 1831 (quotations); Garrison and Garrison, *Garrison*, 1:146–8; Dillon, *Lundy*, 27–30; *GUE*, vol. 3, series 3 (June 1833): 120; Graham, *Baltimore*, 97–108.

made them particularly persuasive.[32] Historians no longer assume that Garrison by himself transformed the antislavery movement during the late 1820s and early 1830s. The concept of immediate abolition was not new. But Garrison's renunciation of the ACS and the initiation of his weekly *Liberator* in January 1831 with a demand for immediate emancipation and citizenship rights for blacks played a crucial role. He pushed other northern white abolitionists toward rejecting gradualism and colonization.

In December 1833 northern immediatists led by Garrison met in Philadelphia to form the American Anti-Slavery Society (AASS), dedicated to achieve these goals through nonviolent means. Although dominated by white men, the AASS attracted support from black male abolitionists and antislavery women of both races. It enlisted only a tiny minority of northerners, but by 1838 it claimed 1,350 affiliate societies and maintained a vigorous propaganda campaign against slavery. By radicalizing abolitionism in the North, immediatism transformed the context of biracial antislavery cooperation in the Chesapeake.[33]

White supporters of the ACS continued throughout the antebellum decades to provide important services to the antislavery cause in this region. Either Chesapeake natives or Yankees who had lived in the region for many years, they contributed to purchases of freedom and supported courtroom efforts. But blacks and whites who subscribed to immediatism determined the agenda of the biracial community. Increasingly, too, the whites involved in this community were Yankee evangelicals rather than local Quakers. Far less

32. Garrison and Garrison, *Garrison*, 1:144–56; Stewart, *Garrison*, 40–59; Walter M. Merrill, *Against Wind and Tide: A Biography of William Lloyd Garrison* (Boston: Little, Brown, 1963), 81–113.

33. David Brion Davis, "The Emergence of Immediatism in British and American Antislavery Thought," *Mississippi Valley Historical Review* 49 (September 1962): 209–30; Anne C. Loveland, "Evangelicalism and 'Immediate Emancipation' in American Antislavery Thought," *Journal of Southern History* 32 (May 1966): 172–88; James Brewer Stewart, *Holy Warriors: The American Abolitionists and American Slavery*, 2d ed. (New York: Hill and Wang, 1997), 35–50; Lawrence J. Friedman, *Gregarious Saints: Self and Community in American Abolitionism, 1830–1870* (New York: Cambridge University Press, 1982), 11–40; Louis Filler, *The Crusade Against Slavery, 1830–1860* (New York: Harper and Row, 1960), 66–7. For a recent assessment of Garrison's importance at this point in the antislavery movement see Robert H. Abzug, *Cosmos Crumbling: American Reform and the Religious Imagination* (New York: Oxford University Press, 1994), 129–57.

impressed with the authority of human law than either Tyson or Lundy, some of them were willing to join blacks in illegal efforts aimed at weakening or destroying slavery. Ironically, the direction of Garrison's own reform ideology after 1831—toward pacifism, anarchism, and disunionism—greatly limited his role and that of his associates in these new initiatives.

The relocation of the regional center of antislavery efforts from Baltimore to the District of Columbia rivaled the rise of immediatism in the development of subversive biracial community in the Chesapeake. The emerging predominance of the District cities of Washington, Georgetown, and Alexandria in the domestic slave trade caused this geographical reorientation. More centrally located in the Chesapeake "buying market" than Baltimore, these municipalities also placed fewer legal restrictions on slavetrading. They enjoyed good access to coastal shipping via the Potomac River and by the mid-1820s had attracted "sundry traders." The establishment in 1828 of Isaac Franklin and John Armfield's slavetrading firm at Alexandria was especially important in the district's emergence as *the* slaveholding center in the region. By the mid-1830s, these notorious slavetraders surpassed Austin Woolfolk and others in Baltimore to become the nation's leading dealers in human beings. Yet it was Washington, not Alexandria, that by the early 1830s controlled the slave trade in northern Virginia and "most of Maryland." Abolitionists called Washington the "great Man-Market of the nation."[34]

The slave trade had existed there since the city's founding. Periodically, observers denounced the trade, the kidnapping of free blacks that it encouraged, and the conditions in slave prisons where people were held pending sale. As the trade expanded during the late 1820s and 1830s, criticism became more sustained. As early as 1827 a black journalist writing in New York City asked if the slave trade were more vigorously pursued anywhere else than in the national capital. Northern colonizationist Ethan Allen Andrews in 1835

---

34. Wendell Holmes Stephenson, *Isaac Franklin: Slave Trader and Planter of the Old South* (1938; reprint, Gloucester, Mass.: Peter Smith, 1968), 23–7 (first & second quotations); Bancroft, *Slave Trading,* 45–51, 58 (third quotation); Calderhead, "Woolfolk," 200; J. B. W. Lydia Maria Child, *An Appeal in Favor of That Class of Americans Called Africans,* ed. Caroline L. Karcher. (Amherst: University of Massachusetts Press, 1996), 32; J. B. W. [Jacob Bigelow] to William L. Chaplin, September 1846, in *AP,* 30 September 1846 (fourth quotation); *TL,* 27 October 1842; *PF,* 17 September 1840.

declared it to be "an outrage upon public sentiment" that the United States capital had become "the very seat and centre of the domestic slave-trade."[35]

It was the visibility and shocking inhumanity of this trade that reignited sectional debate in Congress after a period of relative quiescence following the Missouri Compromise. Well before the 1846 war against Mexico revived the issue of slavery expansion, issues related to slavery in the District of Columbia encouraged abolitionism in the North and bitter defense of slavery in the South. While many antislavery northerners accepted the contention that they had no say in what transpired in the southern states, Washington was a different matter. As the national capital, it belonged to all Americans. The oppression of black people within its bounds implicated northerners politically, fiscally, and morally. They believed they had a right and responsibility to interfere there, and improving rail links between the Capital and the North made it easier for them to do so.[36]

In January 1828 Representative Charles Miner of Pennsylvania initiated a lasting focus on slavery and the slave trade in Washington. Northerners, he noted, had responsibility for the trade because their tax money helped pay for jails used as holding pens for slaves awaiting sale. Prodded by Lundy, Miner called for the immediate abolition of the trade and the gradual abolition of slavery in the District. Minor disdained the morals and work ethic of Wash-

35. Green, *Secret City,* 19–20; *Debates and Proceedings of the Congress of the United States,* 14 Cong., 1 sess. (1 March 1816), 1115–7; George Howard Connaughton, "The Anti-Slavery Movement in the District of Columbia," (master's thesis, Ohio State University, 1934), [37–40]; *Freedom's Journal,* 16 November 1817; Ethan Allen Andrews, *Slavery and the Domestic Slave Trade in the United States* (Boston: Light and Stearns, 1836), 122 (quotations). The late Don E. Fehrenbacher incorrectly maintained that "Washington was never a major slave market." See Fehrenbacher, *Slaveholding Republic,* 67.

36. "The extent to which the slave-trade was carried on was well known,—not even the traders themselves tried to keep it secret," wrote Mary Tremain in the 1890s. See Tremain, *Slavery in the District of Columbia: The Policy of Congress and the Struggle for Abolition* (New York: G. P. Putnam's Sons, 1892), 49–50. Power of Congress over slavery in the district: William M. Wiecek, *The Sources of Antislavery Constitutionalism in America, 1760–1848* (Ithaca, N.Y.: Cornell University Press, 1977), 102, 183–90; W[illiam] S[lade] to Editor of the *E,* 18 February 1839, in *PF,* 14 March 1839; *PF,* 3 September 1840; J. B. W. [Jacob Bigelow], Correspondence of the *Boston Whig,* in *AP,* 28 July 1847. Commitment to act in the District: James M. McPherson, "The Fight against the Gag Rule: Joshua Leavitt and the Antislavery Insurgency in the Whig Party," *Journal of Negro History* 48 (July 1963): 177–95; *Great Falls Journal,* quoted in *L,* 9 March 1836.

ington's black population, the resolutions he presented had no chance of passage. But abolitionists long remembered his exposure of the outrages Washington slavetraders perpetrated on African Americans.[37]

In the minds of slaveholders, Miner's words paled in comparison to a series of antislavery assaults that occurred beyond the halls of Congress. In 1829 black abolitionist David Walker published in Boston his incendiary *Appeal . . . to the Colored Citizens of the World* and managed to get it circulated among slaves. In January 1831 Garrison initiated the *Liberator* with a call for immediate abolition. In August of that year Nat Turner led a bloody slave revolt in southern Virginia. These startling events brought on a great proslavery reaction that transformed conditions in the Chesapeake and the rest of the South. Southern states and the District of Columbia tightened controls over slaves, placed further restrictions on free black people, and limited freedom of speech among antislavery whites.

Lundy and Garrison had each independently contemplated moving their antislavery efforts to Washington. As conditions deteriorated, Garrison decided to go to Boston instead. Lundy proceeded to publish the *Genius* in Washington during the fall of 1830, but the proslavery reaction made it impossible for him to sustain the effort for long. While visiting black settlements in Canada in early 1832, he learned that he had been indicted in the District for libel. Convinced that he would be imprisoned or worse if he returned, he stayed away. In October 1833 Evan Lewis, who had replaced Lundy as editor of the *Genius*, retreated with the paper to Philadelphia. By 1835 proslavery forces had overwhelmed the District's local white antislavery movement that had been led by men such as George Drinker and Samuel Janney.[38] There had been earlier proslavery reactions in the Chesapeake, but this time efforts to suppress southern antislavery sentiment were much more thorough.

If reaction in the city discouraged white antislavery activists, it devastated

37. *GUE,* 4 March 1826; *Register of Debates in Congress,* 20 Cong., 2 sess., 167–8, 175–81; William Jay, *Miscellaneous Writings on Slavery* (Boston: J. P. Jewett, 1853), 153–4; William Slade to Samuel D. Darling, 12 October 1838, in *PF,* 1 November 1838.

38. Dillon, *Lundy,* 121–6, 148, 186; Samuel M. Janney to Dillwyn, Parish, et al., 4 June 1875, Samuel M. Jenney Papers, Friends Historical Library, Swarthmore College; Green, *Secret City,* 31–3; *CA,* 2 January 1841; *L,* 18 June 1831; *GUE* 11 (October 1830): 97; *GUE* 12 (August 1831): 49–50, (September 1831): 65, (April 1832): 173–4; *GUE* 13 (October 1833): 177; Connaughton, "Anti-Slavery Movement," 84–6.

their African-American associates. In 1831, as reports of Turner's revolt reached the capital, heavily armed and reportedly inebriated white vigilantes beat and arrested black men and women who were delivering produce during predawn hours.[39] Four years later, fear of collaboration between antislavery blacks and whites, heightened by a recently initiated northern abolitionist effort to send antislavery literature into the South, generated a greater outbreak of proslavery violence.

In August 1835 local newspapers juxtaposed a report that a slave had attempted to murder his female owner with another report concerning the arrest of Reuben Crandall for possessing abolitionist literature. It is unlikely that Crandall, a white northern physician who had recently moved to Georgetown, circulated these materials among either blacks or whites in the District or that the offending slave had read them. But Crandall's acknowledgment after his arrest that he favored immediate emancipation fueled indignation among local whites. So did the fact that Crandall was the brother of Prudence Crandall, an abolitionist noted for her efforts to establish a school for black girls in Connecticut. A mob formed as Washington constables led Crandall to jail. During the following week white rioters physically threatened African Americans and inflicted considerable damage on black homes, businesses, and churches.[40]

No one was killed in this disturbance, known as the "Snow Riot" or "Snow Storm" in remembrance of its principal victim, black restaurateur Beverly Snow. But some black abolitionists fled the city. Among them was John F. Cook Sr., whose later caution is partly explained by his having to run for his life in 1835. Another African American who fled was a Patent Office messenger who, according to a white coworker, had "been a great patron of the abolition journals, and used to get leave of absence every summer to attend the negro Congress at Phila. as the Washington delegate."[41]

These events did not end cooperation between antislavery blacks and

39. *GUE* 12 (October 1831): 177.

40. The best account of this incident is Neil S. Kramer, "The Trial of Reuben Crandall," *RCHS* 50 (1980): 123–39.

41. Cook, q.v., *DANB* (first quotation); Constance M. Green, *The Secret City: A History of Race Relations in the Nation's Capital* (Princeton: Princeton University Press, 1967), 40 (second quotation); William P. Hoyt, ed., "Washington's Living History: The Post Office Fire and Other Matters, 1834–1839," *RCHS* 46–7 (1947): 61–5 (third quotation).

whites in Washington and its vicinity, but they changed its form. Some individuals who had been associated with local antislavery efforts prior to 1835, such as Cook, Drinker, Janney, and the prominent colonizationist Joseph H. Bradley—who served as Crandall's lawyer—remained active after that date.[42] But the rise of immediatism, the emergence of the slave trade in Washington as a galvanizing sectional issue, and the proslavery reaction combined to create a new more radical antislavery community in the capital city. Leadership passed to more-desperate blacks and to whites who represented northern immediatist organizations or northern political constituencies that embraced immediatist precepts.

A petitioning campaign organized by the AASS brought these northern whites to Washington. Lundy, in conjunction with local gradual abolition societies and the American Convention of Abolition Societies, had in 1828 organized the first coordinated campaign to petition Congress for action against slavery and the slave trade in the District. During the mid-1830s the AASS revived Lundy's campaign on a massive scale. Many thousands of petitions calling for abolition of slavery or of the slave trade in the District inundated the House of Representatives. Under southern leadership, the House responded in 1836 with the Gag Rule, banning the presentation of petitions related to slavery.[43]

The story of how former president John Quincy Adams, who represented a Massachusetts district in the House from 1832 to 1848, promoted the growth of antislavery sentiment in the North during his successful eight-year campaign for repeal of the Gag is well known.[44] Just as important, his struggle created the first cadre of white antislavery northerners in Washington. It included Adams's congressional allies, Seth Gates of New York, William Slade

42. On Bradley see Kramer, "Trial of Reuben Crandall," 134–9.

43. Dillon, *Lundy,* 121–7; *GUE,* 17 November 1827, 26 January & 2 February 1828; Gilbert H. Barnes, *The Antislavery Impulse, 1830–1844* (1933; reprint New York: Harcourt, Brace, and World, 1964), 109–45; William Lee Miller, *Arguing about Slavery: The Great Battle in the United States Congress* (New York: Knopf, 1996), 301–11; Stewart, *Holy Warriors,* 81–5.

44. Leonard Richards, *The Life and Times of Congressman John Quincy Adams* (New York: Oxford University Press, 1986), 89–179; Miller, *Arguing about Slavery,* passim. See also Stewart, *Holy Warriors,* 85–7 and Eric L. McKitrick's clarifying review of Miller's book in *New York Review* 43 (14 November 1996): 46–50. All of these emphasize the formal political significance of the congressional effort against the Gag Rule.

of Vermont, and Joshua R. Giddings of Ohio, as well as antislavery lobbyists Joshua Leavitt and Theodore D. Weld. There were also a few northern abolitionist journalists, including David Lee Child and Charles T. Torrey. These men succeeded Tyson, Lundy, and Garrison as whites who were willing to engage with African Americans in antislavery efforts in the Chesapeake.

They found in Washington a more polarized climate of opinion regarding slavery and black rights than had existed during the four decades prior to the great reaction. The city's emergence as the Chesapeake's principal slave market, efforts among African Americans to protect themselves, an increasingly tense sectional conflict, and the northerners' own actions created an environment in which a subversive community could flourish and have an enormous impact on national events.

TWO

Elements of a Biracial Antislavery Community

HE antislavery community that existed in the Chesapeake for nearly forty years united local slaves and free blacks with northern-born white abolitionists, other northern antislavery activists, and a few white southerners. Not until the Civil War could northern black abolitionists participate. Heroic black initiatives in behalf of freedom were at the community's core. The empathy, paternalism, and bravery of antislavery whites—the assistance they provided in freedom suits, purchases of freedom, and escape attempts—helped shape the community's spirit.

Yet the lives of the community's white members contrasted with those of its enslaved and free black members. The whites enjoyed advantages in education, economic and social standing, and in individual liberties. In most instances the whites had observed slavery when they, like Harriet Martineau, traveled through Baltimore to Washington. Local African Americans always had lived in slavery's shadow, subject to the vicissitudes of this regionally declining labor system and to oppressive laws. The community was, therefore, synthetic, resting mainly on physical proximity and on a shared opposition to slavery.[1]

There are two common definitions of *community*. The first pertains to

---

1. Scholars usually emphasize what separated blacks and whites. Brenda E. Stevenson writes concerning Loudoun County, Virginia: "family and community differed profoundly for black and white people." See Brenda E. Stevenson, *Life in Black and White: Family and Community in the Slave South* (New York: Oxford University Press, 1996), x.

local geography. In this sense, *community* means neighborhoods, towns, and cities where people of diverse economic and political standing live close to one another and interact in a variety of ways. In geographical communities there are economic and political relationships, formal and informal educational experiences, and cooperation across class and racial lines. Geographical communities are compatible with social hierarchies in which elites dominate and patronize their economic and social inferiors. Southern plantations and northern mill villages are extreme examples of such hierarchical communities in antebellum America.[2]

Nineteenth-century cities, particularly such villagelike ones as Washington, encouraged interclass relationships because they allowed for intimacy among persons who had different backgrounds and social standing. The employment of free and enslaved African Americans as bellboys, waiters, and servants enhanced social interchange among people of different races. As antislavery whites arrived in the city, local blacks learned who they were and initiated another type of community antagonistic to the slave system.[3]

This second type of community is what sociologist Joseph R. Gusfield calls "relational." When used in this sense, *community* refers to "human relationships, without reference to location." This is what people have in mind when they speak of an ethnic community, a scholarly community, or—of par-

2. Community: Roland L. Warren, *Community in America*, 3d ed. (Lanham, Md.: University Press of America, 1987), 9–10; Joseph Gusfield, *Community: A Critical Response* (New York: Harper and Row, 1975), xv–xvi. Plantations: Eugene D. Genovese, *The World the Slaveholders Made* (1969; reprint, Middletown, Conn.: Wesleyan University Press, 1988), 151–64; John B. Boles, ed., *Masters and Slaves in the House of the Lord: Race and Religion in the American South, 1740–1870* (Lexington: University Press of Kentucky, 1988), 9–14. Mill villages: Gary Kulik et al., eds., *The New England Mill Village, 1790–1860* (Cambridge, Mass.: MIT Press, 1982), xxix–xxx, 347–69.

3. Stewart, "Joshua Giddings, Antislavery Violence, and Congressional Politics of Honor," in John R. McKivigan and Stanley Harrold, eds., *Antislavery Violence: Sectional, Racial, and Cultural Conflict in Antebellum America* (Knoxville: University of Tennessee Press, 1999), 169, 182–3. Ira Katznelson suggests that city residents create community through persistent interaction. See Katznelson, *City Trenches: Urban Politics and Patterning of Class in the United States* (Chicago: Univ. of Chicago Press, 1981), 193–209. Blacks seeking out antislavery whites: *PF*, 24 February 1848 and *NASS*, 16 January 1851. See also James Sterling Young, *The Washington Community, 1800–1828* (New York: Harcourt, Brace, and World, 1966), 87–110; Green, *Washington*, 1:238–39.

ticular relevance here—a radical or reform community. In these extended communities or networks people are linked by what they have in common and by what differentiates them from outsiders. To be a member of such a community, one must acknowledge "being part of a common group where loyalties and obligations rest on affective, emotional elements," rather than on "mutual interest and rational calculation of gain." Empathy and altruism predominate, although expectations that political and social gains may result from community actions are not alien to the concept—particularly in regard to reform communities.[4]

Because of their differences in race, culture, wealth, education, and social status, local African Americans and antislavery whites had to create a relational community through what Gusfield calls "symbolic construction." They made use of shared dangers, broad similarities, and individual relationships to stand in for more profound bonds. These efforts were not entirely successful and the community therefore lacked stability. Aspects of geographical community based on mere proximity always modified its character. So did the transience of community members and their existence within a social climate poisoned by slavery and racism. But on several levels relational community existed among antislavery blacks and whites. There was a shared emotional response to the outrages enslavement and the slave trade imposed on black families. There was mutual awareness that slavery conflicted with principles of individual liberty and Christian morality. There was a common struggle against the status quo. Black and white activists agreed that as allies they could drive slavery from the Chesapeake.[5]

---

4. Gusfield, *Community*, xv–xvi (first quotation), 10–3 (second & third quotations), 25–7, 31–3, 45–6. Donald G. Mathews demonstrates that relational community among blacks and whites was impossible for even the best intentioned slaveholder. See Mathews, "Charles Colcock Jones and the Southern Evangelical Crusade to form a Biracial Community," *Journal of Southern History* 61 (August 1975): 299–320.

5. Gusfield, *Community*, 23–5; Doug McAdam, "Culture and Social Movements," in Enrique Laraña, Hank Johnston, and Joseph R. Gusfield, eds., *New Social Movements: From Ideology to Identity* (Philadelphia: Temple University Press, 1994), 37–41. The resource mobilization model developed by several sociologists maintains that oppressed groups need the help of "outside elites" to provide the skills and resources necessary for effective resistance. Aldon D. Morris contends that this model exaggerates the influence of affluent white liberals on the twentieth-century civil rights movement. It may be more applicable to the antebellum Chesapeake where indigenous black resources were not as well developed as they would be in the South a century

Prerequisite to the formation of a biracial antislavery community in Washington was the local black community. Because the city's pre–Civil War black population, both free and slave, was dispersed throughout its area, this community was mainly relational in character. It centered, nevertheless, on a dozen or so independent churches that included both free and enslaved members and that owned or rented church buildings in the city. The majority of African Americans in Washington were unchurched or attended predominantly white churches. But those who most actively opposed slavery and sought freedom for themselves or others belonged to these independent congregations. Often their buildings housed schools and became centers for black benevolent, temperance, literary, and self-improvement societies.[6]

Increased wealth and education among some black families played an essential role in the formation of these churches. The great majority of free black men in Washington worked as skilled tradesmen or day laborers. Many male slaves who hired their time did similar work. Free and enslaved black women worked as domestic servants, laundresses, and cooks. Most of these individuals and their families were impoverished and uneducated. But a mi-

---

later. See: Anthony Oberschall, *Social Conflict and Social Movements* (Englewood Cliffs, N.J.: Prentice-Hall, 1973); John McCarthy, "Resource Mobilization and Social Movements: A Partial Theory," *American Journal of Sociology* 82 (May 1977): 1212–41; Morris, *The Origins of the Civil Rights Movement: Black Communities Organizing for Change* (New York: Free Press, 1984), 280–1; Clarence Y. H. Lo, "Communities of Challengers in Social Movement Theory," in Aldon D. Morris and Carol McClung Mueller, eds., *Frontiers in Social Movement Theory* (New Haven: Yale University Press, 1992), 227, 238.

6. Constance M. Green, *The Secret City: A History of Race Relations in the Nation's Capital* (Princeton: Princeton University Press, 1967), 16–7, 23–4, 40, 54; *E*, 8 September 1842; John W. Cromwell, "The First Negro Churches in the District of Columbia," *Journal of Negro History* 7 (January 1922): 64–106; Henry S. Robinson, "Some Aspects of the Free Negro Population of Washington, D.C., 1800–1862," *Maryland Historical Magazine* 64 (Spring 1969): 57–63; Frederick Law Olmsted, *A Journey in the Seaboard Slave States*, 2 vols. (1856; reprint, New York: G. P. Putnam's Sons, 1904), 1:16. See also: Ira Berlin, *Slaves without Masters: The Free Negro in the Antebellum South* (New York: New Press, 1974), 269–71; John B. Boles, *Masters and Slaves in the House of the Lord: Race and Religion in the American South, 1740–1870* (Lexington: University Press of Kentucky, 1988), 15. Cromwell points out that these churches often had members who were subject to the slave trade. Melvin R. Williams notes in regard to *free* blacks in 1860 that, while they lived in all the city's wards, there were clusters of black families living in its northwest and southwest sections. See Williams, "A Blueprint for Change: The Black Community in Washington, D.C., 1860–1870," *RCHS* 48 (1973): 360–2.

Daniel Alexander Payne (1811–1893) was a former slave who became an AME bishop. He worked with antislavery whites in Baltimore and Washington from the 1820s through the Civil War. Daniel Alexander Payne, *Recollections of Seventy Years* (Nashville: Publishing House of the AME Sunday School Union, 1888), frontispiece.

nority had achieved a degree of economic success and a few were "quite wealthy owners of real estate." They provided financial resources and leadership in establishing churches, schools, and other institutions.[7]

The earliest black church in the District was the Mount Zion Negro Church, which organized in Georgetown in 1814 and which, like several later black churches, retained institutional ties to a white congregation. Much more significant were those black churches that for antislavery reasons cut these ties. During the early 1820s some black Methodists left the white Ebenezer Church on Fourth Street because its minister owned slaves and because of its segregated seating. They established their own Israel Bethel Church, affiliated with the AME denomination, and acquired a church building near Capitol Hill. The best known of Israel Bethel's ministers was Daniel A. Payne, a light-complexioned black man who had been born free in South Carolina and educated in Pennsylvania. He led the Israel Bethel congregation

7. Green, *Secret City*, 15–6, 27, 50; *E*, 8 September 1842 (quotation); Robinson, "Free Negro Population," 50–7, 63–4.

from 1843 to 1845, and from 1845 to 1850 held a similar post in Baltimore. Although he became an AME bishop in 1853, he continued throughout the antebellum years to be involved in Washington's subversive community.[8]

Two other local black churches were explicitly antislavery. One of them was the Wesleyan Metropolitan African Methodist Episcopal Zion Church—also known as the African Wesleyan Society—located on D Street in South Washington. This church began in 1833 when black worshipers, under the leadership of Abraham Cole, left the nearby Ebenezer Methodist Episcopal Church because that church's white preacher owned slaves. The other was the Fifteenth Street Presbyterian Church, which separated from the Israel Bethel church in 1841. Under John F. Cook Sr.'s pastorship during the 1840s, it played an important role in bringing together black and white opponents of slavery. Cook, who had been forced to leave Washington temporarily during the Snow Riot of 1835, was a mulatto born in the city in about 1810. He gained his freedom at sixteen and became headmaster of the Union Seminary, a Washington school for black children, in 1834. Well educated and in contact with northern black abolitionists, Cook was an influential, if cautious, facilitator of cooperation between slavery's black and white opponents. "I have to be very particular to do nothing knowingly, that would in the least tend to disturb the public weal, or bring upon me and the cause in which I am engaged the indignation of the inhabitants," he declared in 1851.[9]

Cook and other black ministers in Washington began welcoming white abolitionists to their churches—sometimes as guest speakers, sometimes simply as worshipers—during the early 1840s. In the Northeast such practices had begun among black congregations and white abolitionists ten years earlier. Interracial worship without segregated seating was a means by which

8. Green, *Secret City,* 24–5; Cromwell, "First Negro Churches," 65, 69; David Alexander Payne, *Recollections of Seventy Years* (1888; reprint, New York: Arno, 1968), 74–121; Josephus R. Coan, *Daniel Alexander Payne: Christian Educator* (Philadelphia: AME Book Concern, 1935). See also Douglas C. Stange, ed., "Bishop Payne's Protestation of American Slavery," *Journal of Negro History* 52 (January 1967): 59–64.

9. Cromwell, "First Negro Churches," 80–1, 83; "Smallwood v. Cole," November 1842, Case Papers, entry b, RG 21, NA; "Cook, John Francis Sr." q.v. *DANB,* 125–6; Constance M. Green, *Washington,* 2 vols. (Princeton: Princeton University Press, 1962–63), 1:145; Letitia Woods Brown, *Free Negroes in the District of Columbia, 1790–1846* (New York: Oxford University Press, 1972), 141; Cook to Myrtilla Miner, 31 July 1851, MMP (quotation).

John F. Cook Sr. (1810?–1855) was a former slave who became a school principal and minister in Washington. He cultivated interracial ties with white abolitionists. With permission from Moorland-Spingarn Research Center, Howard University, Washington, D.C.

white abolitionists expressed solidarity with the oppressed.[10] In Washington, where black congregations included slaves, that expression directly challenged human bondage.

White abolitionist Charles T. Torrey made a point of attending only black churches when he was in Washington during the winter of 1841–1842. After

10. Leon Litwack, *North of Slavery: The Negro in the Free States* (Chicago: University of Chicago Press, 1960), 197; Clara Merritt DeBoar, *Be Jubilant My Feet: African-American Abolitionists in the American Missionary Association, 1839–1861* (New York: Garland, 1994); Paul Goodman, *Of One Blood: Abolitionism and the Origins of Racial Equality* (Berkeley: University of California Press, 1998), 54–64; *CA*, 24 June 1837; "Fourteenth Annual Report of the AASS," in *PF*, 28 May 1848; Benjamin Quarles, *Black Abolitionists* (New York: Oxford University Press, 1969), 83. In the antebellum South—including Washington—black churches often had white ministers and African Americans often attended white churches. These religious communities were by no means antislavery in orientation. But there had been some earlier interracial worship antagonistic to slavery in the Chesapeake. In 1824 Elisha Tyson spoke at a black church in Baltimore. See Robert L. Hall, "Black and White Christians in Florida, 1822–1861," in Boles, ed., *Masters and Slaves in the House of the Lord*, 81–98; Berlin, *Slaves without Masters*, 292; *CA*, 24 June 1837; [John S. Tyson], *Elisha Tyson, the Philanthropist* (Baltimore: B. Lundy, 1825), 106–10.

a service at the African Wesleyan church, he told his wife, "I have not enjoyed the 'communion of saints,' so much, for a long time, as when mingling with that little band of despised colored people, partly slaves." Torrey estimated that 1,300 people belonged to Washington's black churches and, while he disdained the "shouting, jumping, and dancing" he observed during services, he found most of the black ministers to be "men of fine talents." The black congregations' "standard of piety and morals," he maintained, equaled if they did not surpass that of white churches. "None of the colored churches would ask a man-stealer [slaveholder] to its communion," he drolly pointed out.[11]

Besides Torrey, antislavery whites who attended black church services in Washington prior to the Civil War included northerners Joshua Leavitt, William L. Chaplin, and Josiah Bushnell Grinnell as well as Virginia-born Thomas C. Connolly. Chaplin reported to New York abolitionists in 1845 that "there are white pulpits and black ones here in almost any quantity. I have listened to numbers of both kinds, and if I were allowed to make a comparison . . . I should say the white pulpits have greatly the advantage in words, and the black ones in *ideas*. . . . The whites resort to the books that are full of words—the blacks to God, who is full of *ideas—light—truth*." During the late 1850s, when there was a white antislavery church in the city, some African Americans attended its services.[12]

Washington's black churches provided a major route to interracial antislavery community in the city. But there were also efforts among antislavery blacks and whites in Washington informally to bridge racial and cultural barriers. Torrey in early 1843 attended a "negro ball," although he regarded dancing as sinful. He went to the ball, he reported, as going was a "way of sharing my *sympathy with the bondmen*." Conversely, Cook cultivated personal

11. Charles T. Torrey to Joshua Leavitt, n.d., in *E*, 8 September 1842; Payne, *Recollections*, 115; Joseph C. Lovejoy, *Memoir of Rev. Charles T. Torrey*, 2d ed. (1848; reprint, New York: Negro Universities Press, 1969), 89–90 (first quotation); P. P. [Torrey] to Editors, 4 December 1841, in *New York Evangelist*, 11 December 1841 (second–fifth quotations).

12. Whites attending black churches: Leavitt to Piercy and Reed, 20 January 1841, in *E*, 28 January 1841; Chaplin to *AP*, 3 February [1845], in *AP*, 12 February 1845 (quotation); John F. Cook, Sr., diary, 14 July 1850, Cook Family Papers, Moorland-Spingarn Research Center, Howard University; Connolly to Gerrit Smith, 3 November 1854, GSP. Blacks attending white antislavery church: Matilda Jones to Myrtilla Miner, 20 April 1848, Emma Brown to Miner, 23 August 1858, MMP; Bettie [Browne] to Emily Howland, 18 February 1860, EHP.

friendships with antislavery whites, including journalist Joseph Evans Snod-grass and United States Senators Salmon P. Chase and Charles Durkee. In a manner reminiscent of northern abolitionism, white antislavery activists de-fied local racial and class prejudices by inviting blacks to their homes. Blacks responded similarly.[13]

It was often in the lodgings of antislavery whites that interracial commu-nity developed. Whig congressman Joshua R. Giddings, from Ohio's radi-cally antislavery Western Reserve, for example, courted the contempt of his proslavery counterparts by welcoming blacks, both slave and free, to his boarding-house. It was not having African Americans in his room, however, that challenged propriety in Washington. Many whites had black servants and African Americans often had white patrons who helped them in times of need.[14] Rather, it was the way Giddings responded to his black visitors and the subject matter of their conversations that made him a subversive. When African Americans came to him, Giddings treated them respectfully as guests and citizens rather than as servants or retainers. He counseled them regarding quests for freedom. Other antislavery whites in Washington acted similarly. They became resources for outraged black people seeking help, protection, and justice.

In February 1848 Ezra L. Stevens, the Washington correspondent for Cleveland's *Daily True Democrat*, was visiting Giddings when his host, at the sound of "a slight rap, opened the door and admitted a woe-begone looking colored man, the picture of despair." Giddings invited the man to take a seat but he was too nervous to comply. According to Stevens, the black man began to weep and said to Giddings, "'O sar . . . our people told me that you had more feeling than the other men here, and the slave driver has taken my girl away. They have got her in the slave pen down thar, and are going to take her to New Orleans.'"

After the man left, Giddings told Stevens of similar cases and declared,

---

13. *AP*, 9 March 1843 (quotation); Correspondence of the Tribune, Washington, 12 June 1849, in *PF*, 5 July 1849; Cook, diary, 13 September 1850, Cook Family Papers; Carlton Mabee, *Black Freedom: The Nonviolent Abolitionists from 1830 through the Civil War* (London: Macmillan, 1970), 91–111.

14. Berlin, *Slaves without Masters*, 338–9.

"My heart bleeds for these poor creatures . . . Oh! that I had the power to break their fetters and relieve them." Stevens asked his readers, "And whose soul would not be weary with anguish to witness, day by day, such exhibitions of unmitigated suffering on the part of the oppressed, and of monstrous depravity on the part of the oppressor?"[15]

These exchanges between local African Americans and antislavery whites encouraged interracial trust and personal relationships that facilitated cooperation in purchasing the freedom of slaves and in helping slaves escape. Meanwhile, open and clandestine conflict with proslavery forces established a unifying sense that black and white antislavery activists shared a common fate as victors over slaveholders or as victims of their wrath. In other words, the danger they faced bound together antislavery blacks and whites in Washington. It had been physically hazardous to engage in antislavery activities in the North during the 1820s and 1830s, but less so during the 1840s and 1850s. In Washington, D.C., and the rest of the border South, the level of danger remained high throughout all four decades and into the Civil War years as well. This was particularly true for blacks because they did not enjoy the same legal and customary protection against arbitrary reprisals as whites. In 1841 the *Pennsylvania Freeman* warned "our colored friends against venturing into any of the slave states," where they could be arrested without hope of release.[16]

Local slaveholders caused much of the danger. They knew that free African Americans undermined the slave-labor system at this vulnerable point and that white abolitionists joined free blacks in helping slaves in freedom suits and escapes. At an 1842 slaveholder convention held at nearby Annapolis one delegate warned "that it was 'now or never.' . . . If they did not put down the colored freeman and those who sympathized with them, they

15. E. L. S., editorial correspondence, 24 January 1848, in *DTD*, 1 February 1848. See also: Giddings to Laura Waters Giddings, 23 January 1848, JRGP; *PF*, 25 December 1851; *CG*, 32 Cong., 1 sess., 531–5; William L. Chaplin to Gerrit Smith, 17 May 1848, GSP; David A. Hall to Salmon P. Chase, 27 June 1848, Salmon P. Chase Papers, Library of Congress.

16. Samivel Weller Jr. to Mr. Editor, 15 November 1842, in *TL*, 15 December 1842; Weller to Mr. Editor, 14 June 1843, in *AP*, 22 June 1843; Thomas Smallwood, *A Narrative of Thomas Smallwood (Colored Man)* (Toronto: Smallwood, 1851), 40; Berlin, *Slaves without Masters*, 99–101; *PF*, 4 August 1841 (quotation).

would be put down themselves."[17] These slaveholders wielded great power in southern Maryland, northeastern Virginia, and the District. Not only was local law usually on their side, they enjoyed support for their interests in Congress and in the judicial and executive branches of the national government.

The power of slaveholders in the District showed itself in a variety of other ways. Washington's police force, headed by Captain John H. Goddard and known as the Auxiliary Guard, acted as a slave patrol and enforced race-specific ordinances on the city's black population. There also existed a disreputable conglomeration of white slavetraders, slave catchers, and kidnappers—aided by numerous black informers—who engaged in surreptitious or openly violent tactics designed to frustrate antislavery activists. Most notorious of all was the Baltimore slavetrader Hope H. Slatter. Between the late 1830s and his retirement in 1848, this devout Methodist engaged in the wholesale sundering of black families in Baltimore and Washington. He entrapped slave rescuers, instigated Washington mobs, brutalized slaves, and lied about his activities. More than any other proslavery figure, Slatter epitomized the common danger African Americans and antislavery whites faced.[18]

While shared dangers exercised a binding force between local African Americans and antislavery whites, the whites' own ethnocentricism strengthened their relationship with African Americans. In contrast to their proslav-

17. Charles T. Torrey to Dear Sir, 24 January 1842, in *E*, 4 February 1842; Berlin, *Slaves without Masters*, 210–1; Early Lee Fox, *The American Colonization Society, 1817–40* (Baltimore: Johns Hopkins University Press, 1919), 30–1.

18. Police force: Washington correspondent for the *Pennsylvania Inquirer*, quoted in *PF*, 12 April 1838; Samivel Weller Jr. to Mr. Publisher, 11 June 1843, in *AP*, 22 August 1843; Weller to Charles, 10 October 1843, in *AP*, 24 October 1843; Walter C. Clephane, "The Local Aspect of Slavery in the District of Columbia," *RCHS* 3 (1900): 226; Green, *Washington*, 160. Conglomeration: Charles T. Torrey to Dear Sir, 24 January 1842, in *E*, 4 February 1842; *TL*, 27 October 1842; *AP*, 7 February 1844; Thomas Garrett to Editor, 16 December 1845, in *PF*, 1 January 1846; *CG*, 30 Cong., 1 sess., 670–1; Berlin, *Slaves without Masters*, 99, 160–1. Black informers: *NASS*, 1 January 1845; *TL*, 15 December 1842; Jacob Bigelow to William Still, 6 October 1855, in William Still, *The Underground Railroad: A Record of Facts, Authentic Narratives, Letters, &c* (1872; reprint New York: Arno, 1968), 180. Interracial bond: Torrey to Dear Sir, 24 January 1842, in *E*, 4 February 1842; *AP*, 2 October 1844 (quotation); *PF*, 5 September 1850. Slatter: *PF*, 12 July 1838, 4 July 1844; Joseph Sturge, "To Hope H. Slaughter," in *E*, 19 August 1841; Samivel Weller Jr. to [editor], n.d., in *AP*, 1 May 1844; *CG*, 30th Cong., 1 sess., 671; E. L. S. editorial correspondence, 22 April 1848, in *DTD*, 29 April 1848.

ery opponents, whites within the subversive community exaggerated the similarities of the oppressed to themselves by focusing on "nearly white" slaves. According to an impressionistic account by a contemporary nonabolitionist white traveler from the North and to statistics compiled by historian Ira Berlin, persons of mixed race were a small minority among slaves in antebellum Washington. Yet, for several reasons, antislavery whites active in the city behaved as if such individuals were very common.

First, caucasoid features *were* more common among the black elite, with whom antislavery whites associated, than among the local black population generally. Second, the existence of mulattoes suited white abolitionist claims that slaveholders were rapists, whoremongers, and slave-breeders. Third, calling attention to "nearly white" slaves served to engage the sympathies of a racially biased northern white audience. Most important, observing the suffering of slaves whom they perceived to be physically similar to themselves intensified antislavery whites' emotional identification with the oppressed group as a whole. In 1841, Torrey told his wife that listening to a "nearly white" woman speak of her suffering in slavery "filled [his heart] with new energy to make war upon that hateful institution." In 1848 Ezra L. Stevens felt drawn to slaves he perceived to be "nearly as white as myself."[19]

Whites within Washington's antislavery community also emphasized cultural convergence between themselves and blacks. They dwelt on the Christian, free-labor, and middle class values they believed the two groups shared.

---

19. Lovejoy, *Torrey*, 89–90 (first–third quotations); Berlin, *Slaves without Masters*, 178; Olmsted, *Seaboard Slave States*, 1:13; Theodore D. Weld, *Slavery and the Interstate Slave Trade in the United States* (London: T. Ward, 1841), 32–7; Weld, *American Slavery as It Is: Testimony of a Thousand Voices* (New York: AASS, 1839), passim; *Liberty Press* (Utica, N.Y.), 26 September 1843; *PF*, 2 January 1845; Robert H. Abzug, *Cosmos Crumbling: American Reform and the Religious Imagination* (New York: Oxford University Press, 1994), 144; E. L. S., editorial correspondence, 22 April 1848, in *DTD*, 29 April 1848 (fourth quotation) Joel Williamson is more supportive of antislavery whites' impressions of the number of mulatto slaves in the Chesapeake. See Williamson, *New People: Miscegenation and Mulattoes in the Unites States* (New York: Free Press, 1980), 63–4. Scholars have thoroughly discussed antebellum white opinion in regard to persons of mixed racial inheritance. For a recent analysis see Nancy Bentley, "White Slaves: The Mulatto in Antebellum Fiction," *American Literature* 65 (September 1993): 501–22. On the subjectivity of race in a different antebellum context, see Walter Johnson, *Soul by Soul: Life inside the Antebellum Slave Market* (Cambridge, Mass.: Harvard University Press, 1999), 155–8.

They perceived in some African Americans the same striving for morality and prosperity that they found in themselves. This is evident in Joshua Leavitt's 1841 insistence that the temperance movement more effectively engaged Washington's black workers than its white workers. "With hardly an exception," he contended, "where you find them employed alike . . . the colored men are the best dressed, and the most sober in their deportment. They are also more economical and provident. Many of them are acquiring real estate . . . and are in all respects useful and meritorious citizens."[20]

The perception among antislavery whites that black family bonds were as strong as their own had particular importance. Rapid economic change in the North and to a lesser degree in the Chesapeake had fostered an idealized image of family. As more men competed in the marketplace, Americans increasingly perceived the family to be a sanctified refuge for religious and feminine virtues. As a result, the threat to the integrity of black families posed by the domestic slave trade seemed particularly heinous.[21] Defense of families became *the* most important bond between local African Americans and their white allies.

Washington's antislavery whites did not ignore the poverty and ignorance that affected the majority of the Chesapeake's free blacks and slaves. They perceived African Americans who called on them to be humble and gave little more than symbolic recognition to an equality between themselves and their desperate allies. Nor were antislavery whites free of racism regarding a people they referred to as a "degraded class." Certain of their own cultural and intellectual superiority, these whites, like their abolitionist counterparts in the North, blatantly patronized the black people with whom they interacted.[22]

20. Leavitt to Piercy and Reed, 20 January 1841, in *E,* 28 January 1841 (quotation). See also C[harles] T. T[orrey] to Leavitt, n.d., ibid., 8 September 1842; *BSV,* 27 January & 17 August 1844.

21. John Ashworth, *Slavery, Capitalism, and Politics in the Antebellum Republic: Commerce and Compromise, 1820–1850* (New York: Cambridge University Press, 1995), 174–81; Ronald G. Walters, *The Antislavery Appeal: American Abolitionism after 1830* (Baltimore: Johns Hopkins University Press, 1976), 91–110. See also Nancy F. Cott, *The Bonds of Womanhood: Women's Sphere in New England, 1780–1835* (New Haven: Yale University Press, 1977).

22. George Drinker to Joseph Bringhurst, 10 December 1804, PASP; *GUE,* 1 January 1830; Horace Mann, "Slavery and the Slave Trade in the District of Columbia," in *LP,* 7 June 1849 (quotation); M. E. Ford to Myrtilla Miner, 29 June 1852, MMP; James Brewer Stewart,

White educator Myrtilla Miner, who during the 1850s conducted in Washington a school for black girls, exemplifies this tendency. When the parents of one of her students objected to her rules regarding proper diet, she accused the pair of ignorantly undermining her mission. "You cannot think as I think, nor feel what I feel!" she exclaimed, and added, "May your eyes be opened to comprehend what dreadful endurance is involved in this mission to raise a people who constantly turn back to their idols, & sigh for the 'flesh pots of Egypt.'"[23]

This smugness on the part of whites limited biracial community. Yet the free black elite also patronized poorer free blacks and slaves. More crucial, condescension toward blacks by Washington's antislavery whites hardly compares to the stultifying paternalism of slaveholders and supporters of the ACS. Slaveholders who claimed to treat slaves as family members assumed that blacks would be permanently subservient. Colonizationists portrayed them as unredeemables who had to be expelled from the United States. In contrast northern antislavery activists who lived in Washington during the period from the 1830s to the 1860s were similar to late-nineteenth-century upper class Britons who settled in industrial neighborhoods to create "a shared community among the well-to-do and the working classes." Just as Victorian British settlement workers hoped to bestow "their superior culture" on their new neighbors, antislavery whites in Washington assumed that they must inculcate their superior values in local blacks—and in southern whites as well.[24]

Holy Warriors: The Abolitionists and American Slavery, 2d ed. (New York: Hill and Wang, 1997), 129–35.

23. *GUE*, 20 November 1829; Miner to Brents, 8 May 1855, MMP (quotations); Lawrence J. Friedman, *Gregarious Saints: Self and Community in American Abolitionism, 1830–1870* (New York: Cambridge University Press, 1982), 165–7; George M. Fredrickson, *The Black Image in the White Mind: The Debate on Afro-American Character and Destiny, 1817–1964* (New York: Harper and Row, 1971), 33–42.

24. Free black elite: *Freedom's Journal* (New York), 23 March 1827; Berlin, *Slaves without Masters*, 283. Slaveholders and the ACS: *Family Friend* (Columbia, S.C.) quoted in *Planters' Advocate* (Upper Marlboro, Md.), 23 March 1853; Mathews, "Jones," 299–320; Fox, *American Colonization Society*, 30–5. Northern antislavery activists: Standish Meacham, *Toynbee Hall and Social Reform, 1880–1914: The Search for Community* (New Haven: Yale University Press, 1987), x; Lewis P. Simpson, "Slavery and the Cultural Imperialism of New England," *Southern Review* 25 (January 1989): 1–29. There are also similarities between white antislavery activists in Washington and a minority of white settlement workers who early in the twentieth century worked

In attempting to make black people more like an idealized version of themselves, white abolitionists in the Chesapeake admonished them to be pious, to train their children for "suitable" employment, to save their money, to pay their debts, to avoid alcohol consumption, and to abstain from licentiousness. These whites assumed that slavery and discrimination caused African-American degradation and could be reversed. Speaking of Washington's slaves in 1849, Representative Horace Mann of Massachusetts noted "their tattered dress and unseemly manners." "Their language," he contended, "proclaims their ignorance." But, as might be expected from the country's leading advocate of public education, Mann blamed what he perceived to be black shortcomings on their exclusion from white schools. Similarly, in 1856 white antislavery journalist Gamaliel Bailey admitted that free blacks were disproportionately represented in the city's jails and almshouses. But, he contended, this was the result of "disadvantages and disabilities" imposed on them by law. He complained that "the thrift and industry of the great mass of them are seldom brought into review, though thrift and industry may everywhere be found among them." Joseph Evans Snodgrass, a white Virginian who published an antislavery newspaper in Baltimore and often visited Washington, went further. He declared it a marvel that, oppressed as they were, so few black people were "'stupefied' and 'degraded.'"[25]

So there was more involved than paternalism and cultural imperialism when white antislavery activists in the Chesapeake exhorted African Americans to improve themselves despite the obstacles. No antislavery whites escaped an ingrained assumption that they were members of a superior race. But an environmental view of racial differences and a romantic faith in human progress led them, despite their often condescending behavior, to align themselves with an oppressed people seeking freedom and advancement. Snodgrass emphasized the cooperative aspect of interracial community in 1846. Discussing his relationship to African Americans, he declared, "While we shall continue ever to give them the best of advice, and to assist

---

to integrate African Americans into white neighborhoods. See Elisabeth Lasch-Quinn, *Black Neighbors: Race and the Limits of Reform in the American Settlement House Movement, 1890–1948* (Chapel Hill: University of North Carolina Press, 1993), 33–5, 39–45.

25. *Liberty Press*, 7 June 1849 (first quotation); *NE*, 27 March 1856 (second quotation); *BSV*, 11 April 1846 (third quotation).

them in their glorious efforts for self-elevation, we pledge ourself to be less than ever sparing of the monstrous cruelty of their law-mongering oppressors!"[26]

If antislavery whites in Washington often patronized their black allies, the black people who approached them were often wary and disingenuous. Ethan Allen Andrews, a white reformer from Boston who visited Washington in 1835, understood this. He reported that local blacks, when threatened with sale south, often sought help from potentially sympathetic northern whites, whom they nevertheless distrusted. "They regard the white man as of a different race from themselves," Andrews wrote, "and as having views, feelings and interests which prevent his sympathizing fully with theirs. Distrust, even of their real friends, is no unnatural consequence of the relation which they and their ancestors have so long borne to the whites."

Despite her sharp words, Miner also recognized this difficulty. She asked herself in 1851, "How long will it take me to convince the colored people that I am sincere in the interest I profess[?]" She answered, "Well I don't know. Some will never see it in a life time but will die & go to judgement without knowing it."[27]

Chesapeake blacks nevertheless responded positively to offers of assistance from antislavery whites. Like other African Americans, they accepted the notion that "the Colored Race" needed "improvement." In the same spirit, they held antislavery whites to a higher standard of benevolence than they might expect from whites generally. Local African Americans called on sympathetic whites to help them gain access to the courts, to help raise money, and, occasionally, to risk their own freedom and lives in rescuing people from slavery. In fact, the subversive biracial community would never have existed, if not for

26. *NASS,* 5 February 1846. See also William Slade to Dear Sir, 13 January 1838, in *PF,* 15 March 1838.

27. Ethan Allen Andrews, *Slavery and the Domestic Slave Trade in the United States* (Boston: Light and Stearns, 1836), 97 (first quotation), 111; undated note next to E.D.E.N. Southworth to Miner, 23 August 1851, MMP (second quotation). Black distrust of whites: Ian Bruce Turner, "Anti-Slavery Thought in the Border South, 1830–1860" (Ph.D. dissertation, University of Illinois at Urbana-Champaign, 1977), 350–1, 358–9; James Oliver Horton, *Free People of Color: Inside the African American Community* (Washington: Smithsonian Institution Press, 1993), 63. I do not agree with Horton's contention that white assistance "was uncommon" or that blacks were unable to identify antislavery whites.

a black commitment to physically challenging the slave system. As masters sold slaves south they prompted a variety of desperate responses among the enslaved, their families, and friends. In turn, those responses impressed white abolitionists, drew them in, and led them to regard blacks as allies rather than clients.[28]

As Washington's black population grew, as its institutions expanded, as a few black families gained literacy and some wealth, the resources to finance purchases of freedom, freedom suits, and slave escapes multiplied. As increasing numbers of slaves hired their time, they too accumulated funds to be put to these purposes. As early as 1833 a slaveholder from nearby Fauquier County, Virginia, complained that African Americans in Washington employed white attorneys to "pry into every man's title to his negroes" and that blacks not only "secreted [escapees] in a labyrinth that has no clue," but paid for their "comfortable ride in the stage via Baltimore" to Philadelphia. By the late 1830s and early 1840s, freedom suits and assisted escapes—both of which destabilized slavery and frightened masters—had become common in the Washington area.[29]

A striking example of the black daring that impressed white abolitionists emerges in the exploits of slave rescuer Leonard A. Grimes. Described as "slightly connected by blood with the oppressed race," Grimes was born free in Virginia. During the 1830s he established himself in Washington as an independent hackman, owning horses and carriages. In late 1839 he drove thirty miles into Virginia in a successful effort to transport northward an enslaved woman and her seven children who had been threatened with sale away from their free husband and father. Three months later the marshal of the District of Columbia arrested Grimes in Washington. After serving two years at hard labor at the Richmond State Prison, Grimes moved to Boston where he became the pastor of a black Baptist church and continued to help fugitive slaves.[30]

28. *GUE* 3, 3d series (May 1833): 99–102 (quotations); Benjamin Quarles, *Black Abolitionists* (New York: Oxford University Press, 1969), 100–15; Horton and Horton, *In Hope of Liberty*, 219–23; Berlin, *Slaves without Masters*, 314–9; *AP*, 22 March 1848.

29. Berlin, *Slaves without Masters*, 284–5, 299, 313; *NI*, 3 August 1833 (quotations); Andrews, *Slavery*, 152; Leavitt to Piercy and Reed, 15 February 1841, in *E*, 25 February 1841.

30. Charles Emery Stevens, *Anthony Burns, A History* (1856; reprint, New York: Arno, 1969), 62–73, 203–10 (quotation); William Cranch to Marshal of D.C., 12 February 1840 and Jos. H. Bradley to William Cranch, [12 February 1840], District Courts of the United States,

Leonard Grimes (1815–1874) was, during the late 1830s, a hackman who helped slaves escape from Virginia to Washington. He later became a prominent minister in Boston. William J. Simmons, *Men of Mark: Eminent, Progressive, and Rising* (Cleveland: Geo. M. Rewell, 1887), opposite p. 664.

Most impressive among these later activities was Grimes's involvement with George Lewis and his family. During the autumn of 1846 Lewis, a Baptist preacher and carpenter, escaped from Virginia to Washington where his daughter Lizzie, who was also a slave, hid him until the following April. After white abolitionists helped the father and daughter to reach Boston, Grimes raised money to purchase the freedom of Lewis's wife and the couple's five remaining children. Then, despite the obvious risks, Grimes went to Richmond to get them.[31]

Far more common in the development of a subversive antislavery community in Washington than the striking bravery of a few prominent individuals like Grimes, were the desperate actions of ordinary black people. Mothers seeking to free their children or husbands seeking to free their wives through court action, purchase, or escape created images of black heroism that white abolitionists cherished. It is crucial to note, however, that most of the African

---

Circuit Court of District of Columbia in and for the County of Washington, Segregated Habeas Corpus Papers, 1820–63, RG 21, NA (hereafter cited as Habeas Corpus Papers); Wilbur H. Siebert, "Underground Railroad in Massachusetts," in *Proceedings of the American Antiquarian Society* 45 (17 April–16 October 1935): 62–3, 70–1, 75–9, 84.

31. Austin Bearse, *Reminiscences of Fugitive Slave Law Days in Boston* (Boston: W. Richardson, 1880), 10–2.

Americans who gained white help were not without resources. They had marketable skills, help from family members, owned land, or could raise money. Antislavery whites regarded them as respectable Christians.

The efforts of ordinary black people to help themselves or others gain freedom also forced more powerful individuals to take a stand for them or against them. This was especially true of slave escapes.[32] The daring November 1841 escape of several black men from Williams's Slave Pen on Maryland Avenue polarized proslavery and antislavery opinion. Thomas Smallwood—the black Washington correspondent for the Albany, New York, *Tocsin of Liberty*—commented, "the whole paternity of man-hunters was thrown into a fever," while "there were many hearts in this city that rejoiced at their escape." A battle at nearby Rockville, Maryland, in July 1845 between about two hundred white men and about seventy armed male slaves who were escaping toward Washington had a similar impact. Although the whites succeeded in recapturing the blacks, this violent escape attempt caused "a terrible state of excitement" among proslavery whites, while local abolitionists welcomed news that slaves were "escaping in shoals."[33]

32. Herbert Aptheker, "The Negro in the Abolitionist Movement," *Science and Society* 5 (Winter 1941): 12. Estimates of the number of fugitive slaves who escaped from the South between 1830 and 1860 vary widely. Even the lower estimates suggest that well over one thousand fugitives left or passed through Washington every few years. See Theodore D. Weld to Angelina Grimké Weld, in Gilbert H. Barnes and Dwight L. Dumond, eds., *Letters of Theodore Dwight Weld, Angelina Grimké Weld, and Sarah Grimké Weld, 1822–1844,* 2 vols. (1934; reprint, Gloucester, Mass.: Peter Smith, 1965), 2:956 (hereafter cited as Barnes and Dumond, *Weld-Grimké Letters*); *PF,* 27 August 1846, 21 October 1847; Wilbur H. Siebert, *The Underground Railroad from Slavery to Freedom* (1898; reprint, New York: Arno, 1968), 44, 341; Joseph C. Carroll, *Slave Insurrections in the United States, 1800–1865* (1938; reprint, Negro Universities Press, 1968), 182; Elwood L. Bridner Jr., "The Fugitive Slaves of Maryland," *Maryland Historical Magazine* 66 (Spring 1971): 33–6; Barbara Jeanne Fields, *Slavery and Freedom on the Middle Ground: Maryland during the Nineteenth Century* (New Haven: Yale University Press, 1985), 16–7; David M. Potter, *The Impending Crisis, 1848–1861* (New York: Harper and Row, 1976), 135–7; John Hope Franklin and Loren Schweninger, *Runaway Slaves: Rebels on the Plantation* (New York: Oxford University Press, 1999), 279–82.

33. Williams's: Samivel Weller Jr. to Nevy, 9 November 1842, in *TL,* 17 November 1842 (first quotation). Rockville: *PF,* 17 & 31 July (second quotation), 1845; *BSV,* 19 July 1845; Chaplin to J. C. Jackson, 30 December 1844, in *AP,* 8 January 1845 (third quotation). The *BSV,* seeking to diminish white fears, estimated the number of escaping slaves in the Rockville

Remarks published by William L. Chaplin in 1848 and Ezra L. Stevens in 1849 illustrate how slave escapes influenced antislavery whites to identify with local African Americans. Chaplin asserted that "the manly attempt to secure one's freedom mankind regard as the highest deed of human virtue. These persons have a strong hold upon our admiration, as they have upon our sympathy." Stevens noted the "excitement" among slaveholders, living in or near the District of Columbia, who wondered why there had been an upsurge in slave escapes. "Somehow," he explained, "an idea has become prevalent among them that they are *men,* and that *man* was not born to be the slave of his fellow man." In 1850 the Washington correspondent for the *New York Evening Post* declared that "beings with brains and legs" could steal themselves away.[34]

Yet escape was not easy. Masters sought to prevent it by discouraging cooperation among slaves and by limiting their knowledge of regional geography. As the battle at Rockville indicates, armed slaves could be overwhelmed by superior numbers. During the mid-1840s the Washington Auxiliary Guard employed eighteen men—nearly all of them *"professional slave catchers"*—who knew how to block potential escape routes. So there had to be advance planning if fugitives were to reach the North. In addition, women and children—especially women *with* children—and often men required northward transportation to effect their escapes. Such transportation was not cheap and financial arrangements became a crucial factor.[35]

Neither was it easy for African Americans to undertake court proceedings or to purchase freedom. Sometimes black church congregations or black fam-

melee to be as low as thirty. Relying on the *Baltimore Sun,* historian Ira Berlin says, "some hundred slaves" were involved. See Berlin, *Slaves without Masters,* 211.

34. Chaplin to [?], 18 May 1848, in *AP,* 24 May 1848 (first quotation); E. L. S. to Ed.[*sic*], 7 November 1849, in *AS,* 17 November 1849 (second & third quotations); *PF,* 5 September 1850 (fourth quotation). John Ashworth places the unwillingness of African Americans to remain slaves at the core of northern abolitionism. See Ashworth, *Slavery, Capitalism, and Politics,* 1:1–10.

35. *PF,* 5 September 1850 (first quotation); *AP,* 7 February 1844 (second quotation); Smallwood, *Narrative,* 17, 20–1, 29–31; *L,* 21 April 1848; Fields, *Slavery and Freedom,* 33; Bridner, "Fugitive Slaves of Maryland," 36–46; David Meaders, *Dead or Alive: Fugitive Slaves and White Indentured Servants before 1830* (New York: Garland, 1993), 33–6; Charles T. Torrey to Gerrit Smith, 23 January 1844, GSP.

ilies raised funds to redeem members who were threatened with sale south. But black churches and families lacked extensive financial resources and real legal standing. Therefore, the willingness of African Americans—such as the man who visited Giddings—to seek out white allies and the willingness of whites to help in escapes, purchasing freedom, and court actions became a central feature of the subversive community. "Is it at all surprising," the *Post*'s correspondent asked, "that where such things [as the slave trade and kidnapping] are practiced, slaves should runaway? Is it at all to be wondered that white men should be found to assist them in their flight?"[36]

While all white members of Washington's antislavery community cooperated with African Americans, not all of them advocated helping people steal away from their masters. There were important differences among these whites regarding ideology, reform methodology and motive—as well as concerning geographical background and gender. Perceiving these differences is essential to understanding the relationship of Washington's antislavery community to the larger northern antislavery movement, which by the late 1830s had begun to fragment.

William Lloyd Garrison's social radicalism—his criticism of organized religion, his devotion to women's rights, his commitment to the anarchistic doctrine of nonresistance, his condemnation of electoral politics—repulsed most black and white abolitionists. After 1840 only a minority of them continued to recognize his leadership and remained loyal to the AASS. This *Garrisonian* minority regarded voting as sinful and the United States Constitution as intrinsically proslavery. Garrisonians advocated the dissolution of the Union as the only means of withdrawing northern support from slavery and forcing abolition. Their views drew them away from the United States government and the South. During the late 1820s, Garrison had helped form the subversive antislavery community in the Chesapeake. In 1843 he declared that it was too dangerous for northern abolitionists to go south. Instead, he

36. Fredrika Bremer, *The Homes of the New World: Impressions of America*, 2 vols. (London: A. Hall, Virtue, 1853), 1:491–2; Mary Beth Corrigan, " 'It's a Family Affair': Buying Freedom in the District of Columbia, 1850–1860," in Larry E. Hudson, Jr., *Working toward Freedom: Slave Society and the Domestic Economy in the American South* (Rochester, N.Y.: University of Rochester Press, 1994), 163–91; *NE*, 24 May 1855; *PF*, 5 September 1850 (quotation).

claimed, they had "enough to do at home," because "it is solely by the aid of the people of the North that" African Americans were held in bondage."[37]

Henceforth the antislavery northerners who joined Washington's subversive community were rarely Garrisonians. Instead they represented groups that were willing to contest against slaveholders in the forum provided by the United States government. They also held aggressive action aimed at alleviating black suffering in the South to be compatible with abolitionist goals. Among them were church-oriented abolitionists, antislavery Whig congressmen, and abolitionists associated with the Liberty party.

After 1840 church-oriented abolitionists constituted the largest group of northern abolitionists. Under the leadership of New York City merchant Lewis Tappan, they organized—in 1840 and 1846 respectively—the American and Foreign Antislavery Society (AFASS) and the American Missionary Association (AMA).[38] These organizations cooperated with Washington's subversives and the AMA played a crucial role in that city during the Civil War.

The antislavery Whig politicians included Giddings, Gates, Slade, and several others. In Congress they often seemed to be more concerned that a slaveholders' conspiracy known as the *slave power* threatened their constituents' interests than that slavery oppressed African Americans. But a large portion of their constituents were abolitionists and these congressmen believed they represented Christian morality and human rights.[39]

37. Aileen S. Kraditor, *Means and Ends in American Abolitionism: Garrison and His Critics on Strategy and Tactics* (New York: Random House, 1967); James Brewer Stewart, "The Aims of Garrisonian Abolitionism, 1840–1860," *Civil War History* 15 (September 1969): 197–209; *L*, 2 June 1843 (quotation).

38. Evangelical and church-oriented abolitionism: John R. McKivigan, *The War against Proslavery Religion: Abolitionism and the Northern Churches, 1830–1865* (Ithaca, N.Y.: Cornell University Press, 1984); DeBoar, *Be Jubilant My Feet;* Bertram Wyatt-Brown, *Lewis Tappan and the Evangelical War Against Slavery* (Cleveland: Case-Western Reserve University Press, 1969), 185–225, 287–309.

39. Leonard L. Richards, *The Slave Power: The Free North and Southern Domination, 1780–1860* (Baton Rouge: Louisiana State University Press, 2000), 1–27; David Brion Davis, *The Slave Power Conspiracy and the Paranoid Style* (Baton Rouge: Louisiana State University Press, 1961); Eric Foner, *Free Soil, Free Labor, Free Men: The Ideology of the Republican Party before the Civil War* (New York: Oxford University Press, 1970), 73–102; Daniel Walker Howe,

The Liberty abolitionists concentrated more narrowly than antislavery Whig politicians in using the political process to spread antislavery sentiment. But from their party's beginning in 1840 to its breakup in 1848, they divided into factions that endorsed conflicting antislavery strategies. Wealthy philanthropist Gerrit Smith and his upstate New York circle led the more militant faction. Influenced by Christian perfectionism, Smith and other *radical political abolitionists* held that slavery—because it violated God's law—could never enjoy the protection of human law. They argued that the Constitution banned slavery, that Congress or the Supreme Court could abolish it in the states, that it was legal for slaves to escape and for others to help them. In physically challenging slavery in the borderlands, cooperating with African Americans, and putting slaveholders on the defensive, the radical political abolitionists surpassed all other abolitionist factions during the 1840s and 1850s. Their provocative actions in Washington and its vicinity shaped the character of the city's subversive community.[40]

The less militant Liberty abolitionists, who had roots in Boston and Cincinnati, had more in common with Giddings and other antislavery congressmen than did the radical political abolitionists. Beginning in early 1847, Gamaliel Bailey represented this faction in Washington as editor of the influential *National Era,* a moderate abolitionist weekly newspaper. Bailey, a close associate of antislavery politician Salmon P. Chase, had previously edited the *Herald and Philanthropist* in Cincinnati, another borderlands city.

Bailey, Chase, and others in this group recognized the legality of slavery within the southern states and advocated direct federal government action only against slavery within the national domain. They, like the congressmen, recognized the legitimacy, if not the morality, of proslavery laws. While Gar-

---

The Political Culture of the American Whigs (Chicago: University of Chicago Press, 1979), 9, 150–80.

40. The discussion in this and the following paragraphs is based on: Douglas M. Strong, *Perfectionist Politics: Abolitionists and the Religious Tensions of American Democracy* (Syracuse, N.Y.: Syracuse University Press, 1999); John Stauffer, *The Black Hearts of Men: Radical Abolitionists and the Transformation of Race* (Cambridge, Mass.: Harvard University Press, 2002), 16–20; Stanley Harrold, *The Abolitionists and the South, 1831–1861* Lexington: University Press of Kentucky, 1995), 6–8; and Harrold, *American Abolitionists* (Harlow, England: Longman, 2001), 61–72. See also William C. Wiecek, *The Sources of Antislavery Constitutionalism in America, 1760–1848* (Ithaca, N.Y.: Cornell University Press, 1977), 202–75.

risonians demanded disunion and the radical political abolitionists endorsed direct action against slavery in the South, these antislavery activists hoped peacefully and legally to spread abolitionist political organization, free labor, and a market economy into the southern states. They and the antislavery congressmen were nevertheless drawn by their more militant black and white associates into direct antislavery action that could be clandestine and illegal.

Prior to the Civil War, white male antislavery subversives who came to Washington from the North greatly outnumbered similarly inclined white women who came from that section. But the sex ratio began to change in 1847 when Virginia-born Margaret Shands Bailey arrived with her husband, Gamaliel Bailey. Soon the Bailey's large Washington home became a center for northern women who wrote for the *National Era* and for Margaret's juvenile antislavery monthly. Unlike Margaret Bailey, most of these women had been only tangentially involved in the antislavery movement prior to arriving in Washington.[41]

Several local white men and women who engaged in antislavery activities in Washington during the 1840s and 1850s had an even more remote relationship to northern abolitionist perspectives. Most of them had been born in the upper South and maintained ambiguous relationships to the subversive community. No one could gainsay the selfless motives of former secretary of war John H. Eaton—a native of Tennessee—and his controversial wife Margaret "Peggy" O'Neale Eaton—born in Washington—when, during the 1840s, they harbored escaped slaves. The same was true of Virginia-born Snodgrass's advocacy of black rights in Baltimore and Washington.[42] But the motivations of such prominent local attorneys as Joseph H. Bradley and Daniel Ratcliffe are difficult to ascertain.

Bradley defended Reuben Crandall in 1835 and Leonard A. Grimes in 1840. During the next two decades, he provided counsel to black and white abolitionists, while also serving masters who sought to recover slaves. Ratcliffe aspired to a place in Washington's slaveholding social set, while perennially representing abolitionists in court. In 1848 he simultaneously led an antiabolitionist mob and helped persuade the mob not to harm Gamaliel Bai-

41. Stanley Harrold, *Gamaliel Bailey and Antislavery Union* (Kent, Ohio: Kent State University Press, 1986), 81–93, 133, 190, 194–5.
42. Eatons: William L. Chaplin to Gerrit Smith, 25 March 1848, GSP. Snodgrass: Harrold, *Abolitionists and the South*, 29, 134.

ley. By 1850 he had an office at the same address as Bailey's home.[43] Antislavery conviction, humanitarianism, and a willingness to represent anyone who could pay were all factors in determining these lawyers' actions.

But generally it was empathy that led a few whites in Washington to cooperate with blacks. Influenced by northern evangelicalism, a sentimental regard for family life, and a popular romanticism that stressed emotion, white abolitionists identified with the poor and downtrodden. Before he ventured into the South, William L. Chaplin referred to members of enslaved black families as "fellow-men & fellow citizens crushed & dumb . . . husbands torn & mangled by the brutality & lust of the lawless despot . . . wives more than widows—mothers more than childless, and orphans more than motherless, made so by the infernal spirit of slavery."[44]

Except for James L. Huston's 1990 article on the "experiential basis of the northern antislavery impulse," recent studies have placed the development of this empathy for African Americans in an exclusively northern context. Abolitionists in their speeches and writings certainly attempted to create a vicarious bond between northern whites and suffering, far off slaves. Chaplin felt the bond well before he personally confronted the suffering. But when white northern abolitionists actually observed the shocking brutality of the slave trade, their identification with African Americans became intense. Their realization that masters and traders exhibited no such identification, no regard

43. Bradley: Bradley to William Cranch, [12 February 1840], Habeas Corpus Papers, and Deposition by D. Hartley Crawford, 11 September 1851, Fugitive Slave Cases, RG 21, NA; S. J. Bowen to Myrtilla Miner, 7 November 1858, MMP; Bradley to William H. Seward, 18 March 1858, in Gamaliel Bailey to Lewis Tappan, 29 March 1858, AMAA. Ratcliffe: Ben: Perley Poore, *Reminiscences of Sixty Years in the National Metropolis*, 2 vols. (Philadelphia: Hubbard Bros., 1886), 1:399; Richard Xavier Evans, "The Ladies' Union Benevolent and Employment Society, 1850," *RCHS*, 39 (1938): 162–3; J. Bremers and Ratcliffe to [Lewis Tappan], 18 November 1850, in Tappan to Gerrit Smith, 19 November 1850, GSP; Edward Waite, comp., *The Washington Directory . . . for 1850* (Washington: Waite, 1850), 4, 72; Tappan to Ratcliffe and Kennedy, 15 October 1856, letter book copy, LTP; *Boyd's Washington and Georgetown Directory . . . 1858* (New York: William H. Boyd, 1858), 413.

44. Chaplin to Gerrit Smith, 21 March 1838, GSP (quotation). Northern abolitionist motivation: Stewart, *Holy Warriors*, 33–49; Friedman, *Gregarious Saints*, 11–42; Bertram Wyatt-Brown, *Yankee Saints and Southern Sinners* (Baton Rouge: Louisiana State University Press, 1985), 1–127; Harrold, *Abolitionists and the South*, 71–2.

for the sanctity of black families, and no sense of black humanity, compounded the shock.[45]

One northern abolitionist wrote in 1847 that "to know the true meaning of slavery, we must look upon a slave; as to know what is meant by death, we must look upon the corpse of one that was near and dear to us. For my own part I never dreamed of the sad influences of slavery, until I had seen them with my own eyes." In Washington antislavery whites forced themselves to view the agony of blacks in slavery. They observed masters mistreating slaves, they went to slave auctions, they visited private slave prisons where men, women, and children awaited sale south. Giddings attests that these were major emotional engagements. On a February morning in 1839 he noticed a newspaper advertisement for a slave auction. Later he recorded in his diary, "I thought upon the subject & finally got my feelings wrought up to the determination of attending it."[46]

It *was* possible for slavery to shock some white Chesapeake natives. Among them were individuals such as Snodgrass and Samuel M. Janney, whose empathy for suffering African Americans was as strong as that of their northern-born counterparts. But usually it was northern abolitionists in Washington who bonded with oppressed African Americans by asking themselves and others to imagine how they would feel if members of their families suffered enslavement. When they called on northern "friends of freedom" for aid, they often recalled the sale during the 1790s of white Americans into slavery in Algeria. They asked potential donors to respond with "the same

45. Abolitionist empathy: Huston, "The Experiential Basis of the Northern Antislavery Impulse," *Journal of Southern History* 56 (November 1990): 609–40; Bertram Wyatt-Brown, *Lewis Tappan and the Evangelical War Against Slavery* (Cleveland: Case-Western Reserve University Press, 1969), viii; Kraditor, *Means and Ends in American Abolitionism,* 21, 237; Friedman, *Gregarious Saints,* 17, 26, 161, 176–7, 183–6, 195; Elizabeth B. Clark, "'The Sacred Rights of the Weak': Pain, Sympathy, and the Culture of Individual Rights in Antebellum America," *Journal of American History* 82 (September 1995): 463–93. Insensitivity of masters and slave traders: Johnson, *Soul by Soul,* passim.

46. *PF,* 15 April 1847 (first quotation); Giddings, diary, 16 February [1839], JRGP (second quotation). Two exceptional Garrisonians reported experiences similar to Giddings's in visiting slave prisons in Washington. See J. Miller McKim to Joshua Leavitt, 14 February 1838, in *PF,* 13 March 1838, and David Lee Child, "Correspondence from Washington," 3 January 1843, in *NASS,* 12 January 1843.

spirit of pity and generosity they would claim from others if themselves were in agony to rescue a wife, mother, or sister, from Algerine bondage."[47]

Throughout its existence the Washington antislavery community was a southern outpost of northern abolitionism. A shared reform culture, a need for funding, and, in many cases, personal background tied the city's antislavery activists to the larger movement. Black and white abolitionists residing in the North cooperated eagerly with men and women in Washington who appeared to be making progress against slavery on its own ground. Those in the North did so because they perceived the strategic and symbolic importance of the capital city, and because antislavery subversives there sent northward frequent appeals for aid in the redemption of slaves, the payment of legal fees, and the financing of slave escapes.[48] Numerous antislavery northerners also visited Washington. Beginning in the late 1840s, the Baileys' large home became a mecca for them.[49]

47. Turner, "Anti-Slavery Thought," 272–5; J. E. Snodgrass to Editors, 9 February 1846, in *PF*, 12 February 1846; Patricia Hickin, "Gentle Agitator: Samuel M. Janney and the Antislavery Movement in Virginia, 1842–1851," *Journal of Southern History* 37 (May 1971): 168–72; [William L. Chaplin] to *Patriot*, 3 February [1845], in *AP*, 12 February 1845 (quotations).

48. Redemptions and legal fees: William L. Chaplin to Smith, 17 May & 11 November 1848, GSP; Myrtilla Miner to Samuel Rhoads, 25 September 1853, MMP; Tappan to Jacob Bigelow, 30 January 1856, Tappan to Ezra L. Stevens, 30 July 1857, letter book copies, LTP. Northern white support for slave escapes: Smith, "Address to the Slaves," in *NASS*, 24 February 1842; Smith to William H. Seward, 11 August 1850, WHSP; W. B. Williams to [Wilbur H. Siebert], 30 March 1896, Wilbur H. Siebert Papers, Ohio Historical Society, Columbus; William Penn to [William Still], 10 November 1855, in Still, *The Underground Railroad* (1871; reprint, Chicago: Johnson, 1970), 181. Northern black donations: Charles T. Torrey to J. Miller McKim, 29 November 1844, William Lloyd Garrison Papers, Boston Public Library; William L. Chaplin to Gerrit Smith, 2 November 1848, GSP; *NYDT*, 10 May 1850. Northern black support for slave escapes: *NS*, 5 September 1850, Still, *Underground Railroad,* 158, 177–82.

49. Joshua Leavitt to S. W. Benedict, 23 January 1834, in *GUE* 1, 4th series (March 1834): 39–41; Cha's L***** to Br. Goodell, n.d., in *Friend of Man,* 22 March 1838; Alvan Stewart to Mr. Hough, 18 October 1841, in *PF,* 24 November 1841; *PF,* 15 January 1846; Harrold, *Bailey,* 82–3; *AS,* 13 April 1850; John Wallace Hutchinson, *Story of the Hutchinsons (Tribe of Jesse),* Charles E. Mann, ed.; 2 vols. (1896; reprint, New York: Da capo, 1977), 1:311–2; G[iddings] to Kind Reader, 29 January 1853, in *AS,* 5 January 1854. Most who visited were from the church-oriented and political wings of abolitionism. The Garrisonian James and Lucretia Mott were an exception. See: Lucretia Mott to Maria [Weston Chapman], 30 November 1842, in Chapman Papers, Boston Public Library; Anna Davis Hallowell, *James and Lucretia Mott: Life and Letters* (Boston: Houghton, Mifflin, 1896), 386.

But there was often friction between antislavery activists stationed on the Potomac and some northern abolitionists. Garrisonians and radical political abolitionists objected to the compromises some of the Washington antislavery community members made in order to function inside the law. Somewhat less pervasively, Garrisonians and some evangelical abolitionists complained that helping slaves to escape violated the antislavery movement's commitment to convincing masters voluntarily to free their chattels. They considered escape attempts wasteful of energies better devoted to agitation in the North for general emancipation. Many northern abolitionists also contended that efforts centered in Washington to purchase the freedom of slaves were counterproductive because the purchases implicitly recognized the legitimacy of owning human property.[50]

Conversely, antislavery activists in Washington who considered themselves to be front-line troops in a war against slavery bristled at reprimands from those in the rear. When Garrison suggested in Boston in 1832 that antislavery veteran Benjamin Lundy in Washington was too timid, Lundy gently objected. Garrison, he noted, "may be safe in pursuing the path that *others have beaten*:—but shall he penetrate the *wilderness of despotism* . . . he must, at least, *philosophize* a little, as he goes along." Gamaliel Bailey in 1848 reminded his northern critics, "We take our stand as far south as we can."[51]

Besides its symbolic significance as the national capital, Washington gained importance as a place, deep within a slaveholding region, that was accessible to the North's more aggressive antislavery activists. These activists allied with African Americans struggling to free themselves. The two dissimilar groups formed a lasting community dedicated to driving slavery from the Chesapeake. Their subversive actions, as well as events in Congress, kept Washington a major focal point of abolitionism into the Civil War years.

---

50. Compromises: "Thirteenth Anniversary of the AASS," 11 May 1847, in *PF*, 20 May 1847; *Liberty Press*, 25 May 1848; *Chronotype*, quoted in *AP*, 26 April 1848. Escapes: Abby Kelley to William Lloyd Garrison, 22 August 1851, Garrison Papers. Purchases: *PF*, 16 January 1845, 6 December 1849.

51. *GUE* 2, 3d series (May 1832): 191 (first quotation); Harrold, *Bailey*, 91–3 (second quotation). See *NE*, 4 August 1859.

THREE

Charles T. Torrey, Thomas Smallwood, and the Underground Railroad

C HARLES T. TORREY died of tuberculosis in the Maryland Penitentiary on May 9, 1846, while serving a six-year sentence for the crime of helping slaves escape. Ten days later his northern white abolitionist colleagues held his funeral at Tremont Temple in Boston, far from the Washington area where he had gained his reputation as a friend of enslaved African Americans. Yet Torrey's reputation preceded his body to Boston.

Joseph C. Lovejoy, the brother of abolitionist martyr Elijah P. Lovejoy, delivered the funeral sermon and directed his remarks to what he perceived to be Torrey's legacy. Torrey's death, he predicted, would "be the beginning of the Hegira of the slave[s]." Lovejoy imagined them "in scores and by hundreds, crossing the long line of border, and treading with a new and wondering emotion, a soil partially free." Their "watchword," he hoped, would be "'Torrey and Liberty!'" Lovejoy also hoped that Torrey's example would convince more whites "of the righteousness and expediency of direct efforts to assist the slaves, individually to their freedom."

Lovejoy recognized that the slaves themselves must take the initiative against the most oppressive aspect of slavery. It was, he said, enslaved black men who had to guard the chastity of their wives and daughters with force if necessary. "The father and husband who will not protect, resisting even to blood, the innocence of his own family," said Lovejoy, "is worthy to be nei-

Torrey Monument, Mount Auburn Cemetery, Cambridge, Massachusetts. Raised over Torrey's grave in 1847, the monument's inscription reads, in part, "The friends of the American slave erect this stone to his memory, as a martyr for liberty." Author's photograph.

ther a father nor a husband."[1] Lovejoy might have included mothers and wives along with fathers and husbands in his endorsement of such efforts. A desire to protect family members motivated African Americans of both genders to escape northward. But Lovejoy's emphasis on interracial cooperation was apropos in remembrance of Torrey, who had labored to promote biracial antislavery communities in Boston and Washington.

African Americans reciprocated Torrey's dedication. Black Bostonians "thronged in great numbers" to Torrey's funeral and black leaders praised him. David Ruggles portrayed Torrey as a Good Samaritan, Frederick Douglass linked him to the will of God, and William C. Nell led an effort to build

1. Joseph C. Lovejoy, ed., *Memoir of Rev. Charles T. Torrey* (1847; reprint, Negro Universities Press, 1969), 294–305.

a monument to him at Mount Auburn Cemetery in Cambridge. AME Bishop Daniel A. Payne, who had known Torrey in Washington, visited the monument in 1850 and thousands of other African Americans from the Potomac to Canada remembered him as well. Among them was Thomas Smallwood, Torrey's chief associate in helping slaves escape. Writing in Toronto in 1851, Smallwood referred to him as "the beloved friend . . . who is now no more."[2]

Between 1842 and 1844, Torrey and Smallwood attempted to challenge slavery in Washington and the surrounding Chesapeake region by creating a clandestine means of black escape along a predetermined route—what contemporaries called an *underground railroad*. Their story, including the black and white men and women who assisted them, illustrates the physical struggle between antislavery and proslavery forces in the eastern borderlands. The area in contention stretched from northern Virginia to southern Pennsylvania and centered on the nation's capital. While debate in Congress concerning slavery could become abstract, Torrey and Smallwood confronted a concrete issue: whether or not slavery would continue to exist in this region. Their struggle changed permanently the way slavery's black and white opponents cooperated in Washington.

Torrey came to Washington as correspondent for a half-dozen antislavery newspapers and worked in conjunction with the cadre of white antislavery northerners that had formed in response to the Gag Rule. Among its members were Whig congressmen John Quincy Adams, Seth M. Gates, Joshua R. Giddings, and William Slade. By 1841 this cadre also included antislavery lobbyists Theodore D. Weld and Joshua Leavitt, with whom Torrey cooperated. For several sessions of Congress, Gates, Giddings, Leavitt, and Weld lived together near the Capitol at Ann G. Sprigg's boardinghouse, which Weld named the Abolition House. Adams acted as counsel before the Supreme Court for the Africans who rebelled aboard the Spanish slave ship *Amistad*, but there is no evidence that he interacted with local African Ameri-

2. Ibid., 294 (first quotation); *L*, 3 January 1845; John W. Blassingame et al., eds., *The Frederick Douglass Papers*, 4 vols. (New Haven: Yale University Press, 1979–1986), 1:116–7; *E*, 26 August 1846; David Alexander Payne, *Recollections of Seventy Years* (1888; reprint, New York: Arno, 1968), 98–9; *PF*, 9 September 1847; Thomas Smallwood, *A Narrative of Thomas Smallwood, (Colored Man)* (Toronto: Smallwood, 1851), 21 (second quotation).

cans on issues related to slavery.[3] The others—albeit often in condescending and awkward ways—all helped to create a biracial antislavery community.

This was especially the case concerning Leavitt, Slade, and Giddings. Leavitt, a pious Liberty abolitionist from Boston, had visited Franklin and Armfield's Alexandria slave prison with George Drinker in 1834. During the early 1840s, he studied the condition of Washington's black population, attended black church meetings, and cultivated contacts with individual African Americans. Slade braved threats of violence from a South Carolina congressman in calling for a ban on the slave coffles that passed along Washington's streets. He denounced the slave trade itself for its "sundering of domestic relationships" among African Americans, and supported private efforts to protect black families from dismemberment. Well after he left Congress, Slade—who was governor of Vermont during the mid-1840s—remained in touch with black people he had known in Washington.[4]

3. William Lee Miller, *Arguing about Slavery: The Great Battle in the United States Congress* (New York: Knopf, 1996), 301–487; Leonard L. Richards, *Life and Times of Congressman John Quincy Adams* (New York: Oxford University Press, 1986); James Brewer Stewart, *Joshua R. Giddings and the Tactics of Radical Politics* (Cleveland: Case-Western Reserve University Press, 1970), 37–83; Gates to Giddings, 2 October & 29 December 1844, JRGP; Gilbert H. Barnes, *The Antislavery Impulse, 1830–1844* (1933; reprint, Gloucester, Mass.: Peter Smith, 1973), 177–90; James M. McPherson, "The Fight against the Gag Rule: Joshua Leavitt and Antislavery Insurgency in the Whig Party," *Journal of Southern History* 48 (July 1963): 177–95 (first quotation p. 180); Hugh Davis, *Joshua Leavitt: Evangelical Abolitionist* (Baton Rouge: Louisiana State University Press, 1990), 176–7; Theodore D. Weld to Angelina Grimké Weld, 27 December 1842, in Gilbert H. Barnes and Dwight L. Dumond, eds., *The Letters of Theodore Dwight Weld, Angelina Grimké Weld, and Sarah Grimké, 1822–1844*, 2 vols. (1934; reprint, Gloucester, Mass.: Peter Smith, 1965), 2:947 (second quotation, hereafter cited as Barnes and Dumond, eds., *Weld-Grimké Letters*). During the early 1840s, Gates joined the Liberty party. Historians do not include Torrey among members of the antislavery lobby, but see: Lovejoy, *Torrey,* 88–9; Seth Gates to James G. Birney, 24 January 1842, in Dwight L. Dumond, ed., *The Letters of James G. Birney,* 2 vols. (New York: Appleton-Century, 1938), 2:667; Gates to Gerrit Smith, 14 March 1842, GSP.

4. Leavitt: William Jay, *Miscellaneous Writings on Slavery* (Boston: J. P. Jewett, 1853), 157; Leavitt to Piercy and Reed, 20 January 1841, in *E,* 28 January 1841; Leavitt to Piercy and Reed, 5 July 1844, ibid., 15 July 1841. Slade: Slade to Leavitt, 7 August 1838, in *PF,* 23 August 1838; Slade to Leavitt, 12 October 1838, in *PF,* 1 November 1838 (quotation); Slade to Editors, 12 February 1839, in *CA,* 16 February 1839; Slade to Leavitt, 18 February 1839, in *PF,* 14 March 1839; *PF,* 11 April 1839; Slade to Joshua R. Giddings, 17 December 1848, JRGP.

Meanwhile Giddings established himself as an ally of African Americans. He was born in Pennsylvania in 1795 and had grown up amid frontier conditions in Ohio's Western Reserve. A successful attorney, a fervent evangelical, and a member of a local antislavery society, Giddings first gained election to Congress in 1838. In 1842 the House of Representatives censured him for defending the right of slaves to revolt. He resigned his seat and was quickly reelected. The next year he challenged a District of Columbia ordinance that allowed for free blacks *falsely* arrested as fugitive slaves to be sold into slavery if they could not pay their jail fees. Along with William Jones, a black Virginian held in Washington Jail, and Jones's white attorney, David A. Hall, the large, muscular, often bellicose Giddings raised a furor in the House of Representatives over this practice. While the Jones case served Giddings's political goal of demonstrating the complicity of Congress in slavery's injustices, the case also helped gain him a reputation as a valuable resource in the black struggle for racial justice.[5] But not even Giddings's efforts in cooperation with Washington-area African Americans during the first half of the 1840s approached Torrey's.

Short, slight, delicately handsome, and subject to poor health, Torrey was born in 1813 to a distinguished if not wealthy Massachusetts family. After tuberculosis took the lives of his parents during his early childhood, his maternal grandparents became his guardians. He attended Phillips Academy and Yale College, while—like other young New Englanders of his generation—struggling introspectively over sin and redemption. In Torrey's case, this struggle led to the Congregationalist ministry and abolitionism. After graduating from Yale in 1833, he attended Andover Theological Seminary, where he established a student antislavery society. Although illness and financial difficulty forced Torrey to withdraw from Andover, he finally gained ordination in 1836 under the guidance of the Reverend Jacob Ide, whose daughter he married. The couple had two children, but a commitment to abolitionism drew Torrey away from his family.[6]

5. Giddings to Laura Waters Giddings, 12 February 1843, JRGP; *CG*, 28 Cong., 1 sess. (28 December 1843), 80; *E*, 4 & 11 January 1844; *AS*, 6 & 20 January 1844. For Giddings's life see Stewart, *Giddings*.

6. Lovejoy, *Torrey*, 1–33; Torrey to Editor, 3 March 1835, in *L*, 7 March 1835. Soul searching among young New Englanders: Lawrence J. Friedman, *Gregarious Saints: Self and Community in American Abolitionism, 1830–1870* (New York: Cambridge University Press,

Charles T. Torrey (1813–1846) was a white northern abolitionist who helped organize an underground railroad in Washington during the early 1840s. J. C. Lovejoy, *Memoir of Rev. Charles T. Torrey* (Boston: John P. Jewett, 1847), frontispiece.

As he became increasingly active in the Massachusetts Anti-Slavery Society (MASS) and the AASS, Torrey became disenchanted with William Lloyd Garrison, who led both groups. In 1838 Torrey emerged, along with Amos A. Phelps, Alanson St. Clair, and Henry Stanton, as a leader among the "clerical abolitionists" who bitterly opposed Garrison's rejection of electoral politics and his denunciation of American churches as bastions of slavery. Torrey feared mainly that abstinence from the electoral process would make abolitionists irrelevant. But his hostility to the participation of women in abolitionist meetings, his reputation as a "'plotter'" against Garrison, and allegations that mental instability contributed to his actions have shaped evaluations of his career.[7]

1982), 11–40 and Bertram Wyatt-Brown, *Yankee Saints and Southern Sinners* (Baton Rouge: Louisiana State University Press, 1985), 42–75.

7. Lovejoy, *Torrey*, 33–42; Wendell Phillips Garrison and Francis Jackson Garrison, *William Lloyd Garrison: 1805–1889*, 4 vols. (New York: Century, 1885–89), 2:220–1, 262–77, 284–9, 296–7, 300–7, 330–31, 338–43; John L. Thomas, *The Liberator: William Lloyd Garrison, a Biography* (Boston: Little, Brown, 1963), 146–51, 220–3, 351; Richard H. Sewell, *Ballots for Freedom: Antislavery Politics in the United States, 1837–1860* (New York: Oxford University

Personal problems certainly disturbed Torrey. His health was never good. He had to borrow to pay for his college education. His career as an abolitionist journalist limited his ability to pay creditors. As a result, he feared that he could not fulfil his masculine responsibility to provide for his family. He also had a strained relationship with his wife, and his enemies charged that he had been unfaithful to her. Raised as an only child by doting grandparents, he had become vain and impetuous. In some contexts, he had difficulty working with others.[8]

Yet Torrey was intelligent, occasionally witty, and a daring organizer. In 1839 he helped put together the Massachusetts Abolition Society (MAS) in opposition to the MASS. In January 1840 he bypassed more senior abolitionists in calling for the national convention that produced the Liberty party, and he continued to help lead that party during the early 1840s. More to the point, he was a white abolitionist who worked harmoniously with African Americans. At its first meeting in May 1839, Torrey committed the MAS to "improvement of the free people of color, in this their native country." Subsequently he hired a black man, Jehiel C. Beman, to coordinate projects for "colored youth." During the spring of 1841, Torrey, rather than his Garrisonian counterparts, organized the biracial Boston Vigilance Committee that served as a bridge to his activities in the Chesapeake.[9]

In June 1841 Torrey had a schooner captain and mate arrested in Boston for kidnapping John Torrance and transporting him into slavery in North Carolina. He also investigated a report that a slave had been illegally brought to Boston from South Carolina and sent back by ship to that state. A few weeks before he removed to Washington in December of that year, he at-

---

Press, 1976), 52 (first quotation), 29–32 (second quotation); Aileen S. Kraditor, *Means and Ends in American Abolitionism: Garrison and His Critics on Strategy and Tactics, 1834–1850* (New York: Pantheon, 1969), 48–51, 96–7, 113, 115.

8. Lovejoy, *Torrey*, 5–6, 32, 86–7, 154–5, 212; *Spirit of the Times* (Philadelphia), quoted in *AP*, 16 October 1844; Torrey to McKim, 29 November 1844, William Lloyd Garrison Papers, Boston Public Library.

9. Kraditor, *Means and Ends*, 51; Wm. B. Dodge to Torrey, 2 April 1839 and Edwin W. Clarke to Torrey, 21 February 1840, Charles T. Torrey Papers, Congregational Library, Boston; Sewell, *Ballots for Freedom*, 52, 58–9, 66, 69–70, 88; *AP*, 9 February, 5 September, & 12 September 1843; *CA*, 23 November 1839 (quotations); Torrey to Joshua Leavitt, 28 June 1841, in *E*, 15 July 1841.

tempted to help a free black man from Baltimore who had been kidnapped, taken aboard a ship registered in Boston, and carried into slavery in New Orleans. In behalf of the Vigilance Committee, he wrote to the man's father in care of Isaac Tyson, son of Elijah Tyson, for proof of the man's free status. By the time Tyson had fully complied with this request, Torrey was himself in the Chesapeake, as a congressional correspondent.[10]

On his way to Washington, Torrey spent a day in Baltimore interviewing black and white leaders. He wanted their assessments of the upcoming Maryland slaveholders' convention scheduled for January 12, 1842 at Annapolis, the first ever held in the United States. He learned that the convention, which had been called by planters who feared antislavery tendencies in the state, would propose legislation to expel free blacks, promote the domestic slave trade, reduce the number of slave escapes, and curtail the circulation of abolitionist newspapers. The slaveholders also planned to denounce the refusal of Governor William H. Seward of New York to extradite three black sailors to Virginia on charges that they had helped a slave escape from nearby Norfolk.[11]

Although it seemed unlikely that the Maryland legislature would adopt the convention's proposals, members of the antislavery cadre at Washington encouraged Torrey to go to Annapolis to report on the convention. They hoped he would expose the slaveholders as rogues and fools while confronting them on their own ground. John Needles, former Baltimore colleague of Elisha Tyson and Benjamin Lundy, had a similar idea. He caused a stir when he entered the Annapolis Courthouse, where 150 slaveholders had convened

10. *L,* 2 July 1841; MASS, *Tenth Annual Report* (1841; reprint, Westport, Conn.: Negro Universities Press, 1970), 81–5; Torrey to J. White, 8 November [December] 1841, Torrey to Robert Wright, 24 November 1841, in Torrey to Isaac Tyson, n.d. and Isaac Tyson to Torrey, 15 January 1842, Torrey Papers.

11. P. P. [Torrey] to Editors, 4 December 1841, in *New York Evangelist,* 11 December 1841; Torrey to Dear Sir, 24 January 1842, in *E,* 4 February 1842. Torrey identifies himself as the Washington correspondent of the *Evangelist* in Torrey to J. White, 8 November [December] 1841, Torrey Papers. Ira Berlin and Lawrence H. McDonald support Torrey's assessment of the slaveholders' convention. See: Berlin, *Slaves without Masters: The Free Negro in the Antebellum South* (New York: New Press, 1974), 210–1 and McDonald, "Prelude to Emancipation: The Failure of the Great Reaction in Maryland, 1831–1850" (Ph.D. dissertation, University of Maryland, 1974), 23–35. Extradition controversy: Paul Finkelman, "The Protection of Black Rights in Seward's New York," *Civil War History* 34 (September 1988): 211–28.

the convention "and stood up before them." But Torrey had greater impact. His remark that a black man in Baltimore had informed him "that the colored people would die before they would leave the State" attracted attention. His resistance to a door-keeper who tried to stop his note-taking produced a confrontation that shaped his future.[12]

In short order Torrey was held against his will by convention delegates, rescued by some Annapolis residents, captured by a mob, and jailed by local authorities. He faced charges of "mutiny," distributing "incendiary matter," and exciting "'discontent' among the colored people." Ably defended by Thomas S. Alexander of Annapolis, Joseph M. Palmer of Frederick, and David A. Simmons of Boston—the last having been dispatched from Washington by Giddings and others—Torrey regained his freedom on January 19 when a local judge dismissed the charges as groundless.

By then Torrey's empathy for black suffering and his commitment to direct action against slavery had intensified. In jail he had shared a cell with thirteen members of a family who were waiting for a court to determine whether they were free by the will of their former master or were the property of his heirs. Torrey feared the worst—that they would be sold to traders. His time with them led, he recalled, "to a solemn re-consecration of myself to the work of freeing the slaves, until no slave shall be found in our land." He claimed to feel "with more force than ever, the biblical injunction to 'remember them that are in bonds as bound with them,'" *and* to identify with his old nemesis Garrison. "When Garrison was thrust into Baltimore jail," Torrey proclaimed, "guiltless of crime, the death of the [slave] system was decreed. And now god has written upon the walls of Annapolis jail also, 'Slavery must die.'" A few white abolitionists reacted negatively to this egotism. A few questioned the wisdom of Torrey's trip to Annapolis.[13] But no black aboli-

12. The discussion in this and the following paragraph is based on: Editorial Correspondence [Leavitt], 15 January [1842], in *E*, 20 January 1842; Lovejoy, *Torrey*, 143; Torrey to Dear Sir, 24 January 1842, in *E*, 4 February 1842; Edward Needles Wright, ed., "John Needles (1786–1878): An Autobiography," *Quaker History* 58 (Spring 1969): 7 (first quotation); Torrey to Dear Sir, 24 January 1842, in *E*, 4 February 1842 (succeeding quotations); Theodore D. Weld to Angelina Grimké Weld, 18 January 1842, in Barnes and Dumond, eds., *Weld-Grimké Papers*, 2:895–6. In June 1841 the *CA* called on black Marylanders to resist colonization schemes "and determine to die upon the soil." See *CA*, 16 June 1841.

13. Lovejoy, *Torrey*, 95 (first & second quotations), 99 (third quotation). See also *AP*, 24 June 1846. White abolitionist criticism of Torrey: Lovejoy, *Torrey*, 99; Theodore D. Weld to

tionist complained and one obscure Washington black man, on reading about the events in Annapolis, perceived in Torrey a kindred spirit.

This was Thomas Smallwood, whose wife Elizabeth washed clothes for Torrey's landlady. Smallwood took advantage of this connection to gain an introduction when Torrey returned from Annapolis to his 13th Street boardinghouse located near the White House. According to Smallwood, Torrey immediately informed him of a plan to rescue a family of slaves whom Secretary of the Navy George E. Badger of North Carolina intended to sell south. This proposed rescue, Smallwood asserted, initiated the underground railroad in Washington.[14]

In 1961 Larry Gara's *The Liberty Line: The Legend of the Underground Railroad* challenged the popular notion that before the Civil War white abolitionists operated a well-organized, clandestine slave escape network that stretched from the southern borderlands to Canada. Gara correctly pointed out that there was no monolithic organization that coordinated escapes throughout the United States. He also was right in emphasizing that African Americans who escaped were not just passive recipients of white abolitionist help. But he was incorrect in two respects: first, in suggesting that there were few, if any, coordinated escapes along predetermined routes and, second, in denying that white abolitionists played an important role in escapes from the South. The biracial underground railroad network established by Smallwood and Torrey remained for over twenty years a central facet of Washington's subversive community. The organizing, planning, and financing in which the two men engaged, as well as the obstacles they faced, indicate that slaves—especially enslaved women and children—often required assistance if they were to escape successfully.[15]

Angelina Grimké Weld, 18 January 1842, in Barnes and Dumond, eds., *Weld–Grimké Papers,* 2:895–6.

14. Smallwood, *Narrative,* 17–8; Anthony Reintzel, comp., *Washington Directory, and Governmental Register, for 1843* (Washington: Reintzel, 1843), 67.

15. Larry Gara, *Liberty Line: The Legend of the Underground Railroad* (Lexington: University of Kentucky Press, 1961). The recently published memoir of black underground railroad operative John P. Parker, and Kathryn Grover's study of escapees and abolitionists in New Bedford, Massachusetts, confirm that white abolitionists cooperated with African Americans in coordinated escape efforts. See Stewart Seely Sprague, ed., *His Promised Land: The Autobiography of John P. Parker, Former Slave and Conductor on the Underground Railroad* (New York: Norton, 1996), and Grover, *The Fugitive's Gibralter: Escaping Slaves and Abolitionism in New Bedford,*

Before his meeting with Torrey, Smallwood's life had been markedly different from that of his new friend, although the two men had several things in common. Twelve years older than Torrey, Smallwood was born a slave in Prince George's County, Maryland, just to the east of the District of Columbia. When his first master died, Smallwood, then a small child, passed by inheritance to the Reverend John B. Ferguson, who Smallwood recalled was "no friend of slavery." Ferguson taught Smallwood how to read and write, and later agreed to free him at age thirty in return for $500. Smallwood paid installments while living and working with a Scottish immigrant named John McLoad, who also contributed to his education. In the process, Smallwood developed a fondness for British literature—especially the works of Charles Dickens—which he later shared with Torrey.[16]

Free in 1831, Smallwood became "a shoemaker, in making and selling shoes in the City of Washington," married, and started a family. By the time he met Torrey, he also worked at the Washington Navy Yard and he, his wife, and four children occupied a large house on the outskirts of the city. He owned valuable furniture and had a garden in the rear. In addition, Smallwood had been a class leader at the African Wesleyan Church until May 1840, when he initiated a bitter quarrel with its pastor, Abraham Cole. Influenced by black abolitionist David Walker's *Appeal to the Colored Citizens of the World*, Smallwood charged that Cole and other local black leaders lacked "energy" and "courage." Cole responded by expelling Smallwood from the church. Therefore Smallwood, like Torrey in regard to Garrison, was moti-

---

Massachusetts (Amherst, Mass.: University of Massachusetts Press, 2001). Earlier, C. Peter Ripley portrayed the underground railroad network centered in Washington to have been an exclusively black operation. See Ripley et al., eds., *The Black Abolitionists Papers*, 5 vols. (Chapel Hill: University of North Carolina Press, 1985–92), 3:39–40, and Ripley, *Witness for Freedom: African-American Voices on Race, Slavery, and Emancipation* (Chapel Hill: University of North Carolina Press, 1993), 15.

16. The discussion in this and the following paragraphs is based on: Smallwood, *Narrative*, iii–xii, 13 (first quotation), 14–7, 23–4, 30, 32–4, 37–8, 55–6 (third & fourth quotations); "Smallwood v. Cole," November 1842, entry 6, Case Papers, RG 21, NA (second quotation). Samivel Weller Jr. to Editor, 22 October 1842, in *TL*, 3 November 1842; Weller to Editor, 14 June 1843, in *AP*, 22 June 1843; Seth M. Gates to Joshua R. Giddings, 5 December 1848, JRGP. Ferguson remained on friendly terms with Smallwood up to the time Smallwood and his family left Washington. See "Slave Manumissions," 3:486, RG 21, NA. Navy Yard: John B. Ellis, *Sights and Secrets of the National Capital* (Chicago: Jones, Jenkins, 1869), 331–3.

vated to demonstrate his own superior bravery in comparison to Cole and other local black leaders.

During the 1820s Smallwood had favored African colonization because he believed that the ACS aimed at general emancipation. By the early 1830s, he had concluded—like other abolitionists—that instead it aimed to reduce unrest and perpetuate slavery by draining away free blacks. He later maintained that he resisted an attempt by slaveholders to bribe him into promoting black migration to Liberia. Yet, before he met Torrey, he saw few opportunities for effective antislavery activity. He could talk privately but in a slaveholding region he could not organize abolitionist lectures and meetings. Torrey offered him a clandestine alternative and, because of Torrey's career as a journalist, a chance to boast about it in print.

The behavior and motivation of Torrey and Smallwood in risking their freedom and their lives in helping slaves to escape reveals a great deal about them and the subversive community. The "desperate courage" and bravado they and others exhibited in attempting to undermine the existing order is characteristic of revolutionary vanguards.[17] They challenged the slaveholding power structure in order to undermine slavery in the District and its vicinity.

The two men differed in race, class, and regional background and they each had their own motives for undertaking this dangerous work. But they shared a perception of slavery as an institution that oppressed blacks, corrupted both races, and violated Christian precepts. Like many other Americans of his time, Smallwood warned that, unless the people of the United States repented their tolerance of slavery, God would "leave them to their folly to work out their own destruction." Torrey believed that the fate of his soul depended on his willingness to follow the example of Christ in rejecting obedience to human law that conflicted with God's.[18]

Both men abhorred the treatment of women and children in slavery and especially the sexual abuse of black women. The masters, Smallwood believed, had destroyed the chastity of black women and thereby the respect of

17. S[tephen] P[earl] A[ndrews], Washington Correspondence of the New York *Tribune*, 26 August [1850], in *PF*, 5 September 1850 (quotation). Difficulty of slave escapes: John Hope Franklin and Loren Schweninger, *Runaway Slaves: Rebels on the Plantation* (New York: Oxford University Press, 1999), 116, 212, 228, 279; *L*, 21 April 1848.

18. Smallwood, *Narrative*, 20 (quotation); *AP*, 3 October 1843.

black men for them. In September 1843 he declared that scenes associated with the Washington slave trade "would make the devil blush." His own family's insecure and limited freedom inspired his prediction that because of an insatiable demand for slaves in the Deep South that year "many more heartstrings will be broken before the winter sets in, by sundering all the ties of life."[19]

In contrast to Smallwood's natural identification with the oppressed, Torrey's commitment to them grew out of his religious beliefs, his dedication to immediate emancipation, and the shock that he, like other northerners, experienced on observing the physical and emotional cruelties associated with slavery. Concerning the time he spent imprisoned in 1842 with a slave family, Torrey recalled, "I could not help weeping as I looked at the two little infants . . . in their mothers' arms, mewling in sweet unconsciousness of the bitter doom their parents were anticipating, a sale to the trader." Two years later he decried the sexual "impurity" of slavery and its mockery of family morality. It was common, he reported, for slaveholders in the Baltimore-Washington area not only to have children by their female slaves but to have additional children by their enslaved daughters and to sell them all to traders.[20]

Why did these two individuals take the lead in organizing slave escapes, while others who held similar views provided only tacit support or avoided involvement? Torrey had always been impulsive. Or, from a different perspective, he had always acted forthrightly when others might equivocate. Torrey also sought distraction from worries over his increasing financial difficulties, estrangement from his wife, and his role in shattering the antislavery movement. He wanted tangible proof that he could effectively fight slavery. As he put it to Gerrit Smith in January 1844, "Do you ask: 'Why waste your time so, and run these risks?' I reply. . . . *Private* causes of personal misery render me—perhaps *reckless*. In toil and excitement the misery one cannot relieve, may be forgotten. . . . And, for a time to come, I shall relieve *individual* cases of suffering, while, I hope, I am not unfitting myself for duty to the whole cause."[21]

19. Smallwood, *Narrative*, 58–9; Samivel Weller, Jr. to Printer, 12 September [*sic*], 1843, in *E*, 12 September 1843 (quotations).

20. Torrey to Sir, 24 January 1842, in *E*, 4 February 1842 (first quotation); "Notes on Southern Travel," *AP*, 6 March 1844 (second quotation); Lovejoy, *Torrey*, 89–90.

21. Torrey to Smith, 23 January (quotation) and 3 August 1844, GSP.

Torrey arrogantly believed he could challenge the proslavery status quo in the Chesapeake, and there was arrogance in Smallwood's character as well. He felt deeply the humiliations imposed on him by American racism. He assumed he was superior morally and intellectually to others, both black and white. Helping slaves to escape allowed him to defy a black elite that he believed collaborated with proslavery forces and gave him a chance to outwit slaveholders and law enforcement agents, whom he held in contempt. When, for example, he learned that a Georgetown slaveholder had "frequently boasted that a neger [*sic*] could not beat his time," Smallwood replied that he "would beat his time, though a neger, according to his sense of the word . . . and by the assistance of the Lord always could beat his time and any of the rest of the slaveholders' time, but for the treachery of some of my own colour."[22]

Moral and strategic considerations also shaped Torrey's and Smallwood's actions. According to Smallwood, neither he nor Torrey approved of purchasing the freedom of individual slaves. Although such purchases later became an important function of Washington's antislavery community, the two men agreed with the widely held abolitionist view that paying slaveholders for freeing a slave amounted to rewarding thieves for their crimes. Strategically, they believed that fostering slave escapes served the larger purpose of driving human bondage from the Chesapeake. Relying on interviews with persons who had cooperated with Torrey, Robert Clemens Smedley concluded during the 1880s that Torrey believed assisted escapes would render "property in slaves . . . so insecure that it would hasten emancipation." In February 1844, Torrey lectured northern abolitionists: "Too long have we delayed assaults on slavery in her own dark dominions. The very spirit of cowardice has infested us, and we have called it 'prudence.'"[23]

The plan to rescue the family owned by Secretary Badger fell through when the mother informed Smallwood that her husband preferred to seek money in the North to purchase the freedom of herself and her children

22. Smallwood, *Narrative*, 23 (quotation), 32–3, 52–3; Samivel Weller, Jr. to Editor, 14 June 1843, in *AP*, 22 June 1843.

23. Smallwood, *Narrative*, 18–20; Robert C. Smedley, *History of the Underground Railroad in Chester and Neighboring Counties in Pennsylvania* (1883; reprint, New York: Arno, 1969), 81 (first quotation); *AP*, 14 February 1844 (second quotation).

rather than risk an escape attempt. But during the months that followed, Smallwood, Torrey, Elizabeth Smallwood, and Mrs. Padgett (Torrey's southern white landlady) created what Smallwood called "our new underground railroad." By necessity flexible in their illegal and dangerous operations, they provided a degree of organization to slave escapes from Washington and its vicinity that, according to Smallwood, had hitherto been lacking.[24]

They relied on constantly changing secret meeting places where potential escapees could rendezvous with their guide. They established "places of deposit between Washington and Mason's and Dixon's line" to conceal their "passengers" to the North. Among potential clientele, they favored families threatened with sale south, as well as those who could help pay the costs of transportation and subsistence during a three-day trip northward. They harbored escapees at Smallwood's and Padgett's homes or elsewhere in order to elude pursuers, and they usually traveled at night by carriage to reach Pennsylvania where the escapees could continue by train.

Prominent among the escapees were church members, whom Torrey characterized as "Christian fathers and mothers, with their little children, whom they sought to rescue from a life of slavery." Such people, Torrey carefully pointed out to his northern readers, belonged "not [to] a pro-slavery white church, but a *colored abolition* church." They were the sort of middle-class-oriented African Americans whom Torrey met at the black churches he attended in Washington; the sort whom Smallwood taught as an African Wesleyan class leader or encountered while working at the Navy Yard. They were, Torrey noted, "men and women of every color, from the deepest black to the clearest white." But he and Smallwood in their published writings called attention to those of light complexion in order to convince their white readers that persons like themselves could be oppressed. "Some" of the escapees, Torrey admitted, were ignorant and superstitious. He emphasized, however, that "in the manly energy and partial education of others, we have seen indications

24. The discussion in this and the following paragraph is based on: Samivel Weller Jr. [Smallwood] to Editor, 19 November 1842, in *TL*, 8 December 1842 (first quotation); Smallwood, *Narrative*, 17–28 (second & third quotations); Lovejoy, *Torrey*, 89; Washington correspondence of *New York Commercial*, in *TL*, 10 November 1842; [Torrey], "First Annual Report of the Albany Vigilance Committee," in *TL*, 22 December 1842.

of a noble character, which could rise above the most depressing condition of life, and assert its native dignity and worth."[25]

Torrey, Smallwood, Elizabeth Smallwood, and Mrs Padgett did not work alone in helping people to escape slavery. Instead they relied on an extensive biracial network stretching from Washington northward and to a lesser extent southward. It included white Quakers and African Americans in Delaware and southern Pennsylvania, the black Philadelphia Vigilant Association, and white abolitionists in Albany, New York. It also involved the escapees themselves, who frequently provided funds and logistical support for their northward journeys.[26]

An important aspect of the network was the role of women in it. Mrs. Padgett and Elizabeth Smallwood were the two men's closest collaborators and a division of labor by gender existed within their underground railroad organization. While the men recruited and guided, the women harbored, an undertaking that could be risky. Since Padgett, whom Torrey described as "lame," employed enslaved African Americans as servants at her boardinghouse, she had, as a white woman, adequate cover against unwarranted police searches of her property. This was not the case for Elizabeth Smallwood and other black women who took fugitive slaves into their homes. When Captain Goddard entered the Smallwood residence looking for fugitive slaves in October 1843, it was up to Elizabeth and other women to spirit a female escapee "through a back door into the garden" in order to hide her "in some corn."[27]

The gender line, though, was permeable. Men sometimes harbored and women sometimes planned and guided. Smallwood reported that, in October 1843, Captain Goddard arrested two free black women on charges that they intended to take two slaves with them to Canada. Sometimes black women contacted Torrey or Smallwood and helped plan the escapes of their husbands and children. In January 1844 Torrey reported to Gerrit Smith that he planned to cooperate "with a shrewd woman" in an effort to get some recaptured fugitives "out of bondage." Later that year Torrey maintained that it was

25. [Torrey], "First Annual Report of the Albany Vigilance Committee," (quotations).

26. Escapee funding: Smallwood, *Narrative*, 29–31.

27. Lovejoy, *Torrey*, 89 (first quotation); Smallwood, *Narrative*, 18, 25, 34 (second & third quotations); *Baltimore Sun*, 27 November 1843.

"a most respectable lady of Baltimore" who planned his effort to help several slaves escape from that city. It is not surprising that by 1844 Torrey had "materially modified" his view of what he called "the 'confounded woman question.'"[28]

Still, men most often served as agents or guides. Smallwood and Torrey sometimes personally transported or led escapees northward. On other occasions they hired black men to do this work. This was especially the case during the fall of 1842 when Smallwood "sent . . . off" groups of slaves in rapid succession. Most of those he employed were peripheral members of the antislavery community, poor individuals who took risks primarily for the sake of the money they could earn. Others cooperated with Torrey and Smallwood in hope of earning help for their families. This was so in the case of John H. Fontain, a Winchester, Virginia, free African American who was arrested and imprisoned for ten weeks under suspicion of having aided Torrey.[29]

On a more regular basis, Torrey and Smallwood relied on an obscure free black man named Jacob Gibbs. According to Smallwood, Gibbs led an underground railroad operation in Baltimore similar to the one in Washington. Smallwood also claimed that he had black competitors in Washington's underground railroad business, who, he charged, were motivated by greed. "There were plenty of champions of my own colour," he maintained, "who for the sake of filthy lucre attempted to build upon the foundation I had laid." He responded by attempting to deny them access to Gibbs and the northward stretching support network[30]

28. Smallwood, *Narrative*, 25–8; Torrey to Smith, 23 January 1844, GSP (first & second quotations); *BSV*, 23 May 1845 (third quotation); Torrey to J. Miller McKim, 29 November 1844, Garrison Papers (fourth quotation). Torrey by this time had also concluded that churches were too corrupt for antislavery work. See Lovejoy, *Torrey*, 134.

29. Smallwood, *Narrative*, 24–32 (quotation); *AP*, 6 March 1844; *L*, 9 August 1844.

30. Smallwood, *Narrative*, 28, 30; Henry Wilson, *History of the Rise and Fall of the Slave Power in America*, 3 vols. (Boston: James R. Osgood, 1876), 2:80. Smallwood identifies Gibbs as "G." An article published in the *Elevator* (San Francisco)—a black newspaper—on 15 September 1865 also mentions Gibbs. This article is part of a series of partially fictional articles describing underground railroad activities in Washington and Baltimore. Because they conflict with the information I have adduced from contemporary sources, I am reluctant to credit them. See *Elevator* (San Francisco), 15, 22, & 29 September 1865; 27 October 1865 in *The Black Abolitionist Papers Microfilm Edition*, 17 reels (New York: Microfilming Corp. of America, 1981–83 and Ann Arbor: University Microfilms International, 1984–92).

There also were some prominent blacks and whites in Washington who had inside information about Torrey's and Smallwood's activities. Besides Congressmen Gates, Giddings, and Slade, they included black clergymen Daniel Payne and William Nichols, white abolitionist Joshua Leavitt, and white attorney David A. Hall—a colonizationist. The three congressmen knew several of the first escapees to depart Washington with Torrey's and Smallwood's help. When Torrey made his first clandestine trip north in August 1842 with a total of fifteen men, women, and children, among them was Robert, a cook, who had been employed in behalf of his owner at Ann Sprigg's boardinghouse. In a letter to his son, Giddings provided an informed if disingenuous account of the escape and the underground railroad. Robert, he reported, had "left Wednesday evening . . . and the next he was heard from he was 'way up there in York State,' full tilt for Canada. . . . Some swear that there is a *Subterranean rail road* by which they travel *underground*. Men, women & children all go. Whole families disappear like the baseless fabric of a vision & leave not a wink behind."[31]

In fact, the assisted escape of Robert and the others was both difficult and contingent. Torrey and Smallwood could find no teamster who would take the escapees north "at any price" and the men had to purchase a "huckster's wagon" and a "not very good" team of horses at a total cost of $118. This delayed Torrey's departure, and as a result, slave catchers headed out "on all the roads leading North" *before* Torrey and his party left the city. Only the breakdown of the old wagon, requiring Torrey to pull off the road, kept his group from being caught as the search party returned south from Baltimore, having erroneously concluded that the escape must have been by a water route. Smallwood saw the hand of God in this and Torrey was able to proceed to Troy, New York where he put his charges on a canal boat for Canada.[32]

31. Payne, *Recollections*, 98; Payne, *History of the African Methodist Episcopal Church* (1891; reprint, New York: Arno, 1969), 176–7; Giddings to Joseph Addison Giddings, 13 August 1842 (quotation) and Seth M. Gates to Giddings, 5 December 1848, JRGP. In late 1843 the Auxiliary Guard discovered the baggage of a female slave, who allegedly belonged to Hall, in a wagon Torrey proposed to drive north. That this woman intended to go with Torrey without Hall's knowledge is unlikely. Otherwise Hall would not subsequently have agreed to provide legal counsel to Torrey and a black associate. See *Baltimore Sun*, 27 November & 16 December 1843.

32. Smallwood, *Narrative*, 21–4.

Shortly thereafter Torrey moved with his wife and children, who had remained in Massachusetts while he was in Washington, to Albany, where he became editor of the *Tocsin of Liberty,* published by Abel Brown as the organ of the Eastern New York Anti-Slavery Society. In December Torrey and Limaeus P. Noble, who later joined the Washington antislavery community, purchased the *Tocsin* and renamed it the *Albany Patriot.* Meanwhile Brown, a Baptist minister who, a few years earlier, had himself aided slaves to escape from the District of Columbia, joined with Torrey to organize the Albany Vigilance Committee, which welcomed fugitive slaves arriving from the Chesapeake. This left Smallwood in charge of underground railroad operations in Washington, which he reported in letters Torrey edited and published in the *Tocsin* and *Patriot* over the name *Samivel Weller Jr.,* after a character in Dickens's *Pickwick Papers.*[33]

During the early fall of 1842 Smallwood led two more escapes that are as revealing of the nature of his and Torrey's work as was Torrey's earlier venture. Once again some of the escapees were acquaintances—in one case a personal friend—of antislavery congressmen. In September Smallwood conducted a party of eighteen on foot to just north of Philadelphia where he put it on a train to Albany. Among the escapees was John Douglass, who, hiring his time from his Georgetown master, worked as a waiter at Ann Sprigg's. He had nursed Gates through an illness and when, several months before the escape took place, his master threatened to sell him to a trader, Gates directed him to Torrey, who "told him how to get off."[34]

In October Smallwood helped Douglass's brother, Lewis, who faced a similar threat of sale. In this case, according to Gates, Smallwood harbored Lewis in the "garret" of Washington attorney and peripheral subversive com-

33. Lovejoy, *Torrey,* 104–5; *TL,* 5 & 19 October 1842; 17 November 1842; *Philanthropist,* 4 January 1843; *AP,* 16 February 1843; Catherine S. Brown, *Memoir of Rev. Abel Brown, by His Companion* (Worcester, Mass.: C. S. Brown, 1849), 87–8. Torrey indicated that *Weller* was a pen name and that the letters were written in Washington. He denied that the writer was either Abel Brown or himself and indicated that the writer was not a Yankee but an "old settler" in Washington. In his *Narrative,* published in 1851, Smallwood reveals that he had written the *Weller* letters. See *TL,* 3 November & 1 December 1842; Smallwood, *Narrative,* 56, 60.

34. The discussion in this and the following paragraph is based on: Gates to Joshua R. Giddings, 5 December 1848, JRGP (quotations); Weller to Printer, 19 November [1842], in *TL,* 1 December 1842.

munity member Joseph A. Bradley, a slaveholder and leading colonizationist. Lewis remained at Bradley's for "3 weeks, till another gang were ready to start north." Gates maintained that Bradley was away from his home during part of this time. But at the very least this arrangement suggests that Smallwood believed he had little to fear from an attorney who had earlier defended white abolitionist Reuben Crandall and black slave rescuer Leonard Grimes.

In November *Samivel Weller Jr.* claimed that the Washington branch of the underground railroad had helped 150 escapees since the previous March at an estimated total cost to slaveholders of $75,000. On April 12, 1843, after the inclement weather and mud of winter had passed, *Weller* announced that "spring business has begun." He brazenly assured local masters that they would lose as many of their chattels as they had during the previous year. But by early June Smallwood had sent off only nine "passengers" and had grown fearful of exposure. He knew that several escapees had been recaptured and he distrusted several of the black men he employed as agents. His dispute with Cole and other local black leaders continued and he believed they had informed slaveholders concerning his activities. He concluded, therefore, that he was no longer safe and left for Toronto on June 30. He returned to Washington in August to arrange to move his family in early October to that Canadian city.[35]

Rumors spread that Smallwood intended to take slaves with him and, the day before he planned to leave, Captain Goddard and the Auxiliary Guard searched his house unsuccessfully seeking fugitives. The next day Smallwood placed his wife and children on a steamboat to Baltimore, hoping to auction his furniture before following them. But, increasingly fearful of arrest, he instead hid until 4:00 a.m the next day, when he set out on foot to rejoin his family. When he arrived, they took a stage from Baltimore to Philadelphia and proceeded by train to Albany. There, they enjoyed the hospitality of abolitionist friends before going on to Toronto.[36]

During these months, from the fall of 1842 until the summer of 1843,

35. Weller to Editor, 19 November 1842, in *TL*, 8 December 1842; Weller to Printer, 12 April 1843, in *AP*, 27 April 1843 (first quotation) and 6 June 1843, in *AP*, 15 June 1843 (second quotation); "Smallwood vs. Cole," November 1842, entry 6, Case Papers, RG 21, NA; Smallwood, *Narrative*, 23–8, 30–3, 37–8.

36. Smallwood, *Narrative*, 33–6.

Torrey edited the *Patriot,* struggled to make it a financial success, and prepared for the Liberty national convention in August 1843. He also kept in contact with Smallwood, meeting with him in Toronto, and remained committed to direct action against slavery in the Chesapeake. When Smallwood, late in October, informed Torrey that four black men had approached him in Toronto asking that he help their enslaved wives and children leave Washington, Torrey responded by proposing a more ambitious scheme.[37]

Smallwood recalled that he agreed to Torrey's suggestion "that we should try and obtain a team [of horses] and proceed to Washington, and bring away as many slaves as we could." They raised a small amount of money in New York and Vermont, and in late November headed south to renew their unequal struggle. They were not, however, without logistical support. They spent a night at the home of Thomas Garrett, the white Wilmington, Delaware, abolitionist who, a decade later, provided similar aid to black underground railroad operative Harriet Tubman. White abolitionists at Kennett Square, Pennsylvania, supplied a wagon and horses. Smallwood made advance arrangements with John Bush, an African American who had a house "in low grounds" east of Washington's city hall, to harbor prospective escapees.[38]

In Baltimore Smallwood and Torrey successfully arranged for the northward departure of two of the four families whom Smallwood had agreed to help. But when the men reached Bush's house on the evening of November 24, Captain Goddard and the Guard, who had been tipped off by a black informant, were waiting. Mrs. Bush did her best to dissuade the guardsmen from searching her stable, where the fugitives had gathered, but the men

37. *AP,* 13 July, 3 August, 5 September, & 12 September 1843; Torrey to Gerrit Smith, 23 January 1844, GSP; Smallwood, *Narrative,* 36–7. Torrey said his object in visiting Toronto "was to make some arrangements and inquiries connected with the UNDERGROUND RAILROAD." Although as a matter of policy he did not mention Smallwood's name, I assume that he consulted with Smallwood.

38. Smallwood, *Narrative,* 37–8 (first quotation); Smedley, *Underground Railroad,* 81; J. S. of Oldtown to [editor], 25 November 1843, in *BS,* 27 November 1843 (second quotation); Priscilla Thompson, "Harriet Tubman, Thomas Garrett, and the Underground Railroad," *Delaware History* 22 (September 1986), 1–21. During the 1850s, Garrett continued to direct fugitive slaves through the same locality in Pennsylvania that Torrey got the wagon. See Garrett to Eliza Whigham, 27 December 1856, Quaker Collection, Haverford College, Haverford, Pennsylvania.

pushed her aside. They captured ten would-be escapees, including two women and four children already in the wagon, and arrested John Bush. Torrey and Smallwood themselves barely avoided capture and the guard identified Smallwood before he escaped once again on foot to Baltimore. There Jacob Gibbs, with financial support from Torrey, helped Smallwood on his way north and, after a series of adventures, he reached Toronto. Meanwhile Torrey remained in Washington to engage David A. Hall as attorney for Bush. Incredibly, Torrey revealed his own complicity in the escape attempt by having Hall file a claim in his behalf to recover possession of the horses and wagon that the Guard had seized at Bush's residence.[39]

This debacle ended Torrey's and Smallwood's collaboration. Thereafter Smallwood, who operated a saw mill in Toronto, established himself within that city's black community, emerged during the 1850s as one of its leaders, and lived into the 1880s. In contrast, following his narrow escape, Torrey expanded his underground railroad activities. He used the Philadelphia home of his black friend, James J. G. Bias, a dentist and a leader of the local vigilance association, as his base of operations. From there, between December 1843 and June 1844, Torrey made a series of forays into Virginia and Maryland that would lead to his arrest, imprisonment, death, and legendary status among abolitionists and fugitive slaves.[40]

In December, at the behest of a free black women named Emily Webb, he traveled by carriage south through Gettysburg and Harpers Ferry to Winchester, in Virginia's Shenandoah Valley. There he rescued Webb's husband, John Webb, and five of their children from Bushrod Taylor, who held legal title to all six of them. Pursued by local authorities, Torrey was nearly cap-

39. *BS,* 16 December 1843; *PF,* 1 February 1844; Smallwood, *Narrative,* 39–41. Joshua R. Giddings was also involved in the defense of Bush, who was eventually acquitted. See Giddings to C. P. Giddings, 24 December 1843, JRGP; Lovejoy, *Torrey,* 105.

40. Smallwood: Smallwood, *Narrative,* xii, 36, 57–60; *Provincial Freeman* (Toronto), 24 March, 3 & 17 June, 29 July, 5–26 August, & 14 October 1854; 20 & 24 March, 5 & 12 May 1855; 25 November 1856; 18 June 1859. On Smallwood's life in Toronto see Richard Almonte's recent edition of Smallwood's *Narrative* (Toronto: Mercury Press, 2001). Bias: Payne, *Recollections,* 98; Jacob C. White, Sr., "Minute Book of the Vigilant Committee of Philadelphia (4 June 1839–30 March 1844)," American Negro Historical Society Collection, 1790–1903, Historical Society of Pennsylvania, Philadelphia, and Julie Winch, *Philadelphia's Black Elite: Activism, Accommodation, and the Struggle for Autonomy, 1787–1848* (Philadelphia: Temple Univ. Press, 1988), passim.

tured in Chambersburg, Pennsylvania, before he succeeded in putting the Webbs on a northbound train at Philadelphia. In March he addressed a special meeting of the black-led Philadelphia Vigilant Association, probably seeking financial support for his continued efforts, which he envisioned as reaching into North Carolina and Louisiana. In early June he helped three slaves escape from William Heckrotte of Baltimore, and once again pursuers nearly captured him and the escapees.[41]

It was an effort to negotiate the release of Big Ben, a free black man kidnapped in Bucks County, Pennsylvania, from Hope H. Slatter's slave prison that ended Torrey's clandestine campaign. When Slatter recognized Torrey, he contacted Bushrod Taylor, who secured a warrant from the state of Virginia for Torrey's arrest. Shortly thereafter Baltimore authorities charged Torrey in the escape of Heckrotte's slaves. Torrey and his friends, including black bishop Daniel Payne, maintained that slaveholders had plotted his arrest. They charged that his December 1844 conviction in the Heckrotte case rested on perjured testimony. This was all true, but Torrey never denied the substance of the charges against him. He boasted to local attorney Reverdy Johnson, who assisted in his defense, that he had helped one of Johnson's slaves escape![42]

Initially Torrey believed that his trial might help the antislavery cause in the borderlands. After Bush's arrest in November 1843, he had hoped to use slave rescue cases to obtain court rulings against slavery. As an early advocate of an independent abolitionist political party, he had in 1838 argued against the Garrisonian interpretation of the U.S. Constitution as a proslavery document. Instead he joined those who held the Constitution to be antislavery, and slavery to be illegal, throughout the country. Torrey had hoped to use the

41. Lovejoy, *Torrey*, 105–25, 173–202; Torrey to Gerrit Smith, 23 January 1844, GSP; [Torrey], "Notes of Southern Travel by a Negro Stealer," in *AP*, 7 & 21 February, 6 & 13 March 1844; White, "Minute Book of the Vigilant Committee;" Smedley, *Underground Railroad*, 80–1; *E*, 7 August 1844.

42. *PF*, 28 March, 6 June, & 4 July 1844; *E*, 17 July & 7 August 1844; Payne, *Recollections*, 98; Torrey to Gerrit Smith, 16 November 1844, GSP; Torrey to J. Miller McKim, 29 November 1844, Garrison Papers; Joseph E. Snodgrass to Horace Mann, 26 July 1848, Horace Mann Papers, Massachusetts Historical Society, Boston; S[tephen] P[earl] A[ndrews] to NYT, 26 August [1850], in *PF*, 5 September 1850.

Bush case to gain a federal court ruling against slavery in the District of Columbia.[43]

Now, following his own arrest, Torrey and others—including John Quincy Adams—set broader goals for courtroom action. They believed they could use his case to foster assisted slave escapes throughout the borderlands. If they could get into federal court, they hoped to argue, in Torrey's words, "that by the laws of God and nature, by the common law, by the Constitution of the United States, and of Maryland, and of Virginia even, it is no crime for a slave to escape if he can, and therefore it *can* be no *crime* to help him." If the Supreme Court agreed, Torrey predicted, "Slavery cannot be maintained in any of the border States; and wherever the border is . . . the result must be the same. It takes from the master all means of keeping his victims but force. Slaveholders, as a class, are too effeminate and cowardly to hold their victims when that is the case, even if their numbers were not too small."[44]

By giving the Heckrotte case precedence and avoiding extradition to Virginia, local prosecutors deprived Torrey of a chance to seek a writ of habeas corpus from a federal district court and, therefore, from making his case in a federal court. But Torrey's statement concerning physical force and the character of slaveholders has wider significance in understanding his and Smallwood's methods and goals. Both men challenged the masters' masculine self-image. Torrey, in addition, disputed their portrayals of northern abolitionists as less than manly—and he was not just talking. He and Smallwood and those who succeeded them in helping slaves escape from the Washington area were ready to act on an assumption that they were tougher than the slaveholders. This is not surprising in regard to black males whom historians agree sought traditional means of asserting their manhood, but it does run counter to recent depictions of white male abolitionists.[45]

43. Torrey to Gerrit Smith, 23 January 1844, GSP; *AP*, 7 February 1844; Lovejoy, *Torrey*, 135. See also William W. Wiecek, *The Sources of Antislavery Constitutionalism in America* (Ithaca, N.Y.: Cornell University Press, 1977).

44. Amos A. Phelps to Joshua Leavitt, 12 July 1844, in *E*, 17 July 1844; *PF*, 18 July 1844; Lewis Tappan to John Scoble, 31 July 1844, in Annie H. Abel and Frank J. Klingberg, eds., *A Side-Light on Anglo-American Relations, 1839–1850* (Lancaster, Pa.: Association for the Study of Negro Life and History, 1927), 189; Lovejoy, *Torrey*, 136 (quotations).

45. *BSV*, 24 August & 21 September 1844; *E*, 21 August 1844; Bertram Wyatt-Brown, *Southern Honor: Ethics and Behavior in the Old South* (New York: Oxford University Press,

Historians of gender have found in northeastern male reformers of the 1830s and 1840s evidence of a more feminine concept of masculine honor than flourished in the antebellum South and West. The reformers' empathy for those in distress, their relations with women, and their intellectual commitment to nonviolence reflected their embrace of feminine values. Yet, as Torrey and Smallwood engaged in clandestine subversive activities, they *both* embraced an aggressive masculinity foreshadowing that of John Brown.[46] They found risk-taking to be emotionally exhilarating and this feeling in turn provided them additional motivation for continuing their dangerous work.

Local slaveholders—relying on the Guard, constables, other law enforcement agents, slavecatchers, and black informants—engaged Torrey, Smallwood, and their associates in a physical struggle that provides an essential context for understanding the character of the Washington antislavery community during the 1840s and 1850s. In October 1842 Dr. William H. Gunnell swore out an arrest warrant for Torrey, charging him in the escape of a slave. The following spring a group of Baltimore slaveholders offered a $500 reward for him. Months before Slatter engineered Torrey's arrest, local newspapers circulated accounts of his assistance in the escape of John Webb and the Webb children. Slaveholders had more difficulty in identifying Smallwood, in part because his last name was common in Washington. Although Gunnell knew that Torrey had a black accomplice, he mistakenly focused on *Dennis* Smallwood, a free black hackman and, in league with a local postmaster, searched this man's mail.[47]

Masters also offered rewards for the return of escapees and drew members of Washington's Auxiliary Guard into their service. Shortly before Small-

---

1982), 34–5; Christopher Dixon, "'A True Manly Life': Abolitionists and the Masculine Ideal," *Mid-America* 77 (Fall 1995): 227–30; James Oliver Horton, *Free People of Color: Inside the African American Community* (Washington: Smithsonian Institute Press, 1993), 76–7, 80–96.

46. Dixon, "'A True Manly Life,'" 213–36; Donald Yacavone, *Samuel Joseph May and the Dilemmas of the Liberal Persuasion, 1797–1871* (Philadelphia: Temple University Press, 1991), 95–103; Kristan Hoganson, "Garrisonian Abolitionists and the Rhetoric of Gender, 1850–1860," *American Quarterly* 45 (December 1993): 558–95; Wyatt-Brown, *Yankee Saints and Southern Sinners*, 123–6.

47. Samivel Weller Jr. to Editor, 22 October 1842, in *TL*, 3 & 15 November 1842, in *TL*, 15 December 1842; *AP*, 27 April 1843 & 29 May 1844. It may be that Smallwood confused William H. Gunnell, a lumber yard employee, with James S. Gunnell, a "surgeon dentist." See Anthony Reintzel, comp., *Washington Directory . . . for 1843* (Washington: Reintzel, 1843), 36.

wood decided to move to Toronto during the summer of 1843, *Samivel Weller Jr.* complained that the Guard seemed to do nothing but engage in "*hunting the colored people.*" To protect escapees and themselves, Torrey and Smallwood bribed members of the Guard. Meanwhile masters bribed "subordinate agents" of the underground railroad to get information.[48]

All of this was far removed ethically from the righteous atmosphere of Torrey's Liberty conventions or Smallwood's African Wesleyan class meetings. Although the level of violence was low by twentieth and twenty-first century standards, Torrey, Thomas Smallwood, Elizabeth Smallwood, Mrs. Padgett, and others in Washington's antislavery community were engaged in border skirmishes against proslavery forces. Consequently they came into contact with members of black and white underclasses who followed rules quite different from those of polite society.

Torrey visited a disreputable part of Washington where he observed slave-traders and slavecatchers making deals. "Here," he reported, "bargains are made by which life's dearest ties are broken asunder; the cup of anguish filled, and forced upon the suffering poor, by monsters accustomed to, and hardened in their guilt." Farther north, along the Mason-Dixon Line, Torrey found men he called "border miscreants." They were, he said, "a set of vicious, degraded, crazy scoundrels, whose . . . business is to arrest fugitives." He charged that they also engaged in "counterfeiting, stealing sheep, stabbing, killing men, and debauchery in its lowest forms." Torrey went on to write that "associated with them is a set of females, not a whit more elevated in moral character."[49]

As Torrey and Smallwood reveled in outsmarting such people, they adopted some of their opponents' ruthlessness. Since their ultimate objective was to destroy masters' confidence that they could continue to hold slaves in the Chesapeake, the two men played on the masters' fear of aggressive abolitionism. They taunted, goaded, and belittled slaveholders in what amounted to psychological warfare. Copies of *Samivel Weller Jr.*'s letters reporting as-

48. Weller to Editor, 15 November 1842, in *TL*, 15 December 1842; Weller to Printer, 11 June 1843, in *AP*, 22 August 1843 (first quotation); Weller to Charles, 10 October 1843, in *AP*, 24 October 1843; *AP*, 7 February 1844 (second quotation); Smallwood, *Narrative*, 25–8; Weller to Printer, 6 June 1843, in *AP*, 15 June 1843.

49. *TL*, 27 October 1842 (first quotation), *AP*, 7 February 1844 (second–third quotations), 1 May 1844 (fourth quotation).

sisted escapes arrived in the masters' mail. Copies of the *Tocsin of Liberty* and the *Albany Patriot,* sent to individuals who had lost slaves, promoted the impression that underground railroad agents were omnipresent. In November 1842 *Samivel Weller Jr.* claimed that they had baffled "the most experienced [slave] hunters" and greatly alarmed "the nabobs." *Weller* openly raised Torrey's name in the context of slave escapes and called the Baltimore police "poor puppies!"[50]

Torrey and Smallwood also encouraged others to take direct action against slavery. Like other black abolitionists, Smallwood believed it was his duty to prod African Americans into confronting oppression. Torrey approached whites similarly. "If there is a spark of manhood left in the hearts of the American people," he wrote in 1843, "they *will* speedily *demand* the overthrow of this damning system, despite legal technicalities and all constitutions in the world, *if they come in their way* in doing it." Of nonslaveholding southern whites, he wrote, "We look for the day when the common people at the south will get their eyes open, and their feet placed where they can stand up against slavery." When, following his arrest, some white abolitionists condemned Torrey's *imprudence,* he replied from Baltimore Jail, "The question of my prudence, I must adjourn to Judgement day. I *have* done, many things in the South, that prudent men *dared* not do. . . . I am *bold* & *decided.* God made me so. He did not make me *cautious.*"[51]

In Torrey's case confrontational tactics led to the advocacy of violent means against slavery and threats of violence against enemies. Exhilarated by his actions, frequently frightened—Smallwood noticed that he shook in fear at Bush's residence—Torrey embraced a concept of masculine honor more characteristic of the men he opposed than of many of his northern abolitionist colleagues. He and his northern friends later denied that he had contemplated, let alone engaged in, forceful action against slavery's defenders. But the facts belie such assertions. It may be true, as Torrey declared following his conviction, that he "never raised a hand or finger, or used any weapon or

50. *TL,* 27 October 1842; Weller to Nevy, 9 November 1842, in *TL,* 17 November 1842; Weller to Editor, 15 November 1842, in *TL,* 15 December 1842 and 19 November 1842, in *TL,* 8 December 1842 (first quotation); Weller to Printer, 17 April 1843, in *AP,* 27 April & 6 June 1843, in *AP,* 15 June 1843 (second quotation).

51. Smallwood, *Narrative,* 38–9 (first quotation); *AP,* 15 June 1843 (second & third quotations); Torrey to Gerrit Smith, 3 August 1844, GSP (fourth quotation).

instrument whatever, in violence against any human being!" But he was *not* telling the truth when he went on to say, "I never even *threatened* violence to any one."[52]

Writing in Washington in March 1842 he suggested that, if annexation of Texas led to civil war between the sections, the North should employ black as well as white troops to invade the South. In March 1843 he approved the forceful resistance to slavecatchers offered by some residents of Wilkesbarre, Pennsylvania. By February 1844 he had become menacing in his pronouncements against those who opposed his underground railroad operation. He reported that he had warned blacks who served as police informers that they remained in Washington "on peril of their lives." He said of a Gettysburg constable who had received a reward for the capture of fugitive slaves, "I saw the poor tool at Gettysburg . . . and *marked him!* He will do few more such deeds." According to the man who prosecuted his case, Torrey carried pistols at the time of his arrest.[53]

Torrey, Smallwood, and their collaborators engaged in guerilla war against slavery in Washington and its vicinity. The Baltimore correspondent of New York's *Christian Advocate* reported that Torrey had "declared *war against the State* [of Maryland], invaded her territory, and *plundered her citizens.*" Antislavery journalist Stephen Pearl Andrews noted that Torrey, during his imprisonment in Baltimore Jail, "employed his leisure in . . . instructing a dozen slaves confined along with him, in the ways and means of elopement, and nearly all of them escaped within a few weeks after they left the prison." Andrews characterized Torrey as "the regular Rob Roy MacGregor of dare-devil philanthropy." Since Torrey maintained that proslavery laws were not binding, he was consistent in planning to break out of jail in September 1844 when he realized that his case would not get into federal court. It was just as

---

52. Smallwood, *Narrative*, 38–9; *L*, 26 July 1844; Timothy Stowe, "Sermon on the Death of Rev. C. T. Torrey," in *AP*, 24 June 1846; Lovejoy, *Torrey*, 310, 312; Torrey to [?], 1 December [1844], in *E*, 11 December 1844 (quotation). Contrary to historian Aileen Kraditor, Torrey was never a nonresistant although, like some other non-Garrisonian abolitionists, he had rejected even defensive violence. See Kraditor, *Means and Ends*, 105, 115.

53. Torrey to John W. Alden, 19 March 1842, in *E*, 31 March 1842; *TL*, 1 December 1842 (first quotation); *AP*, 2 March 1843 & 7 February 1844 (second & third quotations); *BSV*, 21 December 1848.

consistent, considering his underclass contacts, that he confided in an imprisoned forger who betrayed his plan to the police. Thereafter Torrey's physical
and mental health failed and he died in May 1846.[54]

Some northern abolitionists maintained that he had been too impulsive.
Gamaliel Bailey, who visited Torrey in Baltimore Jail, worried that his type of
clandestine action would lead abolitionists into self-defeating deceit. To gain
legitimacy, Bailey believed, abolitionists must seek to change laws, not break
them. In addition some Garrisonians never reconciled with Torrey even after
his death. This was especially the case with such feminists as Abigail Kelley,
who denounced efforts to aid Torrey's family. But most abolitionists made a
martyr of him. They regarded him as a Christian hero and a prophet of a
more aggressive attack on slaveholders.[55]

Of the many appreciative letters following Torrey's death, one from by "A
Citizen of Maryland" has special relevance. If more abolitionists were like
Torrey rather than "sneaking cowards," asserted this writer, "we might storm
the infernal castle of slavery in the next twelve months, and make the blood-
stained soul of the guilty slaveholder 'quake with more terrific fear.'. . . May

54. *Christian Advocate*, quoted in *L*, 22 May 1846 (first quotation); S. P. A., Correspondence of the *Tribune*, in *PF*, 9 September 1850 (second quotation). Torrey's escape attempt: *L*,
27 September 1844; Torrey to Gerrit Smith, 16 November 1844, GSP; Lovejoy, *Torrey*, 148–
59. Torrey claimed that the "powder and balls" found in his possession at the jail had been sent
to him by "mistake," and that he did not personally intend to use them. See Lovejoy, *Torrey*,
158–9. According to his wife, Mary I. Torrey, and others, Torrey wrote vicious letters to friends
while in prison. They attributed the tone of the letters to declining emotional stability and destroyed most of them. But one in which Torrey expresses anger toward Lewis Tappan survives,
and his anger in this case was not irrational. Tappan initially opposed raising a defense fund for
him. See Tappan to John W. Alden, 8 July 1844, to Joseph E. Snodgrass, 28 October 1844, to
Torrey, 11 November 1844, to Joshua Leavitt, 25 January 1845, letter book copies, LTP; Tappan to Amos A. Phelps, 28 October 1844, Torrey to Phelps, 4 November 1844, Mary I. Torrey
to Phelps, 15 September 1846, Amos A. Phelps Papers, Boston Public Library; Lovejoy, *Torrey*,
152, 160–1, 266–7.

55. Lovejoy, *Torrey*; *Philanthropist*, 31 October 1841; *Cincinnati Weekly Herald and Philan-
thropist*, 25 September 1844; Torrey to Gerrit Smith, 3 August & 15 November 1844, GSP;
William Lloyd Garrison to Samuel E. Sewell, 15 May 1846, in Walter M. Merrill and Louis
Ruchames, eds., *The Letters of William Lloyd Garrison*, 6 vols. (Cambridge, Mass.: Harvard
University Press, 1971), 3:338; *L*, 7 August 1846; Benjamin Quarles, *Black Abolitionists* (New
York: Oxford University Press, 1969), 164–5.

God in mercy multiply the Torreyites a thousand-fold per annum, and speed the operations of the Patent Rail-road to freedom! Amen."[56]

From an antislavery perspective, Smallwood deserved equal praise with Torrey. He did not receive it in part because of his race and in part because his avoidance of arrest preserved his anonymity. Others, too, within the Washington antislavery community contributed to the four hundred escapes abolitionists credited to Torrey. Among them were Elizabeth Smallwood, Mrs. Padgett, John Bush, David A. Hall, Joshua R. Giddings, the many black harborers and agents, and the escapees themselves.

But Torrey and Smallwood stand as symbols of this community during the early 1840s. Smallwood represents the local black element that felt deeply the outrages imposed by the slave system and took the initiative to engage sympathetic whites. Torrey epitomizes an increasingly aggressive northern abolitionism aligned with the radical political abolitionist wing of the Liberty party. He had counterparts in the early 1840s in such slave rescuers from the North as Alanson Work, James E. Burr, and George Thompson, all arrested in Missouri in 1841; Jonathan Walker, arrested in Florida in 1844, and Calvin Fairbank and Delia Webster, arrested in Kentucky that same year.[57] But it was primarily in Washington that black and white antislavery components came together to form a radical community of action.

Between them, Torrey's and Smallwood initiated a strategy of subverting the peculiar institution through assisted slave escapes. They made Washington the center of an organized escape route that served the needs of black families and challenged slavery in the Chesapeake. The network continued to exist in altered form into the Civil War years. Their efforts also solidified cooperation between local African Americans and antislavery whites against slavery and racial oppression. Torrey's death ensured that other northern white abolitionists would commit themselves to carrying on where he left off.

---

56. Lovejoy, *Torrey*, 345–6.

57. Herbert Aptheker, *Abolitionism: A Revolutionary Movement* (Boston: Twayne, 1989), 94–122; Harrold, *Abolitionists and the South*, 68–9. See also Randolph Paul Runyon, *Delia Webster and the Underground Railroad* (Lexington: University Press of Kentucky, 1996). Starting in the late 1840s, former slave John P. Parker cooperated with white abolitionists led by John Rankin in helping slaves to escape from Kentucky into Ohio. See Sprague, *His Promised Land*.

[FOUR]

The Bureau of Humanity and the Sectional Struggle

AFTER the final departure of Thomas Smallwood for Toronto in December 1843 and the jailing of Charles T. Torrey in Baltimore the following June, an underground railroad network continued to function in the Chesapeake. Several of the slaves Torrey met in jail later escaped northward, and in August 1845 a constable from Fredericksburg, Virginia, arrested in Washington a black man named Mayo for "enticing away certain slaves." Slaveholders had good reason to fear Torrey's "ghost."[1] But from early 1845 through early 1848 antislavery blacks and whites who cooperated in the city concentrated on purchasing the freedom of individuals threatened with sale south rather than on the more dangerous tactic of engineering their escape. Initiated as a defense against the interstate slave trade, this tactic aimed to further weaken slavery in the District of Columbia and the entire Chesapeake region. It helped alter abolitionist conceptions of antislavery strategy and influenced the sectional conflict.

The change in emphasis among members of the subversive community came as that conflict entered a more confrontational stage. In May 1846, as Torrey lay dying in the Maryland Penitentiary, Congress declared war on

1. *Niles National Register,* 23 August 1845 (first quotation); S. P. A[ndrews], Correspondence of the Tribune, Washington, 26 August [1850], in *PF,* 5 September 1850; *BSV,* 19 July 1845; William L. Chaplin to J. C. Jackson, December 1844, in *AP,* 8 January 1845 (second quotation); *E,* 25 June 1847. Mayo received a ten-year sentence in the Virginian penitentiary. See also *Cincinnati Morning Herald,* quoted in *AP,* 21 January 1846.

Mexico. To abolitionists, antislavery members of Congress, and a large portion of the northern population, this war seemed to be part of a plot to expand slavery. Most of them believed the plot had begun in 1836 when Americans in Texas rebelled against the Mexican government to form a slaveholding republic. Then, in 1844, James K. Polk, a Democrat from Tennessee running on a platform demanding the annexation of Texas, had won the presidential election over Whig candidate Henry Clay of Kentucky. In 1845 Congress responded to this victory by taking Texas into the Union as a slaveholding state. Now Polk had begun a war to further expand slavery into the Mexican provinces of New Mexico and California. Many northerners believed that if this effort succeeded it would undermine the interests of the free states.[2]

As a result, in August 1846, after American troops had captured large portions of Mexico, a northern majority in the House of Representatives passed the Wilmot Proviso banning slavery in all territories gained as a result of the war. The Senate defeated the Proviso, but in conjunction with southern fears of rising slave escapes, it catalyzed a major sectional crisis in which many southern leaders threatened secession to protect what they regarded as the interests of their section. Washington's subversive antislavery community perceived both a threat and an opportunity in this polarizing crisis. Recognizing that they could have a major impact, subversives acted to weaken the political power of slaveholders, to defend black families, and to counteract racial stereotypes.

While John F. Cook Sr. and other black ministers continued their ties to antislavery whites during this crisis, less prominent African Americans played more crucial roles. Among them were Luke and Sarah Carter, Henry and Sylvia Wilson, and Mathew Mathews. Each of their personal struggles gained national significance. Meanwhile antislavery whites such as Joshua R. Giddings and David A. Hall expanded the interracial work that they had engaged in since the late 1830s. They were joined by local attorney Jacob Bigelow, Congressman Edward S. Hamlin of Cleveland, Hamlin's journalist friend Ezra L. Stevens, Gamaliel Bailey, Margaret Shands Bailey, and the

---

2. Don E. Fehrenbacher, *The Slaveholding Republic: An Account of the United States Government's Relations to Slavery* (New York: Oxford University Press, 2002), 118–26; Leonard L. Richards, *The Slave Power: The Free North and Southern Domination, 1780–1860* (Baton Rouge: Louisiana State University Press, 2000), 1–27; Larry Gara, "Slavery and the Slave Power: A Crucial Distinction," *Civil War History* 15 (March 1969): 4–18; Michael F. Holt, *The Political Crisis of the 1850s* (New York: John Wiley and Sons, 1978), 1–138.

National Era's business manager Limaeus P. Noble. By far the most important of these newcomers, however, was William L. Chaplin, Torrey's successor as the unofficial representative in Washington of New York's radical political abolitionists.

Although these antislavery whites cooperated among themselves as well as with African Americans, most of them belonged to separate factions. Giddings, Hamlin, and Stevens, who were all from Ohio's Western Reserve, formed one. Chaplin and Bigelow, who were both natives of Massachusetts, and Noble, who had worked with Torrey and Chaplin in New York, formed the other. Hall acted on his own or served both of these groups. The relatively conservative but socially engaging Baileys developed ties to all the other white subversives. Margaret Bailey, who had been born in Virginia to a slaveholding family in 1812, was particularly effective in promoting informal gatherings.

While Giddings remained active in interracial antislavery efforts and the other whites engaged in them as well, Chaplin and Bigelow most closely followed Torrey's example of day to day involvement with African Americans. Giddings's primary duty in Washington was after all to represent his district in Congress. Most of the other antislavery whites had similarly time-consuming responsibilities. Chaplin and Bigelow had both the inclination *and* the time to concentrate on interracial cooperation.

Bigelow, who was born near Boston in 1790, belonged to an old Massachusetts family. As a young man he engaged in business with his father and brothers in Montreal and Indiana before moving by himself to Washington in 1843. (One of his sons had died at age nine in 1832, his wife had died in 1839, and his other son was attending Harvard College and medical school.) Bigelow was a lawyer, patent agent, newspaper correspondent, congressional reporter, and a founder of Washington's first gas company. A devout Congregationalist, he lived frugally in a room adjacent to his office on E Street, while maintaining ties to northern evangelical abolitionists and antislavery politicians. Much of his time went to charitable—if not always purely benevolent—action in behalf of the African-American population in Washington and adjacent portions of Maryland.[3]

---

3. Jacob Bigelow of Washington was a first cousin of Jacob Bigelow, the prominent physician and botanist who taught at Harvard. G. B. Howe, *Genealogy of the Bigelow Family of America* (Worcester, Mass.: privately published, 1890), 62–3, 115, 201, 203–4; Mary L. Cox to

William L. Chaplin (c1795–1871) succeeded Charles T. Torrey as the white abolitionist in Washington who cooperated most closely with African Americans in opposing slavery. *Case of William L. Chaplin* (Boston: The Chaplin Committee, 1851), frontispiece.

Chaplin was more influential than Bigelow and by far better remembered by historians. He was a worthy successor to Torrey, with whom he shared a nearly identical religious, political, and ideological orientation. He also shared Torrey's empathy for suffering black families, which he publicly expressed as early as 1838. In 1841, as editor of the Rochester *American Citizen,* he endorsed the duty of abolitionists to help fugitive slaves reach safety in Canada. But in appearance and personality Chaplin and Torrey differed substantially. Torrey was short, thin, frail, and young. Chaplin was tall, "plump," muscular, middle-aged, and "considerably bald" by the time he arrived in the national capital. He was a bachelor and womanizer, as well as a charming, polished

Gamaliel Bailey, 1 December 1852, MMP; *NE,* 17 January 1850, 23 May 1851; Robert R. Hershman, "Gas in Washington, Some Notes on the Washington Gas Light Company," *RCHS* 50 [40] (1948–50): 144–5; *E,* 16 July 1846; Lewis Tappan to Joshua Leavitt, 2 February 1847, in *E,* 10 March 1847; Tappan to Bigelow, 7 January 1848, letter book copy, LTP; Bigelow to William H. Seward, 23 January 1858, WHSP; William Still, *The Underground Railroad: A Record of Facts, Authentic Narratives, Letters, &c.* (1872; reprint, New York: Arno, 1968), 178.

gentleman, in contrast to the arrogant, aggressive, and often irritating Torrey.[4]

Chaplin's friend, Joseph C. Hathaway, described him as "serene, dignified, cheerful, loving, brave and gentlemanly." Antislavery journalist Stephen Pearl Andrews vouched "for the fact that there is not a man in America whose face beams with a more genuine radiance of benevolence, whose whole demeanor exhibits more of the absolute *repose* so much vaunted in the higher circles of society. . . . He is . . . eminently qualified to make friends—to enlist the sympathies of all those by whom he is surrounded." Yet Chaplin had insecurities and weaknesses that became evident as a result of his work in Washington.[5]

Born in 1796 in Groton, Massachusetts, the youngest son of a Congregationalist minister, Chaplin attended Andover Academy and Harvard College. From the 1820s through the mid-1830s, he practiced law and engaged in benevolent reform—especially temperance. In 1836 he gave up his legal practice to serve as an AASS agent. The following year he moved to Utica, New York, to become the general agent of the New York State Anti-Slavery Society (NYSASS). An able administrator thereafter known among New York abolitionists as "General Chaplin," he advocated political abolitionism and by 1840 had become a tireless worker in behalf of the Liberty party.[6]

4. Chaplin to Gerrit Smith, 21 March 1838, GSP; *CA*, 10 April 1841; *NASS*, 16 January 1851 (first & second quotations); J. B. W. to Editor of the *Patriot*, 7 March 1846, in *E*, 1 April 1846; S. P. A., Correspondence of the Tribune, Washington, 26 August [1850], in *PF*, 5 September 1850.

5. *Liberty Party Paper*, in *NS*, 5 September 1850 (first quotation); S. P. A., Correspondence of the *Tribune*, Washington, 26 August [1850], in *PF*, 5 September 1850 (second quotation).

6. *The Case of William L. Chaplin* (Boston: Chaplin Committee, 1851), 14–7; Henry Wilson, *History of the Rise and Fall of the Slave Power in America*, 3d ed. (Boston: James R. Osgood, 1876), 2:80–1; *Courtland Standard*, 2 May [1871], in *New National Era* (Washington), 11 May 1871; William Goodell, *Slavery and Antislavery: A History of the Great Struggle in Both Hemispheres* (1852; reprint, New York: Negro Universities Press, 1968), 445–6 (quotation); Lawrence J. Friedman, *Gregarious Saints: Self and Community in American Abolitionism, 1830–1870* (New York: Cambridge University Press, 1982), 97–123; Walter M. Merrill and Louis Ruchames, eds., *The Letters of William Lloyd Garrison*, 6 vols. (Cambridge, Mass.: Harvard University Press, 1971–81), 2:527n; A. B. Smith to Gerrit Smith, 26 September 1841, GSP. Lawrence J. Friedman's portrayal of Chaplin as "the plodding antislavery administrator" is belied by Chaplin's activities in Washington.

Chaplin knew Torrey well, shared his view that slavery could nowhere enjoy the protection of law, and admired his daring actions. When Chaplin first arrived in Washington, in December 1844, to replace Torrey as correspondent of the *Albany Patriot*, he traveled with Joshua Leavitt to Baltimore to consult with Torrey and his attorney concerning a request for a pardon. But Chaplin doubted that he could measure up to Torrey. In January 1845, in response to an editorial in Gamaliel Bailey's *Cincinnati Morning Herald* repudiating clandestine operations as detrimental to the antislavery cause, Chaplin declared, "As I am a living man, I believe that one hundred men like Charles T. Torrey, in courage and devotion to his object, would do more to deliver the slave speedily, than all our paper resolutions, windy speeches, presses and *votes* into the bargain. His may not be the best way for either the Herald or me to work; I am sorry to say it, we have got neither his courage nor devotion!"[7]

Chaplin found, nevertheless, that he could to a degree emulate Torrey. Washington's black community drew him in, just as it had Torrey. He attended black churches, became acquainted with local black ministers—especially Cook—and learned first hand the anguish suffered by black families.[8] Then the case of James Baker, a legacy left to him by Torrey and Smallwood, led Chaplin to believe that, as a means of undermining slavery, he might substitute purchasing the freedom of slaves for the more dangerous tactic of helping slaves escape.

Baker, who had been the legal property of R. W. Hunter, a tobacco planter residing in nearby Prince George's County, Maryland, had joined a group of slaves that Smallwood sent north from Washington in September 1842. Conscientious and pious, though illiterate, Baker, like others whom Torrey and Smallwood helped, belonged to a black church in the city. He was the sort of upstanding individual whom abolitionists liked to portray as victims of slavery. On reaching Albany, he teamed on the local antislavery lec-

---

7. Joseph C. Lovejoy, *Memoir of Rev. Charles T. Torrey*, 2d ed. (1848; reprint, New York: Negro Universities Press, 1969), 283; Chaplin to J. C. Jackson, 3 January 1845, in *AP*, 8 January 1845 (quotation). See also W. L. C. to *Patriot*, 12 January 1846, in *AP*, 21 January 1846. Following Torrey's death, Chaplin declared him to be "more Christ-like than any of us." See *AP*, 26 December 1846.

8. [Chaplin to *Patriot*], 3 February [1845], in *AP*, 12 February 1845; Cook to Myrtilla Miner, 31 July 1851, MMP.

ture circuit with Abel Brown, the dynamic white leader of the Eastern New York Anti-Slavery Society.[9]

Baker suffered considerable anguish because he had left behind in Washington a pregnant wife and a one-year-old son, who were owned by a government clerk. During a speaking tour in Vermont in 1843, he and Brown raised forty dollars to help fund Torrey and Smallwood in an attempt to transport this growing family and others to Albany. But, in November of that year, the attempt failed at John Bush's Washington residence. The Guard, which nearly apprehended Torrey and Smallwood, succeeded in arresting the would-be escapees as they sat in Torrey's wagon. Baker's wife, Mary, and her children went to jail, her infant died there, and Baker assumed that from jail Mary and their son had been sold south.

When Brown became terminally ill during the late fall of 1844, Baker "proceeded to meet the appointments which had been made for Mr. Brown and himself." This impressed Eber M. Pettit, a white Versailles, New York, abolitionist, who in December wrote to Washington requesting that Chaplin make inquiries concerning Mary and her son. By early February Chaplin had located them in the city, still residing with their master. Rather than plot their escape, as Torrey and Smallwood might have done, he entered into what he described as an amicable agreement with the master to purchase their freedom. With just a hint of sarcasm, Chaplin described the man as "*very religious,*" wishing the best for Baker, but demanding three hundred dollars for the woman and child. As was usually the case in such transactions, it was up to Baker to raise the money, which he did with the help of Pettit and an ap-

9. The discussion in this and the following paragraphs is based on: Samivel Weller Jr. to Mr. Printer, 12 April 1843, in *AP,* 27 April 1843; Thomas Smallwood, *A Narrative of Thomas Smallwood, (Colored Man)* (Toronto: Smallwood, 1851), 37; [Chaplin to *AP*], 3 February [1845], in *AP,* 12 February 1845 (quotations); Homer Uri Johnson, *From Dixie to Canada: Romance and Realities of the Underground Railroad* (1896; reprint, Westport, Conn.: Negro University sities Press, 1970), 39–43. Baker served on two committees at the Cazenovia, New York Fugitive Slave Convention in 1850 and as a delegate to the Liberty party national convention in Buffalo in 1851. See *NS,* 5 September 1850 and *FDP,* 25 September 1851. Johnson's book contains slightly altered copies of letters from Pettit to Chaplin and Chaplin to Baker. They are altered to bring them into conformity with a fictionalized and slightly racist account of Baker written by Pettit during the 1870s. In Johnson and Pettit's accounts Baker is called "Jo Norton." See Pettit, *Sketches in the History of the Underground Railroad* (1879; reprint, Freeport, N.Y.: Books for Libraries, 1971), 34–49.

peal in his behalf by Chaplin to New York abolitionists. When Congress adjourned in March 1845, ending Chaplin's reporting duties, he escorted the now free Mary and child to Utica, where they reunited with Baker.

There was nothing new about purchases of freedom and, because there were no legal restrictions on manumission in the District of Columbia, Washington was an excellent location to negotiate them. African Americans had been purchasing themselves, their families, and others for many years. Black churches and white individuals helped them. As historian T. Stephen Whitman points out, help from whites was not always benevolent. White "manumission brokers" lent money to enslaved persons at exorbitant rates of interest and stood, on default, to gain possession of their erstwhile clients. But John Needles and Elisha Tyson had no ulterior motives when, early in the 1800s, they helped purchase the freedom of slaves in Baltimore. Between 1839 and 1842, William Slade, David A. Hall, and Seth M. Gates acted similarly in Washington. Several African Americans with whom Torrey and Smallwood dealt preferred purchase as a safer route to freedom than escape.[10]

Most abolitionists—including Chaplin—were, nevertheless, initially reluctant to purchase freedom. As in the case of proposals for compensated general emancipation, abolitionists perceived that *paying* slaveholders to free their bondpeople amounted to recognizing a right to own slaves in the first place. Purchase seemed to condone criminal and sinful activities and to involve the purchasers in those activities. It amounted to doing business with the devil. In 1830 William Lloyd Garrison suggested that it would be right for abolitionists to help purchase the freedom of slaves only when masters could prove they had a legitimate title *from God* to their chattels. Garrisonians, in particular, maintained that purchasing freedom—and, for that matter,

---

10. Ira Berlin, *Slaves without Masters: The Free Negro in the Antebellum South* (New York: New Press, 1974), 157, 314; C. T. T. to Joshua Leavitt, n.d., in *E*, 8 September 1842; T. Stephen Whitman, *The Price of Freedom: Slavery and Manumission in Baltimore and Early National Maryland* (Lexington: University Press of Kentucky, 1997), 126–31 (quotation); Graham, *Baltimore*, 63; Whitman, "Slavery, Manumissions, and Free Black Workers in Early National Baltimore (Maryland)" (Ph.D. dissertation, Johns Hopkins University, 1993), 170–1; W. S. to Editor of the Emancipator, 18 February 1839, in *PF*, 14 March 1839; D. A. Hall to Julia Butler and her children, deed of manumission, 11 September 1840, in "Slave Manumissions," 3:277, RG 21, NA; Seth M. Gates to Gerrit Smith, 25 March 1842, GSP; Smallwood, *Narrative*, 21–2; Samivel Weller, Jr. to Editor, 15 November 1842, in *TL*, 15 December 1842.

helping slaves to escape—aided only a few people, misappropriating resources that might be better used in efforts to achieve general emancipation.[11] It took, therefore, several considerations to get Chaplin, Bigelow, and others in Washington to move from regarding purchase as an isolated necessity in particularly distressing circumstances—as in Baker's case—to endorsing it as a comprehensive antislavery policy.

Of particular importance in this transformation was the example of Chaplin's friend and mentor, Gerrit Smith. During the early 1840s Smith spent large sums of money to free Maryland slaves who had belonged to his wife and her late father. Soon he began purchasing the freedom of other slaves and countering abolitionist contentions that he was wrong to do so. Those who rejected purchase, Smith informed one of his Garrisonian critics, injured their cause by engaging in mental "calculations" that led them away from benevolence and setting moral examples for slaveholders. A year later Chaplin echoed Smith's reasoning by calling on those opposed to slavery to repudiate "all that class of *cute* philosophers, who raise doubt about *buying people out of bondage!*" As for the broad impact of such purchasing, Chaplin said, "Let us wholly reject the dogma, that money is lost which is paid for slaves. Every dollar thus paid is a most effective sermon to the conscience of the guilty."[12]

Yet exposure in Washington to the agony of black families facing dismemberment was much more important than Smith's example in convincing Chaplin, Bigelow, and others to try to systematize purchases of freedom. As Bigelow in 1853 looked back over the previous decade, he declared, "On the subject of paying for slaves, to secure their freedom, I acknowledge that I once *theorised* against it; but was, long ago very summarily cured of my theory,

11. Betty L. Fladeland, "Compensated Emancipation: A Rejected Alternative," *Journal of Southern History* 42 (February 1976): 169; Wendell Phillips Garrison and Francis Jackson Garrison, *William Lloyd Garrison, 1805–1889,* 4 vols. (New York: Century, 1885–89), 1:151, 176; *PF,* 16 January 1845, 28 January 1847; *Liberty Press* (Utica, N.Y.), 3 June 1847.

12. Joseph Sturge, *A Visit to the United States in 1841* (London: Hamilton, Adams, 1842), 115–6, appendix k; Smith to J. Worthington, 15 July & 25 August 1841, to W. E. Channing, 17 August 1841, to Nathaniel Crenshaw, 30 December 1841, letter book copies, GSP; Smith to Myrtilla Miner, 10 January 1848, MMP; Smith to Sarah Pugh, 5 April 1847, in *AP,* 14 April 1847 (first quotation); W. L. C. to Pat, n.d., in *AP,* 22 March 1848 (second quotation); *AP,* 24 May 1848 (third quotation).

when I came to practise upon it."[13] Of particular importance in changing the men's minds was an association with two extraordinary individuals, Luke and Sarah Carter.

The Carters worked in Washington for Thomas Monroe, an elderly former postmaster who lived not far from the White House. Sarah, a slave, was the Monroe family "cook and *maid of all work.*" In 1845 she was about fifty-two years old, had "a hale, good constitution," and carried on a business as a laundress in addition to her work for the Monroes. According to Bigelow, she was also "for years an intelligent and approved midwife." The mother of seven children and grandmother to seven more, she had ten years earlier weaned a child of her own in order to wet-nurse one of Monroe's grandchildren. Her life, testified Bigelow, "had been filled up with such acts of fidelity and kindness as call forth a corresponding kindness and sympathy, wherever there are hearts that can feel."[14]

Luke Carter, Sarah's husband since 1820, was about seventy years old and had been free since before the War of 1812. He had been a sailor during the 1810s and a member of a Methodist Church, "without taint or reproach," since 1814. He earned twelve dollars per month as Monroe's coachman, with two dollars per month deducted to rent a cottage on Monroe's property that he shared with Sarah and their younger children. The rest of Luke's earnings went to support this family, without help from Monroe.

When Chaplin returned to Washington from Albany in early December 1845 to once again serve as the *Albany Patriot*'s correspondent and as an anti-slavery lobbyist, he learned from Horace Wheaton, a Democratic member of Congress from Syracuse, that disaster had struck the Carters. Several years of worsening relations between them and Monroe had culminated in the sale

13. *ASR* 1, 3d series (1 May 1853): 114.

14. The discussion in this and the following paragraphs is based on: W. L. C. to Charles A. Wheaton, 30 December 1845, in *AP*, 7 January 1846 (first, second, & fifth–seventh quotations); J. B. W. [meaning Jacob Bigelow in Washington] to Editor of the Patriot, 7 March 1846, in *E*, 1 April 1846 (third & fourth quotations); Luke Carter, certificate of freedom, 25 April 1843, in "Slave Manumissions," 3:469, RG 21, NA; Old Neighbor to Editors of the Evening Journal, 31 January 1846, in *AP*, 18 February 1846; Frederic Bancroft, *Slave-Trading in the Old South* (Baltimore: J. H. Furst, 1931), 56–8; *Washington Directory and National Register for 1846* (Washington: Gaither and Addison, 1846), 84; W. L. C. to Charles A. Wheaton, 25 February 1846, in *AP*, 4 March 1846.

of Sarah and her children and grandchildren to William H. Williams, the city's principal slave trader, who immediately shipped them south to Richmond, Virginia. A distraught Luke Carter followed in early 1846, made a futile attempt to negotiate the purchase of his family from a local slave trader, and saw all but Sarah depart for Georgia. She spent fourteen days in a bare cell in a Richmond slave pen before Mrs. J. C. Walsh, the wife of a naval officer stationed in Washington, purchased her for $250 and allowed her to return to the city. Walsh indicated, however, that if she were not reimbursed by March, she would resell Sarah.

Chaplin's visits with the Carters and his identification with their plight led him to turn his considerable organizational talents to an effort to institutionalize purchasing freedom. He proposed to create what he grandly called a *"bureau of humanity"* to protect black families and undermine slavery in the Washington area. Chaplin's immediate task, which he undertook in partnership with Bigelow, was to help the Carters raise the money to pay back Walsh and liberate Sarah. He hoped later to do something toward the more difficult goal of redeeming her children and grandchildren. He also realized that he could use the Carter case and others like it to arouse sentiment in Washington and the North against slavery.

His carefully researched accounts of the family's plight circulated widely in such northeastern newspapers as Horace Greeley's *New York Daily Tribune* and Thurlow Weed's *Albany Evening Journal.* Deliberately understating the barbarity of the Carter story, Chaplin noted that theirs was not "a peculiarly striking case" and that Monroe was *not* especially evil. Instead, the Carters' experiences "were of a class of every day's occurrence in slaveholding life, and simply the natural offshoot of the system." It was their very ordinariness that revealed that system's oppressiveness and argued for its abolition.

Although the Carter children and grandchildren remained out of reach, the effort to redeem Sarah Carter was a great success as an exercise in interracial cooperation against slavery. By the time Luke Carter purchased and manumitted his wife on April 6, 1846, the couple—by washing clothes and appealing to their friends and neighbors—had raised $114.14. Abolitionists in New York, Pennsylvania, and Ohio had contributed $68.50. Chaplin provided the balance due Walsh on assurances that Gerrit Smith would reimburse him. During June, as Luke Carter continued to raise funds, that reimbursement became unnecessary. In September Bigelow reported that there was enough money left over from the Carter campaign to purchase the freedom of another slave woman—a daughter of a black member of one of Washington's white churches.[15]

Soon Luke Carter, despite having broken several ribs, went into business "hauling wood and sand." This underlined a point that Chaplin had made throughout the fund-raising effort. The Carters were upstanding members of Washington's black middle class—just the sort of family-oriented people white abolitionists met at black churches. They had a free-labor ethos that led antislavery whites to consider them worthy allies in the struggle against dissolute slaveholders. It would be easy, Chaplin maintained, for the Carters to continue to "work hard" for the rest of their lives "if they could only *know where their children are, and see them once more.*" Appealing to northern family values, he emphasized that "fathers and mothers will readily understand this language." In a very middle-class way, too, Bigelow and a correspondent using the *nom de plume* "John Henry" empathized with the Carter's loss of the possessions that Monroe had seized when he repossessed their cottage. Just as significant in cementing interracial ties was the Carters' emergence as antislavery activists ready to harbor fugitive slaves and help raise funds for others.

Chaplin's close relationship with the Carters intensified his commitment to working "directly for the slave, and through him for all poor men." But he left Washington in June 1846 for Albany in order to replace the ailing James C. Jackson as editor of the *Patriot*. That fall he served as the New York Liberty party's candidate for lieutenant governor and resumed his duties as general agent for the NYSASS. Throughout the first four months of 1847 his editorial work, speaking agenda in behalf of the Liberty party, and the perilous financial state of the *Patriot* prevented his return to Washington. As a result, the Bureau of Humanity deteriorated.[16]

15. The discussion in this and the following paragraphs is based on: "Slave Manumissions," 3:587–8, RG 21, NA; W. L. C. to [*Patriot*], n.d., in *AP*, 15 April 1846; Chaplin to Smith, 28 June 1846, Smith Papers; J. B. W. to Chaplin, September 1846, in *AP*, 30 September 1846 (first quotation); W. L. C. to Charles A. Wheaton, 30 December 1845, in *AP*, 7 January 1846 (second quotation); W. L. C. to [*Patriot*], n.d., in *AP*, 15 April 1846 (third quotation); John Henry to Pat, 12 January 1846, in *AP*, 21 January 1846; J. B. W. to Editor of the *Patriot*, Mar. 7, 1846, in *E*, Ap. 1, 1846.

16. W. L. C. to [*AP*], n.d., in *AP*, 15 April 1846; Chaplin to Gerrit Smith, 28 June & 25 November 1846, GSP; *AP*, 8 July, 13 September, & 16 December 1846 (quotation); 20 & 27

Chaplin's antislavery colleagues in Washington missed him. "Will you 'come over and help us,' for we are weak and need help," Bigelow begged him in July 1847. Yet the work of purchasing freedom went on. That month Bigelow hoped to free a sixty-year-old woman and her twenty-year-old daughter. The Marshall of the District of Columbia had seized the women from their master and proposed to sell them in order pay a fine owed to the United States government. The case attracted attention because it involved the government directly in slave trading and because the women were church members with ties to the subversives. As he and Chaplin had done in the case of Sarah Carter, Bigelow saved them from sale south by finding a Washington resident willing to pay the $530 purchase price and to hold them as human collateral until reimbursed.[17]

Bigelow was as aware as Chaplin of the capacity of such cases to arouse antislavery sentiment. A year and a half earlier he had joined Giddings in publicizing a gruesome case of physical abuse. The two men had visited a middle-aged woman, who at her request resided in Washington Jail after her master had severely beaten her. Appalled at her condition, they determined to use her case to expose, in Giddings's words, "the brutal and savage barbarity of slaveholders." Now, in his capacity as the Washington correspondent of the *Boston Daily Whig*, Bigelow reminded his readers that "it is the *voters* of the North who have made [Washington] the *Man-Market of the Nation*."[18]

With Chaplin unavailable to help in securing the freedom of the mother and daughter, Bigelow turned to Gamaliel Bailey, who was personally indebted to Bigelow for the aid he had provided in getting AFASS funds to establish the *National Era*.[19] Bailey was more circumspect than Chaplin. But he was at least as skilled in fund-raising. Bailey was born in New Jersey in 1807 and graduated from Philadelphia's Jefferson Medical College in 1828. He had gained a reputation as an antislavery journalist in Cincinnati as editor

---

January 1847, 17 March–28 April 1847; Lewis Tappan to Joshua Leavitt, 28 February 1847, in *E*, 10 March 1847.

17. [Bigelow] to Chaplin, 16 July 1847 (quotation) and J. B. W., Correspondence of the *Boston Daily Whig*, 13 July 1847, both in *AP*, 18 July 1847.

18. Giddings to Laura Waters Giddings, 8 March 1846, JRGP (first quotation); J. B. W. to Editors of the *Patriot*, 7 March 1847, in *E*, 1 April 1846 (second quotation).

19. Stanley Harrold, *Gamaliel Bailey and Antislavery Union* (Kent, Ohio: Kent State University Press, 1986), 83, 89.

of the *Philanthropist* during the late 1830s and early 1840s. His commitment to spreading Liberty-party abolitionism southward had led to his relocation to Washington. The immediate success of the *Era* allowed him to reach a far larger audience than could Bigelow, Chaplin, or Giddings.

In response to Bigelow's request, Bailey sent "a circular to friends in different sections of the country, explaining the case, and soliciting aid." After noting that the women—because of Bigelow's intervention—had benefitted from being sold, Bailey emphasized that as things stood "the Government of the United States may hold or sell slaves, and seem[s] to regard it as a thing of course." This, he charged, involved "every American citizen" in "the guilt of trading in human beings."[20]

Bailey called on the press to speak out. In response northern newspapers representing a wide spectrum of antislavery opinion echoed his demand that the practice be ended. The Whiggish editor of the *Pittsburgh Gazette,* for example, commented: "Under the very dome of the Capital, beneath the stars and stripes of the nation, women, Christian women, are sold by the appointed officer of the President, and the money put into the bag of the United States Treasury. Judas, for his thirty pieces of silver, hardly did worse than this."[21] In this manner, by encouraging a rising northern sentiment in favor of the abolition of slavery and the slave trade in the District of Columbia, the Washington subversive community contributed to the mounting national crisis of the late 1840s. Interaction with oppressed African Americans had led white subversives to take actions that directly affected the sectional struggle.

The relationship between the subversives and national politics became especially clear a few months later as, during the winter of 1847–1848, Giddings once again became a central figure in a case involving a servant at his boardinghouse. This case, which arose as Congress debated the polarizing issues of slavery in Washington and the territories gained from Mexico, not only helps illuminate the personal ties between antislavery blacks and whites that characterized the subversive community. It also shows how the weakening of slavery in the Chesapeake region intensified—with one surprising exception—the struggle between antislavery and proslavery forces.

Throughout his congressional career, Giddings challenged proslavery in-

20. *NE,* 30 December 1847 (first quotation), 22 July 1847 (second–fourth quotations).
21. *NE,* 12 August 1847.

Joshua R. Giddings (1795–1864) was a congressman from Ohio who, from the late 1830s through the late 1850s, was at the center of Washington's subversive community. Giddings, *Speeches in Congress* (Boston: John P. Jewett, 1853), frontispiece.

terests and courted reprisals. In December 1847 he opposed the election of the Whig candidate for Speaker of the House, Robert C. Winthrop of Massachusetts. He contended that Winthrop had been too supportive of the war against Mexico and too willing to appoint slaveholders to House committees. Then, in early January 1848, Giddings won a moral victory over slaveholders. He gained unanimous support from northern Whigs in his successful effort to refer to committee—rather than to table—a petition "from sundry citizens of the District of Columbia" calling for abolition of the slave trade"[22]

Circumstances suggest that someone among the proslavery leaders in Congress determined to strike back at him in a way that would cause him personal anguish *and* weaken his reputation as a protector of African Americans. Proslavery congressmen regarded the degree of respect and friendship that Giddings accorded to African Americans to be unbecoming in a gentleman and subversive of the existing order. In particular they knew that Giddings esteemed Henry and Sylvia Wilson, a married black couple who worked as a waiter and a maid at Ann Sprigg's boardinghouse. It seems more than coincidental, therefore, that on the evening of Friday, January 14,

22. James Brewer Stewart, *Joshua R. Giddings and the Tactics of Radical Politics* (Cleveland: Case-Western Reserve University Press, 1970), 141–66; *AS*, 10 January 1848.

1848—a week after Giddings presented the slave trade petition—"three ruffians" entered the lower room of the boardinghouse and violently seized Henry Wilson, while Sylvia looked on. The intruders gagged Henry and "placed him in irons and with loaded pistols" dragged him away to Williams's Slave Pen.[23]

Wilson, whom Giddings described as "a stout athletic fellow, tolerably intelligent," had an agreement with his owner, a widow who lived at the Navy Yard, to purchase his freedom in installments totaling $350. He owed her only sixty dollars when she sold him to Williams for $550. As might be expected, Sylvia Wilson, who had always been free and who had been a servant of William Henry Harrison during his brief presidency, reacted emotionally to what had happened to her husband. So did Giddings (who had been "out on an evening walk" when the slavetraders accosted Wilson), Sprigg, and Giddings's Whig messmates, Pennsylvania congressmen Abraham R. McIlvanie and John Strohm.[24]

The cross-racial bonds were strong enough that Sylvia "at once" turned to Giddings and his colleagues "for relief." At first they felt powerless to respond to the outrage. "We were in a barbarous land," Giddings recalled, "controlled by barbarous laws." Yet he "could not sit down quietly in the midst of so much distress." Instead he and McIlvanie walked to Williams's Pen at the corner of Maryland Avenue and Seventh Street. Approaching the forbidding building on a dimly moonlit night, Giddings reflected "that within its gloomy walls were yet retained all the horrid barbarity of the darker ages." Inside, two of Williams's agents, who sat by a fire "smoking segars," told Giddings, "*The negur has gone. We took him immediately on board ship at Alexandria, and he has sailed for New Orleans.*"

23. James Brewer Stewart, "Joshua Giddings, Antislavery Violence, and Congressional Politics of Honor," in John R. McKivigan and Stanley Harrold, eds., *Antislavery Violence: Sectional, Racial, and Cultural Conflict in Antebellum America* (Knoxville: University of Tennessee Press, 1999), 167–92; [Giddings] to Edward L. Hamlin, 15 January 1848, clipping from *Democrat and Freeman*, n.d., Giddings Scrapbook, JRGP (first quotation); *AS*, 7 February 1848 (second quotation). The Giddings to Hamlin letter is also in *DTD*, 24 January 1848.

24. The discussion in this and the following paragraph is based on: [Giddings] to Edward L. Hamlin, 15 January 1848, in clipping from *Democrat and Republican*, n.d., in Giddings Scrapbook, JRGP (quotations); and *DTD*, 24 January 1848. On McIlvanie and Strohm see *Biographical Dictionary of the United States Congress, 1774–1985*, Bicentennial Edition (Washington, D.C.: U.S. Government Printing Office, 1989), 1468, 1888.

Disbelieving this claim, Giddings, with the aid of McIlvaine and Strohm but without much hope of success, initiated habeas corpus proceedings aimed at securing Wilson's release. Then, on Monday, Giddings rose in the House of Representatives to demand, on the basis of what had happened to Wilson, that Congress either abolish the slave trade in the District of Columbia or "remove the seat of government to some free state." Following a sectionally polarized debate that served Giddings's broader antislavery goals, enraged slaveholders tabled Giddings's resolution by a significantly narrow vote of 94 to 88.[25] Once again a gross injustice perpetuated against a member of Washington's biracial community directly influenced the sectional struggle by forcing northern members of Congress to take a stand against the slave trade. Real personal ties rather than a theoretical abhorrence of slavery and its geographical expansion played a central role in this political confrontation in the House.

If it had been otherwise, Giddings might have given up his effort to rescue Henry Wilson once his resolution had served its strategic purpose. According to Ezra L. Stevens, however, Giddings sought doggedly to help Wilson. Stevens reported to the *Daily True Democrat* of Cleveland that Giddings called on "the former owner of Henry, but [that] the old Jezebel was indifferent, stern, immovable in her avariciousness." Giddings met with a similar reaction on a return visit to Williams's Pen. As a last resort, he "laid the case in all its hideous enormity before Duff Green," who owned Sprigg's boardinghouse.[26]

It was Green who proved to be the surprising exception in this story of increasing sectional animosity in Washington. A staunchly proslavery—though somewhat eccentric—southern Whig and former ally of John C. Calhoun, Green readily agreed to intervene in behalf of Wilson. Green saw more clearly than many southern leaders that the publicity the Wilson case generated did the proslavery cause little good. By browbeating "the old Jezebel" *and*

25. [Giddings] to Hamlin, 15 January 1848, clipping from *Democrat and Freeman*, n.d. in Giddings Scrapbook, JRGP; *CG*, 30th Cong., 1 sess., 179–80 (quotation); [Ezra L. Stevens to Hamlin], 18 January 1848, in *DTD*, 27 January 1848; *AS*, 7 February 1848.

26. The discussion in this and the following paragraph is based on: E. L. S., Editorial Correspondence of the *True Democrat*, 10 February 1848, in *AS*, 14 February 1848; *NE*, 24 February 1848. Green: Fletcher Green, "Duff Green, Militant Journalist of the Old School," *American Historical Review* 52 (January 1947): 247–66; David E. Woodward, "Abraham Lincoln, Duff Green, and the Mysterious Trumbull Letter," *Civil War History* 42 (September 1996): 210–4.

the slavetraders, Green elicited an agreement to have Wilson returned to Washington and be manumitted in exchange for $195. Sixty dollars of this amount paid what Wilson owed the woman for his freedom and $135 covered the amount she had spent out of what Williams had paid her. Giddings raised the money by soliciting five dollar donations from Whigs in Congress, and in early February Wilson received his free papers.

All of this had an great impact on Stevens, who had just arrived in Washington from Cleveland. This pious Western Reserve Yankee, who had been outraged that ministers in Washington did not denounce dancing, bowling, and pool-shooting, quickly bonded with Washington's subversives. Dissenting from a perception that blacks lacked the sensibilities of whites, he emotionally described the scene at Sprigg's following Wilson's manumission. "Was he [Wilson]," Stevens asked his readers, "insensible to benevolence and kindness so disinterested? Oh, no!—Could you have seen him after the manacles were taken off—after the chattel had become a man! standing at the door with hat in hand awaiting the egress of Mr. G., and witnessed how enthusiastically and affectionately he grasped the extended hand of that good man, you would not doubt."[27] Stevens might have added that in extending his hand to Wilson, Giddings—symbolically at least—recognized Wilson's social equality with himself.

Even as Wilson gained his freedom, however, it was clear that ad hoc manumissions could not diminish the threat posed by sale south to individuals and families in Washington and its environs. This was especially evident to Giddings and to Chaplin. While the Wilson drama unfolded, numerous other desperate African Americans had sought help from each of them in efforts to save loved ones who were about to be sold to traders. One black man called on Giddings to help his daughter and another appealed in behalf of his five children. "I am constantly beset by the poor miserable wretches here who have their wives, their husbands or children sold to the slave dealers," Giddings lamented to his wife. Chaplin—who, though short of funds, had returned to Washington in mid-December 1847 as the *Patriot*'s congressional reporter—told New York Liberty abolitionists that the few in Washington

27. E. L. S., Editorial Correspondence, in *DTD*, 26 & 27 January, 28 February 1848; E. L. S., Editorial Correspondence of the *True Democrat*, 10 February 1848, in *AS*, 14 February 1848 (quotation).

who had previously helped in such cases had their "time and means . . . severely taxed." He added, "I am only a temporary resident here, and yet a score of these distressed people draw upon my time and sympathy day after day, and week after week."[28]

Chaplin believed by this time that northern antislavery petitions, combined with the efforts of Giddings and John Quincy Adams in Congress, had undermined the slave system in the District of Columbia. He believed, as well, that abolition in the District would be "a prelude to a mightier and more decisive conflict" destined to end in the extermination of slavery throughout the South. But, while he cherished this vision, he knew that the "precarious" existence of slavery in the District—combined with a steeply rising demand for slave labor in the Southwest—spread distress among local African Americans. Furthermore he was far less "*sanguine*" than Giddings that Congress might quickly relieve the suffering by repealing "all slave laws in the District." Consequently Chaplin searched for alternative means of helping people avoid the anguishing dislocations associated with the trade. This search led him in early 1848 once again to become the white agent of black families struggling to avoid "inhuman outrages."[29]

The best documented of Chaplin's activities relate to his cooperation with Mathew Mathews and the Carters. Mathews had been a slave in Richmond until 1831, when his master and friend Philip Harrison manumitted him "in consideration of his *good conduct and uniform good character*." Literate, well-traveled in the Northeast, and experienced in business, as well as a long-time member of a Baptist church in Washington, Mathews—like James Baker and the Carters—impressed white abolitionists. Sixty-two years old in 1848, he had over the years purchased the freedom of three of his four children, leaving only his daughter, Lavinia, in bondage. Anticipating that she might be sold,

28. *AP*, 10 November & 29 December 1847; Giddings to Laura Waters Giddings, 23 January 1848, JRGP (first quotation); E. L. S., editorial correspondence, 24 January 1848, in *DTD*, 1 February 1848; Chaplin to Gerrit Smith and Charles A. Wheaton, 15 February 1848, in *AP*, 23 February 1848 (second & third quotations).

29. W. L. C. to Pat, n.d., in *AP*, 22 March 1848; Chaplin to Gerrit Smith, 25 March 1848, GSP (first quotation); W. L. C. to Gerrit Smith and Charles A. Wheaton, 15 February 1848, in *AP*, 23 February 1848 (second quotation). See also Michael Tadman, *Speculators and Slaves: Masters, Traders, and Slaves in the Old South* (Madison: University of Wisconsin Press, 1996), 116.

he had negotiated with her master during the summer of 1847 to purchase her freedom for $350, and had traveled north to raise part of that amount. When he returned to Washington in November, he had a total of $375. But the master raised the price to $450 and, when Mathews could not pay that amount, sold Lavinia to a trader in Alexandria. She would go south unless Mathews could raise an additional seventy-five dollars.[30]

The Carters, meanwhile, in seeking to reunite their family had made a striking acquisition for Washington's subversive community by drawing in Major John H. Eaton and his wife Margaret "Peggy" O'Neale Eaton. The Major, formerly of Tennessee, had been Andrew Jackson's secretary of war from 1829 until 1831, when the scandal caused by his marriage to disreputable Washington native Peggy O'Neale forced his resignation. In early 1848 John H. Eaton located some of the Carter family in Nashville and learned that others had been "transferred" to Tallahassee, Florida. He informed Luke and Sarah Carter that the freedom of those in Nashville could be purchased for a total of $3,600 and that he would go to Nashville in their behalf.

As Chaplin related these stories to his New York readers, he emphasized that Sarah Carter was, as a result of Eaton's revelations, "full of hope" that she would get "a part" of her family back. Her bravery and determination captivated Chaplin and increased his commitment to direct action against oppression. "I wish you could see her," he wrote. "She is decidedly one of the highest specimens of womanhood I ever set eyes upon. . . . I wish to heaven she could once stand before one of your fat-hearted, rich congregations and tell the story of her family."

---

30. The discussion in this and the following paragraphs is based on Chaplin to Smith and Wheaton, 15 February 1848, in *AP*, 23 February 1848. In early 1843 Charles T. Torrey wrote in Washington, "Some months since a lady, a native of this city, of which she has long been a bright ornament, called to interest me in the case of a colored woman whom she had long known, and whose freedom she very much desired to have secured." If Torrey was referring to Peggy Eaton in this passage, her involvement in such matters cannot be credited to the Carters. See P. P. to Friend, n.d., in *NASS*, 12 January 1843. Almost nothing has been written concerning the Eatons' later years. See Eaton, Peggy, q.v., *American National Biography*, 24 vols. (New York: Oxford University Press, 1999), Eaton, John Henry, and O'Neale, Margaret, q.v., *Dictionary of American Biography* 11 vols. (New York: Scribner's, 1964), and Eaton, Margaret O'Neale, q.v., *Notable American Women, 1607–1950: A Biographical Dictionary*, 2 vols. (Cambridge, Mass.: Belknap Press, 1971).

Peggy Eaton, too, impressed Chaplin. She was, he testified, ready to so-licit funds for the Carters. He was careful, however, to assure his evangelical audience that she was not what she once had been. "The notoriety of her name, at a certain time, in the political circles will readily recur to you," he wrote. "She was then a gay, fashionable woman. She is now a zealous and devout Methodist."

To help Mathews, the Carters, and many others in Washington whose families were threatened by the slave trade, Chaplin called for a reconstitution of his Bureau of Humanity. In February 1848 he asked northern abolitionists of "all shades of opinion" to forgo their opposition to purchasing freedom in order to help him establish a fund for *"the redemption of meritorious captives."* In March he added a request for financial support in retaining two Washing-ton lawyers, in order to create "a regular system" for prosecuting freedom suits. Two years earlier a Washington woman named Lucy Crawford had won her freedom in a suit against Hope H. Slatter. Chaplin hoped to systematize such legal action not just to free "a few poor people" but to generate antislav-ery sentiment and "prepare the way for definitive legislation by Congress" aimed at driving slavery "from the Capital."[31]

Little came of these plans for an enhanced Bureau of Humanity as the issue of slavery expansion into the territories gained from Mexico disrupted the Liberty party on whose supporters Chaplin relied for contributions. Gid-dings and other antislavery Whigs from Ohio and Massachusetts were pre-paring to leave their party over the territorial issue. So were northern Demo-crats, such as David Wilmot of Pennsylvania and Martin Van Buren of New York. These movements led to the formation of the Free Soil party, which mainly opposed slavery's expansion rather than its continued existence in the South. Gamaliel Bailey, his friend Salmon P. Chase of Ohio, and Henry B. Stanton of Massachusetts were ready, although with reservations, to lead the majority of Liberty abolitionists into this new party. But Chaplin, Gerrit Smith, and other radical political abolitionists, most of whom were from New York, insisted that the Liberty party remain an independent avant-garde de-

---

31. Chaplin to Smith and Wheaton, 15 February 1848, in *AP,* 23 February 1848 (first & second quotations); W. L. C. to Pat, n.d., in *AP,* 22 March 1848 (third & fourth quotations); *PF,* 6 August 1846.

voted to the destruction of slavery in the South as well as its prohibition in the new territories.[32]

Because of these political developments, antislavery financial resources that might have funded Chaplin's Bureau of Humanity went instead to help pay for the organization of the Free Soil party during 1848. By the end of March Chaplin had raised only fifty dollars for Mathews. Rather than being freed, Lavinia went from the slave pen in Alexandria to a Virginia slaveholder. Other black families in Washington faced imminent disruption. The Carters' children and grandchildren remained in slavery, while Luke, Sarah, and Chaplin contemplated a more radical way to free Washington slaves.[33] Experiencing extreme trepidation and anxiety, Chaplin was about to discover that he had some of Torrey's desperate courage after all.

32. Richard H. Sewell, *Ballots for Freedom: Antislavery Politics in the United States, 1837–1860* (New York: Oxford University Press, 1976), 131–69; Frederick J. Blue, *The Free Soilers: Third Party Politics, 1848–1854* (Urbana: University of Illinois Press, 1973), 1–80; Harrold, *Bailey*, 70–80, 109–23.

33. Chaplin to Gerrit Smith, 25 March 1848, GSP. The Virginia slaveholder was willing to resell Lavinia for an additional $100 over what the slave trader had asked.

[FIVE]

The Pearl *Fugitives and the Subversives*

O
N the evening of Thursday April 13, 1848, the schooner *Pearl,* having sailed south from Philadelphia, arrived off Washington on the
Potomac River. It docked with a load of firewood at the city's
steamboat wharf located in a sparsely settled area at the foot of Seventh Street
one mile to the south of Pennsylvania Avenue. The tiny vessel's crew consisted of three white men: Edward Sayres, Chester English, and Daniel
Drayton. Sayres was the *Pearl's* owner and captain. English, a young and in-
experienced seaman, served as cook and deck hand. Drayton, a tough, semi-
literate bay trader, had paid Sayres $100 to charter the *Pearl* to transport
slaves to the North and freedom.[1]

At ten o'clock the following Saturday night, after a total of seventy-seven
men, women, and children had crowded below the *Pearl*'s deck, the crew cast
off. They planned to sail down the Potomac into Chesapeake Bay and then

1. The discussion in this and the following paragraphs is based on: Stanley Harrold, "The
Pearl Affair: The Washington Riot of 1848," *RCHS* 50 (1980): 140–3 (second quotation); *Na-
tional Intelligencer* (Washington), 19 April 1848; *NS,* 28 May 1848; *NYH,* 20 April 1848 (first
quotation); E. S. H., editorial correspondence, 17 April 1848, in *DTD,* 20 & 26 April 1848, in
NS, 12 May 1848; *True Wesleyan* (New York), 23 September 1848. See also Richard C. Rohrs,
"Antislavery Politics and the *Pearl* Incident of 1848," *Historian* 56 (Summer 1994): 711–24.
There are incomplete lists of slaves who sailed on the *Pearl* in Entry 45, Records of the United
States District Court for the District of Columbia, 1838–61, RG 21, NA, and *Daily Union*
(Washington), 19 April 1848. These lists usually omit surnames.

Daniel Drayton (1802–1857) was the northern bay trader who, under the direction of William L. Chaplin, rented the schooner *Pearl* in 1848 in an attempt to help seventy-seven slaves to escape from Washington. Drayton, *Personal Memoir of Daniel Drayton* (Boston: Bela Marsh, 1855), frontispiece.

head north through the Chesapeake and Delaware Canal to Frenchtown, New Jersey. But things went awry. The *Pearl* lay idle at the wharf for several hours until, near daybreak, a wind arose. On Sunday evening as the vessel approached the river's mouth about one hundred miles to the southeast of Washington, a strong north wind led Sayres to lay over until Monday morning rather than venture into the bay. This decision permitted the steamer *Salem*—sent out from Georgetown on Sunday after masters in that city, as well as in Washington and Alexandria found slaves missing—to overtake the *Pearl.*

On board the *Salem* were thirty white volunteers under the command of Washington magistrate W. C. Williams. "Armed to the teeth" with small arms and two field pieces, the pursuers found the *Pearl* at two o'clock in the morning. The fugitives, caught by surprise, had no opportunity to resist. Yet a rumor circulated in Washington that "the runaway slaves had been captured [only] after a desperate struggle, in which seven of their number were killed." A vindictive excitement arose among many proslavery whites, while the would-be escapees' friends and relatives became apprehensive.

Williams had the fugitives locked below deck on the *Pearl* and brought Drayton, Sayres, and English aboard the *Salem* for interrogation as the steamer slowly towed the schooner upriver. When they reached the steamboat wharf at seven-thirty Tuesday morning, April 18, a small crowd met them. The crowd grew as Williams marched the prisoners toward the city jail. Drayton and Sayres, manacled and with a guard at each side, led the procession. Then came English and the male slaves, tied together in double file and closely guarded. Finally there were the women and children, who were not bound. In the case of the women, this was because many of them held babies in their arms. In all, the *Pearl* fugitives comprised thirty-eight adult and adolescent men, twenty-six adult and adolescent women, and thirteen children.

It was the crisis created by the demand for slaves in southwestern cotton fields that had led those old enough to reason for themselves to board the *Pearl.* When other methods, including Chaplin's Bureau of Humanity, failed to prevent sales south, some African Americans in the Washington vicinity turned to this dangerous means of holding their families together.[2]

Similar predicaments brought similar individuals to the *Pearl.* Many who boarded the vessel were members of the AME Church. Many belonged to families that functioned as economic units independent of their masters. Others possessed special skills or remarkable trustworthiness. A significant minority were light-complected. All of them were representative of the *respectable* people of color who constituted the African-American component of Washington's biracial antislavery community. Their religious orientation, their middle-class aspirations, their devotion to family, and, to a degree, their physical appearance encouraged antislavery whites to identify with them. This portrait is by no means based on all of the people who sailed on the *Pearl.* The histories of most of them are unknown. But a few are recoverable in some detail and what can be gleaned about others attests to their standing.

Among the more prominent of them were Daniel Bell, who was free, his

2. The discussion in this and the following paragraphs is based on: Washington correspondence, 17 April 1848, in *NYH,* 19 April 1848; *Daily Union* (Washington), 19 April 1848; Chaplin to [?], 18 May 1848, in *AP,* 24 May 1848 (quotation); *PF,* 4 January 1849; HAMPDEN to Editor of the *AP,* 19 February 1848, in *AS,* 20 May 1848; Harriet Beecher Stowe, *The Key to Uncle Tom's Cabin* (1854; reprint, New York: Arno, 1968), 334–9; J. R. Bradley to Frederick Douglass, 9 May 1848, in *NS,* 26 May 1848; Chaplin to Gerrit Smith, 25 March 1848, GSP; *NYH,* 20 April 1848; *L,* 21 April 1848; E. L. S., editorial correspondence, 22 April 1848, in *DTD,* 29 April 1848. Stowe confuses *Grace* Russell with her better known sister, *Emily.* See: Stowe, *Key,* 331 and John White Chadwick, ed., *A Life for Liberty: Anti-Slavery and Other Letters of Sallie Holley* (New York: G. P. Putnam's Sons, 1899), 170.

enslaved wife, Mary, and their eight enslaved children. There were also two daughters and four sons of Paul and Amelia Edmonson. Others among the *Pearl* fugitives were Grace Russell, Ellen Steward, and the wife of Thomas Ducket. Russell was a devout, light-complexioned young woman, whom Chaplin described as "a beautiful girl of eighteen, of slender constitution, intelligent and capable." Steward was the enslaved fifteen-year-old daughter of Dolly Madison's nurse. The elderly former first lady reputedly had for some time sold slaves to cover her living expenses and this young woman feared she would be next. Ducket's husband was a literate black man who helped plan the escape and who was well acquainted with Chaplin, Jacob Bigelow, and Gamaliel Bailey.

Thomas Taylor, a young resident of Georgetown who had been attempting to purchase his freedom, boarded the *Pearl*. So did three sisters from that same city, who had been harbored within the antislavery community for weeks before the vessel set sail. There also were two slaves belonging to a local black hackman, a man who shined shoes at the National Hotel on Philadelphia Avenue, and a slave owned by a Presbyterian minister.

The Bells were central to the enterprise. As described by a white member of Washington's antislavery community, Daniel Bell was "a robust, worthy, industrious man." Born a slave in Prince George's County, he worked for twenty years molding and casting iron at the Washington Navy Yard, where, it is tempting to assume, he came into contact with Thomas Smallwood. When his sale to traders disrupted his life, Bell rebounded in 1847 by purchasing his freedom for a total of $1,630, part of which a local white nonabolitionist merchant named Thomas Blagden provided. Later that same year Bell's wife, their children, and two grandchildren faced sale south. On the basis of a former master's will, they had been free for a number of years. But, despite Bell's engagement of Joseph H. Bradley as counsel in their behalf, the master's widow successfully challenged the will and prepared to sell all eleven to the highest bidder. Arranging to have them shipped aboard the *Pearl* was Daniel Bell's desperate attempt to avoid losing them.[3]

The plight of the Edmonson family was similar to that of the Bells, as well as to that of the Carters. The Edmonsons, however, became more prominent

---

3. *True Wesleyan*, 23 September 1848 (quotation) and Horace Mann, *Slavery: Letters and Speeches* (1851; reprint, New York: Burt Franklin, 1969), 116–7.

Amelia "Millie" Edmonson (c.1779–?)
was an enslaved woman married to a free
black man named Paul Edmonson. Six of
her fourteen children sailed on the *Pearl.*
John H. Paynter, *Fugitives of the Pearl*
(Washington, D.C.: Associated Publishers, 1930), opposite p. 38.

than these other families as a result of their association with Henry Ward
Beecher, a leading northern evangelist, and Beecher's soon-to-be-famous sister, Harriet Beecher Stowe. Paul Edmonson, seventy years old in 1848, was
born in Montgomery County, Maryland, eighteen miles from Washington.
Manumitted by his master at the advanced age of forty-two, Edmonson "by
industry, economy and thrift . . . acquired a comfortable little homestead of
40 acres" near his birthplace. His enslaved wife, Amelia, lived with him and
sewed for her legally incompetent mistress, Rebecca Culver.[4]

4. The discussion in this and the following paragraph is based on: *True Wesleyan,* 23 September 1848 (quotation); *PF,* 4 January 1849; Harriet Beecher Stowe, *The Edmonson Family,
and the Capture of the Schooner "Pearl"* (Cincinnati: American Reform Tract and Book Society,
1856); John H. Paynter, *Fugitives of the "Pearl"* (1930; reprint, New York: AMS Press, 1971),
35; See also: Catherine M. Hanchett, "'What Sort of People & Families . . .': The Edmondson
Sisters," *Afro-Americans in New York Life and History* 6 (July 1982): 21–37, and John H. Paynter, "The Fugitives of the *Pearl,*" *Journal of Negro History* 1 (July 1916): 243–64. Paynter was
a descendent of the Edmonsons. I believe that the Edmonsons' actions rather than their com-
plexions led white abolitionists to praise them. The spelling of their surname varies among *Edmonson, Edmondson,* and other forms.

The Edmonsons had fourteen living children in 1848, all of whom had inherited Amelia's unfree status. Light-complexioned and attractive, they gained renown among antislavery activists because they had "the impulses of manhood and freedom gushing through they veins." An elder son named Hamilton failed in an escape attempt in 1833 and, in response, his master sold him south to New Orleans. Five Edmonson sisters, with the help of their husbands, purchased their freedom and enjoyed "comfortable circumstances" in Washington. The two youngest children lived with their parents. The remaining four brothers—one of whom was coachman for Secretary of the Treasury Robert J. Walker and another of whom worked for subversive community member Bradley—fearing sale south, joined the Bells on the *Pearl*. So did two Edmondson sisters, Mary and Emily. Like the Bells and others on board, all six failed in their quest for freedom.

As the would-be escapees and their would-be rescuers marched from the steamboat wharf along Pennsylvania Avenue toward the jail, a mob lined the street and singled out Drayton and Sayres for special condemnation. Drayton recalled that as the procession passed Gannon's slave market, his guards protected him from James Gannon, who rushed at him with a knife. There were cries of "lynch them! lynch them! the d—n villains!" By the time the procession reached the United States Hotel, Williams, fearing that the threats would be carried out, procured a hack to transport the two supposed ringleaders the rest of the way. The mob followed and soon surrounded the jail. Jacob Bigelow reported to the *Boston Daily Whig* that there he heard "the most bitter imprecations against the abolitionists and the abolition paper (National Era) of the District."[5]

The office of this newspaper, aside from the person of Joshua R. Giddings, was the most prominent embodiment of northern abolitionism in the capital city. Giddings received his share of written, verbal, and physical threats during the days following the recapture of the *Pearl* fugitives. But it was chiefly toward the *Era* building that the mob hurled its anger during the next three nights. The two-story brick structure, located directly across Seventh Street from the United States Patent Office, presented a tempting target to the young men and boys who gathered. It was the home of a busy publishing enterprise during the day. There were four clerks on the first floor. Print-

5. Harrold, "*Pearl* Affair," 143–4.

ers Martin Buell and William Blanchard had their office in the front portion of the second story and Gamaliel Bailey had his small editorial office in the rear. Two black pressmen worked in a contiguous building.[6]

The building was vacant at ten o'clock that Tuesday evening when several hundred people approached it. Amid shouting and threats, some of them threw stones through its windows and smashed at least one of its doors before Captain Goddard, a detachment of the city's Auxiliary Guard, and a drenching rainstorm intervened to halt the destruction. The following night a much larger crowd gathered, together with some local leaders who hoped to "prevent the city from being disgraced."[7]

From the steps of the Patent Office, Walter Lenox of the Board of Aldermen, local attorney Daniel Ratcliffe—who had ties to the subversives—District Attorney Philip Barton Key called on everyone to go home and await further developments before acting. The mob shouted them down, demanding that the *Era* office be torn down "Now! Now! Now!" Finally Ratcliffe negotiated a compromise in which a group of fifty, including himself, would call on Bailey at his home, which—the Washington correspondent of the *New York Herald* wittily observed—was only "a stone's throw from the Patent Office." The delegation aimed to convince Bailey to remove his press from the city in order to keep the peace.

When the delegation arrived at his door, Bailey, who had dealt with mobs in Cincinnati, greeted it politely. But he told Ratcliffe and the others that he would rather die than surrender his rights as a "representative of a free press." After receiving this message, the mob once again marched on the *Era* building. A stone went through a window, a brick hit a door, and someone yelled, "Fire it!" A block away, Bailey's friends rushed into his house, took his six children from their beds, and escorted the entire family to safety. Meanwhile Goddard, the Guard, and a number of specially deputized citizens once again saved the *Era* building.

The following evening President James K. Polk, aware that deteriorating

6. Lewis Tappan to Joshua Leavitt, 28 February 1847, in *E*, 10 March 1847; *Washington Saturday News*, 22 April 1848. On the composition of the mob see Harrold, *"Pearl* Affair," 146–7.

7. The discussion in this and the following paragraphs is based on Harrold, *"Pearl* Affair," 145–60.

conditions in Washington could imperil the Union, appealed to government clerks to act as "conservators of law and order." They joined between seventy-five and one hundred law-enforcement officers from Washington and Georgetown in a show of force that overawed the regathering mob. In response a group of about two hundred Marylanders and Virginians, who had been turned away from the office, made another visit to the Baileys' house. There, with the help of Margaret Bailey and Ratcliffe, Gamaliel Bailey, by denying that he was involved in the escape attempt, persuaded the men to depart peacefully and the riot ended.

Among the anti-abolition urban riots that marked the decades preceding the Civil War, this one in Washington was exceptional in several respects. It came later than those in northern and northwestern cities. It produced little property damage and no injuries. Most remarkably it involved no reported assaults on African Americans or their property. In this the 1848 riot contrasted with Washington's Snow Riot of 1836.

Several factors explain these differences. The city's southern location and the extraordinary impact of a massive escape attempt account for the late date. The minimal damage inflicted is attributable to Washington's "gentlemen of property and standing," who, fearing sectional repercussions, acted to quell the disturbance rather than to encourage it, as white elites sometimes did in northern cities. There were no assaults on African Americans because, while northern white mobs reacted against growing black populations, the Washington mob reacted against an attempt by part of the local black population to leave. Also, while northern urban whites often accused their local power structure of favoritism toward blacks, proslavery whites in Washington were confident that the *Pearl* escapees would be thoroughly punished within the law.[8]

8. Leonard L. Richards, *"Gentlemen of Property and Standing": Anti-Abolitionist Mobs in Jacksonian America* (New York: Oxford University Press, 1970); David Grimsted, *American Mobbing, 1828–1861: Toward Civil War* (New York: Oxford University Press, 1998), esp. viii–32. Grimsted establishes that southern antiabolitionist mobs tended to be more violent toward persons, while northern mobs tended to destroy property. Jonathan Messerli in his biography of Horace Mann claims that the crowd that surrounded the *Pearl* captives later "roamed the streets, beating up hapless blacks who happened to be in their way." But the letter Messerli cites fails to support this claim. See Messerli, *Horace Mann: A Biography* (New York: Knopf, 1972), 464; Mann to Mary Mann, 18 April 1848, Horace Mann Papers, Massachusetts Historical Society, Boston.

What proslavery whites in Washington—from members of Congress to the illiterate day laborers who composed the mob—feared most was not African Americans *per se*. Instead they suspected that the white portion of the city's antislavery community would escape retribution and would continue to cooperate with blacks to subvert slavery in the Chesapeake. Slavery's defenders knew that antislavery members of Congress and local antislavery journalists had been friends of Charles T. Torrey and had helped slaves to escape. In early 1845 Edward Junius Black of Georgia had denounced Joshua R. Giddings on the floor of the House of Representatives as "a co-laborer of Torrey, the thief." Black threatened to knock the large and formidable Giddings down. A few months later Joseph Evans Snodgrass confided to Samuel M. Janney that he faced charges of being "an 'agent of Torrey's friends.'" As the *Pearl* drama unfolded, the *New York Herald*'s Washington correspondent reported that "for some years, slave property has become very unsafe in this quarter, and the presence of several abolitionists in Congress, has encouraged the colored population of Washington to a systematic co-operation with the abolitionists of the North . . . for the gradual elopement of the slaves of this District."[9]

Therefore, when southern congressmen and newspaper correspondents learned of the *Pearl* escape attempt, they assumed that white abolitionists had orchestrated it. Washington's *Daily Union* contended that "many white persons were cognizant of and assisted the adventurers." The *Herald*'s correspondent asserted that "the abolitionists may be safely charged with the transaction," and that "suspicion attaches to several." He described two unnamed individuals in a manner to suggest that he meant Chaplin and Snodgrass. Others in Washington centered their suspicions on Gamaliel Bailey and his employees. "Many persons," reported the *Washington Saturday News*, "insinuated . . . that the conductors of the National Era . . . were cognizant of this movement of the slaves, and had, directly or indirectly, aided them in making their escape."[10]

9. *AS*, 14 February 1845 (first quotation); Snodgrass to Janney, 23 June 1845, Samuel M. Janney Papers, Friends Historical Library, Swarthmore College (second quotation); Washington Correspondence, 17 April 1848, in *NYH*, 19 April 1848 (third quotation).

10. *Daily Union*, 19 April 1848 (first quotation); Washington Correspondence, 17 April 1848, in *NYH*, 18 April 1848 (second quotation); *Washington Saturday News*, 22 April 1848 (third quotation).

Years earlier Torrey had called for driving slavery from the Potomac by making human property insecure. Now slavery's defenders charged that this was the purpose of the *Pearl* venture. Congressman William T. Haskell of Tennessee insisted that, having failed to convince Congress to take action, the abolitionists "were now . . . attempting to abolish slavery in this District by inciting the negroes to leave their masters." Henry Foote, a Democratic senator from Mississippi, asserted that "individuals have resolved . . . to remove by any means whatever all the slaves now in this District, so that those who will have been in the habit of retaining slaves . . . will be discouraged from bringing others here . . . and . . . then, in this covert and insidious manner, the abolition of slavery in the District of Columbia may be accomplished."[11]

Historians characterize such charges of cooperation between white northern abolitionists and enslaved African Americans as proslavery propaganda at best and southern white paranoia at worst. Indeed, those in Washington who suspected white involvement in planning the *Pearl* escape attempt could not prove their case in court.[12] In part this was because they were hamstrung by a ban on black testimony against whites. It was also because Drayton refused to implicate other whites. Despite physical threats and offers of rewards, he never went beyond his initial vague statement that "he was in the employ of abolitionists." Soon he retracted this remark, maintaining instead that, while he had been paid by others to take the slaves and had experience helping slaves escape from Washington, "he had no connection with persons called abolitionists."[13]

As Drayton's trial began in July, his defense team, led by Congressman Horace Mann of Massachusetts, maintained that Daniel Bell himself had

11. *CG,* 30 Cong., 1 sess., 653 (first quotation), *Appendix,* 501–2 (second quotation).

12. See for example: David Brion Davis, *Slave Power Conspiracy and the Paranoid Style* (Baton Rouge: Louisiana State University Press, 1961), 37–50; Steven A. Channing, *Crisis of Fear in South Carolina* (New York: Norton, 1974), 77–8; William L. Barney, *The Road to Secession: A New Perspective on the Old South* (New York: Praeger, 1972), 151–60, 219–20. For a recent exception to this point of view, see Merton L. Dillon, *Slavery Attacked: Southern Slaves and Their Allies, 1619–1865* (Baton Rouge: Louisiana State University Press, 1990), 201–23.

13. *NYH,* 19 April 1848 (first quotation); Daniel Drayton, *Personal Memoirs of Daniel Drayton* (New York: Bela Marsh, 1855), 39 (second quotation). Thomas Orme testified at Drayton's trial that Drayton had offered to name the "principals" in planning the escape only if the slaveholders would let him go. See *NE,* 10 August 1848.

contacted Drayton through a black man in Philadelphia to transport the threatened members of his family northward. All of the other *Pearl* fugitives, the defense contended, had spontaneously decided to escape the day that the *Pearl* departed Washington! Because Drayton had allowed neither Sayres nor English to meet his employers, no qualified witness could contradict this account.[14]

Meanwhile those members of Washington's antislavery community who came under suspicion of involvement in the *Pearl* escape attempt refused to implicate themselves or others. Under intense questioning by John Gayle of Alabama in the House of Representatives, Giddings upheld the right of slaves to escape, while agreeing that it was legally—if not morally—a crime in the District of Columbia to help them. Unlike the radical political abolitionists, Giddings pledged that "where legal constitutional laws of the land enforce penalties on such actions, they are to be obeyed." He denied having seen, heard, or known Drayton or Sayres prior to the escape attempt.[15]

In the Senate, John P. Hale of New Hampshire—an ally of Giddings, a close friend of Bailey, and on his way into the Free Soil party—reacted similarly to charges that he too was involved with the *Pearl*. He could not have been more explicit when he said, "Once and for all, I utterly deny, either by counsel, by silence or by speech, or any other way or manner, having any knowledge, cognizance, or suspicion of what was done, or might be done, until I heard of this occurrence as the other Senators have heard of it."[16]

Bailey went to great lengths to insist that neither he nor anyone associated with the *National Era* had the slightest connection with the *Pearl*. Since his years in Cincinnati, he had been well aware of the vulnerability of abolitionists on the South's border. He was the leading exponent of the argument that illegal, clandestine antislavery activities were not worth the negative publicity they could generate. Throughout the 1840s he criticized those who, like Torrey, undertook the rescue of slaves. In hope of protecting the *National Era* office from further mob violence, he published a handbill "denying the absurd

14. *NYH,* 20 April 1848; Drayton, *Memoirs,* 23–8, 36–9, 46, 63–4, 91, 94; Mann, *Slavery,* 116–7.

15. *CG,* 30 Cong., 1 sess., 654–5.

16. *CG,* 30th Cong., 1 sess., *Appendix,* 502–3. See also Richard H. Sewell, *John P. Hale and the Politics of Abolition* (Cambridge, Mass.: Harvard University Press, 1965).

rumor that myself or any person connected with my office, had anything to do with the abduction of slaves on the *Pearl*." Maintaining his public commitment to peaceful abolition through moral suasion and political action, Bailey denied that he would engage in "illegal measures" or "take part in any movement which would involve strategy or trickery of any kind."[17]

Yet Bailey knew more about the *Pearl* enterprise than he publicly acknowledged. So did Giddings. It is likely that Hale, Horace Mann, and other antislavery whites in Washington did as well. As members of an interracial subversive community, they had knowledge of abolitionist activities they might not approve, but which they could not publicly denounce without hurting the cause and betraying the community. Consequently they shielded from the legally constituted authorities those who undertook dangerous and illegal actions against slavery.[18]

The *Pearl* had come to Washington a few weeks after the European revolutions of 1848. News of these popular uprisings inspired celebration in the city and unintentionally ironic rhetoric praising the advance of republicanism over monarchy. Senator Foote, for example, chose strikingly poor words for a speech delivered in a slaveholding city when he proclaimed, "that the age of tyrants and slavery was rapidly drawing to a close . . . and the recognition in all countries of the great principles of popular sovereignty, equality and brotherhood was at the moment visibly commencing." Foote meant *white* freedom and equality. But antislavery subversives in Washington maintained that the fugitives had spontaneously responded to his and similar speeches. Like the claim that most of the fugitives had taken advantage of Daniel Bell's arrangement with Drayton, this scenario suggested that there had been little advance planning for the escape attempt.[19]

17. *National Intelligencer,* 20 April 1848 (first quotation); *NE,* 27 April 1848 (second quotation). Bailey's outlook: *Philanthropist,* 22 September & 31 October 1841, 6 April 1842; *AP,* 8 January 1845; Stanley Harrold, *The Abolitionists and the South, 1831–1861* (Lexington: University Press of Kentucky, 1995), 80–1.

18. Years later former Republican Vice President of the United States Henry Wilson noted that "little authentic information of the origin of that attempted escape . . . has ever been made public." See Wilson, *History of the Rise and Fall of the Slave Power in America,* 3d ed., 3 vols. (Boston: James R. Osgood, 1876), 2:91.

19. Drayton, *Memoirs,* 27 (quotation); *L,* 21 April 28, 1848; Correspondence of the *New York Tribune,* 29 July [1848], in *PF,* 10 August 1848; [Samuel Gridley Howe], *Slavery at Washington, Narrative of the Heroic Adventures of Drayton, an American Trader* (London: Ward,

In contrast, slaveholders insisted more persuasively that only considerable planning, involving white antislavery leaders as well as blacks, could have produced the massive exodus. "There is no doubt that the matter has been under consideration for some time," reported the *Herald*'s correspondent. "Does he suppose," Foote inquired of Hale, "that this occurrence could have taken place without extensive countenance and aid from men of standing in this District, whether members of Congress or not?" In response Hale conceded that he had "no doubt that those persons could not have got away without some aid."[20]

In fact Hale must have known that Chaplin was the central secret organizer of the escape attempt and that other abolitionists were shielding him from prosecution. In mid-March Chaplin indicated in a letter published in the *Albany Patriot* that he had for months been working with Daniel Bell to protect Bell's family from sale. Then, on March 25, in an extraordinary private letter to Gerrit Smith, Chaplin stated that he had requested someone living in Philadelphia to charter in his behalf "a vessel" that could accommodate a large number of escapees. In this letter, written three weeks before the *Pearl* sailed, a worried Chaplin informed Smith, "The number of persons here, who are anxious to imigrate [*sic*], is increasing on my hands daily. I believe there are no less than 75 now importunate for a passage." Chaplin alluded to the Edmonson brothers and sisters, named "Mrs. Madison's *girl* Helen Steward," and reported that Luke and Sarah Carter were harboring some fugitives in anticipation of the escape attempt. Chaplin had, a month earlier, discussed the undertaking with Drayton in Washington and the two men met again in April after the *Pearl* had docked. The night the vessel sailed with its hopeful passengers, Chaplin saw it off.[21]

Within minutes of that departure Chaplin informed other antislavery whites of his efforts. Among them were the Hutchinson family troop of antislavery minstrels that had been performing in Washington, and *Bailey*.

[1848]), 9. A variation is that Daniel Bell alone planned the *Pearl* escape with Drayton, and then, at the last minute, all the other passengers "begged" to join the Bell family. See Stowe, *Edmonson Family,* 14–6.

20. Washington Correspondence, 17 April 1848, in *NYH,* 19 April 1848 (first quotation); *CG,* 30 Cong., 1 sess., *Appendix,* 503 (second & third quotations).

21. W. L. C. to Pat, n.d., in *AP,* 22 March 1848; Chaplin to Smith, 25 March 1848, GSP (quotations); Drayton, *Memoirs,* 24–5, 28; *Daily Union,* 19 April 1848.

Shortly after the *Pearl* sailed, Chaplin, in company with Bailey, visited the Hutchinsons in their rooms at the National Hotel. According to John W. Hutchinson, Chaplin told the family in Bailey's presence, "'I wish to impart to you what no other people know. I know it will be safe for you are abolitionists. I have chartered a vessel and have offered to take a number of slaves away . . . and I saw them sail down the Potomac.'"[22]

Later that night Chaplin visited Giddings who, looking back from the vantage point of the Civil War years, recalled that he "was sitting in his rooms when a friend called to inform him that . . . [a] schooner . . . had sailed with some eighty slaves on board, bound for the North." Giddings remembered that this was the first he had known of the *Pearl* scheme and that he had "at once pronounced the plan ill-advised."[23] There is no reason to doubt his word. But like Bailey—the extent of whose nocturnal travels with Chaplin remains a mystery—Giddings had come to know considerably more about the *Pearl* escape attempt than he publicly revealed. Community solidarity drove both the congressman and the editor into the deceptive behavior they preferred to avoid.

Solidarity and antislavery strategy also required mobilization in behalf of the recaptured *Pearl* fugitives and their erstwhile rescuers. Black residents gathered in the streets and antislavery whites cooperated in providing help to

22. There are two versions of Hutchinson's account, both of which are based on the same lost diary. The versions are: "Escape of Seventy-seven Slaves. From John W. Hutchinson of Lynn, Mass.," n.d., typescript, Wilbur H. Siebert Papers, Ohio Historical Society, Columbus; and John Wallace Hutchinson, *Story of the Hutchinsons (Tribe of Jesse)*, Charles E. Mann, ed., 2 vols. (Boston: Lee and Sheppard, 1896), 1:237. There are significant differences in phrasing between the two accounts. Both are inaccurate concerning the date and the day of the week. In the typed script Hutchinson misnames Bailey's companion as "Wilson." The book correctly identifies Chaplin as his companion. There seem to be anachronisms in both accounts: the story, associated with later accounts, of slaves begging to be taken on the *Pearl* is included, but in contradiction to Chaplin's contemporary indication of prior planning. Hutchinson also says there were seventy-seven slaves on board, although that number was not clear until after the capture of the *Pearl*.

23. Joshua R. Giddings, *A History of the Rebellion: Its Authors and Causes* (New York: Follet, Foster, and Co., 1864), 272–3. Giddings's biographer believes that Giddings had earlier knowledge of the escape plan and maintains that Giddings approved of it. See James Brewer Stewart, *Joshua R. Giddings and the Tactics of Radical Politics* (Cleveland: Case-Western Reserve University Press, 1970), 152.

the fugitives and their families. Extending legal counsel to Drayton and Sayres and raising funds to ransom African Americans in imminent danger of sale south were benevolent activities that had wide appeal among opponents of slavery who would not themselves engage in illegal clandestine actions. By providing aid to the would-be escapees and their abettors, individuals could embrace them and challenge slavery without violating the law. Meanwhile efforts in behalf of the *Pearl* captives served to further polarize public opinion, draw in local sympathizers to the antislavery community, attract northern support, and produce dramatic confrontations with a proslavery power-structure.

Limited as they were by the city's ten p.m. curfew, local African Americans showed their sympathy for those who had sailed on the *Pearl*. Raucous crowds of "cursing, and threatening, and blaspheming" whites dominated the route traversed by the captives from the wharf to the jail. But Edward S. Hamlin reported that there were also "several small collections of blacks" with "tears rolling down many cheeks." During the following days, the white crowd that surrounded the city jail received more publicity, the proslavery correspondent of the *New York Herald* noting that there was also "a crowd of blacks." Throughout the crisis local African Americans continued publicly to demonstrate their concern for the *Pearl* fugitives.[24]

In each instance these African Americans, some of whom were relatives of the captives, drew encouragement from antislavery whites who shared their concern and who in turn welcomed the black presence as they engaged angry proslavery whites. At no point was this interracial relationship clearer than when Giddings, Hamlin, and David A. Hall went to the jail on Wednesday, April 19, to offer their services as lawyers to the three white prisoners *and* to symbolically embrace the *Pearl* fugitives.

On the previous morning, as the House of Representatives convened, Giddings set the stage for confrontation at the jail. Rising from his seat, he presented a resolution demanding to know on what authority "men, women, and children" were held "without being charged with crime . . . other than an attempt to enjoy that liberty for which our fathers encountered toil, suffering,

24. E. S. H., editorial correspondence, 17 April 1848, in *DTD*, 26 April 1848 (first quotation); *NYH*, 21 April 1848 (second quotation); E. L. S., editorial correspondence, 21 April 1848, in *DTD*, 28 April 1848.

and death itself." This resolution—which had no chance of passage—enraged slavery's defenders because it encouraged slaves to escape and assumed that African Americans had rights.[25]

Therefore, when Giddings and Hamlin went to the jail on Wednesday morning, they knew they risked bodily harm. At the interior rear of this "large three-story stone building" a winding stone staircase rose from administrative offices on the ground floor to reach dimly lit and poorly ventilated cellblocks. The jailor courteously led the two men up the staircase, allowed them to look in on the fugitives, and let them meet with Drayton, Sayres, and English. But the mob, led by slave trader Hope H. Slatter, who had arrived from Baltimore, pressed into the stairway so that Giddings and Hamlin experienced difficulty leaving the building. Giddings, who took pride in his coolheadedness, grew angry when Slatter demanded—without effect—that "'violent hands'" be laid on him. Later Giddings bitterly complained that a congressman could be exposed to harassment "by a miserable mass of moral putridity, called slaveholders and slavebreeders."[26]

Hamlin and Hall faced similar threats that afternoon when they went to the jail for the initial formal examination of the *Pearl* crew. United States Attorney for the District of Columbia Philip Barton Key, who prosecuted the case, advised Hall to leave the jail or face mortal danger. The crisis pushed Hall, who was nominally a colonizationist, toward a more radical position. During the spring and summer of 1848, he redoubled his commitment to freeing people he habitually referred to as "darkies."[27]

25. *CG,* 30 Cong., 1 sess., 641 (quotation), 664.

26. Drayton, *Memoirs,* 43–4 (first quotation); , *CG,* 30 Cong., 1 sess., 664 (second quotation), 671 (third quotation); E. S. H., editorial correspondence, in *DTD,* 26 April 1848, and in *DTD,* 25 April 1848; Giddings, *History of the Rebellion,* 274–5. In his history Giddings recalls that Lawrence Brainerd, a senator from Vermont accompanied him and Hamlin to the jail. No contemporary account indicates that this was the case. On Giddings's pride in his ability to remain calm, see Giddings to Molly, 23 April 1848, JRGP.

27. Drayton, *Memoirs,* 45–6; E. S. H., editorial correspondence, 20 April 1848, in *DTD,* 25 April 1848. Hall reported that he took the case "against the earnest entreaty of some of my friends." See Hall to Charles Francis Adams, 3 May 1848, Charles Francis Adams Papers, Massachusetts Historical Society, Boston. Hall's use of the term "darkies": Ibid. and Hall to William H. Seward, 30 September 1850, WHSP. Hall's expanded efforts: Hall to Salmon P. Chase, 27 June 1848, Salmon P. Chase Papers, Library of Congress; and William L. Chaplin to Gerrit Smith, 11 November 1848, GSP.

But the antislavery community could not prevent the punishment of nearly all of the *Pearl* fugitives. That same Wednesday aggrieved masters had congregated at the jail in the company of numerous newspaper correspondents to identify their disobedient slaves and to begin the process of making examples of them by selling them south. Some of the slaves wept, others stood silent, and several women cast scorn on their tormentors. One domestic servant, who had attempted to flee with her child, rejected a chance to repent and return to her master. When a reporter asked her why she had taken such a risk, she replied, "Have I not the same right to my freedom that you have, and could you have neglected a chance of gaining it, had you been a slave?" Another woman, described as "a fine-looking, intelligent mulatto girl, about seventeen," shook Drayton's and Sayres's hands, "exclaiming, 'God bless you, sirs, you did all you could; it is not your fault that we are not free.'"[28]

It was this gathering that had attracted a "grey-headed," soon-to-be-retired Slatter to come from Baltimore, and he purchased the bulk of the fugitives. At sunset the following Friday, with the business completed, he marched fifty human beings to the Baltimore and Ohio railroad depot at the corner of Second Street and Pennsylvania Avenue for shipment to his slave pen, pending resale south.[29]

Ezra L. Stevens, Congressman John I. Slingerland of Albany, New York, and a crowd of between one hundred and two hundred African Americans reacted in horror to what they observed at the depot. The departing men and boys were "ironed together," their guards appeared to be "the very impersonation of hardened villainy," and several of the women seemed destined for prostitution. Relatives came to bid their wives, husbands, children, or siblings final farewells. A "sobbing" mother aboard the train told her teenage son, "Be a *good* boy, and take care of your little sister,—We shall meet soon in heaven."

28. Washington correspondence, 19 April 1848, in *NYH,* 21 April 1848; E. S. H., editorial correspondence, 20 April 1848, in *DTD,* 25 April 1848; *CG,* 30 Cong., 1 sess., 662; *Boston Transcript,* quoted in *L,* 12 May 1848 (first quotation); [Edward S. Hamlin], editorial correspondence of the *DTD,* quoted in *NS,* 12 April 1848 (second quotation). See also *Liberty Press* (Utica, N.Y.), 25 May 1848.

29. E. L. S., editorial correspondence, 22 April 1848, in *DTD,* 29 April 1848 (quotation); Giddings, *History,* 275; *NYH,* 20 & 21 April 1848; *CG,* 30 Cong., 1 sess., 671; Frederic Bancroft, *Slave-Trading in the Old South* (Baltimore: J. H. Furst, 1931), 373.

A guard knocked from the train a man who insisted that he had free papers for his wife.[30]

More than anything else, what struck Stevens and Slingerland, who was a friend of the Bells, was the insensitivity of Slatter, United States Senate Chaplin Henry Slicer, and others. Slatter was a professing Christian and a family man who rended the families of other Christians. Slicer, a Methodist minister, boarded the train—ostensibly to say farewell to one of his enslaved parishioners—and shook Slatter "heartily by the hand." According to Stevens, Slicer talked with Slatter "in a very light and cheerful manner, and seemed to view the heartrending scene before him, with as little concern as we would look upon so many cattle in the Cleveland market."

Chaplin had for good reason left Washington before this crime against humanity occurred. He left not only because he was a prime suspect in the escape attempt but because his involvement with the oppressed had drained him emotionally. He reported to Gerrit Smith that since the previous winter "by night & day, at all hours they have thronged my room & [I] have listened to their tales of sorrow & outrage till my heart sickened." Yet Chaplin returned to Washington in May to reengage himself in this distressing work.[31]

The Carters, he found, were "great sufferers." They had assisted several of the *Pearl* fugitives prior to its voyage and had "fallen somewhat under suspicion among spies of the slaveholders." Meanwhile John and Peggy Eaton had reached an impasse in their effort to locate and negotiate a purchase of the Carters' children and grandchildren. "How sad & withering to the poor mother's heart!" Chaplin exclaimed. More encouragingly, he renewed his cooperation with Mathew Mathews, who had gone to Alexandria to purchase,

30. The discussion in this and the following paragraph is based on: E. L. S., editorial correspondence, 22 April 1848, in *DTD,* 29 April 1848 (quotations); Correspondence of the *Evening Journal,* 7 May 1848, in *LP,* 25 May 1848; *PF,* 25 May 1848; *HAMPDEN* to Preston King, 25 August 1848, in *PF,* 19 October 1848. On the contradiction between the South's paternalistic image of slavery and the realities of the slave trade see Michael Tadman, *Speculators and Slaves: Masters, Traders, and Slaves in the Old South* (Madison: University of Wisconsin Press, 1996), 9–10; Walter Johnson, *Soul by Soul: Life inside the Antebellum Slave Market* (Cambridge, Mass.: Harvard University Press, 1999), 117–213. Slingerland published a portion of Stevens's letter over his own name in the *Albany Evening Journal.* See *NS,* 12 May 1848.

31. The discussion in this and the following paragraph is based on Chaplin to Smith, 17 May 1848, GSP (quotations).

with Smith's financial assistance, the freedom of his daughter Lavinia. But responding to the capture of the *Pearl* dominated Chaplin's thoughts and time. He felt responsible for the recaptured fugitives—just as Torrey had earlier for those arrested at Bush's stable—and, although he had considerable help from Bigelow, he believed that he alone had the wherewithal to coordinate efforts in their behalf.

The cases Chaplin emphasized in a fund-raising appeal he sent North indicate that these efforts were interracial as well as intersectional. Grace Russell, who was then for sale for about $675 in Richmond, had a free mother in New York City who acted in her behalf and an uncle who pledged three hundred dollars toward her redemption. In Washington Ellen Steward's mother engaged similarly in the effort to manumit her daughter. Chaplin promised—as he had previously in regard to the Carters—that the entire Edmonson family would contribute to raising the estimated $5,800 required to free the two teenage sisters and their four brothers. Chaplin and Bigelow also stressed that Russell, Steward, the Edmonsons, and others who had sailed on the *Pearl* were estimable people with religious and family orientations like those of middle-class white northerners. "The manly attempt to secure one's freedom mankind regard as the highest deed of human virtue. These persons have a strong hold upon our admiration, as they have upon our sympathy," Chaplin insisted.[32]

This cultivated empathy worked particularly well in behalf of several of the Edmonsons. Giddings and Bigelow had met Richard Edmonson, Secretary Walker's coachman, prior to the escape attempt. Years later Giddings, in complacently racialist phraseology, recalled how the young man had impressed him. "His complexion was light," Giddings maintained, "his features were caucasian, his phrenological development bespoke a high order of talent, his language was good and his deportment and bearing gentlemanly." In an appeal in behalf of Mary and Emily Edmonson, Bigelow stressed the degradation that awaited Richard's equally light complexioned sisters. Because of their "rare beauty," Bigelow reported, Slatter "had set a heavy price upon them" expecting that some "southern libertine" would pay dearly for them.[33]

32. Chaplin to [?], 18 May 1848, in *AP*, 24 May 1848.
33. Giddings, *History of the Rebellion*, 279 (first quotation); NORTH to Whig, 28 April 1848, in *AS*, 20 May 1848 (second–fourth quotations); NORTH, correspondence of the Boston Whig, n.d., in *AS*, 20 May 1848. I assume Bigelow is NORTH based on his prior service

Mary Edmonson (c.1830–1853) and Emily Edmonson (c1833–?) were the best known of the *Pearl* fugitives. After gaining their freedom, they attended Oberlin College. Mary died there and Emily returned to Washington to work with Myrtilla Miner at Miner's school. Paynter, *Fugitives of the Pearl*, opposite p. 64.

By June Chaplin's efforts had produced some positive results. That month Snodgrass went to Campbell and Company's Baltimore slave prison—formerly Slatter's—to "receive into freedom" Ellen Steward. By mid-August Richard, Mary, and Emily Edmonson had been brought back to that same prison from New Orleans. According to Edmonson family tradition, the poor health of Richard's wife and children convinced a grandson of fur-trade millionaire John Jacob Astor to pay nine hundred dollars toward freeing him. Bigelow went to Baltimore to execute the transaction and to escort Richard back to Washington. Shortly thereafter Thomas Blagden, who had earlier helped Daniel Bell, redeemed Bell's wife and one of their children for four hundred dollars in anticipation that Chaplin's fund-raising effort would provide reimbursement. At some point Grace Russell gained freedom as well,

---

as Washington correspondent of the *Whig* and internal evidence. Walker had without success tried to prevent Richard's sale south. See William L. Chaplin to [?], 18 May 1848, in *AP*, 24 May 1848.

Price, Birch, & Co. Dealers in Slaves had its slave prison in Alexandria, Virginia. Former owners of the building included the slavetrading firms of Franklin & Armfield and Bruin & Hill. The building was deserted when this photograph was taken during the Civil War. Courtesy of Still Pictures Branch, National Archives.

although two years later her sister Emily, her aunts, and several cousins were sold south.[34]

Chaplin himself arranged the most famous and expensive of the *Pearl* redemptions. Negotiations for freeing Richard Edmonson had preceded his return to Baltimore. But this was not the case in regard to his sisters Mary and Emily. Instead, immediately on their return to Baltimore, Campbell and Company sold them to the firm of Bruin and Hill, which had succeeded Franklin and Armfield as Alexandria's principal slavetrading company. Satis-

34. J. E. S., Correspondence of the Tribune, 20 June 1848, in *NS*, 14 July 1848; Snodgrass to Horace Mann, 26 July 1848, Mann Papers; HAMPDEN to Preston King, 25 August 1848, in *PF*, 19 October 1848; Paynter, "Fugitives of the *Pearl*," 252–4; Stowe, *Key*, 320, 334. On the Russells see: Chadwick, *A Life for Liberty*, 170; [Ezra L. Stevens] to *Democrat*, 9 February 1850, in *Free Democrat and Western Citizen* (Milwaukee), 9 March 1850.

fied that there existed in the South a great demand for attractive young women, Bruin and Hill now demanded $2,250 for the pair.[35]

To raise that daunting sum, Chaplin and Paul Edmonson, whom Harriet Beecher Stowe described as a "venerable-looking black man," traveled to New York City. There they presented the plight of the sisters and other *Pearl* fugitives to Henry Ward Beecher, other prominent New York divines, and Beecher's wealthy Brooklyn congregation. In response Beecher organized a meeting at the Broadway Tabernacle that produced the funds, and Chaplin and Paul Edmonson went to Alexandria on November 7, 1848, to purchase the sisters' freedom. This episode created a bond between the Edmonson and Beecher families as well as between the Beechers and others within Washington's subversive community.

In reference to the manumission of the sisters, Chaplin told Gerrit Smith, "The result of this effort has been most happy upon this city community." But for the great majority of *Pearl* fugitives there were no happy results. Although their families, together with Chaplin, Bigelow, and other community members, continued working on their behalf, most did not return. In June 1848 approximately twenty were still in Washington Jail and their fate is unknown. The same is true of a large percentage of those whom Slatter purchased. Emily Edmondson was still raising money in 1855 in an attempt to redeem a brother who had remained in New Orleans.[36]

The legal defense of Drayton, Sayres, and English had similarly mixed results. Prosecutor Key brought in the U.S. Criminal Court for the District of Columbia forty-one indictments for slave stealing against each of the ac-

---

35. The discussion in this and the following paragraph is based on: Chaplin to Gerrit Smith, 2 & 11 November 1848, GSP; *True Wesleyan,* 9 December 1848; J. C. H. [Joseph C. Hathaway] to Editors, 29 October 1848, in *NS,* 10 November 1848, *Christian Contributor,* quoted in *NS,* 17 November 1848; Stowe, *Key,* 323–4 (quotation); *PF,* 4 January 1849. Chaplin does not mention Paul Edmonson in his account of the trip and Stowe does not mention Chaplin. Based on the sources in this note, I portray Beecher as more actively involved in efforts taken in behalf of the sisters than does Beecher's biographer Paxton Hibben. See Hibben, *Henry Ward Beecher: An American Portrait* (1927; reprint New York: Readers Club, 1942), 10–2, 15. A more recent biography of Beecher does not include this incident. See Clifford Edward Clark, *Henry Ward Beecher: Spokesman for Middle-class America* (Urbana: University of Illinois Press, 1978).

36. Chaplin to Smith, 2 November 1848, GSP (quotation); *Non-Slaveholder* 3 (July 1848): 165; *FDP,* 1 January & 27 July 1855.

cused—one indictment for each of the forty-one masters in the District whose slaves had sailed on the *Pearl*. In addition Key brought against each defendant seventy-four indictments for transporting slaves out of the district. Giddings recruited Hall to defend the three men and simultaneously during that April a group of political abolitionists and antislavery Whigs in Boston organized a defense fund, to which Gerrit Smith immediately pledged five hundred dollars. Although Salmon P. Chase and William H. Seward showed interest in the case, other commitments prevented them from joining the defense. Consequently the Boston committee chose that city's new member of Congress, Horace Mann, to work with Hall. When Hall withdrew in early July, local Washington attorney J. M. Carlisle replaced him.[37]

Since English had not been aware of the purpose of the *Pearl's* voyage and Sayres did not know who had hired Drayton, their cases were uncomplicated. In July, with Daniel Ratcliffe as his attorney, English won a dismissal of the charges against him. After juries that same month acquitted Sayres on two counts of slave stealing—since he did not intend to keep or sell them—he pleaded guilty to having transported the slaves. Key then dropped the remaining slave stealing charges against him. Fined $140 per transporting indictment, Sayres returned to the Washington Jail pending payment of a total of $10,360.[38]

Drayton's case, however, had dramatic potential. Key hoped to use the bay trader's fear of a long prison sentence to force him to name his white collaborators. Testimony leading to an indictment of a prominent abolitionist, particularly one linked to Gerrit Smith, Key believed would curb interference with slavery in the District much more effectively than making an example of Drayton.

Meanwhile those who paid for Drayton's defense had several goals. They wanted to test the legal argument that slavery was unconstitutional within

37. Drayton, *Memoirs,* 61–9; *True Wesleyan,* 23 September 1848; Hall to Charles Francis Adams, 3 May 1848; Messerli, *Mann,* 481; Frederick W. Seward, *William Henry Seward, 1801–1872,* 3 vols. (New York: Derby and Miller, 1891), 72. Wilhelmus Bogart Bryan maintains that Joseph A. Bradley aided Key in the prosecution. See Bryan, *A History of the National Capital,* 2 vols. (New York: MacMillan, 1916), 387. Incomplete manuscript records of the trial are in Case Papers, U.S. v. Drayton, Sayres, and English, RG 21, NA.

38. The discussion in this and the following paragraph is based on: Drayton, *Memoirs,* 25–6, 36, 46, 63–4, 68, 99–100; *DU,* 19 April 1848.

Congress's exclusive jurisdiction. They wanted to make a hero of Drayton. They wanted to keep Drayton quiet concerning Chaplin. Like Torrey before them, they failed to get a hearing for their constitutional viewpoint. Mann, rather than arguing that if slavery were unconstitutional in the District of Columbia it could not be a crime there to help slaves escape, used the same argument in Drayton's behalf, that had won an acquittal for Sayres on the slave stealing charges. If Drayton did not intend to keep the slaves for himself or to sell them for profit, Mann maintained, he should not be found guilty of stealing them.[39]

In contrast the attempt to make a hero of Drayton succeeded, despite reservations that Bailey and Snodgrass expressed concerning his character. Northern abolitionists Samuel Gridley Howe and Richard Hildreth, who served on the Boston committee, wrote flattering accounts of Drayton. Antislavery meetings across the North objected to punishing individuals who acted in behalf of black freedom.[40]

Even more successful was the effort to keep Drayton from implicating Chaplin. While abolitionists—especially radical political abolitionists—despised proslavery laws, they realized that there could be a damaging public reaction to the arrest of one of their colleagues. In addition, a federal indictment of Chaplin would at, the very least, terminate his activities in Washington. So, throughout Drayton's ordeal, the subversives sought ways to keep him quiet. Before the *Pearl* sailed, Chaplin had promised Drayton that if he were arrested abolitionists would provide financial help for his wife and children. One of the reasons Giddings and Hamlin risked danger to go to Washington Jail was to assure Drayton and his accomplices that they would have

39. Constitutional challenge: *NS,* 12 May 1848; Gerrit Smith to Elizur Wright, 1 May 1848, in *NS,* 19 May 1848; Salmon P. Chase to Samuel E. Sewell, 27 May [1848], in Edward G. Bourne et al., eds., "Diary and Correspondence of Salmon P. Chase," *Annual Report of the American Historical Association for the Year 1902,* 2 vols. (Washington: Government Printing Office, 1903), 2:133–4; Joshua P. Blanchard to Gerrit Smith, 9 December 1848, GSP. Mann's defense strategy: Mann, *Slavery,* 88–108.

40. *NE,* 18 May 1848; Snodgrass to Gerrit Smith, 30 June 1848, GSP; Snodgrass to Horace Mann, 26 July 1848, Mann Papers; [Howe], *Slavery at Washington;* Donald Eugene Emerson, *Richard Hildreth* (Baltimore: Johns Hopkins University Press, 1946), 131, 145; MASS, *Seventeenth Annual Report* (Boston: MASS, 1849), 38. Bailey and Snodgrass also questioned Sayres character. Emerson establishes that Hildreth wrote Drayton's *Memoirs.*

legal counsel. In June Hall added to the bargain that at the very least Drayton would not go to the District's penitentiary. "Drayton . . . has kept up a very good courage till now," Hall informed Chase, "but has great terror of being sent to the Penitentiary: he says he can stand anything but that: from that he recoils."[41]

As it turned out, Mann's strategy of questioning the applicability of the larceny charges solved this problem. Juries convicted Drayton on two counts of stealing slaves and he initially received a penitentiary sentence of twenty years. But Mann appealed the verdicts to the Circuit Court and in late November won new trials. During the spring of 1849 two new juries, acting under guidelines established by the Circuit Court, found Drayton not guilty on all of the larceny charges. He then pled guilty to the transportation indictments and, like Sayres before him, received a $10,360 fine, with the same stipulation that he remain in Washington Jail until he paid.[42]

This was a prospect little better than years in a penitentiary and Drayton continued to use Chaplin as leverage to get help from abolitionists. After several years of failed efforts undertaken by Mann, Bailey, and Chase to get a presidential pardon for both Drayton and Sayres, or to raise money to pay their huge fines, Drayton pressed the issue. In February 1851, at a time when Chaplin faced other charges in Washington, Drayton threatened "to turn state's evidence" concerning "Chaplin's connection with the Pearl case." He told Gerrit Smith's associate William R. Smith, who visited him at the jail, that he had "been sorely tried under the inducements held out" by the prosecutor's office. He warned that the abolitionists "must not blame him, if the chains weigh so heavily upon his limbs he should lose his power of endurance and seek that relief which his fellow citizens have not afforded him."[43]

When he received this news, Gerrit Smith wrote to Senator Charles Durkee of Wisconsin pledging his financial resources in behalf of an intensified

41. *Daily Union*, 19 April 1848; [Howe], *Slavery at Washington*, 6; *CG*, 30 Cong., 1 sess., 654; David A. Hall to Charles Francis Adams, 3 May 1848, Adams Papers (quotation). On the District penitentiary see Stephen Dalsheim, "the United States Penitentiary for the District of Columbia, 1826–1862," *RCHS* 53–6 (1959): 135–44.

42. Messerli, *Mann*, 62–87, 494–5, 500–1; Drayton, *Memoirs*, 69–102.

43. Messerli, *Mann*, 501; *NE*, 17 October 1850, 16 October & 6 November 1851; Chase to [Charles Dexter] Cleveland, 10 May 1852, Salmon P. Chase Papers, Historical Society of Pennsylvania, Philadelphia; W. R. Smith to Gerrit Smith, 19 February 1851, GSP (quotations).

campaign to free Drayton and Sayres. Within a year Massachusetts's new Free Soil U.S. Senator Charles Sumner, presented a request for a pardon to President Millard Fillmore. Fillmore responded positively in August 1852. Once free, Drayton and Sayres immediately left Washington to avoid being rearrested on a Virginia warrant in behalf of the Alexandria masters whose slaves had boarded the *Pearl.* Lewis Clephane, the *National Era*'s chief clerk, drove them by carriage through a driving rainstorm to Baltimore where they boarded trains for Philadelphia and Harrisburg. Sayres thereupon dropped out of antislavery circles, while Drayton maintained a limited connection with the movement as a certified hero until his suicide in early 1857.[44]

Aside from what the *Pearl* escape attempt reveals about the secret workings of Washington's subversive community, the incident serves as an example of how that community influenced the course of the sectional conflict. Sympathetic accounts of the slaves' daring strike for freedom, of the pathetic scene at the railroad depot, and of the benevolent effort to preserve the virtue of the Edmonson sisters reached huge audiences in the North. They not only aroused indignation concerning slavery, and especially the slave trade, they embarrassed Henry Slicer and other Washington residents whose commitment to protecting the trade declined as a result.[45]

Because of this impact on northern and local popular opinion, both antislavery and proslavery leaders in Congress realized that, while the slaves and their allies had suffered a tactical defeat, they had won a strategic victory that further weakened slavery in the nation's capital. The escape attempt had also

44. Smith to Giddings, 21 March 1852, letter book copy, GSP; David Donald, *Charles Sumner and the Coming of the Civil War* (New York: Knopf, 1960), 220–2; Drayton, *Memoirs,* 115–9; *Cincinnati Enquirer,* 14 September 1895, clipping in Siebert Papers; Walter C. Clephane, "Lewis Clephane: A Pioneer Washington Republican," *RCHS* 21 (1918): 267–9; *Liberty Party Paper* (Syracuse), quoted in *L,* 24 January 1851; MASS, *Twenty-First Annual Report* (Boston: MASS, 1853), 42–3; A. G. B[eman?] to Editor, 10 September 1855, *FDP,* 14 September 1855; *NE,* 9 July 1857. Drayton was reported to be in poor health early in 1854. See *FDP,* 6 January 1854. For an account of Drayton's last years that portrays him as a dedicated abolitionist, see Kathryn Grover, *The Fugitive's Gibralter: Escaping Slaves and Abolitionism in New Bedford, Massachusetts* (Amherst: University of Massachusetts Press, 2001), 257–60.

45. John I. Slingerland to Slicer, 10 May 1848, in *NS,* 26 May 1848; QUINTEN to *Boston Atlas,* 9 May [1848], in *NS,* 9 June 1848; Constance M. Green, *The Secret City: A History of Race Relations in the Nation's Capital* (Princeton: Princeton University Press, 1967), 45–6.

demonstrated the vulnerability of slave property in Washington, the ineffectiveness of mob action against subversives, and the limited ability of legal authorities to bring them to account.

No one was more aware of the significance of what had happened than Giddings, who led the few antislavery members in pressing the issue on the floor of Congress. According to the staunchly proslavery *Daily Union*, Giddings threw "firebrands" when he contended that blacks had the same right to freedom as whites. Maintaining on April 20 that anyone who interfered with that right "did so at his peril," Giddings declared "the slaves of this District, when they felt the hand of oppression bearing on them, possessed before the universal world and before God himself the right to free themselves by *any means* God has put into their power."[46]

These were extremely provocative words, but not nearly so provocative as the escape attempt itself. In response, Representatives Robert Toombs of Georgia and Abraham W. Venable of North Carolina applauded mob action against Giddings and the *National Era* as a proper reaction to an abolitionist outrage. Representative William T. Haskell of Tennessee charged that "members of this body . . . had been engaged . . . in the deliberate attempt to scatter the seeds of insurrection and insubordination, if not rebellion, among the slaves in this District. . . . for which they ought to swing as high as Haman."[47] If Giddings and his friend Gamaliel Bailey did not themselves aid escaping slaves, slaveholders knew they sustained persons who did. When John G. Palfrey of Massachusetts called in the House of Representatives for an investigation of mob threats to Giddings, and when John P. Hale introduced legislation in the Senate aimed at protecting the *National Era* building, southern leaders could not contain themselves.

In the Senate, John C. Calhoun of South Carolina, the venerable champion of the rights of slaveholders, declared, "The crisis has come!" Describing slave escapes to be "the gravest and most vital of all questions to us and the whole Union," Calhoun interpreted the *Pearl* venture as a northern attack on a southern port. Unless something were done to protect slave property in

46. *Daily Union*, 21 April 1848 (first quotation); *CG*, 30th Cong., 1 sess., 641, 654 (second & third quotations; my italics).

47. *CG*, 30th Cong., 1 sess., 655 (quotation). See also ibid., 652–5, *Appendix*, 502; *L*, 28 April 1848.

Washington and to counteract northern resistance to the Fugitive Slave Act of 1793, he predicted that there would be a "worse" slave revolt than the one that began in the French Caribbean colony of Saint Domingue in 1790 and resulted in the independent black republic of Haiti in 1804. Agreeing with Calhoun, Senator Jefferson Davis of Mississippi asked, "Is this District to be made the field of abolition struggles?" If so, there could be no debate. Rather, Davis, maintained, it was "ground upon which the people of this Union may shed blood." He concluded, "if this is to be made the centre from which civil war is to radiate here let the conflict begin!"[48]

South Carolina's other senator, Andrew P. Butler, joined Calhoun and Davis in linking the *Pearl* to resistance to the Fugitive Slave Act in the North and in predicting civil war. But no one went further than Davis's fellow Mississippian, Foote, who denounced Hale for trying to protect incendiaries from angry slaveholders. Hale, said Foote, aimed to conduct "a sort of civil war . . . in behalf of the liberties of . . . the blacks—the slaves of the District of Columbia," and therefore deserved to be hanged. If Hale ever came to Mississippi, Foote promised to "assist in the operation."[49]

While these southern leaders were sincere in their outrage and broadly accurate in their perception of the tactics employed by Washington's subversive community, their response did their cause little good outside their own section. They had begun to lose northern support in Congress when they insisted on expanding slavery, and their response to the *Pearl* hastened the process. Stephen A. Douglas of Illinois, a champion of sectional compromise, bluntly told the senators from South Carolina and Mississippi that "if they had gone into a caucus with the Senator from New Hampshire [Hale], and . . . devised the best means to manufacture abolitionism and abolition votes in the North, they would have fallen upon precisely the same kind of procedure which they have adopted today."[50]

Although Garrisonian and radical political abolitionists criticized Bailey and Hale for not publicly endorsing the actions of Drayton and Sayres, they

48. *CG,* 30 Cong., 1 sess., *Appendix,* 501 (first & second, fourth–sixth quotations), 505 (third quotation).

49. Ibid., 502 (quotations), 508.

50. Ibid., 506; Leonard L. Richards, *The Slave Power: The Free North and Southern Domination, 1780–1860* (Baton Rouge: Louisiana State University Press, 2000), 134–61.

did take heart in the outcome of the *Pearl* crisis. At the annual meeting of the AASS in May, Garrisonians expressed a hope that other slaves would follow the example of those who had boarded that vessel. A large majority of the delegates became so enthusiastic as to pass resolutions declaring slavery to be unconstitutional in the District of Columbia, even though such an assertion directly contradicted the organization's official position that the Constitution protected slavery.[51]

Meanwhile the interim editor of Hamlin's and Steven's *Daily True Democrat* hoped that the *Pearl* episode would inspire more slave escapes, more northern sympathy for them, and, finally, congressional action to abolish slavery throughout the country. Giddings's hometown newspaper, the *Ashtabula Sentinel,* advised, "Inform the freemen of the North of the character of the institution they are maintaining in the [capital] of this land of *liberty*—show the vile spirit of despotism they are fostering there and the constitutional power they possess by one bold act forever to blot it from existence,—and slavery in the District of Columbia is doomed."[52]

Writing in Rochester, black abolitionist leader Frederick Douglass declared, "Slaves escaping from the Capital of the 'model Republic!' What an idea!—running *from* the Temple of Liberty to be free!" Nothing, he predicted, could cure the shock such a spectacle delivered to slavery. The slaves' boldness, the mob, the "violent" proslavery speeches in Congress, the indomitable, "noble-hearted Giddings, Palfrey, and Hale," Douglass claimed, portended the overthrow of slavery. Like other wavering Garrisonians, Douglass hoped that growing antislavery sentiment would lead the Supreme Court to declare slavery unconstitutional in the District of Columbia.[53]

Chaplin himself regarded the *Pearl* escape attempt to have been as much a strategic victory as slavery's defenders feared. In May he confided to Gerrit Smith that "this attempt of the 77 to 'conquer' their freedom is the grandest event for the cause of anti-slavery that has occurred in years. It is working

51. Abolitionist criticism of Bailey and Hale: *AP,* 26 April & 14 June 1848; *NS,* 5 May 1848; *PF,* 25 May & 1 June 1848; *L,* 5 & 12 May 1848. AASS meeting: *PF,* 18 May 1848.

52. *DTD,* 24 April 1848; *AS,* 29 April 1848 (quotations). Others in and out of Washington hoped the *Pearl* fugitives sold south would carry the seeds of mass escape with them. See correspondence of the *Boston Whig,* quoted in *L,* 28 April 1848; *PF,* 18 & 25 May 1848.

53. *NS,* May 5, 1848.

great good here & elsewhere. If our Abolitionists will take hold we can drive slavery out of this District at once!"[54]

Yet no abolitionist emerged from the *Pearl* crisis more optimistic than Giddings. He knew that the recent events in Washington had a reciprocal relationship with the rising Free Soil party that he was helping to organize. The *Pearl*, he believed, encouraged the emergence of the new party and strengthened antislavery congressmen. "We have gained much by the contest," he informed his wife. "It has thrown forward the cause of freedom and we are more firm than we were before."[55]

In response to the proslavery diatribes against him and the *Pearl*, Giddings on April 25 once again challenged his adversaries. As reported in the *Congressional Globe*, he observed on the floor of the House of Representatives that "the slave power had once reigned triumphant here. Not so at this time; we had regained the freedom of debate and it would never again be surrendered. Gentlemen in making such threats appeared to forget they were not now on their plantations, exercising their petty tyranny over slaves." When warned that slaves might hear these words, Giddings reportedly said, "he would not hesitate from this forum to tell the truth to all who heard him, even if slaves were listening to him. He would open their minds to understand the oppression that weighed down their intellects and shut out the knowledge and truth from their comprehension."[56] As Giddings well knew, many slaves in Washington and its vicinity already resisted oppression. The real value of his words lay in expressing in the United States Congress his solidarity with them.

54. Chaplin to Smith, 17 May 1848, GSP.
55. Giddings to Laura W. Giddings, 20 April 1848, JRGP.
56. *CG*, 30 Cong., 1 sess., 670–3. On Giddings and the Free Soil party see Stewart, *Giddings*, 141–66.

SIX

Subversives in 1850:
Persistence, Change, Limits

O N Saturday, August 10, 1850, the *National Intelligencer* reported
that Captain Goddard and a detachment of the Washington Guard
had the previous Thursday night arrested William L. Chaplin following a ferocious battle. The Guard had apprehended Chaplin at the District of Columbia-Maryland boundary as he attempted to transport two escaping slaves northward. The slaves, Allen and Garland, were body servants,
respectively, of two prominent congressmen from Georgia, Alexander H.
Stephens and Robert Toombs. Relying on a well-tested strategy, the escapees
had left their masters in mid-July and taken refuge among black friends in
Washington. Then Chaplin went to Pennsylvania—as had Charles T. Torrey
before him—to hire an enclosed carriage for a clandestine dash to the North.[1]

When Chaplin returned with the carriage to Washington, Goddard was
ready for him. Well aware of Chaplin's activities among slaves and encouraged by Stephens's and Toombs's offer of five hundred dollar rewards for the
capture of their slaves, Goddard monitored the movements of Chaplin and
his free black associate, Warner Harris. So the captain knew in advance of
Chaplin's intention to drive the two-horse carriage north with Allen and
Garland inside. With four officers and at least two civilian "slave-catchers,"

---

1. The discussion in this and the following paragraphs is based on: *L*, 16 August 1850;
Gerrit Smith to William H. Seward, 11 August 1850, letter book copy, GSP; *NYDT*, 10, 13 &
19 August 1850; *National Intelligencer*, quoted in *NE*, 15 August 1850 (quotations); *The Case
of William L. Chaplin* (Boston: Chaplin Committee, 1851), 20–6.

he prepared an ambush where several routes out of the city joined the main northbound road and where an incline forced the carriage's horses to slow their pace.

As Goddard halted the vehicle by jamming a fence rail through the spokes of a rear wheel, his colleagues stormed it. According to the police, Chaplin "fired a pistol ball" at the head of the man who attempted to "seize the reins" and barely missed his target. Thereupon, the *Intelligencer* maintained, "the runaways in the carriage having each a revolver, fired several times at the officers, who also fired at the Negroes." The newspaper reported that "not less than twenty-seven shots were fired, and the fight continued for five or six minutes."

Chaplin, who later denied being armed or knowing that Allen and Garland carried weapons, suffered a number of painful minor injuries as several of the arresting group threw him to the ground during a "desperate struggle." Allen might have been killed had his watch not kept a bullet from penetrating his body, and Garland—who fled the scene—received a bullet wound to his hand. One or two of Goddard's men had minor wounds and the carriage was "riddled" with bullet holes. Shortly after the battle Goddard had Chaplin and Allen placed in the city jail where Garland, who gave himself up, and Harris, who was arrested, soon joined them.[2]

This frightening engagement brought to a close Chaplin's six-year involvement in Washington's subversive community. Since his efforts had continued those of Smallwood and Torrey, his departure had significant repercussions, particularly regarding the role of radical political abolitionists in Washington. The reduction of that role, the creation in 1848 of the Free Soil party, and Congress's passage of the Compromise of 1850 helped reshape the character of the community and the context within which it functioned.

The Free Soil party, representing a major northern antislavery effort based on that section's economic and political self-interest, changed the political circumstances of the community's white members. The new party also further polarized sectional relations. In contrast the Compromise, which passed

2. Harris: William Blanchard to Lewis Tappan, 31 August 1851, AMAA; *NS*, 5 September 1850. Two weeks later the *L* reported that Garland had a shoulder wound. See *L*, 30 August 1850. Chaplin's lawyer Charles H. Pitts later conceded that the "weight of evidence" was against Chaplin. See Pitts to Lewis Tappan, 18 November 1850, GSP.

within six weeks of Chaplin's arrest, aimed to quell sectional disputes over slavery. It also contained two provisions that had particular relevancy to the community's place in the broader antislavery movement. First, there was legislation concerning the slave trade in the District of Columbia that modified the form, if not the substance, of this threat to black families. Second, there was a new fugitive slave law that, by encouraging masters more vigorously to pursue escapees in the North, began a new era in the antislavery struggle. The circumstances that led to Chaplin's arrest, in association with the new party and the compromise measures, redirected and limited Washington's antislavery community.

The story begins with the continued impact of the *Pearl* escape attempt on the community and its activities. As Chaplin, Giddings, and John C. Calhoun understood, the *Pearl* struck a strategic blow against slavery in Washington and the Chesapeake. It provided slaveholders with a graphic example of increasing cooperation among African Americans and antislavery whites. Yet, by frightening masters, the *Pearl* episode also increased the day-to-day suffering of local black families. In conjunction with abolitionist-inspired proposals that Congress abolish slavery and the slave trade in the District, it encouraged slaveholders to sell their slaves south while they still could.

Driven by southwestern demand, the two principal slavetrading firms in Washington, as well as several smaller ones in that city, and Bruin and Hill in Alexandria continued to promise to pay the highest prices for slaves. They thereby provided masters with a profitable way of dealing with the local instability of slave property. The lure of profits also led to increased kidnappings of free blacks. As Congress considered curtailing the trade during 1849 and 1850, sales in Washington and its vicinity surged. Chaplin maintained that during the spring of 1850 "scarcely a day passed that gangs of chained slaves did not pass through the city."[3]

3. Correspondence of the *Express,* in *New York Evening Post,* 12 August 1850; *Liberty Press* (Utica, N.Y.), 25 May 1848; *NE,* 4 January & 3 May 1849, 17 October 1850; *PF,* 9 September 1850; Fredrika Bremer, *The Homes of the New World: Impressions of America* (London: A. Hall, Virtue, 1853), 492–3; Constance M. Green, *The Secret City: A History of Race Relations in the Nation's Capital* (Princeton: Princeton University Press, 1967), 46; *NASS,* 16 January 1851 (quotation); *L,* 16 August 1850; *NYDT,* 10, 13, 24, & 29 August 1850. See also Carol Wilson, *Freedom at Risk: The Kidnapping of Free Blacks in America, 1780–1865* (Lexington: University Press of Kentucky, 1994).

As black families faced increasingly precarious circumstances, interracial bonds within the city's subversive community tightened, more slaves escaped, and less dangerous efforts to free those threatened with sale south multiplied. In other words, the *Pearl* escape attempt, reactions of masters to it, and the sectional crisis of the late 1840s enhanced a practical local abolitionism. African Americans, attempting to free themselves or their loved ones, resorted to the courts, to fund raising, or to escape, all of which led them to approach their relatively affluent and powerful white allies. "Those here who feel for the bondsmen are called upon almost every hour in the day by some of these unfortunate victims of the lash for aid to prevent a father, a mother, a son, brother, daughter, or sister from being sold to the Southern trader," observed Ezra L. Stevens in November 1849.[4]

In response to such requests, white antislavery activists in Washington continued to track slave sales, to attend slave auctions, to visit slave pens, and to investigate kidnappings. They published what they observed in mass circulation northern dailies as well as in abolitionist weeklies. Shortly after the sale south of most of the *Pearl* fugitives, Stevens observed the auction of a woman and found several "flesh traders . . . examining her minutely." A year later a correspondent of the *New York Tribune* reported that masters continued to lodge in the city jail slaves, including pregnant women, intended for sale south. "You, at the free North, know little of the miseries endured by the colored people here," the correspondent advised readers. Yet, as taxpayers, he reminded them, they helped maintain the jail and therefore shared responsibility for inflicting those miseries.[5]

African Americans readily identified Stevens and other antislavery whites who could be relied on to provide assistance. As Chaplin noted, blacks actively engaged antislavery whites who enjoyed access to civil institutions, wealth, and physical mobility. Thomas Ducket, for example, who, because of his involvement with the *Pearl*, had been sold south to Louisiana, was quite familiar with Jacob Bigelow, Joshua R. Giddings, Chaplin, and Gamaliel Bailey. Ducket wrote to Bigelow for help in February 1850, "Mr. Bigelow i hope

4. E. L. S. to Ed., 7 November 1849, in *AS*, 17 November 1849.

5. E. L. S., editorial correspondence, 10 May 1848, in *DTD*, 16 May 1848 (first quotation); Correspondence of the New York Tribune, June 12, 1849, in *PF*, July 5, 1849 (second quotation).

yo will not for[get] me. . . . I hop[e] you will name me to Mr. Geden [Giddings], Mr. Chaplen, Mr. Baly [Bailey] to help me out. . . . I beleve that if [they] would make the les move to it that it cod be den."[6]

Long-term Washington resident David A. Hall also maintained a reputation as a white person who would help African Americans challenge an oppressive status quo. In June 1848 Hall called on Salmon P. Chase to help locate the daughter and son-in-law of an elderly black woman who had called at Hall's Washington law office. The woman feared that the young couple had been kidnapped as they returned to Washington after visiting Illinois. The last she had heard, they were attempting to reach Cincinnati after being threatened in Tennessee. In attempting to locate the couple, Hall revealed a good deal about himself and Chase. He assumed that Chase had contacts among the "coloured people" of Cincinnati and would "cheerfully" seek out information from local African Americans concerning the couple. He assured Chase of the gratitude of "a mother whose affections are human even here, where her race are but chattel."[7]

Hall's cooperation five months later with Chaplin in helping a young woman named Harriet Scott to avoid sale south indicates his willingness to work with an abolitionist far more radical than himself. Hall persuaded Harriet's mistress, who lived in Prince William County, Virginia, to allow Harriet's brother, Henry Scott, sixty days in which to raise five hundred dollars to purchase Harriet's freedom, and Hall loaned Henry two hundred toward that sum. Chaplin, with the assistance of his friend Limaeus P. Noble of the *National Era* and of abolitionists in New York City and Boston, raised the balance.[8]

Gamaliel and Margaret Bailey engaged in similar biracial work during these years. In May 1849 Gamaliel went to considerable lengths to restore to freedom Edward Brooks, a free black minister from Winchester, Virginia, who had been arrested in Washington as a fugitive slave. Bailey worked for several months helping Brooks. He visited Brooks at Washington Jail and he

6. W. L. C. to Gerrit Smith and Charles A. Wheaton, 15 February 1848, in *AP*, 23 February 1848; *NASS*, 16 January 1851; A SOUTHERNER, Correspondence of the *Tribune*, 16 August [1850], in *NYDT*, 19 August 1850; Harriet Beecher Stowe, *The Key to Uncle Tom's Cabin* (1854; reprint, New York: Arno, 1968), 336–9 (quotation).

7. Hall to Chase, 27 June 1848, Salmon P. Chase Papers, Library of Congress.

8. Chaplin to Gerrit Smith, 11 November 1848, GSP.

Gamaliel Bailey (1807–1859) edited the *National Era* in Washington from 1847 until his death. He was among the more conservative of the subversives. Grace Greenwood, "An American Salon," *Cosmopolitan* 8 (1890): 438.

"procured copies of . . . [Brooks's] free papers from the clerk of the court at Winchester." After a police magistrate rejected this evidence, Bailey filed a writ of habeas corpus that led to a decision from U.S. Circuit Court Judge William Cranch releasing Brooks. Shortly thereafter, the Baileys, who had grown prosperous from the expanding circulation of the *National Era*, decided to forgo "purchasing a piano forte" for their eldest son in order to help a woman whose daughter faced sale to traders. At about the same time, Gamaliel Bailey joined in a law suit in Maryland to recover the freedom of three persons who, he maintained, had been "fraudulently" enslaved.[9]

In January of the following year, Stevens visited "Bruin's Jail" in Alexandria in a failed attempt to purchase the freedom of Emily Russell, the sister

9. *PF,* 9 August 1849; *NS,* 7 September 1849 (first quotation); E. L. S. to Editor, 7 November 1849, in *AS,* 17 November 1849 (second quotation); *NE,* 17 October 1850 (third quotation).

of *Pearl* fugitive Gail Russell. Emily, two of her aunts, and eleven of her cousins had been purchased by Bruin and Hill for resale south. Stevens, acting in behalf of Nancy Cartwright—the mother of Grace and Emily—and of prominent New York City abolitionists had authorization to offer $1200 for Emily. But Bruin, who described Emily as *"the finest looking woman in this country"* and maintained that she was destined to be purchased by a southern *"gentleman,"* refused to sell her to Stevens for less than $1,800. A few weeks later the beautiful young woman died in Georgia.[10]

An evangelical commitment to "disinterested benevolence" contributed to these efforts and, on occasion, proslavery whites helped blacks similarly situated. But there were more radical motives as well. The contention that slavery was illegal under the U.S. Constitution shaped the actions of Chaplin and other radical political abolitionists. So did the conviction that a combination of court action, purchases of freedom, and assisted escapes could weaken slavery in the Chesapeake and throughout the nation.[11] Just as important for radical political abolitionists, like Chaplin and others, such as the Baileys, Hall, and Stevens, was empathy with the oppressed and antagonism toward the slaveholding culture. They continued to perceive suffering people of color as respectable, hard-working, Christians who deserved their help.

Hall informed Chase that he respected the woman who sought his assis-

10. E. L. S. to *Democrat,* 9 February 1850, in *Free Democrat and Western Citizen* (Milwaukee), 6 March 1850 (quotations); [Joshua R. Giddings] to editor, 4 April 1850, in *AS,* 13 April 1850. I thank Mark J. Stegmaier for sending me a copy of Stevens's letter. See also Stowe, *Key to Uncle Tom's Cabin,* 331–4. Stowe mistakenly indicates that Emily Russell had sailed on the *Pearl.*

11. "Disinterested benevolence": Ronald G. Walters, *The Antislavery Appeal: American Abolitionism after 1830* (Baltimore: Johns Hopkins University Press, 1976), 38 (quotation) and Robert H. Abzug, *Cosmos Crumbling: American Reform and the Religious Imagination* (New York: Oxford University Press, 1994), 79–80. Help for blacks among those who supported slavery: Henry Slicer to John I. Slingerland, 5 May 1848, in *NE,* 11 May 1848; W. L. C. to [?], 18 May 1848, in *AP,* 25 May 1848; Mark J. Stegmaier, "The Case of the Coachman's Family: An Incident of President Fillmore's Administration," *Civil War History* 32 (December 1986): 318–24. The illegality of slavery: *Chaplin Case,* 17–8. Weakening slavery: *AP,* 15 April 1846; W. L. C. to Pat, n.d., in *AP,* 22 March 1848; *NS,* 5 September 1850. When Gerrit Smith learned of Chaplin's arrest, he declared, "God grant that this event may contribute to hasten the extinction of at least this part of American slavery." See Smith to William H. Seward, 11 August 1850, letter book copy, GSP.

tance in locating her daughter and son-in-law "for her industrious habits and upright life." Chaplin described Henry Scott as "industrious & worthy" and Hall affirmed that Scott's sister, Harriet, was a "most worthy girl," who would certainly repay money loaned to purchase her freedom. Stevens described Nancy Cartwright as an "esteemed" and "respected colored woman." Antislavery whites in Washington continued to feel especially bound to African Americans who were church members. In contrast they distanced themselves emotionally from slaveholders, whom they portrayed as decadent idlers and, in Stevens's words, representative of "the vilest and most diabolical passions of the human heart."[12]

With cooperation between antislavery blacks and whites came shared anxiety, frustration, and anger. As Washington area African Americans endured stress caused by threats to themselves and their families, the emotional equilibrium of their white friends suffered too. At the time of the *Pearl* escape attempt, Stevens twice threatened violence against his proslavery antagonists. During the more memorable of these instances a member of the mob surrounding the *National Era* office asked Stevens if he was an abolitionist. "I am," he replied, "and what are you going to do about it?" Within moments he "raised a good hickory cane" and demanded of his interrogator, "If you wish to save your skull, you'd better move out of my way." One of Stevens's companions prevented him from carrying out this threat. Still, Stevens asserted "that fifty good men, such as I could pick out in old Cuyahoga [County, Ohio], could drive the entire barbarous slavery horde into the Potomac at the point of the bayonet."[13]

Giddings, who liked to think of himself as a rough frontiersman, had better control of his demeanor. But he could not avoid anxious moments. "Well," he remarked to his daughter during the *Pearl* crisis, "I suppose you and your brothers by this time have become weary of looking to find an account of my being lynched." In 1850, when Giddings escorted Jane Gray Swisshelm to a

12. Hall to Chase, 27 June 1848, Chase Papers, Library of Congress (first quotation); Chaplin to Gerrit Smith, 11 November 1848, GSP (second & third quotations); Correspondence of the *New York Tribune*, 12 June 1849, in *PF*, 5 July 1849; E. L. S. to *Democrat*, 9 February 1850, in *Free Democrat and Western Citizen*, 6 March 1850 (fourth & fifth quotations); E. L. S., editorial correspondence, 10 May 1848, in *DTD*, 16 May 1848 (sixth quotation).

13. *NS*, 26 May 1848 (quotations); E. L. S., editorial correspondence of the *True Democrat*, n.d., in *AS*, 6 May 1848.

White House reception, a fellow guest derided them as a "pair of abolitionists" and that same year Bailey, a dyspeptic worrier, complained that his Maryland lawsuit had cost him "much time, anxiety, and money." A year later, as Myrtilla Miner considered establishing her school for black girls in Washington, E. D. E. N. Southworth, a local novelist who wrote for the *National Era,* advised her that if she went ahead with the project she was bound to experience "inconvenience, loss, and distress."[14]

No white person active against slavery in Washington during these years more willingly exposed himself to physical, mental, and emotional stress than Chaplin. Following the capture of the *Pearl,* he increased his already impressive engagement with desperate African Americans in the city and its vicinity. Not only did he cooperate with black people in court cases and efforts to purchase freedom, he became—with the possible exception of Bigelow—the most active white conductor of the area's underground railroad.

From June 1848, when the suspension of the chronically insolvent *Albany Patriot* released him from editorial duties, until his arrest in August 1850, Chaplin devoted his time, his diminishing financial resources, and his enormous energy to cooperation with African Americans of the Chesapeake in their struggle for freedom. Gerrit Smith later informed William H. Seward that Chaplin "had an agency in helping off the slaves." But he was more broadly engaged than this suggests.[15]

Choosing his words carefully, Chaplin told a group of northern abolitionists in January 1851 that during the preceding years "he did not go to Washington—nor did he remain there—to aid slaves in their escape." Rather, when he was there, he talked "of Slavery as hard as the fanatical Abolitionists of New York. . . . [and] it was natural that the colored people—for poor people are apt to find out their friends—should find him out." For years, he maintained, African Americans in Washington "had been in the habit of consulting him" in regard to contacting their northern relatives, to education, "to their troubles.—and also in regard to their legal rights." Therefore, for

14. Giddings to Molly, 23 April 1848 (first quotation); Joseph A. Slavedealer to Giddings, 4 May 1848; Giddings to Laura Waters Giddings, 18 June 1848, JRGP; Jane Grey Swisshelm, *Half a Century,* 2d ed. (Chicago: Jansen, McClurg, 1880), 127 (second quotation); *NE,* 17 October 1850 (third quotation); Southworth to Miner, 23 August 1851, MMP.

15. Smith to Seward, 11 August 1850, letter book copy, GSP (quotation). Chaplin's finances: James C. Jackson to Gerrit Smith, 9 September & November 1848, GSP.

Chaplin, aiding slaves to escape was not in itself a reason for going to Washington but a product of his daily interaction with black people.[16]

Although the details of most of Chaplin's efforts during the years from 1848 to 1850 are lost, his activities during the fall of 1848 provide an indication of their scope. In October of that year he teamed with prominent northern black abolitionist Henry Highland Garnet to hold "three fine meetings among the colored people" of Philadelphia. While there Chaplin arranged for Garnet to conduct to western New York two young female fugitive slaves, whom Chaplin had brought north with him. In early November Chaplin was in New York City to complete the fundraising campaign in behalf of Mary and Emily Edmonson. While there he wrote to inform Gerrit Smith that he had a black boy from Delaware under his care and that Garnet would apprise Smith of an effort to free the boy's sister. Almost incidentally Chaplin added, "There are forty persons near Hagerstown, who ask assistance in attempting to escape from slavery." By the middle of the month he was back in Washington preparing to escort the Edmonson sisters to New York, cooperating with Hall to raise funds to free Harriet Scott, and commuting to Baltimore, where he sought through the courts to free Madison Pitts—another of the *Pearl* fugitives—from Joseph S. Donovan's slave prison.[17]

"Chaplin is a 'host,'" an AMA agent reported from Baltimore to William Harned. "If properly backed," the agent predicted, he "will accomplish much good." White radical political abolitionists and most black abolitionists would have agreed with this evaluation. They were aware that Chaplin had "collected at least $5000" during the previous few years and had spent most of it to help people in Washington. But so dedicated had Chaplin become to such community-oriented work in the borderlands that other abolitionists who focused on politics and agitation in the North wondered what had happened to him. "Has Chaplin quit the ranks?" George Bradburn asked Gerrit Smith in early 1849.[18]

In addition to empathy and the other forces that motivated white mem-

16. *NASS*, 16 January 1851 (quotations); *L*, 16 August 1850.

17. Chaplin to Smith, 2 & 11 November 1848 (quotations), GSP.

18. William [?] to [William] Harned, 20 November 1848, AMAA (first–third quotations); A SOUTHERNER, Correspondence of the *Tribune*, 16 August [1850], in *NYDT*, 19 August 1850 (fourth quotation); Bradburn to Smith, 10 January 1848, GSP (fifth quotation).

bers of Washington's antislavery community, a concept of Christian manliness underlay Chaplin's willingness to undertake such arduous and sometimes dangerous labors in behalf of the oppressed. In seeking to be Christ-like in his benevolence to the poor, Chaplin modeled his actions on those of Charles T. Torrey, whom he identified with Jesus Christ. To do less, Chaplin believed, would destroy him as a man. In explaining why he risked a prison sentence by helping Allen and Garland, he declared, "I knew that a life in Jail was hard . . . but I also knew other things were more calamitous. . . . It is more calamitous for any man to deny his manhood." Black and white abolitionists—not all of whom shared Chaplin's courage—understood what he meant and honored him as a result. "Chaplin has the heart of a man, quickened by the spirit of the Son of man," observed his friend, James C. Jackson.[19]

Chaplin, however, did not work alone but led an alliance of black and white abolitionists. He became involved with Allen and Garland mainly because he feared that if captured by the guard the two men would implicate members of this alliance, and his fears were well founded. After Garland turned himself in, he revealed to the Guard that a free black man named Noah Hanson was harboring two slaves who had escaped from South Carolina congressman William F. Colcock. It may be that Chaplin and Hanson, who was arrested along with the slaves he sheltered, had begun a coordinated effort to embarrass proslavery members of Congress by aiding their slaves to escape during debate of the compromise measures.[20]

19. *AP*, 26 December 1846; W. L. C. to Charles A. Wheaton, 30 December 1845, in *AP*, 7 January 1846; James C. Jackson to Gerrit Smith, 2 September 1850 and Chaplin to Smith, 9 September 1850, GSP; *NASS*, 16 January 1851 (first quotation); Jackson, "Circular from the Chaplin Fund Committee," 22 August 1850, in *PF*, 5 September 1850 (second quotation). Antebellum concepts of Christian manhood: E. Anthony Rotundo, "Learning about Manhood: Gender Ideals and the Middle-Class Family in Nineteenth-Century America," in J. A. Mangan and James Walvin, eds., *Middle-Class Masculinity in Britain and America, 1800–1940* (New York: St. Martin's Press, 1987), 35–51; Christopher Dixon, "'A True Manly Life': Abolitionism and the Masculine Ideal," *Mid-America* 77 (February 1995): 213–36; Donald Yacavone, *Samuel Joseph May and the Dilemma of the Liberal Persuasion, 1797–1871* (Philadelphia: Temple University Press, 1991), 95–103.

20. *NYDT*, 10, 13, 15, 19, 24, & 29 August 1850; *L*, 30 August 1850; *PF*, 5 September 1850; *CG*, 31 Cong., 1 sess., *Appendix*, 1633, 1635–6, 1652; *NASS*, 16 January 1851; Gerrit Smith to Joshua R. Giddings, 21 March 1852, GSP. Henry Foote charged on September 2 that Chaplin had helped four or five slaves attempt escape that August. See *CG*, 31 Cong., 1 sess., 1635.

In any case, Chaplin's arrest brought change to Washington's subversive community. Washington authorities charged him with stealing slaves. He also faced indictments in Montgomery County, Maryland, the most serious of which was assault with intent to kill. In response, the local antislavery community and northern abolitionists hired a legal defense team that included Joseph H. Bradley, Walter Jones, Daniel Ratcliffe, and J. Brewer—all of Washington—plus Asa Child of New York, and Charles H. Pitts of Baltimore. The two antislavery groups also extended legal assistance to Chaplin's free black associate, Warner Harris, and, more tardily, to Hanson. But radical political abolitionist haste and inadequate communication between western New York and Washington produced a muddled effort on Chaplin's behalf. Misunderstandings and conflicting priorities soon strained relations between the Washington antislavery community and the New Yorkers.[21]

On learning of Chaplin's arrest, several of his New York friends, including James C. Jackson, Joseph C. Hathaway, and Theodosia Gilbert, came to Washington to provide for his needs while he was in jail. Gilbert, a nurse, was an able and attractive young woman whose increasing closeness to Chaplin dismayed many abolitionists. In Washington this New York group cooperated with Giddings, Salmon P. Chase—now a Free Soil senator—and the defense team to negotiate bail so that Chaplin would not suffer the fate of Torrey or of Drayton and Sayres.[22]

Meanwhile, Gerrit Smith, in cooperation with Charles B. Ray, the black leader of the New York State Vigilance Committee, organized a Fugitive

21. Charges against Chaplin: *National Intelligencer,* 16 August 1850; *NYDT,* quoted in *NS,* 3 October 1850; Charles Pitts to Lewis Tappan, 18 November 1850, GSP; *Chaplin Case,* 27–8. Legal Team: Giddings to Louisa, 25 August 1850, Joshua R. Giddings-George W. Julian Papers, Library of Congress; Jackson to Gerrit Smith, 3 September 1850; GSP; *PF,* 5 September 1850; Seward to Gerrit Smith, 15 September 1850, WHSP. Extensive correspondence in the GSP reveals the degree of animosity between the two antislavery groups. For examples see: William R. Smith to Gerrit Smith, 14 September & 8 November 1850, Gerrit Smith to William R. Smith, October 1850, letter book copy, Lewis Tappan to Gerrit Smith, 26 November 1850; Eliza Smith to Gerrit Smith, 11 January 1851.

22. New Yorkers: Gerrit Smith to Chaplin, 11 August 1850, letter book copy, Jackson to Gerrit Smith, 1 September 1850, GSP; *L,* 30 August 1850. Gilbert: Jackson to Gerrit Smith, 21 November 1848, Gilbert to Gerrit Smith, 7 October 1850, William R. Smith to Gerrit Smith, 8 November 1850, Eliza Smith to Gerrit Smith, 10 June 1851, GSP; Samuel Thomas, Jr. to William H. Seward, 12 August 1850, WHSP.

The Cazenovia, New York, Fugitive Slave Convention, August 21–22, 1850, took place in an orchard. This daguerreotype of the speaking platform shows Emily and Mary Edmonson, wearing patterned shawls, standing to the left and right, respectively, of Gerrit Smith, who is gesturing with his left arm. In front of them at the table are Theodosia Gilbert, who later would marry William L. Chaplin, and, to her left, black abolitionist leader Frederick Douglass. With permission from the Madison County Historical Society.

Slave Convention that convened at Cazenovia, New York, on August 21. Between thirty and fifty fugitive slaves and between fifteen hundred and two thousand others, including Emily and Mary Edmonson, attended the convention. With Frederick Douglass presiding, it created a "Chaplin Committee" to raise funds to support legal efforts in Chaplin's behalf. Those attending hoped to assure individuals who might post bond for Chaplin that they would be reimbursed when, as everyone expected, he jumped bail in either the District of Columbia or Maryland, or both. The convention also nominated Chaplin for president of the United States, threatened "revolution" if Washington authorities did not release him, and adopted an address that urged slaves to escape, to carry arms when they did so, and to kill masters who pursued them.[23]

This language suited the evolving conviction among radical political abolitionists that only force could free the slaves. Even the nonviolent Lewis Tappan commented wryly in private that Chaplin "should not have rode with men having fire arms, & especially with those who did not know how to use them effectively." But talk of revolutionary violence in public was tactically inappropriate as—along with mounting slave escapes—it made freeing Chaplin much more difficult. The district attorney in Washington doubled the bond for Chaplin's release from $3,000 to $6,000. David A. Hall, who received assurances from Smith that the Chaplin Committee would reimburse him, countered the district attorney by presenting his note—endorsed by an elderly John Needles and Elisha Tyson's son Isaac—for most of the latter amount. On a similar understanding, two white natives of Washington, William Blanchard, the printer of the *National Era*, and Selby Parker, a local Free Soiler, provided the balance of Chaplin's Washington bail.

Judge Cranch then released Chaplin into the custody of Captain Goddard, who escorted the prisoner to Rockville, Maryland, the county seat of Montgomery County. There a carefully negotiated plan to bail out Chaplin for a few thousand dollars disintegrated. Slaveholders, outraged by escapes and the proceedings of the Fugitive Slave Convention, persuaded a local magistrate to demand an extraordinary bond of $19,000.[24]

23. *National Intelligencer*, 13 August 1850; *L*, 30 August & 13 September 1850; *NS*, 5 September 1850 (quotation); *PF*, 5 September 1850. One of the sisters spoke on Chaplin's behalf and both sang. See also John Stauffer, *The Black Hearts of Men: Radical Abolitionists and the Transformation of Race* (Cambridge, Mass.: Harvard University Press, 2002), 163–4.

24. Radical political abolitionists and advocacy of violence: Gerrit Smith to Dickey and Ellingwood, 21 March 1845, Tappan to Smith, 25 October 1850 (quotation) GSP; *L*, 26 January 1849 and 13 September 1850; Ralph V. Harlow, *Gerrit Smith, Philanthropist and Reformer* (New York: Holt, 1939), 304; *Liberty Party Paper*, quoted in *ASR* 6, n.s. (1 January 1851): 15. Impact of the convention and slave escapes: Silas Cornell to Gerrit Smith, 2 September 1850, James C. Jackson to Smith, 8 September 1850, GSP. Bonds in Washington and Rockville:

After considerable negotiation, misunderstanding, communication break-downs, and posturing, Gerrit Smith pledged most of this sum. Lewis Tappan, one of Tappan's wealthy New York City friends, and Hall took responsibility for the remainder. Chaplin left Rockville on December 19, never to return to the Chesapeake. Over eight months later, Ratcliffe, acting in behalf of the Chaplin Committee, secured the release of Harris. It took much longer to free Hanson. After the failure in 1852 of an effort led by Giddings and backed by Gerrit Smith to raise money to pay Hanson's $1,200 fine, Smith finally secured a presidential pardon for him in 1854. Smith, who was by then a congressman himself, reported to Frederick Douglass that "Hanson was no sooner let out of jail than he hastened to my house. A more grateful creature I never saw." All of the fugitives involved, however, remained in slavery. Stephens and Toombs immediately sold their bondmen, and Colcock sent his back to South Carolina.[25]

When Chaplin arrived in New York, his abolitionist associates assumed he would undertake a speaking tour to raise money to reimburse those who had stood bond for him. Most of his friends also assumed that, while it was too dangerous for him to return to Maryland, it was in the interest of the antislavery cause that he contest in court the charges against him in the District. Initially Chaplin, who had outwardly borne his months of imprisonment extremely well, seemed ready for these challenges. On his way north he "addressed a large public meeting" at a black church in Philadelphia. At a mass meeting at Syracuse in early January 1851 he delivered a rousing address.[26]

NYDT, quoted in NS, 3 October 1850; Gerrit Smith to William H. Seward, 14 August & 15 September 1850, WHSP; Smith to Seward, 29 September 1850, Gamaliel Bailey to Lewis Tappan, 12 March 1851, GSP; *Republic* (Washington), quoted in NE, 21 November 1850.

25. Tappan to Gerrit Smith, 26 November & 11 December 1850, Hall to Gerrit Smith, 7 February 1851, William R. Smith to Gerrit Smith, 19 February 1851, Gerrit Smith to Tappan, 6 April 1851 (copy), Gerrit Smith to Giddings, 21 March 1852, GSP; Smith to Douglass, 25 August 1854, in FDP, 1 September 1854; PF, 9 January 1851; William Blanchard to Tappan, 13 August 1851, AMAA; NS, 5 September 1850; *Washington Republican*, quoted in L, 13 September 1850. The *Republican* reported that Colcock's two slaves again attempted to escape as they began the journey south from Washington. It took a furious struggle to recapture them.

26. Expectations concerning Chaplin: Gerrit Smith to William H. Seward, 11 September 1850, Lewis Tappan to Gerrit Smith, 17 January 1851, Gerrit Smith to David A. Hall, 9 February 1851, letter book copy, H. A. Chittenden to Gerrit Smith, 11 March 1851, Eliza Smith to

On the latter occasion black abolitionists testified to their appreciation for his help in assisting many slaves to freedom. Jermain Wesley Loguen, himself a fugitive slave, told Chaplin, "There are many happy families in New York and Canada, who owe the privilege of breathing free air to your labors." In remarks indicating the importance of the Washington antislavery community, Loguen further addressed Chaplin, "Sir, the black man has many friends—but they are not all of that kind who are ready to go down and meet us at the spot where American tyranny has placed us, and there, where help is most needed . . . to offer themselves as our deliverers. There is where the slave wants help. Had he sufficient aid at that point, his chains would be broken in a thousand fragments. . . . Sir, your name will dwell on the lips of the colored man forever."[27]

But not long after the Syracuse meeting emotional strain caused by Chaplin's ordeal began to tell. He missed speaking engagements, refused to schedule others, and would not return to Washington for trial. He stopped responding to letters and, as a fugitive from justice, became excessively concerned for his physical safety. Finally, having married Theodosia Gilbert, he withdrew from the antislavery movement to join her and Jackson in operating a water cure sanatorium at Glen Haven, New York.[28]

Without its star speaker, the Chaplin Committee raised less than $3,000 of the $24,000 (the equivalent of about $470,000 in 2002 dollars!) required to reimburse those who had stood bail. Mutual recriminations that began

Gerrit Smith, 29 May 1851, William R. Smith to Gerrit Smith, 19 February, 2 June & 9 June 1851, 31 March 1852, William Harned to Gerrit Smith, 22 July 1851, GSP. Chaplin's demeanor and his addresses: S. P. A[ndrews], correspondence of the *Tribune*, 26 August [1850], in *PF*, 5 September 1850; Chaplin to Gerrit Smith, 9 September 1850, GSP; *Chaplin Case*, 26, 33–4, 41; *PF*, 9 January 1851 (quotation); *NASS*, 16 January 1851.

27. *NASS*, 16 January 1851 (first quotation); *L*, 24 January 1851 (second quotation). The Edmonson sisters sang at some of the fund-raising meetings. See Hanchett, "Edmondson Sisters," 28.

28. H. A. Chittenden to Gerrit Smith, 11 March 1851, Eliza Smith to Gerrit Smith, 29 May 1851, William R. Smith to Gerrit Smith, 19 February, 11 March, 2 June, & 9 June 1851, 31 March 1852, William Harned to Gerrit Smith, 22 July 1851, Gerrit Smith to David A. Hall, 27 March 1852, William R. Smith to William H. Seward, 31 March 1852, James C. Jackson to Gerrit Smith, 24 April 1855, GSP; *PF*, 27 March 1851; *New National Era* (Washington), 11 May 1871. Gilbert died in 1855. She and Chaplin had two daughters, one of whom survived Chaplin at his death in 1871.

during the fall of 1850 grew intense and became acrimonious between Gerrit Smith on the one side and Tappan and Hall on the other. Although there were important ideological differences among these three, they argued over trust and money. Tappan, who lost about $3,000, and Hall, who suffered acute financial embarrassment when his notes for about $8,000 expired, held Smith, who claimed to have lost $12,000, responsible for their predicaments—a responsibility Smith bitterly denied.[29]

The result of Chaplin's arrest and this debacle was, therefore, that the long-standing bond between the Washington antislavery community and the radical political abolitionists of upstate New York broke. With Chaplin's departure the direct participation of radical political abolitionists in the activities of the community ended. Albany, which had been a center for sending funds south and for welcoming fugitive slaves headed north since Torrey's time, became irrelevant. Just as significant, the Washington community could no longer draw on Gerrit Smith's huge financial resources. Smith, whose indirect involvement in antislavery efforts in the Chesapeake dated back to the 1830s, continued to fund challenges to slavery throughout the 1850s. But, except for the months in 1853 and 1854 when he served in Congress, the focus of his benevolence shifted from the vicinity of Washington vicinity to Kansas Territory and finally to John Brown's raid at Harpers Ferry.[30]

Others during the remaining antebellum years served as replacements for Chaplin and Smith. In Washington Bigelow became the principal white underground railroad agent. Increasingly Bigelow worked with William Still, a black abolitionist residing in Philadelphia, to coordinate escapes from Washington to that city. Loguen and other black abolitionists escorted fugitive slaves from Philadelphia to Canada. There were new financial backers as well.

29. Funds raised: Receipt [1851?], GSP; *PF*, 9 January 1851; Gerrit Smith to Chaplin Committee, 3 July [1851], in *FDP*, undated clipping, GSP; Harlow, *Smith*, 291–3. Recriminations: letters, 1850–1852 in GSP and Hall to William H. Seward, 3 June 1854, WHSP. Losses suffered: Gerrit Smith to Lewis Tappan, 6 April 1851, Smith to Hall, 11 June 1852, and Smith to Chaplin Committee, 3 July [1851], GSP.

30. Smith in Congress: Smith to Frederick Douglass, 25 August 1854, in *FDP*, 1 September 1854. Smith and Brown: Jeffrey S. Rossbach, *Ambivalent Conspirators: John Brown, the Secret Six, and a Theory of Slave Violence* (Philadelphia: University of Pennsylvania Press, 1982); Stauffer, *Black Hearts of Men*, 236–45.

They included Henry Ward Beecher, Harriet Beecher Stowe, and, especially, Tappan. None of them were as committed to using confrontation to drive slavery from the Chesapeake as Smith had been, nor were they as wealthy as Smith. Tappan, whose financial resources approached Smith's, was far more parsimonious in allocating them.[31]

Chaplin's arrest also widened the breach between the radical political abolitionists and Gamaliel Bailey. During Chaplin's first days in Washington Jail he had helped quell calls for mob action against the *National Era* office by releasing a statement exculpating Bailey and pointing out their disagreement concerning tactics. Bailey responded, somewhat disingenuously, by publishing an editorial denouncing all clandestine action as detrimental to the antislavery cause and wishing that neither Chaplin nor Torrey had ever engaged in such activities.

Gerrit Smith and others in western New York then denounced Bailey as cowardly and heartless. They suggested that it would be better to allow the *National Era* to be destroyed than for abolitionists to give up their commitment to rescuing slaves. One knowledgeable individual called Bailey a hypocrite because Bailey himself had helped slaves escape when he lived in Cincinnati. This acrimony, linked as it was with the failure of the New Yorkers to reimburse Hall and the others, confirmed Bailey in his distrust of radical political abolitionists.[32]

While the Chaplin case produced a realignment of the Washington antislavery community's relationship to northern abolitionism, it simultaneously confirmed slaveholders in their charge that the antislavery movement aggressively subverted southern institutions. This perception became particularly important at a time when measures designed to compromise sectional differences neared passage in Congress.

The divisive issues included the status of slavery in the former Mexican

31. See Chapter 8.

32. *Chaplin's Portfolio* (Albany), quoted in *New York Evening Post,* 10 August 1850; *NYDT,* 13 August 1850; *NE,* 15 & 29 August, 12 September, 10 & 31 October, 7 & 14 November 1850; Bailey to Lewis Tappan, 12 March 1851 and Smith to Tappan, 6 April 1851, GSP; Calvin Fairbank to William Lloyd Garrison, 24 April 1850, in *L,* 3 May 1850; Fairbank, *Rev. Calvin Fairbank during Slavery Times* (1890; reprint, New York: Negro Universities Press, 1969), 21.

provinces of California and New Mexico that had been ceded to the United States in early 1848, the location of the boundary between New Mexico and the slaveholding state of Texas, the status of slavery in the District of Columbia, and the southern demand for a stronger fugitive slave law. In January 1850 Henry Clay of Kentucky, who had based his brilliant political career on an ability to reconcile sectional differences, introduced into Congress a comprehensive plan to deal with these issues. He proposed to admit California as a free state, to organize New Mexico as a territory without restriction regarding slavery, to settle the boundary dispute in favor of New Mexico while compensating Texas, to pass a new fugitive slave law, and keep to slavery in the District while curtailing the slave trade there.[33]

The relationship between the compromise proposals and local issues is clear. Anticipating congressional restrictions on the slave trade, local masters increased sales south. Anticipating a stronger fugitive slave law, local African Americans attempted to escape before the new law went into effect. Conversely, the actions of Chaplin, Harris, Hanson, Allen, Garland, and others influenced debate in Congress. The perception among southern congressmen that slavery was under attack on its northern periphery, along with American annexation of California and New Mexico, had a significant role in the sectional crisis that led to the compromise proposals.[34]

Washington's subversive community directly influenced the formulation of the new fugitive slave law and the District slave-trade act, although it had a more significant impact on the latter measure. The debate concerning the slave trade revealed the anxiety among proslavery politicians concerning the community and their fierce desire to suppress it. In contrast, even though action against slavery in the Chesapeake had contributed to demands for a

33. Slaveholders' perceptions: *NYDT,* 10 & 15 August 1850. Compromise of 1850: Holman Hamilton, *Prologue to Conflict: The Crisis and Compromise of 1850* (New York: Norton, 1964) and Mark J. Stegmaier, *Texas, New Mexico, and the Compromise of 1850: Boundary Dispute and Sectional Crisis* (Kent, Ohio: Kent State University Press, 1999). Clay: Robert V. Remini, *Henry Clay: Statesman for the Union* (New York: Norton, 1991).

34. Correspondence of the *Tribune,* 12 June 1849, in *PF,* 5 July 1849. William W. Freehling, *The Reinterpretation of American History: Slavery and the Civil War* (New York: Oxford University Press, 1994), 170–1; Stanley Harrold, *The Abolitionists and the South, 1831–1861* (Lexington: University Press of Kentucky, 1995), 154–5.

stronger fugitive slave law, debate of the fugitive slave bill focused on the re-capture and extradition of fugitives who had reached northern states.[35]

The Committee of Thirteen, which drafted the slave-trade bill, hoped that by limiting the peculiar institution's most barbaric aspect it might placate northern outrage concerning slavery in the national capital. But the Committee also aimed to reassure southern whites that neither slavery nor the most vital part of the slave trade would be abolished in the District. The bill proposed only to end Washington's role as a way station in the interstate trade by banning importation into the District of slaves for resale or transportation elsewhere. District residents could continue to sell slaves south.[36]

Southern senators, nevertheless, undertook to either defeat the bill or transform it into an overtly proslavery measure. Led by James A. Pearce and Thomas G. Pratt of Maryland, and M. T. Hunter and James M. Mason of Virginia, who represented directly affected constituencies, the southerners argued that the bill portended congressional action against slavery itself in the District and against the entire interstate slave trade. Pearce and the others relied on the Chaplin case to justify adding two amendments to the bill. One provided for much harsher penalties in the District for aiding slaves to escape and for harboring fugitives. The other proposed to empower local officials to curtail the growth of the local free black population and, perhaps, to expel portions of it.[37]

In the debate on these amendments, Pearce, John Bell of Tennessee, Henry Foote, and several other senators noted that cooperation between anti-slavery blacks and whites threatened slavery in Washington. They noted Chaplin's activities, declared that they represented a "systematic" effort, and

35. Fugitive Slave Act: Virginia, *Acts of the General Assembly of Virginia, Passed at the Extra and Regular Sessions in 1849 & 1850* (Richmond: William F. Ritchie, 1850), 246–7; *CG*, 31 Cong., 1 sess., *Appendix*, 1582–1630. District slave-trade act: *Albany Evening Journal*, 21 April & 4–6 May 1848; Hamilton, *Prologue to Conflict*, 23, 44; *CG*, 31 Cong., 1 sess., *Appendix*, 1630–74.

36. *CG*, 31 Cong., 1 sess., 946, 1743, *Appendix*, 1641. The law also empowered the municipalities of Washington and Georgetown to close slave prisons.

37. *CG*, 31 Cong., 1 sess., *Appendix*, 1630–8. Antislavery Senator Salmon P. Chase deliberately encouraged this proslavery reaction by characterizing the bill as "the first step" toward abolition in the District. See ibid., 1644.

denounced Washington's free black population as "disorderly, riotous, and troublesome." Despite Clay's assurances that the original bill would strengthen slavery in the district by depriving abolitionists of a divisive issue, these senators succeeded temporarily in adding Pearce's amendments. Clay gained the political leverage to delete them only when antislavery senators Seward, Chase, and Hale threatened to vote against the amended bill. Then, on September 16, the Senate passed the original bill and sent it to the House of Representatives, which passed it more easily a few days later. By supporting Pearce's amendments, southern senators had demonstrated their commitment to protecting slavery in the District against the efforts of the subversive community.[38]

Because the slave-trade act did not end the local sale of slaves south when it went into effect on January 1, 1851, it had limited impact on conditions in Washington and the vicinity. As both southerners and northerners had predicted before the act passed, interstate slave traders simply moved their operations beyond the District's borders—principally to Alexandria, which had retroceded to Virginia in 1846. Public slave auctions continued in Washington, slave prisons remained in operation, and slave coffles—though rarer than previously—still wended their way through the city's streets.[39] Blacks and whites within the antislavery community continued to cooperate to prevent sales and to rescue victims of the slave trade.

Like the slave-trade act, the new fugitive slave law had a tangential rather

38. Remarks of Pearce, Bell, and Foote: ibid., 1636 (quotations), 1669, 1651–2. Chaplin is mentioned by name on pages 1652 and 1665. Clay's reassurances: ibid., 1631, 1647. Seward, Chase, and Hale: ibid., 1642, 1644–5, 1652–3. Deletion of Pearce's amendments: ibid., 1673–4. The vote in favor of deleting the amendment providing harsher penalties for helping slaves escape was twenty-six to twenty-two. The vote in favor of deleting the amendment dealing with free blacks was twenty-eight to twenty. Passage of the slave-trade bill: *CG*, 31 Cong., 1 sess., 1837, *Appendix*, 1674.

39. Continuation of sales south, the shift of the traders to Alexandria, and coffles: *FDP*, 2 October 1851; *CG*, 32 Cong., 1 sess., 532; *NE*, 13 May 1852, 17 February 1853, 23 December 1858; *AS*, 10 & 17 February 1853; Bryon Sunderland, "Washington as I First Knew It, 1852–1855," *RCHS* 2 (1902): 201; Hamilton, *Prologue to Conflict*, 178; William T. Laprade, "The Domestic Slave Trade in the District of Columbia," *Journal of Negro History* 11 (January 1926): 33–4; [Jacob Bigelow to Thomas Richardson], 16 March 1853, in *ASR* 1, 3d ser. (1 May 1853): 114. Predictions: *CG*, 31 Cong., 1 sess., *Appendix*, 1639; *Southern Press* (Washington), 27 September 1850.

than direct impact on Washington's antislavery subversives. The act authorized United States marshals to apprehend alleged fugitives, created federal commissioners to determine their fate, and explicitly banned testimony from those accused. The new law also imposed stiffer penalties for aiding slaves to escape than had the Fugitive Slave Act of 1793. While the new law could not always be enforced in the North, it could be in the Chesapeake. Yet, local African Americans, aided by Jacob Bigelow and other sympathetic whites, continued throughout the 1850s to escape.[40]

The real significance of the new fugitive slave law, so far as it concerned Washington's subversive community, lay in how it pushed northward conflict between abolitionists and slaveholders. Violent confrontations resulting from escapes had previously been most characteristic of the Chesapeake and other borderlands. Now localities across the North witnessed them. This geographical relocation contributed to the removal of the radical political abolitionist presence from Washington as members of this group could now act directly against slavery in the North. The new circumstances also diminished the publicity the antislavery press provided to the city's subversives.[41]

But more than either the fugitive slave law or the slave-trade act, the rise of the Free Soil party changed the context within which Washington's subversive community existed. Together with Chaplin's departure, the organization of this new northern party during the summer of 1848 contributed greatly to the community's evolving character. As a political union of antislavery Whigs, such as Joshua R. Giddings, Liberty abolitionists, such as Gama-

40. Full text of the law: *NE*, 3 October 1850. Enforcement: Stanley W. Campbell, *The Slave Catchers: Enforcement of the Fugitive Slave Law, 1850–1860* (New York: Norton, 1968), 148–69. Bigelow's role: see chapter 9. For a thorough analysis of both fugitive slave laws, see Don E. Fehrenbacher, *The Slaveholding Republic: An Account of the United States Government's Relations to Slavery* (New York: Oxford University Press, 2001), 205–52.

41. Campbell, *Slave Catchers*, 148–69; Herbert Aptheker, *Abolitionism: A Revolutionary Movement* (Boston: Twayne, 1989), 118–22; David Grimsted, *American Mobbing, 1828–1861: Toward Civil War* (New York: Oxford University Press, 1998), 74–82. The Jerry rescue at Syracuse is an example of radical political abolitionist participation in such confrontations in the North. See *FDP*, 25 September–6 November 1851. See also Samuel J. May, *Some Recollections of the Antislavery Conflict* (Boston: Fields and Osgood, 1867), 374–81; Thomas P. Slaughter, *Bloody Dawn: The Christiana Riot and Racial Violence in the Antebellum North* (New York: Oxford University Press, 1991); Nat Brandt, *The Town That Started the Civil War* (Syracuse, N.Y.: Syracuse University Press, 1990).

liel Bailey and Salmon P. Chase, and Democrats opposed to the extension of slavery, such as David Wilmot of Pennsylvania, the Free Soil party enhanced the role of northern antislavery sentiment in national politics. For the first time an explicitly antislavery political party had enough support in the North to elect members of Congress. By 1850 the presence of fourteen Free Soilers in that body, including Chase and John P. Hale in the Senate, encouraged greater sensitivity to antislavery issues among other northern members.

Yet the Free Soil party also embodied a diminution of the abolitionist commitment to black freedom. Like the Ohio Liberty party that Bailey and Chase had created during the early 1840s, the Free Soil party distinguished between political action against slavery within the exclusive jurisdiction of Congress and moral suasion directed against slavery in the southern states. The Free Soil party committed itself only to the former, leaving individuals and antislavery societies to use moral suasion to convince southern whites to abolish slavery in states where, the Free Soilers maintained, Congress had no authority. While Bailey, Chase, and Giddings never relinquished their abolitionist goals, as Free Soilers they cooperated with politicians who had no such commitment. They also tolerated within the Free Soil ranks former Democrats, like Wilmot, who at times publicly mixed negrophobia with antipathy to slave labor.[42]

Therefore, while the Free Soil party represented a broadening of antislavery sentiment within the northern electorate, it drew the ire of New York's radical political abolitionists. They refused to support the party and gloried in mixing politics with Christian morality. They maintained that Congress could abolish slavery in the southern states and increased their cooperation with black abolitionists in direct action against slavery.[43] This ideological,

42. Richard H. Sewell, *Ballots for Freedom: Antislavery Politics in the United States, 1837–1860* (New York: Oxford University Press, 1976), 131–230; Frederick J. Blue, *The Free Soilers: Third Party Politics, 1848–54* (Urbana: University of Illinois Press, 1973), 1–15, 81–151; Stanley Harrold, *Gamaliel Bailey and Antislavery Union* (Kent, Ohio.: Kent State University Press, 1986), 109–37; Blue, *Salmon P. Chase: A Life in Politics* (Kent, Ohio: Kent State University Press, 1987), 61–92; James Brewer Stewart, *Joshua R. Giddings and the Tactics of Radical Politics* (Cleveland: Case-Western Reserve University Press, 1970), 141–66.

43. Douglas M. Strong, *Perfectionist Politics: Abolitionism and the Religious Tensions of American Democracy* (Syracuse, N.Y.: Syracuse University Press, 1999), 66–90, 137–60; Sewell, *Ballots for Freedom*, 163; *NS*, 5 September 1850; *FDP*, 25 September, 23 & 30 October 1851; *NASS*, 16 January 1851.

emotional, and tactical disjunction between Free Soilers and radical political abolitionists underlay the vehemence in the dispute between the New Yorkers and Bailey concerning clandestine aid to escaping slaves. It also contributed to the failure of the New Yorkers to find an effective replacement for Chaplin in Washington.

With the rise of the Free Soil party, antislavery politics in the capital city quickly began limit interracialism. As the number of antislavery politicians increased in Washington, the percentage who empathized with African Americans declined. Positive racial interaction between antislavery whites and local blacks continued to be far greater than historians have perceived. But the development of a white Free Soil social circle in the city—combined with a desire among Free Soilers to appeal to a regional southern white constituency—circumscribed biracialism, politically, socially, and religiously.

Prior to 1848 there was no local political antislavery organization in the capital. With the formation of a Washington Free Soil Association that year, there began a series of such organizations leading to the influential National Republican Association in 1855. Giddings wrote the Free Soil Association's first address. Over the succeeding years other whites who regularly engaged with African Americans in practical antislavery efforts led these organizations. Among them were Jacob Bigelow and several individuals whom Gamaliel Bailey employed in publishing the *National Era*. Nevertheless these political organizations excluded blacks and did not promote interracial solidarity. Rather they appealed to white antislavery sentiment, divorced from sympathy for the enslaved. Officially they opposed only the extension of slavery, did not advocate abolition in the District, and included slaveholders among their leaders.[44]

Racially exclusive social traditions also developed among Washington's antislavery whites during the late 1840s and early 1850s. As in the case of the antislavery political organizations, these social traditions did not directly

44. Among Bailey's employees who led the associations were William Blanchard, Lewis Clephane, Allen M. Gangewere, and Daniel R. Goodloe. Formation and composition: *NE*, 28 September & 5 October 1848, 15 & 22 July 1852, 23 August 1855, 6 March 1856; Lewis Clephane, *Birth of the Republican Party* (Washington: Gibson Bros., 1889), 8–9; Lewis Tappan to Goodloe, H. S. Brown, and Clephane, 6 March 1856, letter book copy, LTP; *NE*, 21 April 1849. Giddings's address: Giddings, diary, 10 & 16 December 1848, JRGP; American and Foreign Anti-Slavery Society, *Ninth Annual Report* (New York: AFASS, 1849), 22.

interfere with biracial antislavery cooperation. But they did reflect an acceptance of the cultural status quo in the city and an implicit rejection of a more radically inclusive racial policy.

As had been the case in regard to political organization, there was in Washington no formal social life among antislavery whites before 1848. This, among other considerations, led Torrey and others to attend black functions. But Gamaliel and Margaret Bailey, understanding that regular social events could unify slavery's white opponents in the capital, opened their parlor that year to antislavery members of Congress, visiting abolitionists, and others. What began as small, intimate gatherings developed by 1850 into lavish affairs where guests were "sumptuously entertained." While those who visited the Baileys discussed cooperation with African Americans, their hosts' servants were the only people of color in attendance. There is no record that, for example, the Baileys invited the urbane John F. Cook Sr. or the famous Emily Edmonson.[45]

An effort begun by Bigelow in 1847 to create a white antislavery church in Washington better reflected the spirit of biracialism than either the political associations or the Baileys' social affairs. But it also demonstrated the limits of that spirit. With the local help of Gamaliel Bailey and Ezra L. Stevens, and with financial assistance from the New York City-based AMA, Bigelow had by 1851 purchased a church building and hired Josiah Bushnell Grinnell, a young northern abolitionist, as minister.[46] The church refused to admit slaveholders to membership and Bigelow hoped that it would dispense a "free gospel" patterned on John G. Fee's abolitionist evangelicalism in Kentucky. But so daunted was Grinnell by the proslavery climate of the city that he did not directly refer to slavery in his inaugural sermon and soon departed.

Only in 1858, after years of dissension, financial difficulty, and temporary ministers, did the church procure in the person of George W. Bassett a minister who would openly declare that "God Almighty is for the negro." That Bassett did so on slave soil before a biracial congregation is remarkable. Sev-

45. Harrold, *Bailey,* 132–4; [Giddings] to Mr. Sentinel, 2 January 1850[1], in *AS,* 11 January 1851 (quotation).

46. Lewis Tappan to Charles B. Boynton, 11 October 1847, Tappan to Bigelow, 7 January 1848, letter book copies, LTP; Josiah Bushnell Grinnell, *Men and Events of Forty Years* (Boston: D. Lothrop, 1891), 52.

eral young black woman associated with Myrtilla Miner's school regularly attended Bassett's sermons. They included Emma V. Brown, Matilda Jones, and Bettie Browne. Brown rejoiced in March 1858 that "Mr. Bassett . . . dares to preach in this slave-land liberty, justice and humanity." She noted that Giddings and Republican Senator Charles Durkee had joined the small congregation. Yet Bigelow, Stevens, and Bailey believed that Bassett was too close to the radical political abolitionists to make converts to antislavery Christianity among southern whites. This perception and continued financial difficulties led to the failure of the church and Bassett's departure in 1860.[47]

These limits to the biracial commitment of antislavery whites should not obscure continued interracial cooperation against slavery in Washington during the 1850s. Grinnell recalled that the specific reason he left the capital was to avoid prosecution for having advised a "young mulatto couple" in their escape plans. Bailey's public opposition to clandestine acts always diverged from his private reputation among African Americans. In December 1852, for example, a woman in Philadelphia asked him to help finance the escape of her son from slavery in Washington. A white-haired Giddings did not stop encouraging black people to visit him at his rooming house, especially if their families faced disruption through sale south.[48]

Because of his public persona as the most aggressively antislavery con-

47. Bigelow, Grinnell, et al., to Executive Committee, 16 September 1851 (first quotation), William McConnell, Stevens, and B. P. Worcester to Executive Committee, 16 February 1853, Stevens to S. S. Jocelyn, 2 & 15 August 1855; Bassett to Tappan, Jocelyn, and George Whipple, 14 December 1858, Bailey to Tappan, 13 January 1859, AMAA; Grinnell, *Men and Events*, 53–5; George W. Bassett, *Slavery Examined in the Light of Nature* (Washington: privately printed, 1858), 3–8 (second quotation); Bigelow to William H. Seward, 23 January 1858, WHSP; Browne [*sic*] to William Lloyd Garrison, 1 April 1858, in *L*, 16 April 1858 (third quotation); Matilda Jones to Miner, 20 April 1858, Emma Brown to Miner, 23 August [1858], MMP; Bettie [Browne] to Emily Howland, 18 February 1860, EHP. Bassett had been active in behalf of the church since 1855 but did not preach there until 1858. There is extensive correspondence in the AMAA regarding the church. Abolitionists James Freeman Clarke and Moncure Conway, who ministered to Washington's Unitarian Church during the 1850s, fared little better than Grinnell and Bassett. See Clarke, *Anti-Slavery Days* (New York: R. Worthington, 1884); John d'Entremont, *Southern Emancipator: Moncure Conway, the American Years 1832–1865* (New York: Oxford University Press, 1987), 100–12.

48. Grinnell, *Men and Events*, 55 (quotation); Mary L. Cox to Bailey, 1 December 1852, MMP; *PF*, 25 December 1851.

gressman, Giddings's informal social contacts with the oppressed continued to attract the attention of slaveholders. "Who ever saw him, except upon this floor, with a decent man in Washington City?" inquired Representative Edward Stanly of North Carolina in February 1852. "He receives visits from free negroes sometimes. The charity he dispenses no man knows. He never lets his right hand know what his left hand does. . . . He remains with his free negro friends when they call to see him; and this is the way he spends his extra hours." Bigelow and Stevens, though far less prominent than Giddings, spent much of their time in a similar manner.

In addition, as Stanly's remarks indicate, Washington's subversives continued during the 1850s to act in a manner that intensified the sectional conflict. African Americans and their white allies persisted in activities that threatened the continued existence of slavery in the District of Columbia, thereby encouraging divisive countermeasures from the peculiar institution's defenders. In response to the Fugitive Slave Law of 1850, Giddings repeatedly raised in Congress the issue of the right of slaves to escape, by violent means if necessary. On the floor of the House of Representatives in February 1851, he declared, "Were I a colored man, as I am a white man, I would not hesitate to slay any slave-catcher who should attempt to lay hands on my person to enslave me." As result, as Free Soil and, later, Republican congressmen arrived in the capital city, many of them came to share an antislavery outlook that embraced black rights as well as northern white interests.[49]

Events between 1848 and 1850 had altered the subversive community. The departure of Chaplin and the weakening ties between the Washington antislavery community and New York's radical political abolitionists brought an end to well publicized arrests of community members. The spirit of sectional compromise, which during the early 1850s engendered more repressive

49. *CG,* 32 Cong., 1 sess., 535 (first quotation); Joshua R. Giddings, *Speeches in Congress* (1853; reprint, New York: Negro Universities Press, 1968), 451 (second quotation); James Brewer Stewart, "Joshua Giddings, Antislavery Violence, and Congressional Politics of Honor," in John R. McKivigan and Stanley Harrold, eds., *Antislavery Violence: Sectional, Racial, and Cultural Conflict in Antebellum America* (Knoxville: University of Tennessee Press, 1999), 184–8; Paul H. Verduin, "Partners for Emancipation: New Light on Lincoln, Joshua Giddings, and the Push to End Slavery in the District of Columbia, 1848–49" (unpublished paper). I thank James Brewer Stewart for the insight that the subversive community helped shape the spirit of the Republican party during the 1850s.

circumstances in Washington, led subversives to be more discreet and careful in their actions. As fugitive slave cases became common in the North, the community received less coverage in the antislavery press. Meanwhile political and social developments among antislavery whites revealed the limits of interracialism south of the Mason-Dixon Line. Yet a biracial community of action continued to thrive in Washington and to engender bonds of interracial friendship. More than anything else, the story of Myrtilla Miner and the black families with whom she cooperated demonstrates this.

SEVEN

Myrtilla Miner's School:
Education, Feminism, Biracialism

IN 1858 Emma V. Brown, who studied and taught at Myrtilla Miner's Washington "school for colored girls," wrote a letter to William Lloyd Garrison thanking him for sending copies of the *Liberator* to the school's library. Brown praised Garrison for starting the "antislavery agitation," for never forgetting the "oppressed," for publishing "speeches delivered by *colored* men," and for inspiring her "with hope and confidence." Brown then turned to the similar accomplishments of Miner's school. Noting that a local newspaper had called the school "incendiary," Brown commented, "May it indeed prove . . . [so], and may the flame of knowledge, now lit, burn more and more brightly and fiercely, until slavery shall be burned out of our land!"[1]

These views accorded well with those of the school's white founder. Miner had arrived in Washington from western New York in November 1851 and established her school a few weeks later. Thirty-six years old and unmarried, she was a charismatic individual committed to educating free black girls and young women. Education, she believed, was the key to emancipating African Americans from slavery and racial oppression. Her school kept the form she gave it until 1860 and reemerged fifteen years later as Miner Normal School. The history of the school during the 1850s illuminates a central aspect of Washington's subversive community during that final antebellum decade.

1. Brown to Garrison, 1 April 1858, in *L,* 16 April 1858. Brown later attended Oberlin College.

In the promotional literature she produced for her school Miner portrayed herself as a solitary agent of God working in Washington's hostile, proslavery, antiblack, antiabolitionist environment. Although she was a mature and experienced teacher who had worked previously in a slaveholding region, she suggested that she had come to Washington without a definite plan for her school, without money, and—with one major exception—without encouragement from slavery's opponents. "Alone with not fifty dollars at my command and more than one hundred in debt I was pressed by inner promptings to bid farewell to friends and start for Washington to open a school," she recalled. God's will alone, she insisted, allowed her to prevail.[2]

It was a romantic age and Miner was not unique in portraying herself as an independent agent of God. She nevertheless exaggerated her isolation.[3] Her correspondence reveals that her venture in Washington must be understood in terms of her association with northern abolitionism and the city's subversive community. She interacted with radical political abolitionists prior to her removal south. In Washington she enjoyed the support of her students, other African Americans, and local antislavery whites. These relationships. as well as the proslavery reaction to her interracial initiative, are what made her significant in the sectional conflict.

Feminism also shaped Miner's career in Washington. She and her school illustrate the growing role of black and white women in the city's antislavery community during the 1850s. Women had, of course, participated in subversive action prior to that decade. But men dominated in manumissions, court cases, and escape attempts. Men also provided almost all of the records concerning these efforts. In contrast, education lay within the traditionally feminine sphere and Miner and other antislavery women of both races wrote

2. "20a," undated manuscript; [Myrtilla Miner], *The School for Colored Girls. Washington, D.C.* (Philadelphia: Merrihew and Thompson, 1854), 6; [Miner] to Friends, [typed copy, 1854?] (quotation); William H. Beecher, *Normal School for Colored Girls, Washington, D.C.,* printed circular, [December 1856]; Miner to Emily Howland, 23 June 1857, MMP.

3. See for example: Michael Flushe, "Antislavery and Spiritualism: Myrtilla Miner and Her School," *New York Historical Society Quarterly* 59 (April 1975): 150, 157; Philip S. Foner and Josephine F. Pacheco, *Three Who Dared: Prudence Crandall, Margaret Douglass, Myrtilla Miner—Champions of Antebellum Black Education* (Westport, Conn.: Greenwood, 1984), 99; Druscilla J. Null, "Myrtilla Miner's 'School for Colored Girls': A Mirror on Antebellum Washington," *RCHS* 52 (1989): 254, 258–9.

Myrtilla Miner (1815–1864) in 1851 established a school in Washington for black girls and young women. More than any other white woman in the city, she exemplified interracial cooperation against slavery during the 1850s. Ellen M. O'Connor, *Myrtilla Miner: A Memoir* (Boston: Houghton, Mifflin, 1885), frontispiece.

about their experiences as teachers. Their activism during the 1850s anticipated the emergence of women during the Civil War years as leading agents in behalf of thousands of freedpeople who came to Washington from Virginia and Maryland.

Miner was strikingly paradoxical in demeanor. In 1883 Frederick Douglass recalled her 1851 visit to his Rochester, New York, newspaper office just before she left for Washington. She was, he noted, "a slender, wiry, pale (not over-healthy), but singularly animated figure." Another associate remembered that the short, thin Miner "gave the impression from the first of great power,—mental, moral, and spiritual; but . . . [also] seemed to be utterly worn and exhausted." She combined "habitual ill health" with a "vigorous look."[4]

Miner also combined a gentle love of flowers, family, friends, children, and students with a stubborn imperiousness and "terrible wrath" that surfaced

4. Ellen M. O'Connor, *Myrtilla Miner: A Memoir* (1885; reprint, Arno: New York, 1969), 122 (first quotation), 109 (second & third quotations), 118 (fourth quotation). See also Octavius Brooks Frothingham, *Memoir of William Henry Channing* (New York: Houghton, Mifflin, 1886), 404–5.

when she could not achieve the results she desired. Her assistant, Emily Howland, portrayed her as a perfectionist who "grudged waiting for results" and was "often severe in her kindness" toward her students. Fearless Miner, with dark eyes flashing, also unleashed her temper against slaveholders who threatened what they called her "*nigger school*" and on one occasion she berated the president of the United States. Because Millard Fillmore failed to receive her at the White House in 1852 when she called to seek a pardon for Daniel Drayton and Edward Sayres, she compared him to "some aristocratic boor of the South," and lectured him regarding proper "*gentlemanly*" behavior.[5]

Born in 1815 in Madison County, on the eastern edge of New York's Burned-over District, Miner grew up amid the religious revivalism that characterized the region. As historian Michael Flushe notes, religious intensity along with delicate health and an adventuresome spirit shaped her life. They also led her to experience enormous stress and severe emotional breakdowns. Too ill as a young woman to contemplate motherhood and housework as realistic options, she taught at her neighborhood school when she was sixteen, and subsequently enrolled in the Young Ladies Domestic Seminary at nearby Clinton. She taught for several years in Rochester, New York, and Providence, Rhode Island, before taking a position in 1846 at the Newton Female Institute in Mississippi, where her preexisting mild antipathy to slavery blossomed, in Flushe's words, into "unreserved repulsion."[6]

She maintained that she was so "shocked with Slavery" she could not sleep, became deathly ill, and returned to New York during the summer of 1848 expecting to die. Assuming that God had spared her for a reason, she

5. Extremes of Miner's personality: O'Connor, *Miner,* 118–20 (first quotation), 110 (second & third quotations) and F. Holden to Miner, 18 March 1860, MMP. Confrontational posture: manuscript prepared for Harriet Beecher Stowe "in 1852[4]" (hereafter cited as Manuscript for H. B. Stowe) (fourth quotation) and Miner to Fillmore, June or July 1852 (fifth & sixth quotations), MMP.

6. Flushe, "Miner," 149–72 (quotation 156). The best account of Miner's life is Josephine F. Pacheco's in Foner and Pacheco, *Three Who Dared,* 99–219. Pacheco theorizes that Miner contracted tuberculosis as a child. For other accounts of Miner's career see: G. Smith Wormley, "Myrtilla Miner," *Journal of Negro History* 5 (October 1920): 448–57; Lester G. Wells, "Myrtilla Miner," *New York History* 24 (July 1943): 360–74.

determined, as she later told William H. Seward, that her "mission on Earth has some what to do with the oppressed & the afflicted, the cast down & down trodden *colored race* in our own free country."[7]

In this attribution of her antislavery commitment to her experience in Mississippi, Miner serves as an excellent example in support of historian James L. Huston's contention that observation of slavery played an essential role in the orientation of northern abolitionists. It is equally clear that exposure to northern evangelicalism prepared Miner for subversive activity. She never joined an abolitionist organization nor did she attend the women's rights convention that met at nearby Seneca Falls shortly after her return to Madison County from Mississippi. Yet meetings with local radical political abolitionists and her ties to such prominent feminists as Paulina Wright Davis led her to Washington and her school.[8]

Miner was a feminist as early as 1841, when she urged Seward, who was then governor of New York, to support greater access to education for women. Limited educational opportunities, she believed, contributed to the weakness of women in a patriarchal culture. While she was willing to exploit that weakness as a shield against proslavery violence, she believed, like many antebellum feminists, that if women were to improve their status, they had to acquire such masculine traits as bravery and physical strength. Revealing something of the will that made her appear formidable despite her frailty, she described herself in 1850 as "one of Dame Nature's fearless daughters." She admired "manly energy," and in 1853 urged a friend to have her daughter "trained for strength and fitted for great action."[9]

Black women, Miner believed, must become especially strong to escape

7. Miner to Dr. [D. L.] Phares, 26 July 1847, Miner to Gerrit Smith, 16 December 1847, MMP; Miner to Seward, 1 January 1848, in Lester G. Well, "To Teach the Darkened Child: Life and Letters of Myrtilla Miner," 93–4, unfinished typescript, MMP; Miner to Seward, 25 December 1850, WHSP.

8. James L. Huston, "The Experiential Basis of the Northern Antislavery Impulse," *Journal of Southern History* 56 (November 1990): 609–40; Foner and Pacheco, *Three Who Dared*, 179–85.

9. Miner to Seward, 25 December 1850, WHSP (first quotation); Seward to Miner, 27 December 1841, Miner to Gerrit Smith, 11 February 1850, "Feminism and Emancipation," 4 July 1850, Miner to John Murray, 11 February 1856 (second quotation), MMP; Blanche Glassman Hersh, *The Slavery of Sex: Feminist-Abolitionists in America* (Urbana: University of Illinois Press, 1978), 206–9; O'Connor, *Miner,* 44 (third quotation).

sexual exploitation and to help liberate their people. Interracial sisterhood and surrogate motherhood became very important to Miner as her career in Washington progressed. In 1857, while she was in poor physical health and recovering from a severe emotional breakdown suffered two years earlier, she reported to a male friend how much she enjoyed the "sweet-faced world of young [black] women, some of whom," she said, "I am happily able to draw about me for study and amusement while great thoughts are being suggested to them and left to struggle in their minds with miraculous power." She whimsically suggested that this might be enough for her "in this hard, severe, ungenial world." This feeling of feminine community was nearly as important to her as producing teachers and liberators.[10]

Miner would not have become involved with young black women in Washington, however, without prompting from radical political abolitionists. She had for some time been aware of this group's aggressive posture toward the South. She heard Gerrit Smith speak at Cazenovia, New York, during the early 1840s and she was an admirer of William L. Chaplin prior to her sojourn in Mississippi. She and Chaplin had mutual radical political abolitionist friends in Asa B. Smith, his son William R. Smith—who would later spearhead the effort to secure Chaplin's release from jail—and in George W. Clark, a popular antislavery minstrel. The Smiths were orthodox Quakers who lived near Rochester. They had been family friends of Miner prior to her sojourn in Mississippi and they had encouraged Clark to write to her there.[11]

While she was teaching in Mississippi, Miner came under the influence of her slaveholding principal, an advocate of gradual, compensated emancipation. When she naively attempted in December 1847 to enlist the support of Gerrit Smith for this conservative scheme, Smith patiently explained the principles of immediatism. In response Miner began to envision teaching black children in the North as an indirect means of changing the attitudes of white southerners toward slavery. When she returned to New York, her friendship with Smith's abolitionist associates, some of whom had labored in

10. Miner wrote of black women being "subjected to greater temptations to evil." See Manuscript for H. B. Stowe, MMP. Relationship with young black women: Miner to John Murray, 7 November 1857, MMP (quotations).

11. Miner to Gerrit Smith, 16 December 1847, G. W. C[lark] to Miner, 30 May 1847, MMP.

Washington, led her to contemplate the more aggressive strategy of teaching black students in that southern city.[12]

During 1849 Miner lived in William R. Smith's home, teaching his children and recovering from the breakdown in health she had suffered in Mississippi. There she met with "the antislavery hero Chaplin" and Asa B. Smith, both of whom hoped black education in the border South would encourage abolition. They were attempting to raise $7,000 to begin a school in Washington and Asa B. Smith asked Miner "if . . . [she] would take charge of such a school when the hoped-for-time of establishing it should come." Because of her poor health, Miner hesitated to commit herself, but as she gained strength during the succeeding year she became committed to the undertaking. She supposed that it was to be a radical political abolitionist project funded by Gerrit Smith.[13]

She later learned that Smith had made no such commitment. But Chaplin and other radical political abolitionists continued to encourage her to go to Washington. Following his permanent departure from the capital in late 1850, Chaplin assured her, on the basis of his familiarity "with the wants & powers of the free people of color in that city," that an effort to establish a school for their daughters was "both reasonable & practical." Chaplin encouraged her to write to his black friend, John F. Cook Sr. who, because of his standing as an educator could provide invaluable help to her in attracting stu-

12. Miner to Phares, 5 Mach 1847 (in Wells, "To Teach," 85), Miner to Smith, 16 December 1847, Smith to Miner, 10 January 1848 (in Wells, "To Teach," 96), Manuscript for H. B. Stowe, MMP; Miner to William H. Seward, 25 December 1850, WHSP. See also Null, "Miner," 258. Miner wrote a similar letter to William H. Seward two weeks after she wrote to Smith, but apparently received no reply. See Miner to Seward, 1 January 1848, in Wells, "To Teach," 96.

13. *New York Evangelist*, quoted in *NS*, 14 September 1849; Miner to Gerrit Smith, 11 February (quotations) & 17 February 1850, MMP; U.S. Congress, House, *Special Report of the Commissioner of Education on the Condition and Improvement of Public Schools in the District of Columbia*, 41 Cong., 2 sess., H. Exec. Doc. 315, Serial 1427 (1870), 207 (hereafter cited as House, *Special Report*). See also Sadie D. St. Clair's brief Miner entry in Edward T. Jones, ed., *Notable American Women, 1607–1950: A Biographical Dictionary*, 3 vols. (Cambridge, Mass.: Belknap Press, 1971), 2:547. By October 1849 radical political abolitionist women in western New York had formed the "Provisional Committee for the Promotion of Education among the Colored People in Such of the Slave States [as] Are, or May Be Accessible." See *NS*, Oct. 26, 1849.

dents.[14] Thereafter Miner received most of her support from Washington's black middle-class and from more moderate antislavery whites rather than from radical political abolitionists. But the radicals inspired her choice of Washington and in so doing linked her school to their earlier subversive antislavery endeavors in the city.

As she planned her school during late 1850 and early 1851, Miner worked within an extended biracial antislavery community stretching from Rochester to Washington. She wisely sought advice and support from its leaders. Some, like Douglass and prominent white immediatist William Jay, responded cautiously, warning her of the difficulties and dangers she faced. Douglass, impressed with Miner's enthusiasm, feared her Washington school would "prove a vain effort, and bring only persecution and death." Jay, who resided in New York City, questioned the practicality of her endeavor.[15]

But, contrary to Miner's later claims, others embraced her proposal and most of the cautious later gave her generous support. Famous evangelical minister Henry Ward Beecher of Brooklyn—whom Miner later recalled as her *only* early supporter—advised her about raising money and securing books. Chaplin offered his help and so did William Henry Channing, nephew of William Ellery Channing and himself a prominent Unitarian minister. Seward, who had been elected to the U.S. Senate in 1848, directed Miner to Margaret Bailey, whom he described as "a woman of talents and zeal in any good and human[e] work." When Miner visited the AMA office in New York City, Lewis Tappan introduced her to Daniel A. Payne, the AME bishop who had earlier befriended Charles T. Torrey. Payne warned her of the dangers she would face in Washington but also acted in her behalf. Many years later he recalled that "her heroic spirit stirred my soul to its bot-

---

14. "20a" manuscript, Miner to [E.] D. E. N. Southworth, 16 May 1851 (quotations), Cook to Miner, 13 July 1851, MMP. Radical political abolitionist Joseph Hathaway and his sister, Phoebe Hathaway, accompanied Miner during her visit to Frederick Douglass's office in 1851. See O'Connor, *Miner*, 22.

15. "20a" manuscript, MMP (quotation). Douglass in 1883 confirmed Miner's impression of his sentiments. See O'Connor, *Miner*, 20–5. On Jay see Bayard Tuckerman, *William Jay and the Constitutional Movement for the Abolition of Slavery* (1893; reprint, New York: Negro Universities Press, 1969).

tom, and I furnished her with seven letters of introduction to the first colored families in that city."[16]

Washington's antislavery subversives provided additional aid. During the fall of 1851, before Miner arrived in the city, Jacob Bigelow used his connections to black leaders to identify potential locations and students for the school. Considering the risks he had for years run in behalf of fugitive slaves, Miner's claim that she subsequently reacted negatively to her "exampled boldness" seems unlikely.[17] Miner was correct, however, in portraying the hesitation of the Baileys and Cook to commit themselves to her cause.

At first the Baileys wanted nothing to do with her. Rather than responding directly to her letters, they relied on local novelist E. D. E. N. Southworth to inform Miner that they believed her "benevolent scheme utterly impracticable." Like Douglass they feared for her safety. They also disliked her close association with Chaplin and other radical political abolitionists, whose tactics they linked to bad publicity for the antislavery cause and financial embarrassment. But once Miner arrived in Washington and demonstrated that she was not "too much of the Chaplin order," the Baileys provided generous support.[18]

In some respects Cook's initial reaction to Miner's request for advice and assistance was similar to that of the Baileys. He feared to associate himself with her school because its connection to "abolition" could be used by proslavery whites to foment violent reprisals against him and other African Americans. Having been forced to flee Washington during the 1830s and now terminally ill, he wanted to leave his family in safety. Yet, unlike the Baileys, Cook still admired Chaplin and immediately offered Miner as much

16. Octavius Brooks Frothingham, *Memoir of William Henry Channing* (Boston: Houghton Mifflin, 1886), 404 (first quotation); "20a" manuscript, Manuscript for H. B. Stowe, Seward to Miner, 7 January 1850[1] (in Wells, "To Teach," 122) (second quotation), MMP; David Alexander Payne, *Recollections of Seventy Years* (1888; reprint, New York: Arno, 1968), 114–5 (third quotation).

17. Bigelow to Miner, 21 October 1851, "20a" manuscript (quotation), MMP.

18. Miner to Southworth, 16 May 1851, Southworth to Miner, 23 August 1851 (first quotation); Samuel Rhoads to Miner, 6 January & 21 November 1852, undated [1851] manuscript fragment written by Miner beginning "Could Mr. Cook" (second quotation), MMP. Miner attributed "fear" of "the Chaplin order" to Cook but it is more likely that the Baileys felt that way.

support as he could. He praised her willingness "to make sacrifices" in behalf of black education, assured her that "a good female school is needed much," and denied that it would interfere with his own school. In April 1852 he set an example for other African Americans in the city by enrolling his daughter, Mary Victoria, in Miner's school.[19]

It is unlikely that Miner would have succeeded in establishing her school in Washington without this combination of black and white, local and northern antislavery help. An interracial and intersectional effort enabled the school to survive and, for a time, to thrive. It opened on December 3, 1851, with six pupils meeting with Miner and Anna Inman—a New York Quaker who had traveled south with Miner—in a room rented from a black man named Edward C. Younger. Local white hostility forced Miner to move the school repeatedly so that by May 1852 it was in its third location and in its fourth by October 1853.

Enrollment, nevertheless, rose to forty-one by February 1852 and forty-five by the following autumn, with students varying in age from seven to sixteen. There were lessons in arithmetic, reading, grammar, composition, history, geography, deportment, domestic economy, physical fitness, diet, and hygiene. Miner intended to prepare the girls and young women to be teachers for their race. Students also received a thorough grounding in evangelicalism, feminism, and abolitionism.[20]

In order to support this educational endeavor, Miner traveled north each summer to raise funds. She targeted a cross section of abolitionists and antislavery politicians who responded with donations and endorsements. Among the more prominent contributors were Lewis Tappan, Wendell Phillips, Lucretia Mott, Samuel Joseph May, and George B. Cheever. Churches and in-

---

19. Cook to Miner, 31 July 1851 (quotations) and 6 April 1852, MMP.

20. Myrtle Mirror [*sic*] to Julia Griffiths, 31 January 1852, in *FDP*, 26 February 1852; Mary Mann to Frederick Douglass, 3 March 1852, in *FDP*, 25 March 1852; Miner to Hannah, 17 May 1852, in O'Connor, *Miner*, 37–8; *NE*, 27 October 1853; student essays, 21 June 1852–5 July 1854, undated manuscript "circa early 1852 [summer 1852]," Miner to Isaac Newton Miner, 15 March 1852, Samuel Rhoads to Miner, 21 November 1852, *The School for Colored Girls. Washington, D.C.* (Philadelphia: privately published, 1854), MMP; House, *Special Report*, 207–8; Flushe, "Miner," 160; Foner and Pacheco, *Three Who Dared*, 121–6. Miner and Inman "could not labor harmoniously" and Inman soon departed. See Rhoads to Miner, 15 April 1852, MMP.

dividuals from Missouri to Massachusetts donated funds, with the largest amounts coming from Philadelphia, New York, and Boston. Miner also gained the assistance of British abolitionists Anna H. Richardson and Joseph W. Sturge in raising funds in England and Scotland.[21]

Henry Ward Beecher, his sister, Harriet Beecher Stowe, Samuel Rhoads, and Rhoads's associate, Thomas Williamson, comprised the core of Miner's northern antislavery constituency. Beecher provided moral support, purchased "books and furniture," and, as he had in the Edmonson case, raised funds from his wealthy congregation. Stowe, who bonded with Miner and her students on several levels, in 1853 donated $1,000 that British readers of *Uncle Tom's Cabin* had given her during a trip to England. In 1855 she provided an additional $500.[22]

Rhoads and Williamson, wealthy Philadelphia Quakers, became even more intimately involved than Beecher and Stowe in the operation of Miner's school. Rhoads had edited the abolitionist *Nonslaveholder* in Philadelphia from 1846 to 1850 and had helped lead the movement to boycott slave-labor products. Williamson was the father of abolitionist martyr Passmore Williamson, who was jailed in 1855 for resisting the Fugitive Slave Act of 1850. Rhoads and the elder Williamson assumed control of the school's finances and sought a permanent location for it. This effort led, after considerable difficulty, to the purchase of a small frame house and several cabins on a three-acre tract in rural northwestern Washington.[23]

21. Summer trips: Rhoads to Miner, 7 July 1852, 6 July & 18 November 1854, MMP; Flushe, "Miner," 161. Donors: Myrtle Mirror [*sic*] to [Julia] Griffiths, 31 January 1852, in *FDP*, 26 February 1852; list of donors and receipts 1853–59, Samuel Rhoads to Miner, 8 February & 7 May 1854, 14 September 1857, MMP; Tappan to Miner, 14 August 1855, letter book copy, LTP; May to Frances Adeline Seward, 6 August 1857, WHSP; Null, "Miner," 262. Endorsements: *School for Colored Girls*, 9–13. British assistance: Rhoads to Miner, 15 April 1852, 19 January 1854, MMP.

22. Beecher: "20a" manuscript (quotation), Manuscript for H. B. Stowe, William H. Beecher to Samuel Rhoads, 14 September 1857, MMP. Stowe: Rhoads to Miner, 21 February & 9 March 1853, [Miner] to Stowe, 1 October 1853, *School for Colored Girls*, 2, Stowe to Miner, 1 October 1853, 8 November 1855, Miner to [John] Murray, 11 February 1856, MMP; Stowe to Ladies Anti-Slavery Society of Glasgow, 18 November 1853, in *FDP*, 20 January 1854; Foner and Pacheco, *Three Who Dared*, 151–3.

23. Betty Fladeland, *Men and Brothers: Anglo-American Antislavery Cooperation* (Urbana: University of Illinois Press, 1972), 359; Miner to Isaac Newton Miner, 15 March 1852, undated

The roles played by radical political abolitionists and more moderate anti-slavery activists in initiating and maintaining Miner's school perpetuated the tradition of northern involvement in the Washington antislavery community. Also, the white men and women in Washington who aided Miner were usually connected with one branch or another of the northern antislavery movement. Several of them were private citizens who had for years worked in the District of Columbia to subvert slavery. Others were antislavery members of Congress who, often encouraged by their wives and daughters, emulated to a degree Giddings's local involvements.

Matilda A. Jones, who was either a student or a teacher at Miner's school for most of the 1850s, later—as Matilda Jones Madden—listed white residents she recalled to have been its supporters. Among them were Mary Peabody Mann, wife of noted educator and Whig congressman Horace Mann, and Moncure Conway, a Virginia-born Unitarian minister who later became a Garrisonian. Jones also included the Baileys, the family of Senator Seward, and Mary Abigail Dodge, a young journalist and governess for the Bailey children during 1858 and 1859. Gerrit Smith and his married daughter, Elizabeth Smith Miller, were "devoted friends" while Smith briefly served in Congress during 1853 and 1854. For a far longer period, so were Dr. Leonard D. Gale, the chemical examiner for the United States Patent Office, and his wife, A. E. Gale, who lodged Miner in their home during her first two years in Washington.[24]

Seward and Smith were part of a small but powerful coterie of antislavery congressmen—all of whom but Smith became Republicans by 1855. They also visited the school with their families, boarded its students, franked letters, provided testimonials, and countered proslavery criticism of Miner. Among the congressmen were Giddings, Charles Sumner, Norton S. Townshend, Salmon P. Chase, Owen Lovejoy, Charles Durkee, Henry Wilson, and Schuyler Colfax.[25]

manuscript "circa early 1852 [summer 1852]," Rhoads to Miner, 13 January & 17 March 1853, 13 January 1855, MMP.

24. O'Connor, *Miner*, 93–4 (quotations); House, *Special Report*, 209; Miner to Isaac Newton Miner, 15 March 1852, M. C. Horsford to Miner, 25 October 1853; L. D. Gale to Miner, 19 June 1857, undated printed Gale résumé with Miner's note on verso, MMP.

25. O'Connor, *Miner*, 37–8, 96–7; Miner to Isaac Newton Miner, 15 March 1852, Miner to Fillmore, June or July 1852, list of donors and receipts, 1853–1859, *School for Colored Girls*,

Miner also enjoyed the help of two local lawyers and two local business-men, all of whom were northern-born. The lawyers were Allen M. Gangew-ere, a young assistant to Chase and sometime interim editor of the *National Era*, and veteran antislavery attorney David A. Hall. The businessmen were Benjamin B. French and Sayles J. Bowen. French, a New Hampshire native who in 1852 served as president of Washington's board of aldermen, pledged to protect Miner's school against proslavery threats. Bowen, a Free Soiler from western New York, served as her business agent.[26]

While each of these individuals helped Miner to succeed, the Baileys were at the center of the local effort in her behalf. Margaret Bailey had been in-volved in black education since 1841, when the couple lived in Cincinnati. She helped Miner contact similarly inclined women. Gamaliel Bailey publi-cized Miner's school in the *National Era*, contributed financial support, and, in cooperation with Margaret Bailey, introduced Miner to local antislavery activists. With encouragement from Rhoads, Miner made Gamaliel Bailey her most trusted local adviser.[27]

Miner realized, nevertheless, that her school would fail without the sup-port of local African Americans. She constantly interacted with black leaders like Cook and Payne and with black parents. In this endeavor her transparent empathy for the suffering of the oppressed, both slave and free, served her well despite her demanding personality. "I called you good because it is truth," one acquaintance told her. "I did not mean that you was particularly good to me but that you was good to those in bonds—to the oppressed—to

9–12, M. C. Horsford to Miner, 25 June 1854, MMP; Emily Howland to Mother, 13–6 Janu-ary & 23 December 1858, EHP.

26. Gangewere: *NE*, 5 August 1852; Thomas Williamson to Miner, 16 October 1852; Samuel Rhoads to Miner, 13 & 21 February 1853, 18 April 1854, MMP. See also Stanley Har-rold, *Gamaliel Bailey and Antislavery Union* (Kent, Ohio: Kent State University Press, 1986), 132, 156, 194. Hall: Rhoads to Miner, 26 April, 8, 11, 24, & 26 September 1853, MMP. French: Mary Mann to [Frederick Douglass], 3 March 1852, *FDP*, 25 March 1852. Bowen: Foner and Pacheco, *Three Who Dared*, 166–8, 191–2, 196, 198; William Tindall, "A Sketch of Sayles J. Bowen," *RCHS* 18 (1915): 25–6; House, *Special Report*, 208.

27. *Philanthropist*, 9 June 1841; *NE*, 27 October 1853, 1 February 1855; Rhoads to Miner, 6 January & 21 November 1852, 21 February, 22 & 26 September 1853, Miner to Rhoads, 24 September 1853, manuscript entitled "Washington Association for the Education of Colored Youth," 23 May 1856, Rhoads to Miner, 3 December 1857, Bailey to Miner, 31 May 1858, MMP; O'Connor, *Miner*, 46–7.

the needy & to all generally with whom you met tho you sometimes had an odd way of showing it."[28]

Miner's main appeal was, as Bishop Payne suggested, to the local black elite—to those who could afford to have their daughters educated. Using her letters of introduction from Payne, Miner walked from home to home to enlist this class in her subversive enterprise and she continued to visit the homes of her students throughout her stay in Washington. This was remarkable at a time when most whites despised even the black elite as a group little different in character from slaves. In addition, Miner reached beyond the black elite by keeping tuition low, by loaning money to destitute parents, and by accepting a significant number of "charity" students. According to Miner's most thorough biographer, "many of the children [attending Miner's school] were too poor to provide their own school supplies." It was their parents, nevertheless, who urged Miner to acquire a permanent site for the school and who volunteered to construct a schoolhouse.[29]

As this indicates, Washington's African Americans, with some exceptions, accepted Miner and gave her their friendship and moral support. Payne, who visited her school several times, recalled that in times of "troubles and persecutions," Miner had visited the home of his "sister-in-law in Georgetown" seeking "rest and consolation." Similarly Matilda A. Jones recalled that Miner "was a frequent visitor at my father's house." Jones noted that her parents had "a high appreciation of her [Miner's] labors in the community" and "always made her welcome at their home, and assisted her in many ways." Years later a white observer found that "her memory is certainly held precious in the

28. Payne, *Recollections,* 114–5; F. Holden to Miner, 18 March 1860, MMP (quotation). Miner's empathy: Miner to Gerrit Smith, 11 February 1850, Miner to E. D. E. N. Southworth, 16 May 1851, B. Ayer to Miner, 8 April 1855, MMP.

29. Miner's appeal: Miner to William H. Seward, 25 December 1850, WHSP; Payne, *Recollections,* 114–5; Miner to E. D. E. N. Southworth, 16 May 1851, MMP; Lorenzo D. Johnson to Simeon S. Jocelyn, 12 March 1863, AMAA; O'Connor, *Miner,* 83. Most whites: *New York Tribune,* quoted in *L,* 5 June 1857; Miner to Rhoads, 24 September 1853, MMP. Poorer students: Undated fragment [1851], *School for Colored Girls,* 6–7 (first quotation); William H. Beecher, *Normal School for Colored Girls* (circular, December 1856), Rhoads to Miner, 15 April 1852, 15 July 1857, Elizabeth Gale to Miner, 17 December 1856, MMP; O'Connor, *Miner,* 83, 95; House, *Special Report,* 208; Foner and Pacheco, *Three Who Dared,* 121 (second quotation), 127. For reasons discussed below, the school was never built.

hearts of her throngs of pupils, in the hearts of the colored people of this District."[30]

Of all Washington's black families, it was with the Edmonsons that Miner lived most intimately, if not always harmoniously. The white teacher and the black family, which had gained fame due to its connection with the *Pearl*, came together fortuitously as a result of a February 1853 meeting at the Baileys' home. Miner, Samuel Rhoads, and Harriet Beecher Stowe, who had initially published her great novel *Uncle Tom's Cabin* as a serial in Bailey's *National Era*, all attended.

Stowe was in Washington to consult with Bailey before her departure for a promotional tour in England. But she also had come because of her interest in the Edmonsons. She planned to feature Amelia (or Milly) in her *Key to Uncle Tom's Cabin* and hoped to help the Edmonsons to buy freedom for two of their children who remained in slavery. Miner and Rhoads had just consummated the purchase of the lot for Miner's school. By the time the meeting concluded, Stowe had pledged to raise money in England for the school and Miner had agreed to rent a cabin and a large portion of the school grounds to the Edmonsons, where Paul Edmonson, his sons, and one of his sons-in-law could farm.[31]

Because Miner and Paul Edmonson failed to establish a clear tenancy agreement, there was persistent friction between them. But Miner's ties to the Edmonsons involved a great deal more than rent. In October 1853, at Stowe's suggestion, she agreed to allow their daughter and former *Pearl* fugitive Emily to join her school as an assistant teacher. In March 1854 Emily, who, with her recently deceased sister Mary, had attended Oberlin College, became Miner's companion and moved with her into the house on the school

30. Payne, *Recollections*, 114–5 (first & second quotations); O'Connor, *Miner*, 95 (third–fifth quotations); Nancy Day to Geo. T. Downing, 8 June 1855, Matilda Jones to Miner, 20 April 1858, E. Bryon to Miner, 2 June [1858], MMP; House, *Special Report*, 210 (sixth quotation).

31. Rhoads to Miner, 21 February & 9 March 1853, Miner to Rhoads, 25 September 1853, MMP; Harriet Beecher Stowe, *The Key to Uncle Tom's Cabin* (1854; reprint, New York: Arno, 1968), 306–30. Effort to purchase the property: Foner and Pacheco, *Three Who Dared*, 127–32, 137. The best biography of Stowe is Joan D. Hedrick, *Harriet Beecher Stowe: A Life* (New York: Oxford University Press, 1995). Hedrick does not cover this incident.

lot. The house also provided classrooms, dormitory space, and a home for three young black children whom Miner had adopted.[32]

When the elder Edmonsons took up residence at the cottage a month later, Amelia Edmonson began cooking for Miner, Emily, and the children. Much more crucial to Miner, however, was the physical protection provided by the Edmonson men. During the month when Miner and Emily were the only adults occupying the property at night, Miner reported that they had to live there "alone, unprotected, except by God, the rowdies stoning our house at evening." She responded initially by having a fence built and assuming a brave posture: "Emily and I have been seen practicing with a pistol," she noted. She was, nevertheless, relieved when the rest of the Edmonsons "here came, and a dog with them," because then her school was "left in most profound peace."[33]

Had Paul Edmonson only been Miner's tenant and Amelia Edmonson only her cook, one might conclude that Miner, despite her reliance on free labor, had fallen into a typically southern domestic relationship between whites and African Americans. But her correspondence with Rhoads concerning the school lot suggests something closer to a partnership. Depending on a black family for sustenance, companionship, and protection, while finding considerable pleasure in caring for three black children, Miner, during the mid-1850s, drew as much personally from her interracial endeavor as she put into it. She, her white assistants, the Edmonsons, her other black supporters, and her students provide an unsurpassed example of biracialism in the antislavery cause.

32. Miner's relationship with the Edmonsons: Miner to Stowe, 1 October 1853, Rhoads to Miner, 8 & 25 February 1854, 29 March & 7 May 1855, Miner to Paul Edmonson, 16 January 1855, MMP. Mary Edmonson: *The Slave*, no. 31 (July 1853): 27; Hanchett, "Edmondson Sisters," 21–37. Adopted children: O'Connor, *Miner*, 53, 110–1; Miner to [Ruth Church and Family], 14[?] January 1855, MMP. According to Frederick Douglass, "Two of these children appeared to be 'so nearly white as to make it almost impossible for the unpracticed eye to identify them with the African race.'" See *FDP*, 1 September 1854. Stowe provided financial assistance to Emily and Mary Edmonson while they attended Oberlin. See C. E. Stowe to Henry Cowles, 20 July 1852, Stowe to Mary, 2 October 1852, Stowe to [Mrs. Cowles], 12 December 1853, Henry Cowles Papers, Oberlin College Archives.

33. O'Connor, *Miner*, 50–1 (quotations); Rhoads to Miner, 26 September 1854, MMP.

Neither Miner, her friends, her students, nor her proslavery enemies doubted that her school promoted that movement. Some African Americans in Washington questioned her motives. At least one prominent black northern abolitionist challenged her commitment to racial justice. But all agreed that the education of free blacks in a southern city threatened slavery.[34]

Since the time of Elisha Tyson, black and white abolitionists had assumed that African Americans bore some responsibility for the continued enslavement of their race in the United States. Black abolitionists David Walker, Maria W. Stewart, and Henry Highland Garnet preceded such white abolitionists as John Brown and Theodore Parker in contending that black *men* must become more knowledgeable, virtuous, vigorous, and valiant if they were to gain freedom for their people. Miner became the most prominent of a very few individuals who, in order to impart such virtues, actually went among African Americans living south of the Mason-Dixon Line. She also assumed that young black *women* could aspire to these virtues and made abolitionism an explicit part of her school's curriculum.[35]

Her goal, she told Southworth, was to employ "sympathy and love to raise . . . [African Americans] from the prison house of bondage." Miner realized that her "sympathy and love" were insufficient to abolish slavery. While she cared deeply for her students, she believed that it was not her caring but their careers as teachers that would liberate the slaves. Like Chaplin, she linked

34. John F. Cook to Miner, 31 July 1851, *School for Colored Girls*, 3, Manuscript for H. B. Stowe, MMP; Walter Lenox to editors, n.d., *National Intelligencer* (Washington), 6 May 1851; George T. Downing to Frederick Douglass, 6 December 1854, in *FDP*, 22 December 1854. Emily Edmonson left in November 1854 on an extensive fund raising tour. See: O'Connor, *Miner*, 53. It appears that the other members of the Edmonson family had left by late 1857. See Miner to [John Murray], 7 November 1857 and Emily Howland to Miner, 5 December 1858, MMP.

35. David Walker, *David Walker's Appeal . . . to the Colored Citizens of the World*, ed. Charles M. Wiltse (New York: Hill and Wang, 1965), 62; Marilyn Richardson, ed., *Maria W. Stewart, America's First Black Woman Political Writer* (Bloomington: Indiana University Press, 1987), 57–62; Garnet, "Address to the Slaves of the United States," in C. Peter Ripley et al., eds., *The Black Abolitionist Papers*, 5 vols. (Chapel Hill: University of North Carolina Press, 1985–1992), 3:410; Franklin B. Sanborn, *The Life and Letters of John Brown* (1885; reprint, New York: Negro Universities Press, 1969), 130; "Speech of Theodore Parker," 28 January 1858, in *L*, 19 February 1858; Wilhelmus Bogart Bryan, *A History of the National Capital*, 2 vols. (New York: MacMillan, 1916), 1:389.

the education of free blacks with the "abolition of slavery." Years later Ellen O'Connor recalled that "Miss Miner's plan was, really, to sap the slave power by educating its victims, for the free blacks were crushed under its remorseless heel almost as if actually slaves themselves."[36]

To this end, Miner made northern abolitionism part of her school's curriculum. Her students learned about Frederick Douglass. They read his newspaper as well as the *Liberator*, the *National Era*, Jane Grey Swisshelm's *Saturday Visitor*, and the *New York Tribune*. They sang songs from the Hutchinson family's antislavery song book. While a large percentage of their written assignments dealt with the fate of their souls, students also wrote about the movement to provide Bibles to slaves and pondered the prospect of violent abolition. For example, shortly after the passage of the Kansas-Nebraska Act, one student wrote to Miner, "I think there will be blood shed before all can be free, and the question is, are we ready to give up our *own* lives for freedom? Will we *die* for our own people!"[37]

There was much that was patronizing in Miner's relationship to her students. She insisted that she had undertaken her "merciful" or "elevating" mission in Washington because African Americans, without white assistance, would not learn self-reliance or achieve a real desire for freedom. She denigrated the black teachers who preceded her in the capital, believed *she* had to "arouse colored people," and assumed that generations of white helpers would be required "in bringing out & developing these rubbish-hidden treasures." She informed black Washingtonians that, rather than "dwell upon the injustice and inconsistency of white folks," they must "stand firmly and meet all obstacles arising from ignorance and fear among their people."[38]

36. Miner to Southworth, 16 May 1851, MMP (first & second quotations); O'Connor, *Miner*, 19–20 (third & fourth quotations).

37. Myrtle Mirror [*sic*] to Julia Griffiths, 31 January 1852, in *FDP*, 26 February 1852; Miner to Isaac Newton Miner, 15 March 1852, M. A. Beckett to Teacher, 12 July 1854, Marietta Hill to Teacher, 5 July 1854 (quotation), MMP.

38. Miner to E. D. E. N. Southworth, 16 May 1851 (first & second quotations), *School for Colored Girls*, 6, Miner to Harriet Beecher Stowe, 1 October 1853, Miner to Ruth Church and family, 14[?] January 1855 (fourth quotation), MMP; Myrtle Mirror [*sic*] to Julia Griffiths, 31 January 1852, in *FDP*, 26 February 1852; O'Connor, *Miner*, 83, 89, 91 (first, fifth, & sixth quotations, respectively). Miner's attitude toward Washington schools conducted by African Americans was not entirely racial. She embraced Rhode Island educational reformer Henry Barnard's "most advanced ideas for teacher training" and criticized those, regardless of race,

This assumption of cultural and moral superiority, which Miner shared with her white assistants, put off some middle class people of color. But it was precisely this point of view that provided her the strength of character required to forge biracial community and conceive it to be multi-generational. Although she exaggerated when she informed Seward that she was "destitute of those peculiar prejudices which afflict most of my race," she insisted that there were no differences between the races in "natural talent." Although she could, in times of stress, denounce the "stupidity" of her students, she maintained that the shortcomings she perceived were the result of "many generations" of "oppression and degradation."[39]

The thrust of Miner's plan was to train teachers who would prepare free blacks south of the Mason-Dixon Line to become more effective opponents of slavery. Her students got her point. In 1855 Matilda A. Jones observed to a white visitor that while black women faced "severer trials" than white women in obtaining an education, "we need it more than your people do & ought to strive harder because the greater part of our people, are yet in bondage. We that are free," she continued, "are expected to be the means of bringing them out of Slavery." Three years later Emma V. Brown told Garrison that "with education we can no longer be oppressed" and expressed her desire to spread that precept to the "darkened minds of the oppressed all over the land."[40] By 1855 one of Miner's students was teaching in Wilmington and two years later a half dozen were similarly employed in Washington. But black criticism, Miner's physical and emotional frailty, and a proslavery reaction to her school limited her effectiveness just as her plan was beginning to produce results.

In December 1854 George T. Downing, a black abolitionist residing in

---

who did not implement them. See Foner and Pacheco, *Three Who Dared*, 120–1 (quotation), 139.

39. Miner to Seward, 25 December 1850, WHSP (first quotation); Miner to Jane and Elton Brent, 8 May 1855, Matilda A. Jones to Miner, 20 April 1858, *School for Colored Girls*, 3 (second quotation), Miner to Ruth Church and family, 14[?] January 1855 (third & fourth quotations), MMP.

40. *School for Colored Girls*, 3, 6, Jones to Miss Dewey, 25 June 1855 (first & second quotations), Jones to Miner, 20 April 1858, MMP; Brown to Garrison, 1 April 1858, in *L*, 16 April 1858 (third quotation). On occasion Miner appealed for white support by contending that education would make free blacks more tractable.

Providence, Rhode Island, published a letter in *Frederick Douglass' Paper* that portrayed Miner as a racist. Downing indicted her for questioning the effectiveness of black teachers in Washington, for favoring students of mixed race, and, most strongly, for conducting her school as an "auxiliary of the [American] Colonization Society." Miner, Downing maintained, had told him in the presence of Cook and another black minister "that the colored people need not be elevated in this country; that it was our duty to go to Africa."[41]

Nancy Day, one of Miner's students, and Samuel Rhoads defended Miner against Downing's accusations. In a January 1855 letter to Douglass, Rhoads denied that he would have anything to do with a colonizationist school. Miner, he insisted, treated all her students equally and had abolitionist rather than colonizationist goals. Day, writing privately to Downing the following June, countered his criticism of Miner by noting his own disparaging remarks concerning the conduct of African Americans and his failure to promote black education when he had an opportunity to do so. The students at Miner's school, Day contended, were *"not required to go to Africa,* nor taught that it is *best* unless with . . . unbiased judgement they prefer that place to labor as missionaries or teachers."[42]

Miner's striking record of racial interaction bore out this defense. It is true that about half of her students were of mixed race. "Some are very dark & others are fairer & more beautiful than we," she informed her brother in March 1852. While Miner did not claim that the mixed race students were more intelligent than those of "pure African blood," she did regard miscegenation—or racial amalgamation—to be desirable.[43] It was, she believed, a

41. Downing to Frederick Douglass, 6 December 1854, in *FDP,* 22 December 1854. Downing: S. A. M. Washington, *George T. Downing: Sketch of His Life and Times* (Newport, R.I.: Milne Printing, 1910) and Downing, George T., q.v., *DANB.* Downing objected to Stowe giving money to Miner's school instead of to a proposed industrial school for African Americans. See *FDP,* 20 January, 24 March, & 7 April 1854. Employment of Miner's students: Matilda A. Jones to Miner, 25 June 1855; Miner to [John Murray], 7 November 1857, MMP.

42. Rhoads to Douglass, 6 January 1855, in *FDP,* 12 January 1855; Day to Downing, 8 June 1855, MMP (quotation). At least two other of Miner's students wrote anti-colonization letters. See Grace A. Tyson to Teacher, 27 May 1858 and Emma V. Brown to [?], 8 April 1859, MMP.

43. *FDP,* 1 September 1854; Miner to Isaac Newton Miner, 15 March 1852 (first quotation), E. N. Horsford to Miner, 28 December 1853 (second quotation), MMP. On students of mixed race at Miner's school see also: Mary Mann to Frederick Douglass, 3 March 1852, in

long-term solution to racial divisions. Her views on this issue placed her, along with Lydia Maria Child and Frederick Douglass, among the more radical abolitionists. In contrast colonizationists argued that blacks must be separated from whites for the benefit of both groups.

Unfortunately Miner's statements on this subject are lost and references to them occur only in the letters of her colonizationist friend M.C. Horsford, who was outraged by Miner's raising of a sexually touchy issue. "As to your philosophizing upon amalgamation I have not time to go into that," Horsford, who was the wife of a New York congressman, wrote in December 1853, before launching into that very subject. "Whatever may be practicable or desirable at the South," she told Miner, "it is utterly repugnant to a Northern mind to contemplate practical amalgamation. If it is any amusement to you & helps to while away lonely hours—to *speculate* upon the *finished race* which may be *produced* in the course of some five or six generations by crossing the breeds—you will see that the *female* is to be the *colored* party. It is perfectly abhorrent to my mind to think of a white woman being connected with a black man."[44]

While Horsford, like many reformers during the 1850s, believed that interracial contacts between blacks and whites "as equals & associates" were in decline, Miner's experience in Washington led her to a "plan of amalgamation" based on the opposite assumption.[45] Yet Miner's commitment to an extreme version of racial integration does not mean that Downing fabricated the procolonizationist remarks he attributed to her. By the time she talked

---

FDP, 25 March 1852, *School for Colored Girls*, 5, 7, William H. Beecher, *Normal School for Colored Girls*, MMP.

44. Horsford to Miner, 25 October & 14 December 1853 (quotations), MMP. Indications of the radicalness of Miner's ideas regarding miscegenation: Ronald G. Walters, *The Antislavery Appeal: American Abolitionism after 1830* (Baltimore: Johns Hopkins University Press, 1976), 72–6; Lawrence J. Friedman, *Gregarious Saints: Self and Community in American Abolitionism, 1830–1870* (New York: Cambridge University Press, 1982), 168–9, 187; Frederickson, *Black Image*, 117–24; Lydia Maria Child, *An Appeal in Favor of That Class of Americans Called Africans*, ed. Caroline L. Karcher (Amherst: University of Massachusetts Press, 1996), xli, 187–8; Waldo E. Martin, *The Mind of Frederick Douglass* (Chapel Hill: University of North Carolina Press, 1984), 219–24. For years Miner had a crush on a young man whom she believed to be of mixed race. See Foner and Pacheco, *Three Who Dared*, 133–6.

45. Horsford to Miner, 25 January 1854, MMP. On the perceived decline of biracialism see: Friedman, *Gregarious Saints*, 165–87.

with him, she had begun to suffer the emotional depression that forced her temporarily to leave Washington in June 1855. Always irascible and demanding, Miner, like others afflicted by the disease, lost hope, became intensely critical of those she cared about, and wished for her own death.

In January 1855 she complained to a northern white friend that teaching black students "tries the stoutest spirit for most of the colored are more drossy than lead, more heavy than iron, more slippery than clay & such material it is hard to hold—hard to mould & hard to purify." In remarks that revealed her deep emotional distress, Miner went on to write, "My strength & faith almost fail at times but I am still pressed into service & toil on like one doomed to do his task & die." By May she was lashing out at parents, complaining that her "faithfulness" as a teacher had not earned their respect, and bidding them "Farewell—(I only pray God to let me die)."[46]

As early as April of that year, a white physician who was the guardian—if not father—of one of Miner's students had become aware of her depression and some of its causes. He warned her that her fixation on "the dreadful wrongs inflicted by the whites upon this poor despised & down trodden race" and her insistence on producing in her school "perfect specimens of intellectual & moral excellence" were destroying her. He advised her "to take vexatious things more calmly—to turn your back on evils that cannot for the present be overcome." But Miner was unable to heed this counsel. By the time her school ended its spring term in June she was, as she later recalled, "approaching that stage of nervous sensitiveness and irritability which ends in insanity . . . [and] suicidal monomania." Finally during the summer Stowe intervened, sending Miner to the Elmira Water Cure to rest and arranging for Lydia Mann, sister of Horace Mann, to take charge of her school.[47]

That in such a depressed state Miner could express to Downing a loss of hope for black progress in America is entirely plausible. Downing himself, in reply to Rhoads, suggested that difficulties with Miner's "nervous system" had

46. Miner to Ruth Church and family, 14[?] January 1855 (first quotation) and Miner to Jane and Elton Brent, 8 May 1855 (second quotation), MMP. In March Samuel Rhoads urged Miner to "exercise forbearance" in her business dealings with the Edmonsons. See Rhoads to Miner, 29 March 1855, MMP.

47. B. Ayer to Miner, 8 April 1855 (first–third quotations), L. B. Mann to Miner, [31 December], 1855, MMP; O'Connor, *Miner*, 85–7 (fourth quotation). See also Flushe, "Miner," 163–4.

"derange[d] her mind; for there was a time when I never thought of her becoming a Colonizationist." She returned to Washington in the fall of 1855, but soon suffered a relapse. She suspended her school and returned to the Water Cure. There, during 1856, she regained some strength and some optimism concerning interracial community in America. She spent most of 1857 and 1858 raising funds in the North, but her physical health and her relationships with her closest associates continued to deteriorate, while negative publicity stemming from Downing's charges hampered her fundraising.[48]

Proslavery resistance, however, was in itself sufficient to stymie an attempt to expand Miner's school into a central force to promote abolitionism among African Americans in Washington and the vicinity. In 1852 slaveholders had perceived the subversive nature of the school and attempted to intimidate Miner, her black and white supporters, and her students. Miner recalled later that there were threats of "mobs & fires & whippings for me." Mary Mann reported that the students dared not go outside at recess "because the neighbors are so hostile."[49]When she could, Miner responded directly to such threats. She confronted a white lawyer who had pushed her students off a sidewalk, cursed them, and threatened the black woman who rented classrooms to her. "We are not going to have you Northern Abolitionists come down here to teach our niggers," Miner recalled the lawyer saying. She responded that the District was common ground. She said that she would hold men like him responsible for mobbings, that free blacks were not his "niggers," and that she "feared no man." Nevertheless she moved the school to a new location within a month of his threatening behavior.[50]

Miner received similar threats in March 1853, and in 1854 she and Emily Edmonson endured frightening evenings before the rest of the Edmonson

48. Myrtilla Miner to Margaret Burleigh, 17 October 1856, Miner to Howland, 20 August 1858, EHP; Downing to Samuel Rhoads, 13 January [1855], in *FDP*, 19 January 1855; Foner and Pacheco, *Three Who Dared*, 147–8, 154, 171, 191–5. Fund raising: Myrtle to Emily, 8 February & 14 April 1858, Ednah O. Thomas to Howland, 3 July 1858, Elizabeth H. Valentine to Howland, EHP. Miner accepted donations from colonizationists. See Foner and Pacheco, *Three Who Dared*, 156.

49. Miner to Isaac Newton Miner, 15 March 1852, "20a" manuscript (first quotation), undated manuscript circa early 1852 [su. 1852], MMP; Mann to Frederick Douglass, 2 March 1852, in *FDP*, 25 March 1852 (second quotation).

50. Manuscript for H. B. Stowe, MMP.

family arrived at the lot that Rhoads and Williamson had purchased for the school. Thereafter groups of what she usually called "rowdies" continued to harass her and her students. The ability to overcome fear became a criterion by which she judged her assistants. In early 1855 she noted that she valued Margaret Clapp, a young white woman from New York, because "I entirely need *one to stand by my side* & Maggie is able & willing, thank heaven! rarely feeling afraid."[51]

Like Torrey before her, Miner came to relish flirtation with violence. One evening she deliberately approached a group of "rowdies," forcing even the stalwart Clapp to flee. On another occasion, Miner appeared ready to do more than practice with a pistol. "She was one of the bravest women I have ever known," one of her students later wrote. "I am reminded of an incident which occurred one night while I was with her when the evening school was in session. Some rowdies came to the school-house. She stood bravely at the window with a revolver, and declared she would shoot the first man who came to the door. They retreated at once."[52]

In addition to Miner's resistance to physical intimidation, other factors for several years protected her school from determined opposition. A dozen or more influential antislavery congressmen stood behind it. More remarkably, so did Jane Appleton Pierce, the emotionally distressed wife of proslavery President Franklin Pierce. Jane Pierce, with her cousin, Abigail Kent Means, who served as White House hostess during the Pierce administration, took an interest in the school and frequently visited it to help secure "its prospects and safety."[53] That the school served relatively few students also offset in the minds of local slaveholders its subversive orientation.

Powerful local slaveholders were ready to act, however, when Miner and Stowe undertook a campaign to enlarge the school. During the spring of 1856, the two women had formed the Washington Association for the Education of Colored Youth to direct the building of "a suitable edifice" to house

51. O'Connor, *Miner*, 50 (first quotation); Manuscript prepared for H. B. Stowe, Miner to Friends, [1854?], Miner to Ruth Church and family, 14 January 1855 (second quotation), MMP.

52. Miner to Ruth Church and family, 14 January 1855, MMP (first quotation); O'Connor, *Miner*, 57.

53. *New York Tribune*, quoted in *L*, 5 June 1857 (quotation); House, *Special Report*, 208–9; *NE*, 14 May & 29 October 1857.

150 students on Miner's lot. The following December, Stowe's brother, William H. Beecher, began a campaign to raise $20,000 to fund the effort. Beecher was incompetent to manage such an undertaking and Miner's best biographer, Josephine F. Pacheco, contends that an intemperate promotional pamphlet written in part by Beecher in late 1856 caused a disastrous proslavery reaction against the school.[54]

Yet blaming Beecher for the reaction obscures the real conflict between Miner's subversive effort and the interests of local slaveholders. Beecher departed only slightly from Miner's publicly stated goals when he linked the to-be-enlarged school with emancipation, with the enslaved, mixed-race daughters of Maryland and Virginia slaveholders, and with the enrollment of free blacks from those states. It was Miner's plan for enlargement, not the style of Beecher's promotion of it, which led to a proslavery attempt to suppress the school shortly after the Pierce administration ended.

In May 1857 former Washington mayor Walter Lenox published in the *National Intelligencer* an indictment of the plan. Lenox charged that the enlarged school would draw too many undesirable free blacks to Washington. It would also, he claimed, educate African Americans "far beyond their political and social condition," thereby creating a "restless population, less disposed than ever to fill that position in society which is allotted to them." Such powerful individuals as William Seaton, editor of the *Intelligencer,* former member of Congress Elisha Whittlesay, and Francis Preston Blair, an old Jacksonian and now a prominent Republican, supported Lenox in his call for action against Miner's plans.[55]

Lenox was as certain as Miner, her supporters, and her students that she

54. Foner and Pacheco, *Three Who Dared,* 157–60; Washington Association for the Education of Colored Youth (folder), 23 May 1856, William H. Beecher, *Normal School for Colored Girls, Washington, D.C.* (Reading, Pa.: privately printed, [1856]) (quotation), MMP; O'Connor, *Miner,* 59–63. Although Pacheco maintains that Miner had previously avoided publicizing her school, Miner had in fact issued circulars very similar to Beecher's. She also continued to use what she sarcastically termed Beecher's "'dreadful' circulars" as late as February 1858. See O'Connor, *Miner,* 57, 89 (quotation).

55. The discussion in this and the following paragraph is based on: O'Connor, *Miner,* 63–71 (quotations), 74–5; *Star,* quoted in *NE,* 14 May 1857; William H. Beecher to Samuel Rhoads, 14 September 1857, MMP; Allen C. Clark, "Walter Lenox the Thirteenth Mayor of the City of Washington," *RCHS* 20 (1917): 167–93.

and her school were, like "Drayton and Sayres," agents of "abolitionism." He predicted that the expanded school, in cooperation with a yet to be established "incendiary press" and "adherents in Congress" would turn "our District . . . into the headquarters of 'slavery agitation,' from which it may deal forth in every direction its treasonable blows." He therefore demanded "that the advocates of this measure will promptly abandon it" and raised the specter of "tumult and blood, . . . resistance," and disunion if they did not.

Miner was in the North when Lenox's letter appeared but it is unlikely that she would have been more effective than her friend Gamaliel Bailey in attempting to blunt the force of Lenox's words. Bailey's *National Era* ridiculed Lenox's fears that an expansion of the school would, in Bailey's words, "put out the light of white civilization" in Washington. Bailey presented statistics to show that the percentage of free blacks in the city's population had declined and argued that free blacks in Maryland and Virginia had no desire to move to the city. He sarcastically observed that, during six years of existence, Miner's school had "not even shaken the foundations of the Union." According to Bailey, Lenox was the "agitator" seeking to disturb the city's peace. Lenox, nevertheless, correctly perceived Miner's subversive design and Bailey's clever response failed to counteract the reaction that the former mayor had unleashed.[56]

Emily Howland, who had charge of the school in Miner's absence, feared imminent mob violence. Miner's friend, Leonard D. Gale, resigned from the school's board of trustees in a futile effort to save his job at the Patent Office. Beecher resigned as secretary of the board when he realized that Lenox's letter had "*killed*" his fundraising campaign. Potential donors decided not to risk their money on a school likely to be suppressed. Finally, Miner's lawyers determined that the local courts would block the trustees of the school from owning property in the city.[57]

When Miner returned briefly to Washington in the fall, she denounced Seaton to his face for publishing Lenox's letter and for his alleged complicity in the firing of Gale. She and Howland managed to reopen the school and,

56. *NE,* 14 May 1857.

57. Howland to Miner, 17 May 1857, Gale to Miner, 20 May & 16 June 1857, Beecher to Samuel Rhoads, 14 September 1857, Gamaliel Bailey to Miner, 31 May 1858, S. J. Bowen to Miner, 7 November 1858, MMP; *NE,* 29 October 1857.

with Howland and Emma V. Brown doing most of the teaching, it served a respectable but dwindling number of students until 1860. For years Miner continued to plan for a larger school building. But with her physical health deteriorating and her ability to cooperate with others seriously diminished by her continued emotional distress, she never achieved the level of influence to which she had aspired.[58]

Miner began to exhibit symptoms of advanced tuberculosis during a northern fundraising tour in 1858. In Washington in May 1860 she narrowly avoided death when someone set her school and living quarters on fire. Shortly thereafter she moved to San Francisco, hoping to raise money to re-open the school by working as "a clairvoyant and magnetic healer." Like other feminists and abolitionists, she had long been interested in spiritualism and became a convincing practitioner. But she failed to raise much more than enough to cover her living expenses. After suffering a debilitating injury in a carriage accident, she returned to Washington, where she died in December 1864, still hoping that her school might reopen, as it did—*in 1875.*[59]

Because Miner presented herself as a heroic and lonely figure, ordained by God to promote black education and liberation against great odds, she inadvertently obscured her role as a builder of biracial antislavery community. As she cooperated with northern abolitionists, local antislavery whites, the Edmonsons, and other African Americans, she was in fact rarely alone. She always worked with white female assistants and increasingly relied on help from black women, most of whom were her former students. She catalyzed interracial feminine cooperation in a manner that influenced and anticipated a much more extensive cooperative effort among black and white women in educating Freedpeople during the Civil War years.

58. Miner manuscript on back of printed résumé of Leonard D. Gale, 1 October 1857, MMP; O'Connor, *Miner,* 74–9; Samuel Rhoads to Miner, 15 July 1857, Miner to John Murray, 7 November 1857, MMP; Emma Brown to Howland, 14 July 1859, EHP; Foner and Pacheco, *Three Who Dared,* 166–9, 190–5.

59. Miner to Emily Howland, 5 December 1858, EHP; typescript entitled "from Emily Howland's notebook," n.d., MMP (quotation); Foner and Pacheco, *Three Who Dared,* 175–7, 194–205. Pacheco provides the most thorough and accurate history of Miner's school. Convergence of spiritualism, feminism, and reform: Mary Gabriel, *Notorious Victoria: The Life of Victoria Woodhull, Uncensored* (Chapel Hill, N.C.: Algonquin Books, 1998), passim; Barbara Goldsmith, *Other Powers: The Age of Suffrage, Spiritualism, and the Scandalous Victoria Woodhull* (New York: Knopf, 1998), passim; Stewart, *Giddings,* 208–11.

Miner also, during the last antebellum decade, began the transformation of Washington's biracial antislavery community from one primarily concerned with freeing individual slaves to one primarily concerned with overcoming oppression through education. Miner harbored at least one escaping slave during her years in Washington. But, while Torrey, Smallwood, Chaplin, Bigelow, and the Carters embraced interracial community through schemes to purchase freedom, conduct the underground railroad, and pursue court cases, Miner and her associates came together in an effort to liberate African Americans through the spread of knowledge.[60] That slavery's defenders reacted similarly to each sort of biracialism indicates their perception of the dangers posed by both to the peculiar institution.

Beyond the issue of slavery, Miner's mission to Washington foreshadowed changes in the relationship between northern reformers and southern African Americans which became pronounced during the Civil War and Reconstruction. While Chaplin's Bureau of Humanity was, at best, a rudimentary organization, Miner's school anticipated an institutionalization of northern efforts in behalf of blacks that eventually undermined interracial community. Black individuals and families had taken the initiative in enlisting the help of whites in purchases of freedom and in escapes. In the case of Miner's school, whites provided both the initiative and the aid, thereby diminishing the status of African Americans from allies to clients.

Miner was not conscious of this tendency and would have resisted this reasoning. Rather she believed that her school was a part of an attempt to construct a new national community in which black and whites, men and women, would share common rights. It was near the end of her life in December 1862, while she was in San Francisco and the outcome of the Civil War was still in doubt, that she most fully articulated these goals. "It is good," she wrote to her brother, Isaac Newton Miner, "to live in this time when the old is so rapidly giving place to the new! Good to see . . . the grand conflict to overthrow tyranny and establish universal Liberty."

She defined this new liberty in terms of gender as well as race and declared, "When men learn to say *all persons* instead of 'white male citizens,' we shall begin to extricate ourselves from strife." She prayed to "heaven that this generation passes not until every jot and tittle of law be fulfilled which shall

60. Samuel Rhoads to Miner, 17 March 1853, Miner to Students, 16 January 1859, MMP.

open the prison doors and let all go free—in church and State, in house and field . . . over ocean and land, wherever a human soul is found sighing for relief from bonds of all descriptions." Defining her activities in Washington as abolitionist, she provided, in effect, her own epitaph: "I consider Emancipation—human justice—the only effectual contribution and having done what I could to roll that ball I rest in peace."[61]

61. Miner to Isaac Newton Miner, 9 December 1862, MMP.

EIGHT

The Weems Family and the Antislavery Network

I N November 1855 Ann Maria Weems, an enslaved fifteen-year-old, left Washington for Philadelphia disguised as a boy. Her clandestine journey began when she met a white male underground railroad agent near the White House and pretended to be his carriage driver until they passed the city limits. When they stopped for the night at the home of a Maryland slaveholder, the agent introduced her as his slave. On arrival in Philadelphia they went to the home of black underground railroad organizer William Still, who had dispatched the agent. Still had a photograph taken of Ann Maria in boy's attire, as a remembrance for those who had aided her. Then he sent her on to New York City, where she enjoyed the hospitality of the families of black clergymen Charles B. Ray and Amos N. Freeman as well as of prominent white abolitionist Lewis Tappan. A few days later Freeman, escorted Ann Maria to the black settlement at Elgin, near Chatham, Canada West (modern Ontario), where her aunt and uncle awaited her.[1]

1. William Still, *The Underground Railroad: A Record of Facts, Authentic Narratives, Letters, &c.* (1872; reprint New York: Arno, 1968), 182–6; W. B. Williams to [Wilbur H. Siebert], 30 March 1896, typed script, Wilbur H. Siebert Papers, Ohio Historical Society, Columbus; Monroe N. Work, "Life of Charles B. Ray," *Journal of Negro History* 4 (October 1919): 370; *FDP,* 1 February 1856; William H. Pease and Jane Pease, *Black Utopia: Negro Communal Experiments in America* (Madison: State Historical Society of Wisconsin, 1963), 84–108. British publications spell Ann Maria's last name *Weims.* In such cases, I have altered the spelling to *Weems,* which was used in the United States.

Ann Maria Weems (c.1840–?) escaped from Washington in 1855 with the assistance of Jacob Bigelow. In this photograph she is dressed in her disguise as a male carriage driver. William Still, *The Underground Railroad* (Philadelphia: Porter and Coates, 1872), p. 182.

Ann Maria Weems's departure from Washington and her northward journey illustrate two themes: First, the cooperation of blacks and whites in the subversion of slavery. Second, the link between antislavery activists in Washington and abolitionists in the North and beyond. Ann Maria gained freedom within the context of an antislavery network that channeled money into Washington to facilitate the ransoming of slaves and sent escapees northward via the underground railroad.

The story of Ann Maria's escape indicates how this extensive and intricate international network linked Washington's subversives to the northern states, as well as to Canada, Great Britain, and other parts of the Atlantic world. The network was far from perfect. Misconceptions, misunderstandings, prejudices, animosities, and great distances hampered its operation. Yet the Weems story shows how close the cooperation among antislavery subversives of different regions and races had become by the last antebellum decade.

Tensions always threatened to disrupt the network. From Benjamin Lundy's time through the 1850s there existed mutual distrust between antislavery subversives on the Potomac and northern abolitionists. Those in the North sometimes feared that their allies in Washington made too many concessions to the slave power. Those in Washington sometimes claimed that their northern critics did not understand conditions in the Chesapeake or were too cowardly to venture into a region where they must confront slaveholders face to face.[2]

During the 1850s differing strategies were especially important in dividing Washington's antislavery activists and the radical political abolitionists. Antislavery whites in Washington, while working privately and clandestinely to subvert slavery, committed themselves publicly to nonabolitionist mass political parties—first Free Soil and later Republican. These organizations aimed at curtailing the expansion of slavery rather than directly challenging its existence in the South. Meanwhile Gerrit Smith and other radical political abolitionists—including black leaders Henry Highland Garnet, who had identified with this group since the early 1840s, and Frederick Douglass, who left the Garrisonians to ally himself with Smith in 1851—continued to insist that abolitionists must work *both* clandestinely and publicly to destroy slavery wherever it existed.[3]

What slight chance there was that white members of Washington's antislavery community would publicly endorse radical political abolitionist doctrines evaporated as a result of the Kansas- Nebraska Act. Introduced into the Senate in January 1854 by Stephen A. Douglas, a Democrat from Illinois, the act provided that settlers could determine the status of slavery in the Kansas and Nebraska territories. This provision abrogated the Missouri Compromise's exclusion of slavery from these territories. It unleashed northern fears that slaveholders and their slaves would keep free white labor out of Kansas and led to the formation of the powerful, anti-extensionist Republican party, which enjoyed the active support of Washington's white antislavery subversives. Salmon P. Chase, Joshua R. Giddings, Gamaliel Bailey, and other prominent members of Washington's antislavery community helped—with varying degrees of enthusiasm—to establish the new party in Congress, in the northern states, and in portions of the border South.

Unwilling to lower their commitment to U.S. government action against

2. See chapters 2 and 6.

3. Stanley Harrold, *Gamaliel Bailey and Antislavery Union* (Kent, Ohio: Kent State University Press, 1986), 138–83; William W. Wiecek, *The Sources of Antislavery Constitutionalism in America* (Ithaca, N.Y.: Cornell University Press, 1977), 202–27, 249–75; *NS*, 5 September 1850; *FDP*, 25 September 1851.

slavery in the southern states, Smith, Douglass, Lewis Tappan—who joined this faction during the early 1850s—and other radical political abolitionists denounced the Republican party as essentially proslavery. The willingness of antislavery whites in Washington to cooperate with such moderate slaveholders as Francis Preston Blair of Maryland confirmed the radicals in this conclusion. In 1856 Tappan scolded Lewis Clephane and Daniel R. Goodloe—who, together with Martin Buell and Bigelow, had established the National Republican Association in Washington—for failing to commit that promotional body to universal emancipation.[4]

Yet expressions of political animosity masked considerable mutual respect and cooperation between antislavery subversives in Washington and more northerly groups of black and white abolitionists. The subversives constantly interacted with black underground railroad operatives based in Philadelphia and with a group of black and white abolitionists in New York City. These intersectional antislavery ties were longstanding. At the peak of his underground railroading, Torrey worked with James J. G. Bias and other black members of Philadelphia's vigilance committee. Chaplin cooperated with such northern black abolitionists as Henry Highland Garnet and Jermain Wesley Loguen. In 1851 black subversive community member John F. Cook met in Philadelphia with northern black leaders, including Samuel Cornish and William Whipper.[5]

New York's hinterlands were considerably more distant from the Potomac than was Philadelphia. But the commitment among that state's abolitionists to purchasing freedom and helping slaves escape—plus their proximity to Canada—had made them essential supporters of Smallwood, Torrey, Chaplin, and others. After Chaplin's retirement in 1850, Gerrit Smith's brief sojourn in Washington, as a member of Congress during late 1853 and early 1854, kept communications open between the city's subversives and western New York, despite their ideological differences. So did William Henry Channing's extended visit to Washington, where he served as interim pastor of the

4. William E. Gienapp, *The Origins of the Republican Party, 1852–1856* (New York: Oxford University Press, 1987); Harrold, *Bailey*, 155–83; Tappan to John G. Fee, 29 February 1856, Tappan to Goodloe, Brown, and Clephane, 6 March 1856, letter book copies, LTP.

5. David Alexander Payne, *Recollections of Seventy Years* (1888; reprint, New York: Arno, 1968), 98; Chaplin to Gerrit Smith, 2 November 1848, GSP; Cook diary, 1 March 1851, Cook Family Papers, Moorland-Spingarn Research Center, Howard University.

local Unitarian church and helped Miner with her school. While Channing was not a radical political abolitionist, he supported Frederick Douglass's underground railroad activities in Rochester. In turn Douglass regarded Channing's southward relocation as part of the "onward march of free principles." In Washington Charles Sumner, William H. Seward, Gamaliel Bailey, and Salmon P. Chase attended Channing's sermons, Seward invited him to dinner, and Bailey gave him a tour of the Capitol.[6]

The underlying affinities of the New York radical political abolitionists and Washington's antislavery subversives are well illustrated by Julia Griffiths's visit to the capital in early 1854. Griffiths, an Englishwoman who had assisted Douglass with his newspaper since 1849, stayed with Smith's family at their Washington home. When she arrived she found Charles A. Wheaton, who had earlier helped finance Chaplin's Bureau of Humanity, already in residence. Sarah M. Grimké and the Hutchinson family of antislavery minstrels arrived shortly thereafter.[7]Griffiths emphasized how well Smith's entourage interacted with local antislavery activists, some of whom had been publicly criticized by radical political abolitionists. She enjoyed social engagements with Giddings, Gamaliel and Margaret Bailey, and the Seward family. Toward the end of her stay, she visited Myrtilla Miner's school. She praised Miner for "her noble self sacrifice and indomitable perseverance" and reported to Douglass that "our friend Emily Edmonson" was one of Miner's students. Griffiths also met with Emily's mother, Amelia Edmonson, whom she described as "a sweet looking woman, lady-like in manner."[8]

A shared commitment to helping African Americans gain freedom constituted the strongest tie between the Washington antislavery community and

6. *PF*, 22 August 1850; *NS*, 5 September 1850; Ralph V. Harlow, *Gerrit Smith: Philanthropist and Reformer* (New York: Holt, 1939), 312–35; *FDP*, 6 January 1854 (quotation); Octavius Brooks Frothingham, *Memoir of William Henry Channing* (New York: Houghton, Mifflin, 1886), 264–6. Channing served on the original board of trustees for Miner's school.

7. Wheaton to William H. Seward, 14 & 15 October 1851, WHSP. Wheaton was indicted in the Jerry Rescue at Syracuse in 1851. See also Stanley W. Campbell, *The Slave Catchers: Enforcement of the Fugitive Slave Law, 1850–1860* (New York: Norton, 1968), 154–7.

8. Griffiths to [Douglass], 18, 22, & 25 February 1854, in *FDP*, 3 & 17 March 1854; *FDP*, 5 January 1855. On Griffiths's relationship to Douglass see William S. McFeeley, *Frederick Douglass* (New York: Simon and Schuster, 1991), 161–6.

northern abolitionists—particularly those in eastern Pennsylvania and New York. This is clear in the story of how the antislavery network aided Ann Maria Weems and her family. Her father, John Weems, was an illiterate but resourceful free black resident of Rockville, county seat of Montgomery County, Maryland just to the northwest of Washington. Her mother, Arrah Weems, was "a slave-woman of superior culture and endowments," who was allowed to live with her husband in return for paying her master an annual fee.[9]

According to John Weems, that master, who probably was a blood relative of Arrah Weems, had promised to permit John to purchase her and the couple's children, who by law had inherited her unfree status. John Weems realized, however, that slave traders might offer a higher price than he could match for Arrah, Ann Maria, Maria's older sister Catherine, and three older brothers, Addison, James, and Augustus. Several years earlier this contingency had led a third daughter, Stella, to escape northward with her maternal uncle and aunt.

When his wife's master died, John Weems began to raise funds for the purchase of his family members in anticipation of an attempt by heirs to sell them south. Hoping to locate his daughter, Stella, in order to enlist her assistance in his effort, Weems traveled to New York City in early April 1852. This journey was a considerable undertaking for a free black Marylander of limited means. Not only did Weems have travel expenses, but Maryland law required that he have three white men petition the county court of Montgomery County to allow him to leave and return.

While in New York City, Weems visited Charles B. Ray, the black president of the New York State Vigilance Committee and an associate of Lewis Tappan. Ray informed Weems that Stella and her aunt and uncle had left the city for Geneva, New York. Subsequently Weems learned that when the aunt and uncle moved on to Canada West, Stella had remained with the family of Henry Highland Garnet, who at the time preached at the Geneva Tabernacle. During the summer of 1850 when Garnet accepted an invitation from British Quaker abolitionists Henry and Anna Richardson to lecture in behalf

9. The discussion in this and the following paragraphs is based on: Charles B. Ray to Henry Highland Garnet, 27 September 1852, in *ASR* 7, 2d series (1 December 1852): 182; *FDP*, 1 February 1856 (quotation). See also *BSV*, 2 August 1845.

of the Free Produce Movement in England, Stella had gone along with the Garnet family as an "adopted" daughter.[10]

It was on John Weems's return to Maryland that he learned that his wife and other children were in Washington Jail pending sale to traders and that it would cost at least $3,300 to free them. Weems received this daunting information from Jacob Bigelow, who later reported that during the summer of 1852 he had met "the wife and children of John Weems, on their way to our National Man-market [Washington]."[11]

Bigelow soon became the local coordinator of the antislavery network's effort in behalf of the Weemses. He was already, since Chaplin's departure, the most active of the white subversives in efforts to aid black families. In 1853 he claimed, "For years [I have] cheerfully regarded one half of my time as appropriated to aid the oppressed in some form, or to oppose the oppressor." He had met Arrah Weems and her children while venturing into Maryland at the request of Harriet Beecher Stowe, in order to purchase the freedom of another slave "mother and her two children." Despite official abolition of the slave trade in the District, he knew that the city jail still served as a holding pen for slaves destined for sale south, that slave trader William H. Williams still operated in the city, and that public slave auctions remained common.[12]

Bigelow was not alone, however, among Washington's antislavery whites

10. William Harned, Charles Ray, and Andrew Lester to Gerrit Smith, 10 March 1849, circular, GSP; *ASR* 7, 2d series (1 December 1852): 182 (quotation); *FDP*, 1 February 1856; Joel Schor, *Henry Highland Garnet: A Voice of Black Radicalism in the Nineteenth Century* (Westport, Conn.: Greenwood, 1977), 110–1; Benjamin Quarles, *Black Abolitionists* (New York: Oxford University Press, 1969), 68, 79–80; Clara Merritt DeBoer, *Be Jubilant My Feet: African-American Abolitionists in the American Missionary Association, 1839–1861* (New York: Garland, 1994), 16, 30, 84.

11. [Bigelow to Thomas Richardson], 16 March 1853, in *ASR* 1, 3d series (1 May 1853): 114 (quotations). Internal and external evidence indicates that Bigelow is the author of this letter. See also Bigelow to William Still, 27 June 1854, in Still, *Underground Railroad*, 177–8.

12. Bigelow: *AP*, 24 May 1848; Harriet Beecher Stowe, *The Key to Uncle Tom's Cabin* (1854; reprint, New York: Arno, 1968), 320, 334–9; Mary L. Cox to Dr. [Gamaliel] Bailey, 1 December 1852, MMP; W. B. Williams to Wilbur H. Siebert, 30 March 1896, Siebert Papers; [Bigelow to Henry Richardson], 16 March 1853, in *ASR* 1, 3d ser. (1 May 1853): 114 (quotations). See also Bigelow to William Still, 27 June 1854, in Still, *Underground Railroad*, 177–8. Slave trade and Washington Jail: *NE*, 23 December 1848; Harriet Fanning Reed to William H. Seward, 25 September 1860, WHSP. Williams: [Joshua R. Giddings] to Gentlemen, 20 January 1853, in *AS*, 27 January 1853. Auctions: *NE*, 17 February 1853.

in undertaking this work during the 1850s. Joshua R. Giddings, Gerrit Smith, Allen M. Gangewere, and Thomas C. Connolly each acted in behalf of the antislavery community in attempts to free African Americans from either slavery or prison. Giddings played a role in 1853 in recovering the freedom of Solomon Northup, a free black man from New York, who had been kidnapped in 1841 while visiting Washington and transported as a slave to Arkansas. Smith secured a presidential pardon in 1854 for Noah Hanson, the free black Washingtonian convicted in 1850 of harboring the escaping slaves of South Carolina congressman William F. Colcock. Gangewere and Connolly, both of whom were associates of Gamaliel Bailey, raised money to purchase the freedom of a seventeen-year-old female to prevent her sale into prostitution.[13]

Connolly, a native of Virginia and a colonizationist, was one of the more striking white subversives. He developed close ties to black Washingtonians, while eking out a living for himself and his family as a congressional reporter and interim editor of the *National Era*. He enjoyed African-American music, attended black church services, and, like other white members of the local antislavery community, admired the middle class aspirations of black church members. He agreed to help the girl threatened with sale into prostitution in part because she had "an industrious and worthy" mother, who owned a house and lot worth $850, and who, he perceived, would be a partner in the undertaking rather than a passive recipient of aid.[14]

Partnership on a much larger scale characterized the antislavery network's efforts on behalf of the Weemses. Faced with a crisis of greater proportions than he had anticipated, John Weems returned to the North seeking addi-

13. [Giddings] to Gentlemen, 20 January 1853, in *AS*, 27 January 1853; Solomon Northup, *Twelve Years a Slave: Narrative of Solomon Northup* (1853; reprint, Baton Rouge: Louisiana State University Press, 1968); Smith to Frederick Douglass, 25 August 1854, in *FDP*, 1 September 1854; Connolly to Gerrit Smith, 3 November 1854, GSP.

14. *BSV*, 22 August 1846; Connolly to Charles Sumner, 21 August 1854, Sumner Papers, Houghton Library, Harvard University; *NE*, 14 September 1854. During the late 1840s, Connolly came under the influence of Samuel M. Janney, Joseph Evans Snodgrass, and Gamaliel Bailey. See: Snodgrass to Janney, 14 September 1847 and Connolly to Janney, 4 August 1849, Samuel M. Janney Papers, Friends Historical Library, Swarthmore College; Patricia Hicken, "Gentle Agitator: Samuel M. Janney and the Antislavery Movement in Virginia, 1842–1851," *Journal of Southern History* 37 (May 1971): 181–3.

tional help, leaving Bigelow to keep track of his family. When Weems once again visited Ray in New York City, he sparked an international effort. On learning that Weems had raised only $600, Ray wrote to Garnet, asking him to bring the case "before British abolitionists, and solicit a little assistance."[15]

Although Garnet was preparing to leave England for missionary work in Jamaica, he issued a call that October for British abolitionists to act in behalf of the Weemses. With only moderate support from the British and Foreign Anti-Slavery Society, which questioned the "propriety of purchasing slaves," Henry Richardson responded by collecting what became known as the Weems Ransom Fund. In December 1852 Richardson began sending the proceeds—which eventually totaled $5,000—to Ray, who in turn made portions of the fund available to Bigelow. Though he was gratified by the generous British response, Bigelow, like Gerrit Smith and Chaplin before him, could not resist chiding abolitionists who opposed purchasing freedom. Those who were "more immediately in the fight," he insisted, knew better.[16]

The dispatch with which Garnet and Richardson acted in raising funds permitted Bigelow in March 1853 to begin negotiating the liberation of Weems family members. Because all of them had been sold to Charles M. Price, a Rockville trader, and because there was a limited amount of money in the Weems Ransom Fund, these negotiations were difficult. When Price refused Bigelow's offer of $700 for Ann Maria and demanded $1,000—an exorbitant price for a thirteen-year-old girl—Bigelow felt constrained to shift his focus to other family members. He purchased Ann Maria's older sister,

15. Ray to Garnet, 27 September 1852, in *ASR* 7, 2d series (1 December 1852): 182. John Weems had raised $400 in Montgomery County and $200 in northern cities. There was some hope at this point that he would be able to purchase his wife and Ann Maria for $900, but that never materialized. Sarah Jackson Tappan provides a slightly different account of these transactions in "The Weems Family," *FDP*, 1 February 1856.

16. *ASR* 7, 2d series (1 December 1852): 182 (first quotation); Lewis Tappan to Jacob Bigelow, 20 July 1855, letter book copies, LTP; E. L. Stevens to William Still, 8 July 1857, in Still, *Underground Railroad*, 156; [Bigelow to Richardson], 16 March 1853, in *ASR* 1, 3d series (1 May 1853): 114 (second quotation). Ties between British and American abolitionists: Betty Fladeland, *Men and Brothers: Anglo-American Antislavery Cooperation* (Urbana: University of Illinois Press, 1972), 342–58; and R. J. M Blackett, *Building an Antislavery Wall: Black Americans in the Atlantic Abolitionist Movement, 1830–1860* (Baton Rouge: Louisiana State University Press, 1983).

Catherine, for $1,600 and her mother Arrah for $1,000, both of whom were reunited with John Weems and moved to Washington.[17]

Bigelow promised the British subscribers to the Weems Fund that he would soon purchase the freedom of the remaining Weems children. But insurmountable obstacles arose when Price sold the brothers south to Alabama and refused to reduce his price for Ann Maria. In response, and with Ann Maria's brothers at least temporarily out of reach, Bigelow and Ray decided "to run her off." They did so reluctantly since such undertakings were even more dangerous, complicated, and expensive than they had been before the passage of the Fugitive Slave Law of 1850.[18]

Yet slaves still escaped from the Chesapeake and antislavery subversives continued to help them. In Congress Giddings, Gerrit Smith, and Salmon P. Chase provided rhetorical support. Sounding a good deal like Torrey a decade earlier, Giddings declared in January 1851 that there was a border war along the Mason-Dixon Line between the forces of slavery and freedom. He urged African Americans to escape from slavery and expressed his admiration for their "manly firmness" in violently resisting recapture. Smith, in his first remarks on the floor of the House of Representatives, declared in December 1853 that the Golden Rule "justified the deliverance of every slave in this land" and "the shedding of blood" to achieve that goal. The less militant Senator Chase insisted that the Fugitive Slave Law was unconstitutional, having "no more validity than . . . the Alien and Sedition Acts, or the Stamp Act."[19]

This is not to say that Giddings, Smith, and Chase were actively engaged, at this point in their careers, in helping slaves escape. But they knew people who were. In early 1853 Myrtilla Miner arranged for at least two enslaved

17. Still, *Underground Railroad*, 177, 185–6; Tappan to Bigelow, 20 July 1855, letter book copy, LTP; [Bigelow to Richardson], 16 March 1853, in *ASR* 1, 3d series (1 May 1853): 114; *Baltimore Sun*, 27 September 1855–26 October 1855. Price later was a partner in an Alexandria "slave-pen." See Frederic Bancroft, *Slave-Trading in the Old South* (Baltimore: J. H. Furst, 1931), 91.

18. Work, "Life of Charles B. Ray," 369. It is possible that Ann Maria was reluctant to leave Price. See Lewis Tappan to Jacob Bigelow, 20 July 1855, letter book copy, LTP; *FDP*, 1 February 1856.

19. Slave escapes: Ira Berlin, *Slaves without Masters: The Free Negro in the Antebellum South* (New York: New Press, 1974), 347–8. Giddings: *AS*, 11 January (quotation), 18, 1851, 1 & 15 February 1851, 14 February 1852. Smith: *FDP*, 30 December 1853. Chase: Chase to Sir, 31 March 1854, in *FDP*, 5 May 1854.

children to gain freedom by placing them with northern families. Samuel Rhoads, who had learned of Miner's illegal activities, reminded her of the risks she ran but he also recognized that her membership in a biracial community encouraged her to run them. "Thou cannot consent to place the existence of thy school in jeopardy by allowing thy sympathies to lead thee into dangerous enterprises," he warned. Then he added, "If again there are other duties *clearly* demanded of thy hands—even at the risk of such a martyrdom as that of Drayton & Sayres and the sacrifice of thy school—let it be so."[20]

Such "other duties" had for years preoccupied the elderly Bigelow. Abolitionists so highly regarded his penchant for clandestine activities that in May 1851 Gerrit Smith's New York colleague, William R. Smith, credited reports that Bigelow planned to help Drayton and Sayres escape from Washington Jail. Bigelow monitored slaves in Washington who escaped or wished to escape. He knew that the numbers in each category were increasing and in 1854 he organized group escapes on a weekly or biweekly basis. By the spring of 1856, he, William Still, and several black families in Washington and Georgetown were cooperating to help escapees reach Pennsylvania. As had been the case during the 1840s, women with children figured prominently among those who received assistance as did "meritorious" individuals who could pay their own expenses. Years later William Still aptly remembered Bigelow as the "capable conductor of the Underground Rail Road in Washington."[21]

In addition to the Weems story, the case of Jane Johnson illustrates Bigelow's involvement in an extensive, and often clandestine, antislavery network. In 1855 John H. Wheeler, the United States minister to Nicaragua, had taken his slave, Johnson, and her two children with him on a trip from Washington to New York City. As they returned southward through Philadelphia, Passmore Williamson, the son of Miner's benefactor, Thomas Williamson, secured the freedom of the women and children by separating them from Wheeler. Authorities then arrested Williamson. Most accounts of this famous case indicate that Johnson first revealed her desire for freedom while

20. Rhoads to Miner, 17 March 1853, MMP.

21. [Bigelow to Richardson], 16 March 1853, in *ASR* 1, 3d ser. (1 May 1853): 114; Smith to Smith, 22 May 1851, GSP; Still, *Underground Railroad*, 155 (second quotation), 158, 187–9 (first quotation 188).

she was in New York and that Still, who was also charged in the case, forwarded this information to Williamson. But Bigelow volunteered to send witnesses from Washington to Philadelphia to testify in the defendants' behalf that Johnson had determined to escape before she left Washington. She had indicated to Bigelow that if her master, by taking her into a free state, gave her a chance to escape, she would "use it rather."[22]

Bigelow took ironic satisfaction in the protection from prosecution he enjoyed because Johnson, the Weemses, and other African Americans with whom he cooperated in organizing escapes could not testify against whites in either Maryland or the District of Columbia. On rare occasions he engaged in bravado similar to Torrey's. During the late 1850s, he boasted that when Price refused to accept $700 for Ann Maria he had warned Price that Price "had better keep his eye on her or he might call her some morning and she would not answer." But usually Bigelow was very frightened that he might be implicated in escape attempts. In addition to the new Fugitive Slave Law, the District of Columbia and Maryland had stiff local penalties for aiding slaves to escape. Bigelow knew what had happened to Torrey and Chaplin and he feared that his correspondence with Still, Ray, and Tappan could reveal his own illegal activities, so he took elaborate precautions to protect himself. He insisted on complicated procedures and passwords for those who conducted slaves northward. He used a simple code in his letters and included blatantly false claims that he would never break the law. By late 1853 he was signing his letters "William Penn," or not signing them at all.[23]

Bigelow also knew from experience the difficulties involved in slave escapes, particularly those involving women and children who, as he noted to Still, could not walk as fast as the "scores of *men* that are constantly leaving." Since before Torrey's time, black families had harbored fugitives until masters

22. Bigelow to Still, 9 September 1855, in Still, *Underground Railroad,* 179 (quotations); Herbert Aptheker, *Abolitionism: A Revolutionary Movement* (Boston: Twayne, 1989), 119–21.

23. W. B. Williams to Siebert, 30 March 1896, Siebert Papers (first quotation); Campbell, *Slave Catchers,* 148–69; Worthington G. Snethen, *The Black Codes of the District of Columbia in Force September 1st 1848* (New York: William Harned, 1848), 8, 16, 19, 26, 29; [Bigelow] to Still, 27 June & 3 October 1854, 9 September, 12 October, & 10 November 1855, 3 April 1856, in Still, *Underground Railroad,* 178–82, 187–9 (second quotation). Bigelow's fears: Still, ibid., 178, 180–1; [Bigelow] to Charles B. Ray, 17 November 1855, in Work, "Ray," 369–70.

and police reduced surveillance of northward roads and railroad depots. Because there were paid police informants within Washington's black community, and because African Americans enjoyed few constitutional guarantees, such concealment could be dangerous if maintained for long periods. But extended harboring was sometimes necessary in order to make arrangements for the conveyance of fugitives to the North. Whether subversives relied on agents sent by Still from Pennsylvania, or on coastal traders who took fugitives aboard their vessels, they had to invest considerable amounts of time in planning.[24]

Closely related to the need for careful planning was the necessity of paying those who conducted or transported slaves northward. This had been the case in regard to black and white conductors during the 1840s, and it continued to be part of helping slaves escape from Washington during the 1850s. Bigelow used the terms "merchandise," "light freight," "little parcel," and "customers" as code words for the people he helped. These terms indicate that he, Still, and the others were engaged in something very much like a business, albeit a philanthropic one.[25]

When Bigelow suggested in October 1854 that Still find a white man who would reside in Washington and lead parties of slaves northward on a weekly or semiweekly schedule, he also recommended that the agent charge escapees five to ten dollars each. He surmised that such an agent "might make a good living at it." Bigelow knew that a coastal trader code-named *Powder Boy* charged more than ten dollars each for slaves he took on board his vessel. While Bigelow worried about "cruelly treated" slaves who were so "utterly

24. Bigelow to Still, 27 June 1854, 6 October 1855, William Penn [Bigelow] to [Still], 3 April 1856 (quotation), in Still, *Underground Railroad*, 177–82, 187–8; William L. Chaplin to Gerrit Smith, 25 March 1848, GSP.

25. Larry Gara, *The Liberty Line: The Legend of the Underground Railroad* (Lexington, University of Kentucky Press, 1961), 51–4; Eber M. Pettit, *Sketches in the History of the Underground Railroad* (1879; reprint Freeport, N.Y.: Books for Libraries, 1971), 40; Daniel Drayton, *Personal Memoirs of Daniel Drayton* (New York: Bela Marsh, 1855), 24–35; *Norfolk Herald*, quoted in *FDP*, 7 December 1855; B[igelow] to Still, 9 September 1855 (first & second quotations), Wm. Penn [Bigelow] to Still, 3 April 1856 (fourth quotation), in Still, *Underground Railroad*, 178–9, 187–8; [Bigelow] to Ray, 17 November 1855, in Work, "Ray," 369–70 (third quotation).

destitute" that they could not pay such fees, he personally received compensation for half of the slaves he helped and supposed that Still did too.[26]

It was within this mercantile context in mid-1854 that Ray authorized spending $300 from the Weems Ransom Fund to pay for Ann Maria's escape. The money, minus costs for transportation and food in Washington, was to compensate someone to travel south to Washington, pick up Ann Maria, and convey her to Ray's home in New York City. But, before these things could happen, Ann Maria had to be informed of the scheme and brought to Washington from Rockville. This was difficult because Price was on guard and required Ann Maria to sleep in the same room as he and his wife. Ray's preliminary plan to have Arrah Weems and Bigelow rescue the girl fell through. So did Still's to have two of the girl's cousins rescue her in return for their own freedom.[27] By October all rescue plans had reached a standstill.

It took a July 1855 transatlantic inquiry from Henry Richardson to Lewis Tappan, concerning the status of the Weemses, to revive the rescue effort. Tappan prompted Bigelow and Still to renew their efforts, which—despite new difficulties—resulted in Ann Maria departing Price's home for Washington on the evening of September 23. Price, offering a $500 reward for her return, alleged that she had left in a carriage "probably" driven by a white man.[28]

Once Ann Maria was in Washington several factors further delayed her departure for the North. There was the usual harboring, as Still put it, "until the storm passed." In addition, communications broke down between Bigelow and Still. The first agent sent by Still refused to carry out the mission, while the second choice—*Powder Boy*—failed to arrive as scheduled. Still's third choice, a Philadelphia college professor known as "Dr. H.," could not leave for Washington until late November. In the interim, Bigelow worried about the safety of Ann Maria, the black families that concealed her, and himself. He was annoyed at his mounting costs and embarrassed by the fail-

26. William Penn [Bigelow] to Still, 3 October 1854 (quotations), 26 November 1855, B[igelow] to Still, 9 September 1855, in Still, *Underground Railroad,* 187, 182–3, 178–9.

27. Work, "Ray," 396; Still, *Underground Railroad,* 177–8, 185.

28. Tappan to Bigelow, 20 July & 3 December 1855, letter book copies, LTP; B[igelow] to Still, 9 September 1855, in Still, *Underground Railroad,* 178–9; *Baltimore Sun,* 27 September–26 October 1855 (quotation).

ure of Ann Maria to arrive in New York by the time he had promised. While insisting on better planning in future operations, he was relieved when a *"perfectly competent"* Dr. H. met Ann Maria near the White House and proceeded uneventfully with her to Philadelphia on November 22 and 23.[29]

Ann Maria's northward journey and her visits with prominent black and white abolitionists ended on December 1 when, after a trip across New York state by train, Amos N. Freeman delivered her to her overjoyed aunt and uncle in Canada West. The death in Jamaica of Ann Maria's sister Stella that same month and the knowledge that her brothers remained in bondage in the Deep South tempered the good cheer of her family and friends. Nothing could be done for Stella; Garnet took consolation in the fact that she died free. But, regarding the brothers, Tappan wrote to Bigelow, "Those chickens, far away, must be purchased [and] sent to the uncle also. Don't fail to do it."[30]

Bigelow had kept abreast of the whereabouts of the Weems brothers and could use the remainder of the Weems Ransom Fund to purchase their freedom. It was, however, Bigelow's associate, Ezra L. Stevens, who worked most closely with the Weemses to achieve the goal. Between 1856 and 1858 they mobilized the subversive community in Washington and Arrah Weems became an underground railroad agent. The Weemses during that time also demonstrated how the oppressed could assert their own interests against their benefactors. Like the Carters, the Edmonsons, and others, the Weemses were not simply recipients of help from Washington's antislavery community or of an antislavery network. They were a part of both.[31]

In September 1856 Bigelow negotiated the purchase of Addison and James Weems, who were in Alabama, from their owner Bernard Cook, a Washington resident. But Tappan, who was a prudent businessman and re-

29. Still, *Underground Railroad*, 180–4 (quotations); [Bigelow] to Ray, 22 November 1855, in Work, "Ray," 370–1.

30. Still, *Underground Railroad*, 185; *FDP*, 1 February 1856; DeBoer, *Be Jubilant My Feet*, 16; Tappan to Bigelow, 3 & 6 (quotation) December 1855, letter book copies, LTP; "Death of Stella Weims," *Missionary Record of the United Presbyterian Church* 11 (January 1856): 36–7.

31. The discussion in this and the following paragraph is based on: Wm. Penn [Bigelow] to Still, 3 & 23 April 1856, B[igelow] to Still, 12 July 1857, in Still, *Underground Railroad*, 187–8, 155; Tappan to Bigelow, 7 October 1856, Tappan to Ratcliffe and Kennedy, 15 October 1856, Tappan to Gamaliel Bailey, 18 December 1856, Tappan to David A. Hall, 18 December 1856, Tappan to E. L. Stevens, 31 December 1856, letter book copies, LTP.

called the Chaplin bail debacle, balked at Cook's demand—based on prom-
ises to deliver the brothers several weeks later—that he be paid in advance a
total of $1,700. Tappan would neither risk the money in the Weems Fund
nor permit himself to be held accountable if Cook's promise proved to be
worthless. Tappan insisted instead that individuals in Washington handle the
transaction and commit themselves to reimburse the Weems Fund if Cook
failed to fulfill his contract.[32]

Those who agreed to help in this undertaking included three long-time
subversive community members, Daniel Ratcliffe, David A. Hall, and Gamaliel Bailey. A fourth, Benjamin B. French, had helped Miner in 1851 but,
prior to the Kansas-Nebraska Act, had otherwise opposed antislavery activities. None of them would go so far as Bigelow in violating proslavery laws.
But all of them were willing to engage in humanitarian ventures that could,
as in the case of the Weems, involve illegal activities.

In October 1856 Ratcliffe provided legal advice in regard to the purchase
of the Weems brothers. In December Stevens, who during the late 1850s was
a clerk in the U.S. Indian Bureau, and his friend French volunteered to reimburse the Weems Fund if Cook failed to deliver the brothers. Once Tappan
had assurances from Bailey of Stevens's and French's "pecuniary responsibility," he asked Bailey, who owed Tappan a considerable amount of money, to
advance the $1,700. Hall then wrote the sale contract. It was this cooperative
effort that led in early February 1857 to Addison's and James Weems's arrival
in Washington, their reunion with their parents, and their manumission.[33]

Augustus Weems was now the only member of the family still in bondage.
In early July 1857 Stevens learned that Augustus's Alabama master would accept $1,100 for him. But there was less than $800 left in the Weems Fund
and Stevens could only provide an additional $100 on his own, leaving a bal-
ance of $200. Being as precise in money matters as he was willing to break

32. Tappan to E. L. Stevens, 16 December 1856, Tappan to Gamaliel Bailey, 16 December
1856, letter book copies, LTP.

33. Tappan to Ratcliffe and Kennedy, 15 October 1856, Tappan to Stevens, 16 & 18 (quotation) December 1856, 5 February 1857, Tappan to Bailey, 16 & 18, December 1856, Tappan
to Hall, 18 December 1856, Tappan to Bigelow, 5 February 1857, letter book copies, LTP;
Benjamin Brown French, *Witness to the Young Republic: A Yankee Journal, 1828–1870*, ed. Donald B. Cole and John J. McDonough (Hanover, N.H.: University Press of New England, 315,
334; *DMC,* 1 January 1865.

the law, Tappan responded to this difficulty by informing Stevens, "I have a little fund on hand for *fugitives*. If [Augustus] will begin to *run* I can apply it for his relief, but not otherwise."[34] But Augustus was not well and would have had a long way to run.

Instead, Arrah Weems attempted to raise in the Northeast the additional money required to purchase Augustus's freedom. No one thought it extraordinary that she combined a fundraising trip with the rescue of a fourteen-month-old boy, whom Bigelow hoped to reunite with his mother, Emilene Chapman, in Syracuse, New York. Chapman had escaped from Washington in September 1856, leaving her husband and "two little children behind." When she reached Syracuse, black abolitionist Jermain Wesley Loguen, himself a fugitive slave and an underground railroad agent, sent a request to Still that he contact Bigelow in regard to helping her family. When Arrah Weems volunteered her assistance, she followed the example of Sarah Carter and other black women whose own experience had led them to help others.[35]

Leaving her husband and children in Canada West, where the family had been visiting, Weems returned to Washington. She then headed back north with the baby, whom she presented to Chapman in Syracuse that July. But while Weems enjoyed the assistance of Still, Tappan, Freeman, and Frederick Douglass, as she stopped in Philadelphia, New York City, Syracuse, and Rochester, she collected just $20 during five weeks of travel. Only Stevens's willingness to co-sign for a bank loan of $180 enabled her in mid-September to send the full amount for her son to Alabama. Augustus Weems, who was quite ill, arrived in Washington in November and in August 1858 John Weems made his mark on a deed of manumission freeing the last of his children.[36]

It was in regard to the desperate effort to raise funds to redeem Augustus

34. Tappan to Stevens, [28 March], 1 & 4 July 1857 (quotation), letter book copies, LTP.

35. Stevens to Still, 13 July 1857, Loguen to Still, 5 October 1856 (quotation), both in Still, *Underground Railroad*, 155–8. Chapman used the name *Susan Bell*.

36. Stevens to Still, 8 & 13 July 1857, B[igelow] to Still, 12 July 1857, Earro [Arrah] Weems to Still, 19 September 1857 (quotation), in Still, *Underground Railroad*, 155–6, 186–7; Tappan to Stevens, 25, 27, & 30 July, 4 November 1857, letter book copies, LTP; Stevens to Dear Sir, 25 February 1858, AMAA; John Weems to Augustus Weems, Deed of Manumission, 7 August 1858, Records of the District Courts of the United States, District Court of the District of Columbia, "Slave Manumissions" (6 ms. volumes), 4:184, NA.

that Arrah Weems, John Weems, and their daughter Catherine demonstrated that, grateful as they were to those who had aided them, they were willing to challenge what they regarded as improper actions on the part of their black and white benefactors. In July they charged that Bigelow still had $130 of John's money that should be used in the purchase of Augustus's freedom. A month later, as Arrah sought means to pay off the loan, she complained to Stevens and Still that $500 of the money raised in Great Britain for her family had been used instead "to buy the sister of Henry H. Garnet's wife."[37]

When Tappan learned of these charges, he investigated them. He questioned Bigelow, who agreed that John Weems "some years ago" had given him a purse of money. Bigelow indicated—although he had no records to prove it—that he had used the money to help purchase "some" of the Weems family. Tappan accepted this explanation in light of Bigelow's "great" efforts in behalf of the Weems family, while admonishing him for not keeping proper financial records. Tappan similarly found validity in the Weemses' charges of financial impropriety against Garnet. But he once again cited extenuating circumstances. He told Stevens, "Mr. Garnet was instrumental in raising much of the money contributed in England & felt that, under the circumstances . . . he had a claim to some of the money to redeem his sister in law." Garnet, Tappan maintained, was "poor" and could do no more for the Weems family than he already had.[38]

Although Tappan merely reprimanded Bigelow for sloppy bookkeeping and exculpated Garnet, the Weemses' presentation of their complaints indicates a great deal about the nature of the interracial community and the more extended antislavery network. Despite racial and cultural bias among antislavery whites, and some paternalism among black abolitionists, the Weemses levied charges without fear of reprisals, and Tappan took them seriously.[39]

37. Tappan to Stevens, 25 & 30 July 1857, letter book copies, LTP; Earro [Arrah] Weems to Still, 19 September 1857, in Still, *Underground Railroad,* 187 (quotation).

38. Tappan to Stevens, 25 & 30 July (first–third quotations), 4 November 1857 (fourth & fifth quotations), Tappan to Bigelow, [26] & 30 July 1 August 1847, letter book copies, LTP. Garnet's sister-in-law was Diana Williams. A similar network of British and American abolitionists later redeemed her daughter, Cornelia Williams, from slavery in North Carolina. See [Anna H. Richardson], *Anti-Slavery Memoranda* (Newcastle: J. G. Forster, 1860), 6.

39. Still, for example, referred to "the helpless bondman." See Still, *Underground Railroad,* 144 and Stanley Harrold, *The Abolitionists and the South, 1831–1861* (Lexington: University Press of Kentucky, 1995), 49.

That Bigelow was sixty-eight years old in August 1858 may have influenced Tappan's relatively mild admonition to him regarding his bookkeeping. The old underground railroad agent had many years of life ahead of him, but his days as an active member of Washington's antislavery community were over.[40] This was soon to be true as well of other white antislavery veterans, including Giddings, Stevens, Gamaliel Bailey, and Miner.

In 1858 Giddings failed to gain renomination to Congress in his Western Reserve district. In February 1858 Stevens, irritated that responsibility for paying off Arrah Weems's $180 loan had fallen on him alone, informed the AMA that this was "the last time I shall involve myself in such matters to the extent that I have in this." He lived at Duff Green's Row on Capitol Hill until 1864, when he returned to Ohio. Later in 1858 Bailey's health, which had been poor for several years, began a precipitous decline, ending in death in June 1859. Margaret Bailey continued to engage in interracial work, but after 1861 lived in Baltimore rather than Washington. Miner, of course, moved to San Francisco in 1860 and returned to Washington only a few days before her death in 1864.[41]

Washington's subversive antislavery community nevertheless continued to function during the last years of the 1850s. In March 1858 Gamaliel Bailey and Joseph H. Bradley joined forces one last time to raise $353 to finance a suit in behalf of six African Americans who had been kidnapped in Washington in 1854, sold into slavery in Maryland, and then transported to Mississippi. Bradley successfully established that the three adult sisters involved, and the three children of one of them, were legally free. Bailey, as had been his practice for years, raised among sympathetic members of Congress and northern abolitionists most of the money required to pursue the case. When

40. The Bigelow family genealogist, by not including a death date for Bigelow, suggests that he may have been living or recently deceased during the 1880s. See G. B. Howe, *Genealogy of the Bigelow Family of America* (Worcester, Mass.: privately printed, 1890), 115, 204.

41. James Brewer Stewart, *Joshua R. Giddings and the Tactics of Radical Politics* (Cleveland: Case-Western Reserve University Press, 1970), 259–62; Stevens to Sir, 25 February 1858, AMAA (quotation); Earro [Arrah] Weems to William Still, 19 September 1857, in Still, *Underground Railroad*, 187; William L. Coan to George Whipple, 9 September 1864, 2 January 1865, AMAA; Harrold, *Bailey*, 192–4, 207–15; Philip S. Foner and Josephine F. Pacheco, *Three Who Dared: Prudence Crandall, Margaret Douglass, Myrtilla Miner, Champions of Antebellum Black Education* (Westport, Conn.: Greenwood Press, 1984), 198–200.

he died a little more than a year later, black Washingtonians expressed their regret and noted that they considered him to have been a friend.[42]

As such individuals as Bailey, Bigelow, Giddings, Stevens, and Miner died, or became inactive, or left Washington, other white members of the city's antislavery community assumed some of their responsibilities. Most prominent among those who came forward were Washington native Lewis Clephane, long-time business manager of the *National Era* and a leader in both the local and national Republican parties, and Emily Howland, who in 1858 and 1859 served as principal of Miner's school.

A conservative Republican in politics, Clephane had nevertheless been drawn into the subversive community. In 1852, following the pardon of Drayton and Sayres, he had arranged for the two men's hurried northward departure from Washington by carriage as they sought to avoid indictment by Virginia authorities. In 1855 he cooperated with Tappan in aiding black families to purchase their freedom. But it was not until the eve of Bailey's death in June 1859 that such activities became a central part of Clephane's life. In March and April of that year he coordinated with Tappan the trip of Ellen Mitchell, whom he described as a "*white slave* woman," from Fredericksburg, Virginia, to New York City, where Mitchell successfully raised a large portion of the $1,000 she needed to free herself and five children. A few months later Clephane provided similar assistance to Ramona Brice, who had sought funds to purchase the freedom of her daughters. During the same period Clephane served as the agent of Edward Ashe, a resident of Washington, who purchased his own freedom in August 1859.[43]

42. Bradley to William H. Seward [Seward's name crossed out], 18 March 1858, enclosed in Bailey to Lewis Tappan, 29 March 1858, AMAA; Bailey to Gerrit Smith, 4[?] May 1858, GSP; Bettie [Browne], to Emily Howland, 13 July 1859 and Emma V. Brown to Howland, 14 July 1859, EHP. Among those who contributed money to Bailey to help purchase the freedom of slaves was Stephen A. Douglas, whom Bailey described as particularly generous. See Julia Griffiths to [Frederick Douglass], 25 February 1854, in *FDP*, 17 March 1854.

43. Walter C. Clephane, "Lewis Clephane: A Pioneer Washington Republican," *RCHS* 21 (1918): 263–77; Lewis Tappan's journal, entries for 13, 28, & 31 August 1855, LTP; Clephane to Tappan, 15 March 1859 (quotation) and Clephane to Simeon S. Jocelyn, 11 April 1859, in AMAA; D. S. T. to [?], April 1859, in *NASS*, 7 May 1859; Ramona Brice to Henry Ward Beecher, 11 November 1857 and Clephane to J. D. Anderson, 30 December 1859, Beecher Family Papers, Sterling Memorial Library, Yale University; Arianna J. Lyles to Clephane, 4 Au-

Howland, a young Quaker abolitionist and feminist from central New York, had volunteered to teach at Miner's school in 1858 despite having never taught before. While she lacked Miner's knack for demanding the attention of her students, she excelled Miner in working harmoniously with local blacks and whites. Shortly after Howland arrived in Washington she began visiting slaves and, like Clephane, helped black women travel to the North in search of financial support for the manumission of family members. These activities during the late 1850s initiated her long career as a white advocate of black interests.[44]

Howland is especially important because she remained active among African Americans in Washington during the Civil War years. She was a transitional figure between two very different eras as events during the war transformed conditions in the capital city. She also was transitional in the reservations concerning black character that she expressed in late 1860, just after Abraham Lincoln had been elected president.

From Elisha Tyson's time, white antislavery activists in the Chesapeake had cooperated closely with black families. Aware of their economic, educational, and cultural advantages, these whites often patronized the people they helped. Yet they also found much to admire in the Christianity, work ethic, and noble resistance to enslavement that they observed among the region's African Americans. This attitude is exemplified in the high regard Bigelow, Stevens, and others had for the Weems family. It is also apparent in Lewis Tappan's hopes for the future of the Weemses. He assumed that the family would move to the North, or to Canada, and continue to function as a unit. Although he worried that "dishonest men" might take advantage of them, he assumed that Ann Maria's brothers would be "put to their trades" and would help repay the costs of their manumission.[45]

---

gust 1859 and Clephane to Edward Ashe, 4 August 1859, Slave Manumissions, 4:257, RG 21, NA.

44. Judith Colucci Breault, *The World of Emily Howland: Odyssey of a Humanitarian* (Millbrae, Calif.: Les Femmes, 1976), 1–68; Howland to My Pupils, 29 November 1858, typescript, EHP. Visits slaves: Howland to mother, 23 December 1858, EHP. Helps black women in travels to North: Gulielma Breed to Howland, 12 November 1860, EHP.

45. Tappan to Ezra L. Stevens, [28 March], 4 April (first quotation), 1 & 27 July 1857 and to Jacob Bigelow, 5 February 1857 (second quotation), letter book copies, LTP.

In a similar situation Howland reacted differently. Writing to Frances Adeline Seward in behalf of a Virginia woman who had traveled to New York City to raise nine hundred dollars to purchase freedom for one of her two daughters, Howland asserted that she did not believe the woman and her husband were fit parents. In reference to the daughter who was about to be freed, Howland wrote, "I wish the poor little [girl] could have a chance to rise into the decencies of life when she enters freedom; if she must live with her own family, as far as her own prospect[s are] concerned . . . they will be scarcely improved. For they left bondage with all its vices clinging to them, tho not bad-hearted nor hateful."[46]

Miner had on occasion anticipated Howland's remarks. It may be that the day-to-day cultural collision of educators and pupils engendered a pessimistic view of black prospects. It may also be that the family Howland alluded to had suffered more from slavery than had the Weemses. Still, Howland's words in regard to the girl and her family anticipated the reaction of other sympathetic whites to the great influx of black people from the plantation South into Washington and its vicinity, occasioned by the Civil War. An interracial activist community continued to exist there through the war years. But increasingly a perception among whites that blacks were a problem to be dealt with, rather than allies in the struggle against slavery, undermined it.

46. Howland to Seward, 26 November 1860, WHSP.

NINE

Transformation and Disintegration

THE advent of the Lincoln administration and the Civil War transformed the biracial subversive community that had existed in Washington for three decades. Momentous events changed the relationship of the community to the local and national power structure. What had been subversive became government policy. Meanwhile, black refugees from slavery—self-emancipated African Americans called *contrabands* and later *freedmen*—altered relationships between antislavery whites and their black allies.

The war produced an ever increasing number of these refugees who set out for Washington from Maryland and Virginia. What began during 1861 as a stream became a flood during 1862. By late 1864 as many as fifty thousand refugees had moved within the line of forts that surrounded the city. At first local marshals housed some of them at the "Old Capitol Prison" in Washington and at the city jail in Alexandria. As more arrived the Union army appropriated dilapidated buildings at Duff Green's Row. In June 1862 the army moved its refugee center to Camp Barker on the northern edge of Washington. During 1863 military officials greatly reduced the number of refugees at Camp Barker and established new camps at Freedmen's Village in Arlington, Virginia, at other Virginian locations, and at Mason's Island in the Potomac River. About eleven thousand people passed through these camps and the District's total black population increased from 12,929 in 1860 to 38,663 in 1867—from 21 percent of the total population to 44 percent.[1]

Antislavery biracialism had always depended on shared middle-class values. As slavery succumbed to northern arms and the masses of former plantation slaves—who did not share those values—reached Washington, what had been a subversive biracial community became neither subversive nor a community. Instead it evolved into a massive but failed relief effort, in which well-meaning whites sought to control former slaves. What by 1863 had become a war of liberation destroyed Washington's interracial community. Yet biracialism expanded during the war years before it succumbed to altered conditions. During the Civil War, black and white abolitionists continued jointly to help fugitive slaves and kidnap victims. White antislavery missionaries developed close ties with black refugees. Blacks and whites cooperated in raising a black regiment in Washington. The local white-led Union League, like the city's black churches, served as a forum for interracial dialogue. The *National Republican,* as the successor of the *National Era,* became a newspaper for blacks as well as whites.[2]

Danforth B. Nichols's experience in Washington illustrates this continued interaction in the capital between antislavery blacks and whites during the war *and* the limits to that interaction. Nichols, a white Methodist minister and an AMA agent, came to the city from Boston in late May 1862. Almost immediately, a black minister conducted him on a tour of the Capitol and the

1. Ira Berlin et al., *Freedom: A Documentary History of Emancipation, 1861–1867: Selected from the Holdings of the National Archives of the United States,* Series I, 2 vols. (New York: Cambridge University Press, 1985, 1993), 1:159–60, 165, 2:245–6, 248, 253–5, 262 (hereafter cited as *Freedom*); *NR,* 25 June 1861, 26 March 1862; C. R. Vaughan to George Whipple, 18 December 1861, E. Davis to Michael Epaphras Strieby, 7 November 1864, AMAA; Allen Johnston, *Surviving Freedom: The Black Community of Washington, D.C.* (New York: Garland, 1993), 101–13, 120–3; Curtis Carroll Davis, "The 'Old Capitol' and Its Keeper: How William P. Wood Ran a Civil War Prison," *RCHS* 52 (1989): 206–12; Elaine Cutler Everly, "The Freedmen's Bureau in the National Capital" (Ph.D. dissertation, Georgetown University, 1972), 9–11, 26–59; *DMC,* 4 December 1863, 31 July 1864. The population statistics are compiled from tables in Ira Berlin, *Slaves without Masters: The Free Negro in the Antebellum South* (New York: New Press, 1974), 136, 396–9 and Constance M. Green, *The Secret City: A History of Race Relations in the Nation's Capital* (Princeton: Princeton University Press, 1967), 88.

2. *NR,* 10 December 1861, 15, 16, 21, & 23 April, 1 October, 5 November, 31 December 1862, 18 March 1863.

two men shared the burden of having to enter "by a side door." The following Sunday, Nichols preached at two black churches. At the first of these "several white persons were present." Among them was George F. Needham, who later escorted Nichols to a meeting of the local, predominantly white National Freedmen's Relief Association (NFRA), where members of the organization discussed a plan reminiscent of the *Pearl* escape attempt. The aim was "to send a col[ored] brother to Phil[adelphia] & N.Y. to obtain a vessel to transport at least 100 Contrabands *quietly* to the North to get them out of the clutches of southern hounds." As had been the case during the 1850s, the man was to report in New York City to Lewis Tappan.[3]

When this meeting concluded Nichols proceeded to the second church to hear a lecture by white northerners on prison reform. Then, prior to addressing the congregation himself, he dined at the home of the church's black pastor. They discussed "the providences of God in relation to the history of the black man in this country and then sat down to a cup of tea." This ritual convinced Nichols that he was acting within a community of respectable people. "Washington has good tea," he noted, "and the blacks know how to make it and serve it up too according to the rules of etiquette." Nichols later became superintendent of several local black refugee camps, acquiring a reputation for insensitivity toward their less than respectable residents.[4]

The Republican triumph in the presidential election of 1860 had sparked the war. The victory of Abraham Lincoln, who vowed to exclude slavery from United States territories, capped decades of sectional tensions. In response all the states of the Deep South had withdrawn from the Union by February 1861. Following the initiation of armed conflict at Fort Sumter in April, Virginia and most of the other states of the upper South also seceded to joined the new Confederate States of America. It took a Union army to keep Maryland from seceding as well.

A major cause of secession was fear among southern leaders that a Repub-

3. Nichols to George Whipple, 31 May 1862 (first quotation), Nichols to Simeon S. Jocelyn, 2 June 1862, AMAA (second & third quotations); J. R. Johnson to George Whipple, 4 July 1863, AMAA; *Freedom*, 2:247, 329–31.

4. Nichols to George Whipple, 31 May 1862, AMAA. Historian Elaine Cutler Everly portrays Nichols as devoted to the freedpeople but incompetent. See Everly, "Freedmen's Bureau," 47–53.

lican administration would permit a southward expansion of the practical abolitionism that for years had flourished in the Chesapeake. Initially Lincoln promised to prevent such an expansion. He pledged to enforce the Fugitive Slave Law and to preserve the Union without abolishing slavery[5]. He expressed reluctance to move against slavery anywhere in the border South. Yet almost immediately the Lincoln administration transformed government policy concerning slavery and black rights in Washington. It also began employing abolitionists as clerks in the executive departments, thereby swelling the ranks of the local antislavery community.

Secretary of the Treasury Salmon P. Chase, formerly a member of this community, led in replacing proslavery with antislavery bureaucrats. Soon, Treasury Department clerkships supported antislavery activists in Washington and its environs. In January 1862 one abolitionist reported to the AMA from Washington, "All I can do to advance the cause of *God* & Humanity shall be done free of charge as I have an appointment in the Treasury Department under Sec. Chase." Previously many government clerks had been active among the city's defenders of slavery. Chase began a process in which the federal bureaucracy subsidized abolitionism in Washington. A month before Lincoln took office, local white abolitionist Gulielma Breed predicted that such a reversal of government posture would produce a "moral revolution" in the city. In December 1861 the increasingly radical *National Republican* declared that the Civil War was transforming Washington into a "Yankee city."[6]

The policies of an increasingly antislavery national government changed the environment within which Washington's subversive community operated.

5. Stanley Harrold, *The Abolitionists and the South, 1831–1861* (Lexington: University Press of Kentucky, 1995), 149–61; William W. Freehling, *The Reintegration of American History: Slavery and the Civil War* (New York: Oxford University Press, 1994), 170–5; James M. McPherson, *Ordeal by Fire: The Civil War and Reconstruction,* 2d ed. (New York: McGraw-Hill, 1992), 140; McPherson, *The Struggle for Equality: Abolitionists and the Negro in the Civil War and Reconstruction* (Princeton, N.J.: Princeton University Press, 1964), 56.

6. C. R. Vaughan to George Whipple, 25 January 1862 (first quotation), M. French to Brethren, 4 January 1862, William Slade to Simeon S. Jocelyn, 11 January 1864, AMAA; Breed to Emily Howland, 20 February 1861, EHP (second quotation); *NR,* 4 December 1861 (third quotation). The idea that Washington had become a northern city was common. See: *NR,* 18 April 1862; *DMC,* 4 January & 22 February 1864; James Huntington Whyte, *The Uncivil War: Washington during Reconstruction, 1865–1878* (New York: Twayne, 1958), 17.

In April 1862 a Republican Congress emancipated the slaves in the District of Columbia. One month later it repealed the local black code. From the start of hostilities, local black and white abolitionists—like abolitionists in the North—pressed Lincoln to enlist black troops and to transform the war into one for emancipation and racial justice. Lincoln met part of these demands with the Preliminary Emancipation Proclamation of September 1862, the Final Emancipation Proclamation of January 1863, and the wholesale enlistment of black troops later in 1863. In 1864 Congress repealed the fugitive slave laws and Lincoln pushed Maryland to free its slaves. In 1865 Congress initiated local black suffrage legislation and created the Freedmen's Bureau, designed to protect the interests of former slaves throughout the South[7].

A particularly striking change from antebellum conditions in Washington was that during the war African Americans were able to act openly in behalf of racial justice. Therefore the increasingly less subversive antislavery community grew in strength. While most of its antebellum activists were dead or gone, a few veterans continued to engage in biracial undertakings. AME Bishop Daniel A. Payne, for example, worked closely with AMA leaders. White journalist Thomas C. Connolly frequently spoke at black gatherings[8]. More important, though, were younger blacks and whites who during the 1850s had played minor roles in the community. Among them were Daniel and Gulielma Breed, Sayles J. Bowen, Lorenzo D. Johnson, William H. Channing, and Emily Howland—all of whom were white—and John F. Cook Jr. and Myrtilla Miner's student, Emma V. Brown, who were black.

The Breeds had supported Miner's school during the 1850s and were active in the NFRA during the war. Daniel Breed, a surgeon of northern Quaker origins, helped create what became Freedmen's Hospital. He also

---

7. McPherson, *Struggle for Equality,* 39–40, 47–51, 61–5; Danforth B. Nichols to George Whipple, 31 May 1862, AMAA; Elaine Everly, "Freedmen's Bureau," 32; Green, *Secret City,* 59–60, 76–80; James Brewer Stewart, *Holy Warriors: The Abolitionists and American Slavery,* 2d ed. (New York: Hill and Wang, 1997), 191; Barbara Jeanne Fields, *Slavery and Freedom on the Middle Ground: Maryland during the Nineteenth Century* (New Haven: Yale University Press, 1985), 128–9; Michael J. Kurtz, "Emancipation in the Federal City," *Civil War History* 24 (September 1978): 250–67.

8. *NR,* 21 April & 25 November 1862, 9 June 1863, 2 January 1864; Jocelyn to George Whipple, 21 April 1864, Payne to Jocelyn, 29 April 1864, AMAA.

chaired the first board of trustees for local black public schools. Gulielma Breed worked in behalf of black widows, orphans, and the elderly.[9]

Bowen had arrived in Washington from western New York in 1845 as a Democratic appointee to the Treasury Department. In 1848 his support of the Free Soil party cost him his job. During the 1850s he worked with Miner and joined the Republican party, becoming the Senate's disbursing officer in 1861. In that capacity he helped transform what had been subversion into government policy by drafting legislation to curtail the recapture of fugitive slaves in the District and to establish black public schools. Lincoln appointed Bowen as commissioner of Washington's police force, as its Collector of Internal Revenue, and as its postmaster. Bowen's leadership in the NFRA and his advocacy of black suffrage encouraged African Americans to support his political career during the late 1860s.[10]

Like Daniel Breed, Johnson was a physician. He claimed to have been "trying to elevate the colored people of this District" since 1853. But he was not well known in the city until he left a position in Chase's Treasury Department in 1863 to become surgeon at the Lincoln Military Hospital on North Carolina Avenue. There he began a school for black children, employed a local black teacher named Elizabeth A. Smith, and conducted religious ceremonies among the freedpeople. Johnson presided at the NFRA meeting that

9. C. B. Webster to George Whipple, 7 April 1863, AMAA (quotation); Judith Colucci Breault, *The World of Emily Howland: Odyssey of a Humanitarian* (Millbrae, Calif.: Les Femmes, 1976), 39; *NE*, 15 March 1860; printed pamphlet, 14 April 1864, AMAA; Charles Moore, ed., "Historical Sketches of the Charities and Reformatory Institutions in the District of Columbia," in U.S. Congress, *Joint Select Committee to Investigate the Charities and Reformatory Institutions of the District of Columbia. Part III* (Washington: Government Printing Office, 1898), 63; Thomas Holt, Cassandra Smith-Parker, and Rosalyn Terborg-Penn, *A Special Mission: The Story of the Freedmen's Hospital, 1862–1962* (Washington: Howard University, 1975), 3; Gulielma Breed to Emily Howland, 20 February 1861, Gulielma Breed, *Appeal of the National Association for the Relief of Colored Women and Children* ([Washington]: privately printed, 27 February 1863), Maria M. Menyan to Emily Howland, 21 February 1863, Howland to Mother, 11 February & 31 March 1863, Henry Dickinson to Howland, 1 May 1863, EHP.

10. William Tindall, "A Sketch of Mayor Sayles J. Bowen," *RCHS* 18 (1915): 25–30; Whyte, *Uncivil War*, 34; Breault, *Howland*, 38; Bowen to Miner, 7 November 1858, 11 January 1860, MMP; printed pamphlet, 14 April 1864, AMAA; Bowen to Emily Howland, 14 April & 17 September 1859, 31 May 1862, [Mary Bowen?] to Howland, 2 February 1865, EHP.

Nichols attended in June 1862 and Johnson's wife headed that organization's "female committee."[11]

Channing, who had visited Washington and provided support to Miner during the early 1850s, became pastor of the city's Unitarian church in 1861. In 1863 he served as president of the NFRA, spoke at interracial gatherings, and was an early advocate of "a bureau of emancipation" to serve the needs of the freedpeople. In early 1864 he became chaplain of the House of Representatives.[12]

Of all these antislavery whites, none excelled Howland in trying to preserve interracial community in Washington as the Civil War drastically changed circumstances. She had taught at Miner's school from 1857 to 1859 when she left the city following a bitter disagreement with Miner. Having kept in contact with several local black and white women, she returned in January 1863 to teach at refugee camps, distribute food, and nurse the sick. Assisted by fellow Quaker Anna Searing, Howland established a network that channeled clothing from the North to the camps. She maintained close relationships with the refugees and resisted as best she could the tendency within herself and others to dehumanize them.[13]

Among African Americans, Cook, Brown, and several others traced their involvement in biracial activism to the antebellum years. In 1862 Cook, who succeeded his father as an educator, joined other local black leaders in visiting the White House to oppose Lincoln's plan to colonize African Americans in Liberia. In 1863 Cook participated in the biracial effort to raise a regiment

11. Danforth B. Nichols to Simeon S. Jocelyn, 2 June 1862, Johnson to Jocelyn, 12 March (first quotation), 20 May, & 8 October 1863, Johnson to George Whipple, Jocelyn, and Lewis Tappan, 1 June 1864, AMAA; Moore, "Charities and Reformatory Institutions," 35. Mrs. Johnson: H. Hamlin to Jocelyn, 6 September 1862 (second quotation), AMAA. Smith: Lillian G. Dabney, *The History of Schools for Negroes in the District of Columbia, 1807–1947* (Washington: Catholic University of America Press, 1949), 8, 18, 27, 35–40, 41–2, 75.

12. Octavius Brooks Frothingham, *Memoir of William Henry Channing* (New York: Houghton Mifflin, 1886), 310–1, 316–8; Emma V. Brown to Emily Howland, 19 November 1862, EHP; Lorenzo D. Johnson to Simeon S. Jocelyn, 13 June 1864, AMAA; *NR*, 5 January 1863; *DMC*, 5 January & 13 April 1862.

13. Breault, *Howland*, 33, 38, 51–96; Philip S. Foner and Josephine F. Pacheco, *Three Who Dared: Prudence Crandall, Margaret Douglass, Myrtilla Miner, Champions of Antebellum Black Education* (Westport, Conn.: Greenwood, 1984), 148–51.

Emily Howland (1827–1929) taught at Miner's school during the late 1850s and worked in behalf of the freedpeople in an about Washington during the Civil War. With permission from Carl A. Kroch Library, Cornell University.

of black troops, and in 1865 he joined in petitioning for black male suffrage in the District.[14]

Brown, who attended Oberlin College in 1860, was the most prominent of several of Miner's former students who remained in contact with antislavery whites during the war. After returning from Oberlin, she maintained a school for black children in Georgetown and in 1864 began teaching at one of Washington's first black public schools. Racially segregated for students, this school, located in the Ebenezer Methodist Episcopal Church on Capitol Hill, nevertheless exemplified continued interracial cooperation. Not only did Brown enjoy the support of school commissioner Daniel Breed, the New England Freedman's Aid Society engaged a white woman named Frances W. Perkins to assist her. Well acquainted with Gulielma Breed, Emily Bowen, Miner, missionary teacher Anna Searing, and Howland—and conscious of

14. *NR*, 15 August 1862, 8 May 1863; Greene, *Secret City*, 77; Whyte, *Uncivil War*, 36–7; *DANB*, 126.

her own mixed racial inheritance—Brown worked with white women whom she perceived to be advocates of racial equality.[15]

Such people as Brown, Cook, Howland, Johnson, Bowen, and the Breeds linked the antebellum and wartime biracial community. But the great majority of blacks and whites who worked in behalf of the freedpeople during the war years were new to the city. Among African-American men there were two well-known ministers, Henry Highland Garnet and Henry McNeal Turner, whose militancy would not have been tolerated in antebellum Washington. In January 1864 Garnet brought from New York a monetary contribution to the NFRA. He also delivered a speech. Six months later Garnet, who had been a radical political abolitionist during the 1840s and 1850s, became pastor of Washington's Fifteenth Street Presbyterian Church. In February 1865 Garnet, with Channing's help, became the first African American to address Congress. The much younger Turner, who was a South Carolinian by birth, had preached to black and white audiences throughout the South prior to the Civil War. During 1862 and 1863 he headed the Israel Bethel AME Church. Both he and Garnet worked with antislavery whites while they were in the capital.[16]

Less well remembered as black leaders than Garnet and Turner, but more

---

15. Foner and Pacheco, *Three Who Dared*, 188–90, 194–5; Brown to Emily Howland, 9 April & 10 December 1861, 23 September 1862, 1 February 1863, 18 July 1864, EHP; Breault, *Howland*, 74, 83; Dorothy Sterling, ed., *We Are Your Sisters: Black Women in the Nineteenth Century* (New York: Norton, 1984), 286. Another of Miner's students, Matilda Jones, also attended Oberlin and taught in Washington during the war, but left less tangible evidence of her continuing relationship with antislavery whites. See Pacheco, "Miner," 190; A. E. Gale to Miner, 18 January 1861, MMP; *NR*, 21 May 1862.

16. Melvin R. Williams, "A Blueprint for Change: The Black Community in Washington, D.C., 1860–1870," *RCHS* 48 (1973): 366–7; *DMC*, 8 January 1864; W. J. Wilson to Rev. Dear Sir, 6 June 1864, AMAA; Frothingham, *Channing*, 316; Martin B. Pasternak, *Rise Now and Fly to Arms: The Life of Henry Highland Garnet* (New York: Garland, 1995), 132–3. Though inadequate, Mungo M. Ponton's *Life and Times of Henry M. Turner* (1917; reprint New York: Negro Universities Press, 1975) remains the best biography of this important black leader. See also John Dittmer, "The Education of Henry McNeal Turner," in Leon Litwack and August Meier, eds., *Black Leaders of the Nineteenth Century* (Urbana: University of Illinois Press, 1980), 253–74. Prominent white Republicans, including Benjamin Wade, Thaddeus Stevens, and Henry Wilson, spoke at Turner's church during the war years.

constantly involved in biracial efforts, were William Slade and William J. Wilson. Slade, whom Chase appointed as a clerk in the Third Auditors Office, arrived in Washington in early 1862 and immediately became a leader of the NFRA. Possibly the first black appointee to such a government post, Slade was part of the bureaucratization of reform during the Lincoln administration. In January 1864, for example, he took charge of an evening school that was taught "gratuitously by experienced teachers who are clerks in the Departments." In contrast, Wilson, whom the AMA employed to administer a large *contraband* school, was by no means exceptional as a black employee of an abolitionist organization, although he was the most prominent of them in Washington. A former slave and outspoken abolitionist who previously had taught in Brooklyn, Wilson arrived in the capital with his wife and daughter in June 1864. He attended Garnet's church, joined the NFRA, and helped shape AMA policy.[17]

Other northern black abolitionist men, who earlier could not have avoided imprisonment or death in Washington, visited the city during the war. Among the first was John Rock of Boston, who in May 1862 delivered a lecture entitled "A Plea for My Race" before a biracial audience at the Fifteenth Street Presbyterian Church. Frederick Douglass came in August 1863 to discuss black enlistment with President Lincoln. Douglass returned to Washington in November 1864 to give a speech. In January of that same year Charles Lennox Remond, a Massachusetts Garrisonian, spoke before the city's Union League. While these men endured public discrimination in wartime Washington, mortal danger no longer kept them away. This, and the fact that Lincoln agreed—reluctantly—to meet with Douglass and other black leaders,

17. Slade: Danforth B. Nichols to George Whipple, 24 June 1862, Johnson to Simeon S. Jocelyn, 8 October 1863, Baker to Jocelyn, 5 December 1863, Slade to Jocelyn, 11 January 1864 (quotation), Johnson to George Whipple, Jocelyn, and Lewis Tappan, 1 June 1864, AMAA; *Freedom*, 2:356n; *DMC*, 7 January 1864. Wilson: Wilson to Revd. Dear Sir, 6 & 16 June 1864, Wilson to George Whipple, 6 & 30 August, 28 November 1864, 3 March 1865, J. N. Coan to Strieby, 23 September 1864, Geo. F. Needham to Whipple, 14 October 1864, W. S. Tilden to Whipple, 28 May 1865, AMAA. See also Clara Merritt DeBoer, *His Truth Is Marching On: African Americans Who Taught the Freedmen for the American Missionary Association, 1861–1877* (New York: Garland, 1995), 90–3, 350–5; William Wells Brown, *The Rising Son; or, The Antecedents and Advancement of the Colored Race* (1874; reprint, New York: Negro Universities Press, 1970), 444–5. The NFRA also employed a black agent named Edward M. Thomas until his death in April 1863. See *DMC*, 13 April 1863.

further indicates the declining subversiveness of the capital's antislavery community.[18]

Dozens of black women also joined in biracial efforts in Washington during the war years. Four of them—Elizabeth Keckley, Ann Jacobs, Maria W. Stewart, and Sojourner Truth—are well known. Keckley, a former slave, gained renown as Mary Todd Lincoln's dressmaker. Meanwhile she led other African Americans in organizing the Contraband Relief Association, raised money in the North, and worked with white female missionaries. Jacobs, who had lived in western New York after escaping from slavery in North Carolina, published *Incidents in the Life of a Slave Girl* in 1861. A year later the Ladies Anti-Slavery Society of Rochester sent her and white Quaker Julia A. Wilbur to work together among black refugees in Alexandria. Stewart, who three decades earlier delivered militant speeches in Boston, moved to Washington from New York City in 1862. With Keckley's help, she organized a school and later worked at Freedmen's Hospital. Truth traveled to Washington from Michigan in mid-1864, met with Lincoln, and remained in the city until 1868. As she had in the North, she worked closely with white female abolitionists, including Jane Grey Swisshelm, Josephine S. Griffing, and Wilbur.[19]

These two women were among the growing number of white northerners who came to Washington during the Civil War in order to engage in benevo-

18. Rock: *NR*, 20, 22, & 23 May 1862. Douglass: William S. McFeely, *Frederick Douglass* (New York: Simon and Schuster, 1991), 228–9; *DMC*, 22 November 1864. Remond: *NR*, 2 January 1864. Circumstances in Washington: Nell Irvin Painter, *Sojourner Truth: A Life, a Symbol* (New York: Norton, 1996), 200–7; Williams, "Blueprint for Change," 367–8.

19. Keckley: Elizabeth Keckley, *Behind the Scenes: Thirty Years a Slave and Four Years in the White House* (1868; reprint, New York: Arno, 1968), 113–6, 143; Patten to Simeon S. Jocelyn, 21 January & 12 February 1863, AMAA; *NR*, 4 November 1862. Keckley claimed to know twelve "colored girls employed as teachers" in Washington. William Slade's wife accompanied Keckley to Camp Barker in January and February 1863. In 1865 Slade became Abraham Lincoln's White House steward and Mrs. Slade joined Keckley as a confidante of Mary Todd Lincoln. See R. G. C. Patten to Jocelyn, 21 January & 12 February 1863, AMAA and Keckley, *Behind the Scenes*, 308–10. Jacobs: Ann Jacobs, *Incidents in the Life of a Slave Girl*, ed. Jean Fagan Yellin (Cambridge, Mass.: Harvard University Press, 1987), xv–xvi, xxv; *Freedom*, 2:283, 302; Anna Searing to Howland, 27 January 1863, Mary H. Thomas to Howland, 30 January 1863, Wilbur to Howland, 5 February 1863, EHP. Stewart: Jessie Carney Smith, ed., *Notable Black American Women* (Detroit: Gale Research, 1992), 1083–7; Dabney, *History of Schools for Negroes*, 78n. Truth: Painter, *Truth*, 179–81, 200–7, 210–6.

lent work among the black refugees. Like the antebellum white subversives, these northerners were dedicated to interracial cooperation. But they greatly outnumbered their predecessors and a much larger proportion of them were women than had been the case before the war. The wartime white reformers were also more paternalistic toward African Americans and were much more likely to depend on interracial work for their livelihood.

Several factors favored the increased involvement of women. Miner's school had attracted their interest. The war drained away men into the Union armies. Most important, the war shifted the focus of biracial efforts from courtrooms and underground railroading, where men dominated, to refugee camps and schoolrooms, where women could be employed cheaply. Prominent among the many antislavery white women who first came to Washington during the war were Wilbur, Griffing, Rachel G. C. Patten, May June Doxey, and Georgiana Willets. Wilbur, who teamed with Jacobs in Alexandria, worked for better housing for refugees and sought to become "assistant superintendent" for them in that city. Griffing, a Garrisonian from Ohio, worked during 1864 for the NFRA, distributing wood, blankets, bedsteads, and clothing to refugees. She also organized a campaign to lower the rents they paid for their shacks. Patten and Doxey, who, like Wilbur and Jacobs, came from New York, were appointed under the NFRA as refugee camp "matrons" during 1862. They later taught at Lorenzo D. Johnson's school at Lincoln Hospital. Willets, who was from Jersey City, distributed clothing and taught school at a Washington refugee camp during 1863 and 1864.[20]

Among the newly arrived white men who became prominent in biracial efforts was Nichols, who, though lacking in managerial skill, successively su-

20. Women working more cheaply: John M. Perkins to George Whipple, 7 October 1864, AMAA; Everly, "Freedmen's Bureau," 56. Wilbur, Griffing, Patten, Doxey, and Willets: *Freedom*, 2:250–1, 275–6, 281–3 (first quotation), 329–31; Keith E. Melder, "Angel of Mercy in Washington: Josephine Griffing and the Freedmen, 1864–1862," *RCHS* 63–5 (1966): 246, 253–3, 255–6; Griffing to Gerrit Smith, 2 & 4 August 1864, Griffing to W. E. Whiting, 15 August 1864, Griffing to George Whipple, 20 August 1864, James I. Ferree to George Whipple, 13 January 1864, H. Hamlin to Jocelyn, 6 September 1862, Patten to Jocelyn, September, 15 November, & 20 December 1862, Danforth B. Nichols to Jocelyn, 3 December 1862 (second quotation), Johnson to Jocelyn, 12 March 1863, George E. Baker to Simeon S. Jocelyn, 19 February 1864, clipping enclosed in Lorenzo D. Johnson to Jocelyn, 9 July 1864, AMAA; *DMC*, 28 November 1863; unsigned to Emily Howland, 2 November 1863, EHP.

pervised the refugee camps at Duff Green's Row, Camp Barker, and Freedmen's Village. Other leading figures were Albert Gladwin, James I. Ferree, William L. Coan, and George E. Baker. Gladwin, who arrived in Alexandria as an agent of the northern Free Baptist Mission Society, became "superintendent of contrabands" in that city in 1863. Ferree, a Methodist minister from Florida, became a NFRA leader. As temporary superintendent at Camp Barker in January 1863, his humanitarian concerns led him to delay the removal of the last freedpeople in that camp to Freedmen's Village. Coan, of New Haven, Connecticut, headed the AMA's missionary effort in Washington from August 1864 to March 1865. Baker, who became a State Department employee in 1862, served as treasurer of the NFRA[21].

Meanwhile prominent northern white abolitionists continued to visit Washington. AMA administrators Simeon S. Jocelyn, George Whipple, and Michael Epaphras Strieby often traveled from New York City to Washington during the war years. Among others there were veteran radical political abolitionist William Goodell, who spoke at the Smithsonian Institution in 1862, antislavery evangelist George B. Cheever of New York City, who spoke on behalf of the freedpeople that year, and Harriet Beecher Stowe, who attended a benefit for sick *contrabands*.[22]

As these black and white men and women from various backgrounds interacted among themselves and with the refugees, evidence of continuing interracial community abounded. Nichols and other white ministers preached at local black churches and to the refugees. They also worshiped under the

---

21. Johnston, *Surviving Freedom,* 121; *Freedom,* 2:247–8, 250–1, 254, 283n, 286–7n, 294n, 300, 356n; Everly, "Freedmen's Bureau," 33–7, 41–53; George Whipple to Simeon S. Jocelyn, 11 March 1862; Danforth B. Nichols to Whipple, 24 June 1862, Baker to [Simeon S. Jocelyn], 28 June 1862, Lorenzo D. Johnson to Jocelyn, 20 May 1863, Ferree to Whipple, 13 January 1864, Coan to Whipple, 11 February 1864, William J. Wilson to Whipple, 30 August 1864, John M. Perkins to Whipple, 6 October 1864, Coan to W. E. Whiting, 27 March 1865, AMAA; *DMC,* 13 April 1863. Coan, who had previously been employed by the AMA in Virginia, rented E. L. Stevens's house. See Coan to Whipple, 9 September 1864, AMAA.

22. On visits by AMA administrators, see the AMAA Washington file. Cheever: Yarnell Cooper to Simeon S. Jocelyn, 27 February 1862, AMAA. Goodell: *NR,* 21 March 1862; Rachel G. A. Patten to Jocelyn, 21 January 1863, AMAA. Stowe: Emma V. Brown to Emily Howland, 9 November 1862, EHP. James Redpath also visited Washington during the war. See Julia A. Wilbur to Howland, 5 February 1863, EHP.

direction of black ministers. In December 1862 Patten and Doxey attended a convention of delegates from Washington's black churches that aimed to create several black institutions, including an orphanage, a home for the aged, and a hospital. As a member of the NFRA and as the organizer of evening schools, black activist Slade cooperated closely with white missionaries and teachers. Like Miner before her, Howland maintained friendships with a number of young black women. White teachers also continued to visit the homes of their black students and white camp workers developed personal relationships with black refugees. When Frederick Douglass spoke at Bethel Church in November 1864, a local Republican newspaper reported that whites comprised one quarter of his audience.[23]

Four undertakings were especially important in perpetuating interracial bonds during the war years. They included efforts in behalf of escaped slaves and threatened free black people, recruitment of a black regiment, organization of a Union League, and humanitarian aid to the newly free. The last of these affected the largest number of people and had the most profound impact on the existence of the biracial community.

Many times during the war, antislavery whites joined African Americans in protecting free blacks from being kidnapped into slavery. In undertakings evocative of underground railroading, blacks and whites also cooperated in arranging northward transportation of people threatened with reenslavement. As the war progressed, it was slave catchers and local constables, rather than abolitionists, who defied government policy in such matters. But neither Secretary of State Seward's decree of December 1861 ordering the arrest of Vir-

---

23. Interaction: Nichols to Simeon S. Jocelyn, 6 & 19 June, [7 August] 1862, Patten to Jocelyn, 20 December 1862, L. C. Lockwood to Brother, 5 January 1863, I. Cross to Jocelyn, 1 July 1863, Lorenzo D. Johnson to Jocelyn, 8 October 1863, Slade to Jocelyn, 11 January & 1 February 1864, William J. Wilson to Sir, 1 & 16 June 1864, AMAA. Friendships: Bettie [Browne] to Howland, 7 July 1861, Emma V. Brown to Howland, 10 December 1861, 1 February 1863, Anna [Searing] to Howland, 27 January 1863, EHP. Visiting: Laurie C. Gates to George Whipple, 1 August 1864, Josephine S. Griffing to Gerrit Smith, 4 August 1864, William L. Coan to Michael Epaphras Strieby, 23 September 1864, AMAA; *Freedom*, 2:329–31. Relationships: unsigned to Howland, 2 November 1863, Carrie Naebok to Howland, 4 December 1863, Cap to Emily [Howland], 17 May 1865, Howland's journal on Mason Island and Camp Todd, 1863–1866, Howland to Mother, 1 February & 31 March 1863, EHP. Douglass: *DMC*, 22 November 1864.

ginians who attempted to reclaim slaves in the District, nor the local abolition of slavery in April 1862 ended the struggle. Plenty of proslavery Democrats retained government jobs. Many Washington residents sympathized with the Confederacy. The constables continued to enforce proslavery laws. Local politicians opposed emancipation and the great majority of whites never accepted equal rights for African Americans. Washington remained a center of contention over escaped slaves until the repeal of the fugitive slave laws in June 1864 and the enactment of abolition in Maryland later that year.[24]

There were many violent confrontations. In May 1862 kidnappers shot and killed a black girl. In June 1863 constables arrested three women and four children who had escaped from Prince George's County, Maryland. The following September masters recaptured a band of thirty slaves attempting to escape from the same county to Washington[25]. In response black and white abolitionists, aided by Union troops, employed several tactics to secure the freedom of African Americans.

The effort to transport fugitive slaves quietly northward that Nichols witnessed in June 1862 was not an isolated event. The NFRA, in cooperation with District of Columbia military governor General James S. Wadsworth, the Freedmen's Relief Association of Pennsylvania, and the AMA, hoped to get "six or seven hundred 'contrabands'" to the North in order to protect them from slave catchers. Similar endeavors persisted into 1864. Meanwhile abolitionists among Union soldiers and refugee camp administrators protected fugitives from recapture. White abolitionists cooperated with local black activists in sheltering *contrabands* in their homes and—as had been the case before the war—they hired lawyers to represent alleged fugitive slaves. In May 1862

24. Democratic officeholders: Gulielma Breed to Emily Howland, 28 May 1861, EHP. Confederate sympathizers: Breed to Howland, 20 February 1861, EHP; A. E. Gale to Myrtilla Miner, 18 January 1861, MMP; *NR*, 29 December 1860. Local politicians: *Freedom*, 1:164–5; *NR*, 5 March 1862; Whyte, *Uncivil War*, 19–20, 31. Slave-catching and kidnapping: *NR*, 7 & 9 December 1861, 28 February, 13 May, 17 July, 14 August, 11 October 1862, 10 June, 16 October 1863. Public opinion: [Mary Bowen?] to Howland, 2 February 1865, HP; *NR*, 21 & 22 May 1862, 10 February 1864; Johnston, *Surviving Freedom*, 3, 170–1; Whyte, *Uncivil War*, 31, 49, 68, 249. Center of contention: *Freedom*, 1:175; *NR*, 10 & 12 April 1862; *DMC*, 14 May 1863, 19 June & 19 October 1864.

25. *NR*, 13 May 1862, 10 June 1863; *DMC*, 16 September 1863.

Bowen wrote a bill sponsored by David Wilmot that was designed to end slave hunting in the District.[26]

When unemployment among black refugees in Washington during 1863 became a more pressing issue than reenslavement, local abolitionists assumed that this new problem could also be alleviated by helping people to relocate northward. Former slaves often did not want to go and many northern whites opposed black immigration. But getting freedpeople into northern jobs seemed to be a humanitarian duty and a means of countering proslavery claims that African Americans could not succeed in freedom.

Therefore Howland established an informal agency that placed former slaves as "helps" in the homes of northern white families. By 1865 Josephine Griffing had persuaded the Freedmen's Bureau to create the Freedmen's Intelligence and Employment Agency to find jobs in the North for former slaves. When the bureau gave up the effort in 1867 after helping about five thousand, Griffing and Truth continued on their own, aiding about three thousand more.[27]

Interracial cooperation also characterized efforts to raise black Union regiments in the district. When a local black man named Jacob Dodson offered to raise three hundred black troops in April 1861, Gulielma Breed informed

26. Hannibal Hamlin (not the vice president) to Freemen's Relief Association of Pennsylvania, 6 June 1862 (quotation), William H. Channing to Dr. Furness, 6 June 1862, Hamlin to Jos. M. Truman, 15 June 1862, Pennsylvania Abolition Society Papers, Historical Society of Pennsylvania, Philadelphia; Baker to Jocelyn, 28 June 1862, AMAA; *Freedom*, 1:160, 169–70, 173–5, 177, 397–81, 2:260; *NR*, 28 March & 7 May 1862, 7 & 9 April, 17 May, 17 & 18 July, 5 November 1862, 12 September 1863; *DMC*, 17 November 1862; Bowen to Emily Howland, 31 May 1862, EHP.

27. Johnson, *Surviving Freedom*, 187–91, 198–9; Everly, "Freedmen's Bureau," 25, 71, 78, 84, 95–6; Howland to Mother, 11 March 1863, Howland to Father and Mother, 7 May 1863 (quotation), M. J. Burleigh to Howland, 11 December 1864; Sallie Holley to Howland, 3 April 1865, EHP; Painter, *Truth*, 217–8; Carlton Mabee, "Sojourner Truth Fights Dependence on Government: Moves Freed Slaves off Welfare in Washington to Jobs in Upstate New York," *Afro-Americans in New York Life and History* 14 (January 1990): 7–26; Melder, "Griffing," 259. Johnson indicates that 8,519 former slaves received assistance between November 1865 and August 1868. While Howland's agency is praiseworthy, it raises some disturbing images. She reported in her March 1863 letter that a northern family had put in a request for a "nearly white" black boy.

Howland that young black men in the city were eager to fight. Although Lincoln rejected the offer, Breed hoped the men would still be able to serve. In 1862 George Weston of the *National Republican* joined in urging the enlistment of black troops. A northern-born conservative Republican, Weston had advocated colonization before the war. Now he published Henry M. Turner's call on black men to fight for their "beloved country" and *"universal liberty."*[28]

During 1863 local blacks and whites raised the first of the District's three black regiments. This effort paralleled similar ones in the North in its biracialism and in recognizing that white officers would lead black military units. In May, prospective regimental colonel J. D. Turner, a white Baptist minister from New York, called to order a recruitment meeting in a black church where Deacon Gunder Snowden presided. A black speaker observed that Colonel Turner and his second-in-command "are men of our choice" and Turner responded that he had spent months attending black churches, Sunday schools, literary societies, and celebrations. By early June, when General William Birney, son of Liberty abolitionist James G. Birney, spoke at a meeting chaired by Henry M. Turner on the "south side of the Capitol," about 550 men had volunteered.[29]

Meanwhile antislavery whites in Washington, through the organization of a local Union League, plunged into interracial politics. Union Leagues had emerged a year earlier in the North as white patriotic clubs. Following the northern victory in 1865, biracial leagues initiated Republican parties in the former Confederate states. The League in Washington held a middle position. At its first meeting, in 1863, James H. Lane, a white Republican from Kansas, advocated racial separation. By January 1864 it was a biracial organization that included many of the same men who had raised the District's black regiment. Members celebrated the first anniversary of the Emancipa-

28. Johnston, *Surviving Freedom*, 113; Breed to Howland, 28 May 1861, EHP; *NR*, 24 January, 28 April, 1 August (quotations) 1868; Green, *Secret City*, 70–1, 78.

29. *NR*, 5 & 8 May, 9 June (quotation) 1863, 2 January 1864; *Freedom*, 2:254n; Arthur J. Larsen, ed., *Crusader and Feminist: Letters of Jane Grey Swisshelm, 1858–1865* (Saint Paul: Minnesota Historical Society, 1934), 231. Melvin R. Williams indicates they met at the black Ebenezer Church and that 770 men eventually served in the regiment. See Williams, "Black Community," 368. Howland claimed to know some of the black men who enlisted. See Howland to Father and Mother, 7 May 1863, EHP.

This photograph of freedpeople's shanties in Washington during the Civil War indicates the dire conditions in which black refugees lived. Courtesy of Still Pictures Branch, National Archives.

tion Proclamation, provided a forum for northern black abolitionist Charles Lenox Remond, and sang "the John Brown song."[30]

Far more significant for the antislavery community, however, was the effort on behalf of black refugees from slavery. This huge, government-supported undertaking involved two sorts of interracial cooperation: that between blacks and whites in providing aid and that between white missionaries and the refugees. Unlike underground railroading, raising a black regiment, or forming a Union League, aiding the newly free redirected and undermined biracial activism in Washington.

The population of the refugee camps consisted mainly of women, children, the infirm, and the elderly. Most healthy adult male refugees gained employment with the Union military, or with local private business, or in the North. Even as the local job market stagnated and able-bodied black men experienced difficulty in finding employment, they remained under-represented

30. Eric Foner, *Reconstruction: America's Unfinished Revolution, 1863–1877* (New York: Harper and Row, 1988), 283; Whyte, *Uncivil War,* 54–7, 62–4; Johnston, *Surviving Freedom,* 172, 195; Green, *Secret City,* 77–81; *NR,* 23 March 1863, 2 January (quotation), 6 January 1864.

in the camp populations. Therefore it was the most vulnerable of the refugees who suffered the deplorable conditions that existed in the camps and who came most directly into contact with those who dispensed aid.

In an attempt to alleviate camp conditions, a variety of local and northern benevolent associations provided clothing, shelter, employment, schools, religious services, and hospitals for camp inmates and other refugees. Although there were separate black-led and white-led relief organizations, they cooperated with one another and there was biracial support for each of them[31]. These interracial efforts continued earlier trends within the subversive community and, as was the case during the antebellum years, they depended on aid from the North.

The AMA was by far the most active northern abolitionist organization in the region. It recruited northerners to travel to the capital city, while providing financial and administrative support to the efforts of the NFRA. The northern-based American Tract Society engaged in similar work in the area, although NFRA and AMA agents questioned its motives—reflecting prewar abolitionist criticism of the Tract Society as proslavery. A variety of other northern groups provided funds, missionaries, and teachers. Among them were several Quaker societies, the Free Baptist Mission Society, the Pennsylvania Freedmen's Relief Association, the Reformed Presbyterian Missions, the New England Freedmen's Aid Society, and Garnet's African Civilization Society.[32]

31. Larsen, *Crusader and Feminist*, 250–2; *Freedom*, 1:165, 2:247–50, 255, 330, 356n; *NR*, 6 July 1861, 15 & 28 March 1862; *DMC*, 13 November 1862; C. R. Vaughan to George Whipple, 18 December 1861, Danforth B. Nichols to Simeon S. Jocelyn, 3 December 1862; Rachel G. C. Patten to Simeon S. Jocelyn, 21 January 1863, Slade to Jocelyn, 11 November 1864, Lorenzo D Johnson to George Whipple, Jocelyn, and Lewis Tappan, 1 June 1865, AMAA; Johnston, *Surviving Freedom*, 122, 138–41 155–63, 179; Everly, "Freedmen's Bureau," 37; Green, *Secret City*, 62–4; Keckley, *Behind the Scenes*, 113–4.

32. AMA: Danforth B. Nichols to George Whipple, 24 June 1862, George W. Baker to Simeon S. Jocelyn, 19 February 1864, AMAA; Joe Martin Richardson, *Christian Reconstruction: The American Missionary Association and the Southern Blacks* (1909; reprint, Athens: University of Georgia Press, 1986); DeBoar, *His Truth Is Marching On*. Tract Society: George E. Baker to Simeon S. Jocelyn, 19 February 1864, AMAA; J. R. Johnson to Emily Howland, 14 November 1863, EHP. Quakers: Rachel S. C. Patten to Simeon S. Jocelyn, 20 December 1862, AMAA; *NR*, 11 August 1862; Henry Dickinson to Emily Howland, 1 May 1863, William Evans to Howland, 21 May 1865, EHP. BFMS: *Freedom*, 2:282–3n. PFRA: W. J. Wilson to George Whipple, 26 October 1864, AMAA. RPM: Lorenzo D. Johnson to Jocelyn, 9 July 1864,

As had been the case before the war, shared dangers and hardships bound antislavery blacks and whites together. Black refugees faced recapture and white abolitionists confronted death threats. As late as October 1864 William L. Coan, superintendent of AMA schools in the city, wrote of himself and his coworkers, "We shall have here no *society* outside of our own circle, bitterly hated by almost all around us." Those who labored with the former slaves shared with them the crowding, temperature extremes, and disease that characterized the camps. They nursed the sick, became sick themselves, and worried about the deplorable conditions. White camp workers resisted racial taboos and affirmed their solidarity with the oppressed.[33]

Empathy among antislavery whites for suffering African Americans continued. Anna Searing, a Quaker, internalized the dangers faced by freedpeople. She could not resist, she informed Howland, being "of some service in some way to this people who are passing through this perilous . . . stage from bondage to freedom. I say perilous because their position and condition may be such as to dishearten & degrade perchance if success comes not." Others sympathized with the plight of black families, with black men exploited by overzealous Union army recruiters, and with the difficulties faced by newly free black workers. Black leaders and refugees in turn often expressed affection and respect for the white missionaries.[34]

Yet most antislavery whites in and about wartime Washington acquiesced

---

AMAA. ACS: L. D. Johnson to Jocelyn, 9 July 1864 and Harriet E. Rogers to Whipple, 10 April 1865, AMAA. See also Everly, "Freedmen's Bureau," 60, 64.

33. A. E. Gale to Myrtilla Miner, 18 January 1861, MP; *NR*, 29 March 1862; Yarnell Cooper to Simeon S. Jocelyn, 10 February 1862, Coan to George Whipple, 7 October 1864 (quotation), Rachel G. C. Patten to Simeon S. Jocelyn, 20 December 1862, C. B. Webster to Jocelyn, 5 September 1863, AMAA; Emma V. Brown to Howland, 10 December 1861, 18 July 1864, Mary H. Thomas to Howland, 30 January 1863, Hannah to Sister, 6 March 1863, Emma V. Brown to Howland, 18 July 1864, Ann [Searing] to Howland, 27 January 1863, Julia A. Wilbur to Howland, 5 February 1863, M. J. Burleigh to Howland, 11 December 1864, Howland , 1863–1864 journal, entry for 16 January 1865, Howland to Father, 20 June 1865 (typescript), EHP.

34. Empathy: Ann [Searing] to Howland, 27 January 1863 (quotation), Howland, "Report to Col. Eaton," 1865, Howland to Mother, 1864 (typescript), EHP; *NR*, 31 March & 10 April 1862; *Freedom*, 2:312–3, 332–4; George E. H. Day to Whipple, 2 February 1865, AMAA. Affection: C. B. Webster to Simeon S. Jocelyn, 5 September 1863, AMAA; Emily Howland, journal, 1863–1864, Howland to Father, 20 June 1865, typescript, EHP.

in military-bureaucratic methods that were, at best, insensitive toward the predicament of the newly free. In response to the unforeseen demographic crisis caused by black refugees, Union military leaders provided short-term humanitarian relief while seeking to control former slaves and quickly transform them into tractable wage laborers. At Freedom's Village and other government-run farms near Washington, white administrators implemented heavy-handed policies that led black refugees to fear that they were being reenslaved. Contacts between antislavery whites and the African Americans they assisted became more hierarchically structured than they had been before the war. As refugees from slavery poured in, it became more difficult for white missionaries to perceive them as individuals. As a result biracial antislavery community gradually ceased to exist. When Congress terminated the Freedmen's Bureau in late 1868, and northern aid societies shifted their attention southward, little remained beyond interracial political cooperation.[35]

A growing cultural distance between antislavery whites and African Americans contributed to this transformation. As extremely poor and previously isolated *contrabands* replaced relatively affluent and acculturated black families as the main beneficiaries of abolitionist help, what had always been a synthetic community disintegrated. Nichols, for example, never developed the rapport with the uneducated and disoriented freedpeople that he had had with Washington's black churchmen. He and other white missionaries complained that refugees from slavery were "violating constantly the laws of chastity & honesty." White teachers in black schools observed that the children were "wild" and had to be taught order and morals as well as academics[36]. Emily Howland's reaction to the arrival of a large group of refugees at Freed-

35. Everly, "Freedmen's Bureau," 43–4, 47, 50–2, 119–25; Johnston, *Surviving Freedom,* 122, 155–9, 172, 192–3; Danforth B. Nichols to Simeon S. Jocelyn, 3 December 1862, C. B. Webster to George Whipple, 7 April & 16 July 1863, AMAA; *Freedom,* 2:254; *NR,* 11 & 28 August, 11 October, 4 & 17 November 1862; Breault, *Howland,* 54; Painter, *Truth,* 218–9; James Oliver Horton, *Free People of Color: Inside the African American Community* (Washington: Smithsonian Institution Press, 1993), 186, 190; Foner, *Reconstruction,* 67–8.

36. Everly, "Freedmen's Bureau," 8, 33, 38, 50–1, 61–7; George E. Baker to Simeon S. Jocelyn, 19 February 1864 (first quotation), Lorenzo D. Johnson to W. J. T., 1 June 1864 (second quotation), Ann Frances Carter to George Whipple, 1 & 5 June 1865, AMAA. Poor conditions contributed to a student rebellion at Washington's 3d Street School in 1865. See J. M. Mace to Whipple, 25 April 1865, William S. Tilden to Samuel Hunt, 12 May 1865, Tilden to Whipple, 29 May 1865, AMAA.

men's Village in May 1863 reflected the cultural divide. When the new arrivals "collected in the yard and sang and clapped their hands in time swaying their bodies," she perceived it to be a "strange barbarous scene." She observed to her father, "You might have thought yourself in Central Africa."[37]

Within this disjunctive context, even the more empathic antislavery whites, such as Howland—exercised authority over blacks in institutional settings. They frequently supervised black assistants in camps, schools, and hospitals and only rarely themselves assisted black teachers and missionaries. They regarded the refugees as clients—representatives of a social problem that had to be solved rather than as allies in a heroic struggle for freedom. In such circumstances white abolitionist paternalism toward African Americans degenerated into condescension. Antislavery whites habitually referred to the refugees as "my people," "our colored people," "our freedmen," "these poor people," and "poor things." One white female camp worker observed to Howland, "They seem as tho they belonged to me almost."[38]

William L. Chaplain's proposal in 1846 for a Bureau of Humanity had anticipated a bureaucratic response to the problem of black transition to freedom. But Chaplain's intention was to help African Americans to become free, not to control how they lived. As a military-governmental bureaucracy drew in abolitionists during the Civil War, they fell victim to forces that favored control. Some joined in callous treatment of camp residents. Many engaged in policies that circumscribed black liberation.[39]

Abolitionists, government officials, and slavery's die-hard advocates debated the length and nature of the transition process from slavery to self-

37. Howland to Father, 28 May 1863, EHP. See the 27 November 1864 entry in Howland's 1863–1864 journal for a more positive view of black music.

38. Danforth B. Nichols to Simeon S. Jocelyn, 3 December 1862, C. B. Webster to Jocelyn, 8 May 1863, Lorenzo D. Johnson to Jocelyn, 28 May 1863, J. R. Johnson to George Whipple, 6 November 1863 (first quotation), Rachel G. C. Patten to Simeon S. Jocelyn, 21 January 1863 (second & third quotations), J. B. Johnson to George Whipple, 18 July 1864, AMAA; L. C. Lockwood to Emily Howland, 17 March 1862, Julia A. Wilbur to Emily Howland, 5 February 1863 (fourth & fifth quotations), Howland to Mother, 11 February 1863, Sallie to Emily, 18 February 1863 (sixth quotation), Carrie Naebok to Howland, 2 November 1863, EHP.

39. J. R. Johnson to Simeon S. Jocelyn, 6 November 1863, C. B. Webster to George Whipple, 9 July 1863, W. S. Tilden to Whipple, 23 May 1865, AMAA; *Freedom*, 2:250–2, 311–2.

sufficiency. Slavery's defenders contended that the newly free would become idle, unruly, and dangerous. Proponents of black freedom, such as the *National Republican,* maintained that they could easily be transformed into tractable free workers. Administrators like Nichols and Gladwin, conscious of the costs involved in maintaining the camps and under pressure from their military superiors, sought to move people through the camps quickly. Others demanded that the Union government do more for destitute women with children, the elderly, and the infirm. In November 1863 J. R. Johnson called on the Lincoln administration to intervene at Freedmen's Village. He claimed that residents were neglected by camp superintendent Nichols, abused by "proslavery military officers," and mauled by "the *haters* of their race." In early 1862 Julia Wilbur denounced the high rents charged for government-owned refugee housing in Alexandria and her associate Anna M. C. Barnes described Superintendent Gladwin as "a brutal man.[40]"

But these humanitarian concerns meshed with a belief that whites must control the freedpeople in order to maintain social order. Working with traumatized, disoriented, and often sick refugees, the more humanitarian of the camp workers concluded that to function well in freedom most former slaves required white guidance. Otherwise, well meaning whites feared, the newly free would lead immoral, criminal lives and risk falling prey to "sharpers.[41]"

In retrospect the confusion in goals is obvious. In November 1862 the *National Republican* asserted that whites could be the "guardians" of blacks without being their "oppressors." The government had to "control" the black transition to freedom. In July 1864 Lorenzo D. Johnson maintained that the NFRA sought "controlling influence over the colored people" in the "cause of humanity and freedom.[42]" It seemed that the mass of black people were no longer allies with antislavery whites against a rapidly diminishing slave power. Instead they were a burden to be borne and a disruptive force to be controlled.

As they became camp officials, missionaries, teachers, and relief functionaries, a few of Washington's antislavery whites joined former slaves and black

40. *NR,* 28 September & 1 December 1861, 17 June, 11 & 22 October, 17 November 1862; Howland to Mother, 1864, typescript, EHP; Johnson to George Whipple, 6 November 1863, AMAA (first quotation); *Freedom,* 2:250–1, 280–6 (second quotation 283), 356–7.

41. George E. Baker to Simeon S. Jocelyn, 19 February 1864, AMAA.

42. *NR,* 11 November (first & second quotations) & 24 November 1862 (third quotation); Johnson to Simeon S. Jocelyn, 9 July 1864, AMAA (fourth quotation).

abolitionists in warning that dispensers of aid had become part of an effort to control rather than to liberate. Josephine S. Griffing was an early advocate of a federal agency to help former slaves in their transition to freedom. In 1865 she became assistant to the assistant director for the Freedmen's Bureau in the District of Columbia. Yet she always suspected that the agency could be oppressive. In August 1864, as Congress debated legislation to form the Bureau, she worried that it would take "from the colored man now *free* the right to control his home, his labor, his wages and a part of his money." She said she had "no doubt the intention of the Law is to *protect* him in his right to his manhood. But the phrase 'provide for the general welfare' of the Freedmen is easily interpreted . . . to mean the *control* of [the black man by] the white man."[43]

Aware of these tendencies in federal government policy and among their white colleagues, local African-American leaders sought autonomy for the freedpeople and for themselves. The Lincoln administration's radical revision of local race policies encouraged them to do so. In pushing for local emancipation, in meeting with the president, in raising black regiments, and in petitioning for suffrage, they gained confidence—perhaps ill-founded—that they no longer needed white intermediaries.

J. Sella Martin, a former slave and former AMA agent who came to Washington in 1868 to become pastor of the Fifteenth Street Presbyterian Church, summarized this new black outlook in January 1870. In an early issue of the *New Era*, soon to be renamed the *New National Era*, he praised Gamaliel Bailey and "the Old 'Era'" for speaking for African Americans "when we were dumb." His point was that those days had passed. "There are," he asserted, "interests . . . peculiarly affecting us and opportunities of which we alone know how to take advantage, in connection with the effort to organize the millions of our race in the South into permanent communities of self-supporting, self-reliant and self-respecting citizens."[44]

43. Griffing to W. E. Whiting, 15 August 1864, AMAA. See also Griffing to Gerrit Smith, 4 August 1864, AMAA. Merton L. Dillon summarizes the historical literature concerning Union efforts to control former slaves. See Merton L. Dillon, *Slavery Attacked: Southern Slaves and Their Allies, 1619–1865* (Baton Rouge: Louisiana State University Press, 1990), 263–4.

44. *New Era*, 20 January (first & second quotations), 13 January 1870 (third quotation). On Martin see R. J. M. Blackett, *Beating Against the Barriers: Biographical Essays in Nineteenth-*

The biracial antislavery effort in Washington had produced interracial friendships, interracial worship, and the instruction of black children by white abolitionist women. By the Civil War years black men and women openly acted as members and employees of white-led antislavery missionary organizations. But African Americans were rarely willing to give up their own institutions. By the 1860s there were at least twelve black churches in the city with weekly attendances averaging three hundred, plus many smaller religious groups. There were eight independent black schools, and numerous charitable and benevolent societies, cemetery associations, and libraries[45]. This proliferation of black institutions caused friction between black leaders and antislavery whites whose paternalism clashed with black autonomy.

Most antislavery whites assumed that they or others of their race would exercise authority over black schools and hospitals, if not black churches. Black leaders, in contrast, believed that with general emancipation, it was up to them to control their own institutions. These conflicting perspectives led to hurt feelings and further undermined biracial community. Two instances illustrate the situation. The first concerned the housing of schools for the freedpeople in black church buildings. The second involved the issue of whether black or white teachers should teach the freedpeople.

In the first instance, many antislavery whites thought that African Americans should bear disproportionate financial burdens during a war for emancipation. This perspective provided a rationale for paying black Union soldiers less than white soldiers and for requiring black workers in the District of Columbia to be taxed to help defray costs of housing *contrabands*.[46] It also led white members of the biracial community to assume that local black churches should not charge rent for the rooms the churches allowed the AMA, NFRA, and other benevolent groups to use for schools.

"It really seems hard to have to pay rent for what is to contribute so much to their interests as a people," complained William L. Coan, who in 1864 supervised AMA schools in Washington. But what white missionaries regarded

Century Afro-American History (Baton Rouge: Louisiana State University Press, 1986), 185–285.

45. Churches: *NR*, 27 & 29 March, 15 April 1862. Schools: *NR*, 27 & 29 March, 21 May 1862. Other institutions: *NR*, 29 March 1862; *Freedom*, 2:261–2. Three of the larger churches had white ministers. See also Johnston, *Surviving Freedom*, 60–2, 81–4.

46. *Freedom*, 2:251–3.

as an economic issue, black leaders regarded as an issue of black autonomy versus white control. In 1865 Coan's successor, William S. Tilden, attempted to partition a large room he rented from the Third Street Church. In rejecting Tilden's plan, church leaders informed him that "they did not sell themselves for [the] five hundred dollars" they received annually in rent.[47]

In the second instance, the issue of racial preferences for teachers in black schools contributed to strained relations between William J. Wilson and AMA administrators. Wilson was not the only black teacher employed in refugee schools in Washington and its vicinity. But he was the only African American in charge of an AMA school. Shortly after he, his wife, and his daughter began teaching at the Camp Barker school in June 1864, Wilson complained about their pay, about building maintenance, and about his impression that AMA officials considered his employment as an *experiment*. Wilson soon insisted that only black teachers be hired at his and other schools for black children.

"Give us a change," he advised George Whipple, "not as an experiment, but as an act eminently proper at this stage of the progress of the colored people themselves & the great need of inculcating in the minds of this especial people here the idea of our own ability for self Education, which after all is but true Elevation. We the Colored People must be taught to do our own work. . . . So long as the dominant class are to fill among us the first places . . . we shall be but the same helpless & dependent people. *Slaves.*" Later Wilson insisted on his own behalf that the AMA "must not only employ Colored Teachers, but place competent Colored men in . . . positions of trust & responsibility" as superintendents.[48] Wilson succeeded—with some white support—in having a black woman, rather than a white woman, appointed as an

---

47. Billings, "Social and Economic Conditions in Washington during the Civil War," 193; Johnston, *Surviving Freedom*, 163; Coan to M. E. Strieby, 12 September 1864 (quotation), Tilden to Samuel Hunt, 12 May 1865, AMAA. Coan was concerned mainly with the 4th Street Baptist Church.

48. Wilson to Rev. Dear Sir, 6 & 16 June, 6 August 1864, Wilson to Whipple, 30 August (first quotation) & 26 October 1864 (second quotation), AMAA. Clara Merritt DeBoar finds that Wilson used charges of racism against his white colleagues to mask his "deficiencies as a disciplinarian and administrator." But in 1865 Garnet engaged in a similar struggle aimed at getting the NFRA to hire black teachers for the African Civilization Society School. See Pasternak, *Garnet*, 133 and DeBoar, *His Soul Is Marching On*, 350–5.

additional teacher at his school. By mid-1865 local AMA superintendents had also become more responsive to his requests for improvements. His case illustrates, nevertheless, that white paternalism was no longer acceptable among Washington's black leaders.[49]

The Civil War, which Washington's subversive community had helped to bring about, led to the realization of the community's goal of ending slavery *and* to the community's destruction. Union armies had won the war during the spring of 1865. The Thirteenth Amendment, abolishing slavery, went into effect in December of that year. But well before then the increasingly abolitionist orientation of the Lincoln Administration and the arrival of thousands of black refugees in Washington's vicinity had destroyed the political and social contexts within which the community had flourished. It was no longer subversive to be an abolitionist. White missionaries regarded the *contrabands* as clients rather than allies. Meanwhile, as local black leaders gained protection for their rights and interests, they repudiated a subservient relationship to antislavery whites that had always marked the community and that had grown more pronounced during the war years.

49. Wilson to George Whipple, 7 December 1864, 22 January, 1 & 11 March 1865; George E. Baker to Simeon S. Jocelyn, 15 January 1865; Julia B. Landre to M. E. Strieby, 23 March 1865; Landre to Whipple, 24 April & 4 May 1865; W. S. Tilden to Whipple, 27 May & 1 June 1865, AMAA; Johnson, *Surviving Freedom*, 218. Wilson later became chief cashier at Washington's failed Freedmen's Savings and Trust Company.

CONCLUSION

The Significance of Subversive Biracialism

Following the Union victory over the Confederacy during the spring of 1865, the Freedmen's Bureau took control of the schools that the AMA and other northern-based benevolent associations had established in Washington. By then most antislavery whites in the city were employees of these associations and they left when the associations did. Thereafter the AMA shifted its efforts to the former Confederate states where it supported segregated black colleges. Meanwhile the Freedmen's Bureau accelerated the movement of freedpeople out of the refugee camps, which it shut down in August 1868. When Congress dismantled the bureau itself in late 1868 and local Radical Republicans failed in an attempt to establish integrated schools, what remained of the city's biracial community dissipated. Whites gradually ceased to serve in black schools, hospitals, and other institutions that had brought them together with African Americans in behalf of progressive causes.[1]

For a time black and white Radical Republicans maintained a vestige of the interracial community. In early 1867 white Radicals led by Charles Sum-

---

1. Howard N. Rabinowitz, "Half a Loaf: The Shift from White to Black Teachers in the Negro Schools of the Urban South," *Journal of Southern History* 40 (November 1974): 565–94. Closing of the camps: Elaine Cutler Everly, "The Freemen's Bureau in the National Capital," (Ph.D. dissertation, Georgetown University, 1972), 124. Shifting of benevolent society focus: Constance M. Green, *The Secret City: A History of Race Relations in the Nation's Capital* (Princeton: Princeton University Press, 1967), 100; Everly, "Freedmen's Bureau," 65–7, 119–20, 127–8; Allan Johnston, *Surviving Freedom: The Black Community of Washington, D.C., 1860–1880* (New York: Garland, 1993), 191; James B. McPherson, *Struggle for Equality: Abolitionists and the Negro in the Civil War and Reconstruction* (Princeton: Princeton University Press, 1964), 403–7.

ner succeeded in enfranchising the District's black men, who thereafter constituted a majority of Washington's Republicans and nearly half of the city's registered voters. Each of the city's wards had an integrated Republican organization and black voters were crucial to that party's victory in the local elections held in June.

In 1868 Republicans elected white antislavery activist Sayles J. Bowen as mayor. Simultaneously John F. Cook Jr. and another black man gained positions in local government. At the city's Republican nominating convention in 1871 several white men, including long-time subversive community member Thomas C. Connolly, supported Frederick Douglass's failed attempt to become the party's nominee for delegate to Congress. In 1872, when Congress established a territorial government for the district, three black men—including Douglass—were appointed to its legislative council. Black and white Radical Republicans visited each other's homes on New Year's Day.[2]

But commitment to biracial politics slipped away. Condescension among white Republicans contributed to black demands for their own political organization. By 1874 prolonged factionalism, persistent corruption, and growing racial antipathy had destroyed this last remnant of interracial cooperation in Washington as Congress terminated self-government in the District. Although all of its residents lost the right to vote, the District of Columbia set a precedent for black disfranchisement throughout the former Confederate states.[3]

Most recent studies of the Reconstruction era that followed the Civil War emphasize the roles of laissez faire ideology, white racism, and a related desire to reintegrate the white South into the Union as factors in the nation's failure

2. Thomas R. Johnson, "Reconstruction Politics in Washington: 'An Experimental Garden for Radical Plants,'" *RCHS* 50 (1980): 180–7; James H. Whyte, *The Uncivil War: Washington during Reconstruction, 1865–1878* (New York: Twayne, 1958), 49–64, 106–7, 283–6; Melvin R. Williams, "A Blueprint for Change: The Black Community in Washington, D.C.," *RCHS* 48 (1973): 378–80; James O. Horton, *Free People of Color: Inside the African-American Community* (Washington: Smithsonian Institution Press, 1993), 187; *DMC*, 2 January 1872.

3. Williams, "Blueprint for Change," 380; Whyte, *Uncivil War*, 275–80; Johnson, "Reconstruction Politics in Washington," 189–90; Alan Lessoff, *The Nation and Its City: Politics, "Corruption," and Progress in Washington, D.C., 1861–1902* (Baltimore: Johns Hopkins University Press, 1994), 101–29.

to protect the rights of the freedpeople.[4] But the collapse of northern abolitionism following the ratification of the Thirteenth Amendment banning slavery was also significant. So was the decline of Washington's biracial community, which, had it survived, might have influenced national policy. Instead massive black migration, excessive paternalism among white abolitionists, and the complicity of these whites in efforts to control rather than to liberate, caused the community to disintegrate as African Americans reacted by demanding autonomy.

It seems unlikely that this debacle could have been avoided. The change in the city's political context, the wartime termination of slavery and slaveholding interests, and the cultural gap that separated antislavery whites—and some black leaders—from the refugees destroyed the forces that maintained the community. An antebellum convergence of northern abolitionism and local black self-defense had produced it. As the Civil War brought change, the community lost its character and reason to exist.

The subversive community stands, nevertheless, as an example of how progressive interracial cooperation—if not full mutual understanding—could exist for an extended period in a slaveholding region of nineteenth-century America. By conjoining black resistance and northern white abolitionism, the subversives had a major impact on the course of events, not only in Washington and the Chesapeake but throughout the country. Their history provides a vantage point from which to better comprehend the antislavery movement and the sectional conflict.

From the 1790s through the Civil War years African Americans in the Chesapeake interacted with whites who sympathized with their struggle against enslavement. Elisha Tyson's cooperative effort with enslaved African Americans in Baltimore during the early decades of the nineteenth century are comparable to those of Torrey, Chaplin, and Bigelow during the 1840s and 1850s. In both periods, African Americans took the initiative in seeking out antislavery whites. But it took a series of pivotal events during the late 1820s and early 1830s to create a subversive community of national importance.

4. See for example Eric Foner, *Reconstruction: America's Unfinished Revolution, 1863–1877* (New York: Harper and Row, 1988), 603 and David G. Blight, *Race and Reunion: The Civil War in American Memory* (Cambridge, Mass.: Harvard University Press, 2001), 98–138.

It was within the context of biracial abolitionism that William Watkins, Jacob Greener, and other black leaders in Baltimore encouraged William Lloyd Garrison to create the radical brand of immediatism that transformed northern abolitionism. Combined with the shift of the slave trade from Baltimore to Washington, this movement made possible an *influential* subversive biracial community. Although Garrison and his closest associates pulled back from confrontation in the Chesapeake, other northerners influenced by immediatism joined African Americans in making the nation's capital a center of antislavery activities. Between 1840 and 1850 the more aggressive of these were radical political abolitionists from New York, who led in attacking slavery on its own ground. When the New Yorkers shifted their efforts away from Washington, a diverse group of white abolitionists—within which women were increasingly prominent—continued to support local African Americans in seeking freedom.

For a century historians have noted that the abolitionists failed to convince significant numbers of slaveholders to free their bondpeople and failed as well to convert a majority of northerners to favor emancipation and equal rights for African Americans.[5] Yet Washington's antislavery community, linked to northern abolitionism, succeeded in convincing the South's white leaders that they had to take extraordinary measures to defend slavery in the borderlands. Aware that slavery in this city and its environs could not withstand sustained biracial attack, slaveholding politicians determined on a course of action that affected the entire nation. They demanded that Washington remain a slaveholding city, endorsed mob action against those who threatened its status, and called for a fugitive slave law that angered northerners. When the election of a Republican president made it likely that interracial subversive cooperation in the borderlands would expand, they turned to secession.

In some respects this analysis is compatible with a contention, popular among historians during the first half of the twentieth century, that abolitionists caused the Civil War. The so-called Revisionist historians, who took no interest in African-American perspectives, regarded the abolitionists as fanatics so obsessed with destroying a benign slave system that they plunged the nation into a needless conflict. In response to the Revisionists, liberal histori-

---

5. Albert Bushnell Hart, *Slavery and Abolition, 1831–1841* (1906; reprint, New York: New American Library, 1969), 232–4, 315; Lawrence J. Friedman, "'Historical Topics Sometimes Run Dry': The State of Abolitionist Studies," *Historian* 43 (February 1981): 177–94.

ans during a long period stretching from the 1940s into the 1980s worked assiduously and effectively to establish that slavery was not benign and that abolitionists were neither fanatics nor responsible for the Civil War.[6]

In retrospect it seems unfortunate that these liberal historians defended abolitionists by minimizing their radicalism and their impact on the politics of antebellum America. Despite their own biases, white abolitionists and their antislavery fellow travelers shared a truly radical vision of racial justice. Without that vision northern abolitionists would not have undertaken the aggressive action against slavery in Washington and other vulnerable outposts in the borderlands—action that undoubtedly helped bring on the Civil War.

Aggressive northern abolitionism, in turn, would not have existed without initiatives undertaken by African Americans. As historian John Ashworth points out, a black struggle against slavery was a prerequisite for northern abolitionism.[7] If African Americans had not demonstrated their unwillingness to remain slaves, a northern antislavery movement would have been inconceivable. This was also the case in Washington and its vicinity. Despite racial, cultural, political, and economic disparities between white abolitionists and local African Americans, black antislavery efforts impressed sympathetic whites. The heroism of black families touched the emotions of antislavery whites and inspired them to devote themselves and the resources they could muster in a subversive struggle against slavery in Washington.

The subversive community that resulted was synthetic, unstable, and fated for extinction. Although it rested on black initiative, antislavery whites usually led it. Their class and racial perspectives led them to patronize the African Americans with whom they cooperated. They worked best with black people who shared their middle-class orientation. These characteristics contributed to the destruction of the community during the Civil War years. Yet the fact that the community lasted for so long and achieved so much is a tribute to the spirit of northern abolitionism and to its aggressive determination to confront slavery on southern soil. The subversives remind us that much can be achieved through interracial cooperation.

6. Betty L. Fladeland, "Revisionists vs. Abolitionists: The Historiographical Cold War of the 1930s and 1940s," *Journal of the Early American Republic* 6 (Spring 1986): 1–21; James L. Huston, "The Experiential Basis of the Northern Antislavery Impulse," *Journal of Southern History* 56 (November 1990): 609–40.

7. John Ashworth, *Slavery, Capitalism, and Politics in the Antebellum Republic* (New York: Cambridge University Press, 1996), 1–8.

ESSAY ON SOURCES

Writing about a subversive community, clandestine schemes, and far-flung antislavery networks leads to reliance on widespread and, in some cases, curious sources of information. Although most of the action in this book takes place in Washington and its vicinity, most of the primary documents on which the book is based were published elsewhere or are housed in archives distant from that city. Similarly much of the secondary literature cited in the notes addresses subjects that transcend the local history of Washington and the Chesapeake. This essay discusses briefly the more important of these disparate sources, to explain how they shaped the character of this book, and to inform readers concerning the process of investigation that produced it. For documentation of any given point, readers should consult the notes.

PRIMARY SOURCES

I consulted several sorts of primary sources. They include antebellum and Civil War era newspapers, manuscript collections, and published documents. I also made use of a variety of autobiographies, reminiscences, and contemporary biographies. Many of the newspaper and manuscript collections have been microfilmed and are available more or less easily through interlibrary loan.

Of these primary sources, newspapers are most important throughout this book. Prior to the organization of professional press services, newspapers received out-of-town news from their own correspondents, and northern antislavery newspapers from the late 1830s onward employed correspondents in Washington. Their reports are especially important in regard to the antebellum period. They contain first-hand accounts of events in that city that are not otherwise recorded. Smallwood, Torrey, Chaplin, Snodgrass, Giddings, Stevens, and others report their activities in this manner.

Among the northern papers on which I rely are the *Albany Patriot* (1843–

1848), *Ashtabula Sentinel* (Jefferson, Ohio, 1844–1854), *Colored American* (New York and Philadelphia, 1837–1841), *Daily True Democrat* (Cleveland, 1848), *Emancipator* (New York and Boston, 1833–1848), *Frederick Douglass' Paper* (Rochester, 1850–1857), *Liberator* (Boston, 1831–1865), *National Anti-Slavery Standard* (New York, 1841–1869), *North Star* (Rochester, 1848–1850), *New York Daily Tribune* (1846–1856), *Pennsylvania Freeman* (Philadelphia, 1838–1853), and *Tocsin of Liberty* (Albany, 1842).

Of all the antebellum Washington newspapers, only Gamaliel Bailey's *National Era* (1847–1860) compares in importance with the northern newspapers in reporting events associated with subversive activity in the capital city. In the *Era* are some of Bigelow's and Snodgrass's letters, some African-American news, indications of Bailey's point of view, and excerpts from antislavery and proslavery journals. For shorter periods of time other Chesapeake newspapers provide significant information. Benjamin Lundy's *Genius of Universal Emancipation* (Baltimore and Washington, 1826–1834) is a major source for early interracial antislavery action in Baltimore and Washington. The *National Republican* (Washington, 1861–1865) and the *Daily Morning Chronicle* (Washington, 1860–1865) are vital concerning relations between African Americans and antislavery whites during the Civil War. At various other points, the *Baltimore Sun* (1843 & 1855), *Daily Union* (Washington, 1848), and the *National Intelligencer* (Washington, 1828–1861) provide useful information not available elsewhere. The same is true regarding the semi-official *Congressional Globe* (1833–1865) when its transcriptions of the debates in Congress bear on events in Washington's streets.

Among unpublished sources, several manuscript collections are important in developing an understanding of subversive antislavery activity in the Chesapeake. The Pennsylvania Abolition Society Papers (Historical Society of Pennsylvania) contain letters from Elisha Tyson, George Drinker, and other white antislavery pioneers in the region. Letters in the Gerrit Smith Papers (Syracuse University) provide details about the activities of Charles T. Torrey, William L. Chaplin, and other subversives. The Smith Papers are also a source of information concerning the relationship of New York's radical political abolitionists to events in Washington. It is in a letter to Smith that Chaplin reveals his role in the *Pearl* escape attempt.

The Smith Papers are especially useful for the 1840s and are less so thereafter. For the 1850s, I rely most heavily on the Lewis Tappan Papers and the

Myrtilla Miner Papers (both located at the Library of Congress). The Tappan Papers consist almost entirely of letter book copies of Tappan's outgoing correspondence, which are often difficult to decipher. For the 1860s, the American Missionary Archives (Amistad Research Center, Tulane University) and the Emily Howland Papers (Cornell University) are essential.

Other manuscript collections are not crucial but contribute important isolated material. Among these are the American Negro Historical Society Collection, 1790–1903 (Historical Society of Pennsylvania), Beecher Family Papers (Sterling Memorial Library, Yale University), Cook Family Papers (Moorland-Spingarn Research Center, Howard University), Charles Francis Adams Papers (Massachusetts Historical Society), Charles Sumner Papers (Houghton Library, Harvard University), Charles T. Torrey Papers (Congregational Library, Boston), Henry Cowles Papers (Oberlin College Archives), Horace Mann Papers (Massachusetts Historical Society), Joshua R. Giddings Papers (Ohio Historical Society), Joshua R. Giddings-George W. Julian Papers (Library of Congress), Moses Sheppard Papers and Samuel M. Janney Papers (Friends Historical Library of Swarthmore College), Salmon P. Chase Papers (Historical Society of Pennsylvania), Salmon P. Chase Papers (Library of Congress), William H. Seward Papers (Rush Rhees Library, University of Rochester), Wilbur H. Siebert Papers (Ohio Historical Society), and William Lloyd Garrison Papers (Boston Public Library). Of particular importance among manuscript collections are the Segregated Habeas Corpus, Slave Manumission files, and Case Papers of the District Court for the District of Columbia (Record Group 21) at the National Archives. These provide terse but unique information about relationships of local African Americans with antislavery whites.

Several published collections of primary materials contain useful information. Among them are Herbert Aptheker, ed., *A Documentary History of the Negro People in the United States* 2d paperbound ed. (New York: Citadel, 1963); Gilbert H. Barnes and Dwight L. Dumond, eds., *Letters of Theodore Dwight Weld, Angelina Grimké Weld, and Sarah Grimké, 1822–1844* (1934; reprint, Gloucester, Mass.: Peter Smith, 1965); Donald B. Cole and John J. McDonough, *Witness to the Young Republic* (Hanover, N.H.: University Press of New England, 1989); and C. Peter Ripley et al. eds., *The Black Abolitionist Papers*, 3 vols. (Chapel Hill: University of North Carolina Press, 1991). Most notable by far in this category are the sections on the District of Columbia in the first two volumes of Ira Berlin et al., eds., *Freedom: A Documentary History of Emancipation, 1861–1867: Selected from the Holdings of the National Archives of the United States* Series 1 (New York: Cambridge University Press, 1985, 1993). I rely very heavily on this well edited resource in the final chapter.

A number of contemporary published works are also very important. The variously titled *Proceedings* and *Minutes* of the American Convention for Promoting the Abolition of Slavery contain reports on early biracial antislavery activities in the Chesapeake. Crucial to an understanding of the Washington branch of the underground railroad are Thomas Smallwood, *A Narrative of Thomas Smallwood, (Colored Man)* (Toronto: J. Stephens, 1851) and William Still, *The Underground Railroad: A Record of Facts, Authentic Narratives, Letter, &c* (1872; reprint New York: Arno, 1968). Together with Smallwood's Washington correspondence published under the *nom de plume* "Samivel Weller Jr." and Torrey's newspaper correspondence, Smallwood's narrative provides the basis for my discussion of the two men's clandestine activities. It is also in his narrative that Smallwood reveals that he had written the *Weller* letters. Without that information my account of the underground railroad would be quite different.

Other important contemporary biographies, autobiographies, and reminiscences, some of which contain letters and other documents, are Daniel Drayton, *Personal Memoirs of Daniel Drayton* (New York: Bela Marsh, 1855); Wendell Phillips Garrison and Francis Jackson Garrison, *William Lloyd Garrison, 1805–1889*, 4 vols. (New York: Century, 1885–89); John Wallace Hutchinson, *Story of the Hutchinsons (Tribe of Jesse)*, ed. Charles E. Mann, 2 vols. (1896; reprint, New York: Da Capo Press, 1977); Elizabeth Keckley, *Behind the Scenes; or, Thirty Years a Slave, and Four Years in the White House* (1868; reprint, New York: Arno, 1968); J[oseph] C. Lovejoy, *Memoir of Rev. Charles T. Torrey* 2d ed. (1848; reprint, New York: Negro Universities Press, 1969); Solomon Northup, *Twelve Years a Slave: Narrative of Solomon Northup* (1855; reprint Baton Rouge: Louisiana State University Press, 1968); Ellen M. O'Connor, *Myrtilla Miner, A Memoir* (1885; reprint New York: Arno, 1969); Daniel Alexander Payne, *Recollections of Seventy Years* (1889; reprint New York: Arno, 1968); Harriet Beecher Stowe, *History of the Edmonsons* (n.p.: privately published, n.d.) and *Key to Uncle Tom's Cabin* (London: Sampson, Low, Son, 1853); Jesse Torrey Jun., *Portraiture of Domestic Slavery in the U.S.* 2d ed. (Ballston, Pa.: Torrey 1818); [John S. Tyson], *Elisha Tyson, the Philanthropist* (Baltimore: B. Lundy, 1825); and Edward Needles Wright, ed., "John Needles (1786–1878): An Autobiography," *Quaker History* 58 (Spring 1969): 3–21.

SECONDARY SOURCES

During a period stretching from the 1930s into the 1980s most historians of the antislavery movement portrayed white abolitionists—and to a lesser degree black abolitionists—in terms of antebellum northern culture and almost entirely within northern political and social contexts. By the late 1960s historians had begun to emphasize how white male abolitionist biases in regard to race and gender limited the effectiveness of the antislavery movement. These historiographical tendencies reached a peak in Lawrence J. Friedman's *Gregarious Saints: Self and Community in American Abolitionism, 1830–1870* (New York: Cambridge University Press, 1982), which portrays white northern abolitionists as defensively withdrawn into isolated support clusters, limited by their own racism and sexism, and largely divorced from the sectional struggle.

Several studies produced during the past decade or so influenced my book's alternative portrayal of white northern abolitionists. In this interpretation, racism among white abolitionists does not prevent them from cooperating effectively with African Americans in an antislavery movement that directly affects the South. The studies include: Herbert Aptheker, *Abolitionism: A Revolutionary Movement* (Boston: Twayne, 1989) and *Anti-Racism in U.S. History: The First Two Hundred Years* (New York: Greenwood, 1992); Merton L. Dillon, *Slavery Attacked: Southern Slaves and Their Allies, 1619–1865* (Baton Rouge: Louisiana State University Press, 1990); James L. Huston, "The Experiential Basis of the Northern Anti-Slavery Impulse," *Journal of Southern History* 56 (November 1990): 609–40; Clara Merritt DeBoar, *Be Jubilant My Feet: African-American Abolitionists in the American Missionary Association, 1839–1861* (New York: Garland, 1994); Paul Goodman, *Of One Blood: Abolitionists and the Origins of Racial Equality* (Berkeley: University of California Press, 1998); David Grimsted, *American Mobbing, 1828–1861: Toward Civil War* (New York: Oxford University Press, 1998); John Stauffer, *The Black Hearts of Men: Radical Abolitionists and the Transformation of Race* (Cambridge, Mass.: Harvard University Press, 2002). The intellectual and historiographical parameters for this book are most directly established in my *The Abolitionists and the South, 1831–1861* (Lexington: University Press of Kentucky, 1995).

The extensive literature on northern abolitionism plays a central role in my approach to events in the Chesapeake. The best survey is James Brewer Stewart, *Holy Warriors: The Abolitionists and American Slavery,* rev. ed. (New York: Hill and Wang, 1997). Robert H. Abzug in *Cosmos Crumbling: American Reform and the Religious Imagination* (New York: Oxford University Press, 1994) analyzes the role of evangelicalism in abolitionism and other northern reform movements. He clearly delineates the centrality of William Lloyd Garrison in American immediatism. John R. McKivigan covers the church-oriented abolitionists in *The War Against Proslavery Religion: Abolitionists and the Northern Churches, 1830–1865* (Ithaca: Cornell University Press, 1984). Douglas M. Strong investigates the relationship between religion and politics among western New York's radical political abolitionists in *Perfectionist Politics: Abolitionism and the Religious Tensions of American Democracy* (Syracuse: Syracuse University Press, 1999). Aileen S. Kraditor, *Means and Ends in American Abolitionism: Garrison and His Critics on Strategy and Tactics* (New York: Random House, 1967) discusses the breakup of the AASS. William C. Wiecek in *The Sources of Antislavery Constitutionalism in America, 1760–1848* (Ithaca: Cornell University Press, 1977) describes the various abolitionist interpretations of the Constitution. In *The Antislavery Appeal: American Abolitionism after 1830* (Baltimore: Johns Hopkins University Press, 1976) Ronald G. Walters analyzes the northern abolitionists' negative views of southern culture. Betty Fladeland in *Men and Brothers: Anglo-American Antislavery Cooperation* (Urbana: University of Illinois Press, 1972) explores ties between American and British abolitionists. The best study of northern women in the antislavery movement is Julie Roy Jeffrey, *The Great Silent Army of Abolitionism: Ordinary Women in the Antislavery Movement* (Chapel Hill: University of North Carolina Press, 1998).

Studies of black opposition to slavery also heavily influence this book. Herbert Aptheker's *American Negro Slave Revolts* (1943; reprint New York: International Publishers, 1974) pioneers the view that African Americans actively sought to free themselves from slavery. Ira Berlin discusses the origins, accomplishments, and outlook of southern free blacks in *Slaves without Masters: The Free Negro in the Antebellum South* (New York: Random House,

1974). John Hope Franklin and Loren Schweninger chronicle the ubiquitous phenomenon of slave escape in *Runaway Slaves: Rebels on the Plantation* (New York: Oxford University Press, 1999). John Ashworth's *Slavery, Capitalism, and Politics in the Antebellum Republic* (New York: Cambridge University Press, 1995) demonstrates the role of slaves in encouraging abolitionism in the North. Although focused on the North, James Oliver Horton and Lois E. Horton's *In Hope of Liberty: Culture, Community, and Protest among Northern Free Blacks, 1700–1860* (New York: Oxford University Press, 1997) and Carol Wilson's *Freedom at Risk: The Kidnapping of Free Blacks in America, 1780–1865* (Lexington: University Press of Kentucky, 1994) are extremely useful. The Hortons provide an essential analysis of black perspectives and Wilson illuminates the violent struggle in the border region among masters, slaves, and abolitionists. James Oliver Horton's *Free People of Color: Inside the African American Community* (Washington: Smithsonian Institution Press, 1993) is also very helpful.

There are a number of books dealing specifically with black abolitionists, though, as in the case of most studies of white abolitionists, these do not focus on the border region. Benjamin Quarles's classic *Black Abolitionists* (1969; reprint, New York: Oxford University Press, 1977) stresses interaction between black and white antislavery activists. Jane H. Pease and William H. Pease in *They Who Would Be Free: Blacks' Search for Freedom, 1830–1861* (New York: Atheneum, 1974) emphasize what separated the two groups. Harry Reed's *Platform for Change: the Foundations of the Northern Free Black Community, 1775–1865* (East Lansing: Michigan State University Press, 1994) investigates the role of black culture in the rise of antislavery action. R. J. M. Blackett, *Building an Antislavery Wall: Black Americans in the Atlantic Abolitionists Movement, 1830–1860* (Baton Rouge: Louisiana State University Press, 1983) provides an international perspective. The only book-length study of black female abolitionists is Shirley J. Yee, *Black Women Abolitionists: A Study in Activism, 1828–1860* (New Haven: Yale University Press, 1990).

Several studies regarding the vulnerability of slavery in the Chesapeake deserve mention. They include: Barbara Jeanne Fields, *Slavery and Freedom on the Middle Ground: Maryland during the Nineteenth Century* (New York: Yale University Press, 1985); Gary Lawson Browne, *Baltimore and the Nation, 1789–1861* (Chapel Hill: University of North Carolina Press, 1980); T. Stephen Whitman, *The Price of Freedom: Slavery and Manumission in Baltimore and Early National Maryland* (Lexington: University Press of Kentucky, 1997); and Brenda Stevenson, *Life in Black and White: Family and Community in the Slave South* (New York: Oxford University Press, 1996), which focuses on Loudoun County, Virginia.

A dozen studies are useful in regard to the origins of biracial antislavery action in the Chesapeake. Two that deal with antislavery Quakers are Jean R. Soderlund, *Quakers and Slavery: A Divided Spirit* (Princeton: Princeton University Press, 1988) and Thomas E. Drake, *Quakers and Slavery in America* (New Haven: Yale University Press, 1950). Two others investigate black activism in Baltimore: Leroy Graham, *Baltimore: Nineteenth Century Black Capital* (Washington: University Press of America, 1982) and Christopher Phillips, *Freedom's Port: the African American Community of Baltimore, 1790–1860* (Urbana: Illinois University Press, 1998). On slavetrading, Frederic Bancroft, *Slave Trading in the Old South* (Baltimore: J. H. Furst, 1931) is still valuable. But readers should consult Michael Tadman, *Speculators and Slaves: Masters, Traders, and Slaves in the Old South* (Madison: University of Wisconsin Press, 1996), Walter Johnson, *Soul by Soul: Life inside the Antebellum Slave Market* (Cambridge, Mass.: Harvard University Press, 1999), and William Calderhead, "The Role of the Professional Slave Trader in a Slave Economy: Austin Woolfolk, a Case Study," *Civil War History* 23 (September 1977): 195–211. The roles of Benjamin Lundy and William Lloyd Garrison, as well as their black associates are discussed in Merton L. Dillon, *Benjamin Lundy and the Struggle for Negro Freedom* (Urbana: University of Illinois Press, 1966), Walter M. Merrill, *Against Wind and Tide: A Biography of William Lloyd Garrison* (Boston: Little, Brown, 1963), and James Brewer Stewart, *William Lloyd Garrison and the Challenge of Emancipation* (Arlington Heights, Ill.: Harlan Davidson, 1992).

Gilbert H. Barnes discusses the struggle over the Gag Rule in *The Antislavery Impulse, 1830–1840* (1933; reprint New York: Harcourt, Brace, and World, 1964). So do William Lee Miller, *Arguing about Slavery: the Great Battle in the United States Congress* (New York: Knopf, 1996) and Leonard Richards, *The Life and Times of Congressman John Quincy Adams* (New York: Oxford University Press, 1986).

Several studies by sociologists and social psychologists provide the context for my discussion of the elements of the subversive community. The most important of them for this book are Joseph Gusfield, *Community: A Critical Re-*

sponse (New York: Harper and Row, 1975) and Roland L. Warren, *Community in America* 3d ed. (Lanham, Md.: University Press of America, 1987). My understanding of biracial subversive community action benefits from Aldon D. Morris, *The Origins of the Civil Rights Movement: Black Communities Organizing for Change* (New York: Free Press, 1984); Standish Meacham, *Toynbee Hall and Social Reform, 1880–1914: The Search for Community* (New Haven, Conn.: Yale University Press, 1987); and Elisabeth Lasch-Quinn, *Black Neighbors: Race and the Limits of Reform in the American Settlement House Movement, 1890–1948* (Chapel Hill: University of North Carolina Press, 1993). Also very useful in providing a context for Washington's biracial antislavery community are two books on African Americans in the District of Columbia. They are Constance M. Green, *The Secret City: A History of Race Relations in the Nation's Capital* (Princeton, N.J.: Princeton University Press, 1967) and Letitia Woods Brown, *Free Negroes in the District of Columbia, 1790–1865* (New York: Oxford University Press, 1972).

Several secondary sources contributed to my discussion of Charles T. Torrey, Thomas Smallwood, the underground railroad, and the context within which they operated. Wilbur H. Siebert's *The Underground Railroad from Slavery to Freedom* (1898; reprint New York: Arno, 1968), Larry Gara, *The Liberty Line: The Legend of the Underground Railroad* (Lexington: University of Kentucky Press, 1961), and Kathryn Grover, *The Fugitive's Gibralter: Escaping Slaves and Abolitionism in New Bedford, Massachusetts* (Amherst: University of Massachusetts Press, 2001) present widely differing views of the railroad's nature and significance. James M. McPherson, "The Fight against the Gag Rule: Joshua Leavitt and Antislavery Insurgency in the Whig Party," *Journal of Negro History* 48 (July 1963): 177–95 is the earliest discussion of the antislavery cadre of politicians and journalists in Washington.

Five books are essential for understanding the role of antislavery politics in the antebellum years. They are Don E. Fehrenbacher, *The Slaveholding Republic: An Account of the United States Government's Relations to Slavery,* Ward M. McAfee ed. (New York: Oxford, 2001); Leonard L. Richards, *The Slave Power: The Free North and Southern Domination, 1780–1860* (Baton Rouge: Louisiana State University Press, 2000); Richard H. Sewell, *Ballots for Freedom: Antislavery Politics in the United States, 1837–1860* (New York: Oxford University Press, 1976); Frederick J. Blue, *The Free Soilers: Third Party Politics, 1848–54* (Urbana: University of Illinois Press, 1973); and William E.

Gienapp, *The Origins of the Republican Party, 1852–1856* (New York: Oxford University Press, 1987).

Studies of gender add considerable texture to my understanding of the subversives. Kristan Hoganson, "Garrisonian Abolitionists and the Rhetoric of Gender, 1850–1860," *American Quarterly* 45 (December 1993): 558–95 is very instructive. Among the more important studies influencing my discussions of women within the subversive community are Barbara J. Welter, "The Cult of True Womanhood, 1820–1860," *American Quarterly* 18 (Summer 1966): 151–74; Ellen C. DuBois, *Feminism and Suffrage: The Emergence of an Independent Women's Movement in America, 1848–1869* (Ithaca: Cornell University Press, 1978); and Blanche Glassman Hersh, *The Slavery of Sex: Feminist-Abolitionists in America* (Urbana: University of Illinois Press, 1978). My discussions of the community's masculine ethos draw on Anthony Rotundo, "Learning about Manhood: Gender Ideals and the Middle-Class Family in Nineteenth-Century America," in J. A. Mangan and James Walvin, eds., *Middle-Class Masculinity in Britain and America, 1800–1940* (New York: St. Martin's, 1987); Christopher Dixon, "'A True Manly Life': Abolitionists and the Masculine Ideal," *Mid-America* 77 (Fall 1995): 213–37; and Donald Yacavone, *Samuel Joseph May and the Dilemma of the Liberal Persuasion, 1797–1871* (Philadelphia: Temple University Press, 1991).

Two books contribute to my discussion of antiblack and antiabolitionist riots in Washington. They are Leonard L. Richards, *"Gentlemen of Property and Standing": Anti-Abolitionist Mobs in Jacksonian America* (New York: Oxford University Press, 1970) and David Grimsted, *American Mobbing, 1828–1861: Toward Civil War* (New York: Oxford University Press, 1998). Of the two, Grimsted's is the more comprehensive.

Historians have long debated whether reality or paranoia shaped southern white fear of abolitionists and slave rebels. Those who stress paranoia include Bertram Wyatt-Brown, *Southern Honor: Ethics and Behavior in the Old South* (New York: Oxford University Press, 1982) and Steven A. Channing, *Crisis of Fear in South Carolina* (New York: Norton, 1974). But two books by William W. Freehling establish that southern whites did have cause to believe that slavery must be defended vigorously against its enemies. They are *The Road to Disunion: Secessionists at Bay, 1776–1854* (New York: Oxford University Press, 1990) and *The Reinterpretation of American History and the Civil*

War (New York: Oxford University Press, 1994). I argue similarly in *Abolitionists and the South.*

A number of books influenced my treatment of the Civil War and Reconstruction eras. The best general studies of the war and of abolitionists during the war are James M. McPherson's *Ordeal by Fire: The Civil War and Reconstruction,* 2d ed. (New York: McGraw-Hill, 1992) and *The Struggle for Equality: Abolitionists and the Negro in the Civil War and Reconstruction* (Princeton: Princeton University Press, 1964). The most recent major study of Reconstruction is Eric Foner's *Reconstruction: America's Unfinished Revolution, 1863–1877* (New York: Harper and Row, 1988). Studies dealing specifically with Washington include James Huntington Whyte, *The Uncivil War: Washington during Reconstruction, 1865–1878* (New York: Twayne, 1958); Allan Johnson, *Surviving Freedom: The Black Community of Washington, D.C., 1860–1880* (New York: Garland, 1993); Carlton Mabee, "Sojourner Truth Fights Dependence on Government: Moves Freed Slaves off Welfare in Washington to Jobs in Upstate New York," *Afro-Americans in New York Life and History* 14 (January 1990): 7–26; Melvin R. Williams, "A Blueprint for Change: The Black Community in Washington, D.C., 1860–1870," *RCHS* 48 (1973): 359–93; Elaine Cutler Everly, "The Freedmen's Bureau in the National Capital" (Ph.D. dissertation, Georgetown University, 1972); and Michael J. Kurtz, "Emancipation in the Federal City," *CWH* 24 (September 1978): 250–67. Useful in regard to AMA teachers is Clara Merritt DeBoer, *His Truth Is Marching On: African Americans Who Taught the Freedmen for the American Missionary Association, 1861–1877* (New York: Garland, 1995).

Although this book strives to portray a community of action as it developed over several decades, rather than to analyze deeply the lives of individuals, it seems appropriate to end this essay with a nod to biography. Most of the people, both black and white, who participated in Washington's subversive community are obscure. Not only do they lack biographers, they have left so little evidence about their lives that they probably never will be subjects of biographies. But communities are composed of individuals and in a few cases modern biographies contribute greatly to this study. Some already have been mentioned. Others include: Henry Mayer, *All on Fire: William Lloyd Garrison and the Abolition of Slavery* (New York: St. Martin's, 1999); Hugh Davis, *Joshua Leavitt: Evangelical Abolitionist* (Baton Rouge: Louisiana State University Press, 1990); James Brewer Stewart, *Joshua R. Giddings and the Tactics of Radical Politics* (Cleveland: Case-Western Reserve University Press, 1970); Stanley Harrold, *Gamaliel Bailey and Antislavery Union* (Kent, Ohio: Kent State University Press, 1986); Frederick J. Blue, *Salmon P. Chase: A Life in Politics* (Kent, Ohio: Kent State University Press, 1987); Richard H. Sewell, *John P. Hale and the Politics of Abolition* (Cambridge, Mass.: Harvard University Press, 1965); Clifford Edward Clark, *Henry Ward Beecher: Spokesman for Middle-class America* (Urbana: University of Illinois Press, 1978); Philip S. Foner and Josephine F. Pacheco, *Three Who Dared: Prudence Crandall, Margaret Douglass, Myrtilla Miner—Champions of Antebellum Black Education* (Westport, Conn.: Greenwood, 1984); Ralph V. Harlow, *Gerrit Smith: Philanthropist and Reformer* (New York: Holt, 1939); Joel Schor, *Henry Highland Garnet: A Voice of Black Radicalism in the Nineteenth Century* (Westport, Conn.: Greenwood, 1977); Martin B. Pasternak, *Rise Now and Fly to Arms: The Life of Henry Highland Garnet* (New York: Garland, 1995); Judith Colucci Breault, *The World of Emily Howland: Odyssey of a Humanitarian* (Millbrae, Calif.: Les Femmes, 1976); William S. McFeely, *Frederick Douglass* (New York: Simon and Schuster, 1991).

INDEX